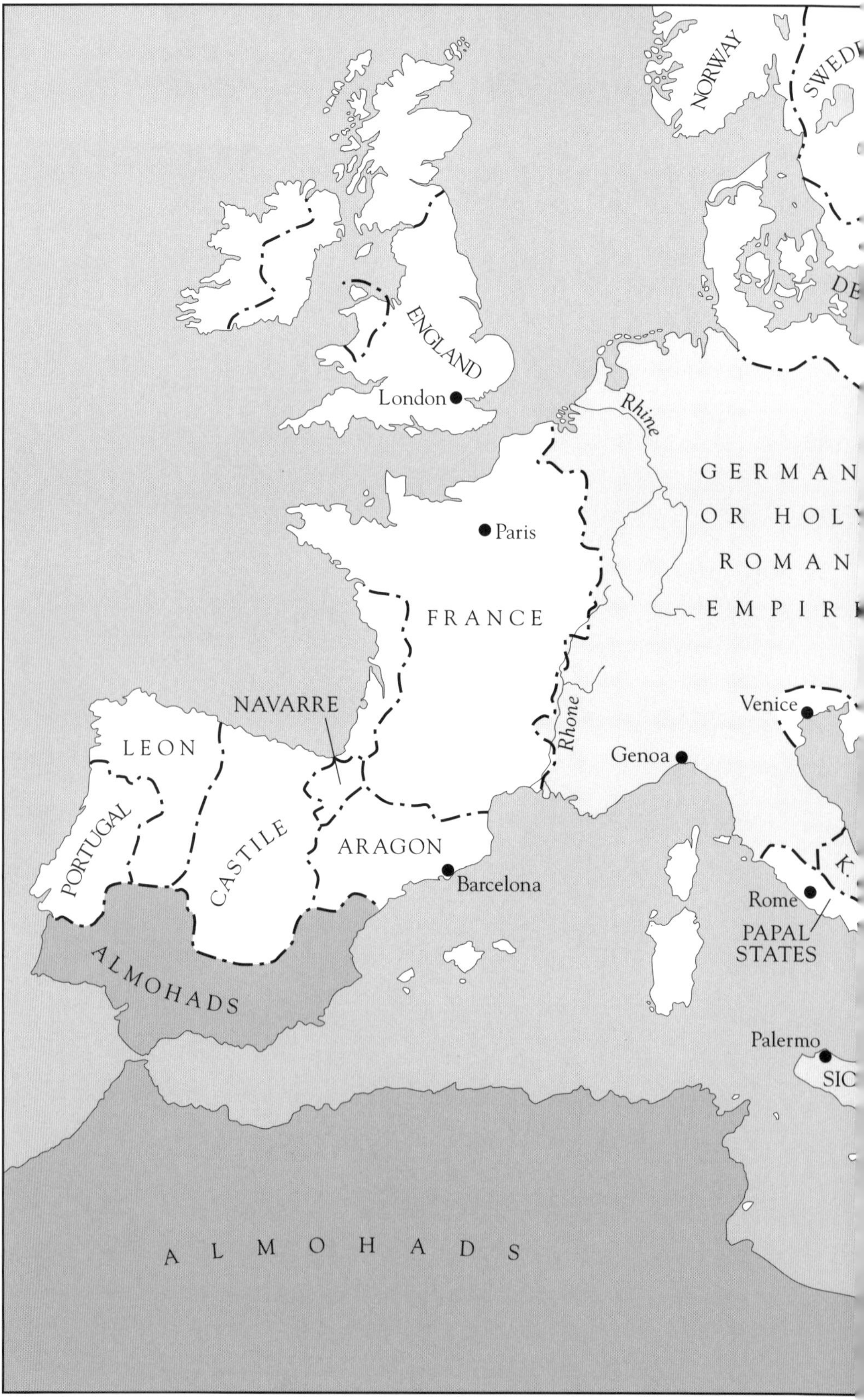
NORWAY
SWEDE
ENGLAND
London
DE
Rhine
GERMAN
OR HOL
ROMAN
EMPIR
Paris
FRANCE
NAVARRE
LEON
PORTUGAL
CASTILE
ARAGON
Barcelona
Rhone
Genoa
Venice
Rome
PAPAL
STATES
K.
ALMOHADS
Palermo
SIC
ALMOHADS

Europe and the Mediterranean
1200–1220
OLAND
HUNGARY
BULGARIA
LATIN EMPIRE
Constantinople
RUM
NICAEA
Antioch
CYPRUS
CRETE
Acre
Jerusalem
Damietta
Nile
AYYUBIDS

Francis of Assisi

Adrian House

Foreword by
Karen Armstrong

HiddenSpring

Jacket art: Margaritone d'Arezzo. Saint Francis of Assisi. Scala/Art Resource, NY.

Published in Great Britain by Chatto & Windus
Random House, 20 Vauxhall Bridge Road, London SW1V 2SA

Library of Congress Cataloging-in-Publication Data

House, Adrian.
Francis of Assisi / Adrian House.
p. cm.
Includes bibliographical references and index.
ISBN 1-58768-009-2 (alk. paper)
1. Francis, of Assisi, Saint, 1182–1226. 2. Christian saints—Italy—Assisi—Biography.
3. Assisi (Italy)—Biography. I. Title.

BX4700.F6 H595 2000
271′.302—dc21
[B]

00-044979

Published in the United States by

HiddenSpring

an imprint of Paulist Press
997 Macarthur Boulevard
Mahwah, New Jersey 07430

www.hiddenspringbooks.com

Printed and bound in the
United States of America

Contents

List of Illustrations

These illustrations are reproduced by permission from, and with gratitude to Peter Meyer for Plates 1 and 2; to Archivo Fotografico, Sacro Convento, Assisi, for Plates 3, 4, 5 (Sermon to the Birds), 7 and 8; and to the National Gallery, London, for the Wolf of Gubbio by Sassetta, on Plate 5.

List of Maps

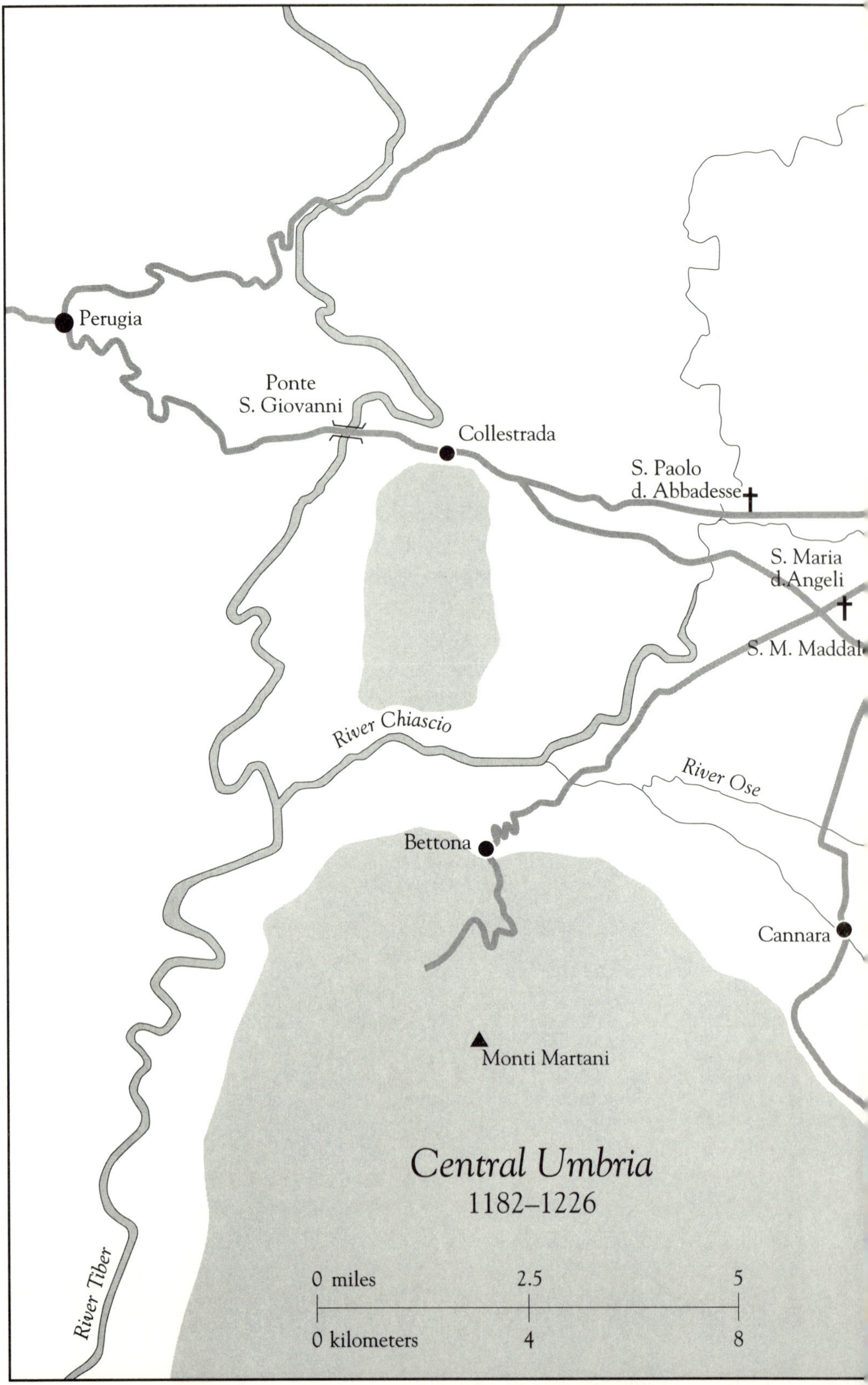
Perugia
Ponte
S. Giovanni
Collestrada
S. Paolo
d. Abbadesse
S. Maria
d.Angeli
S. M. Maddal
River Chiascio
River Ose
Bettona
Cannara
Monti Martani
Central Umbria
1182–1226
0 miles
2.5
5
0 kilometers
4
8
River Tiber

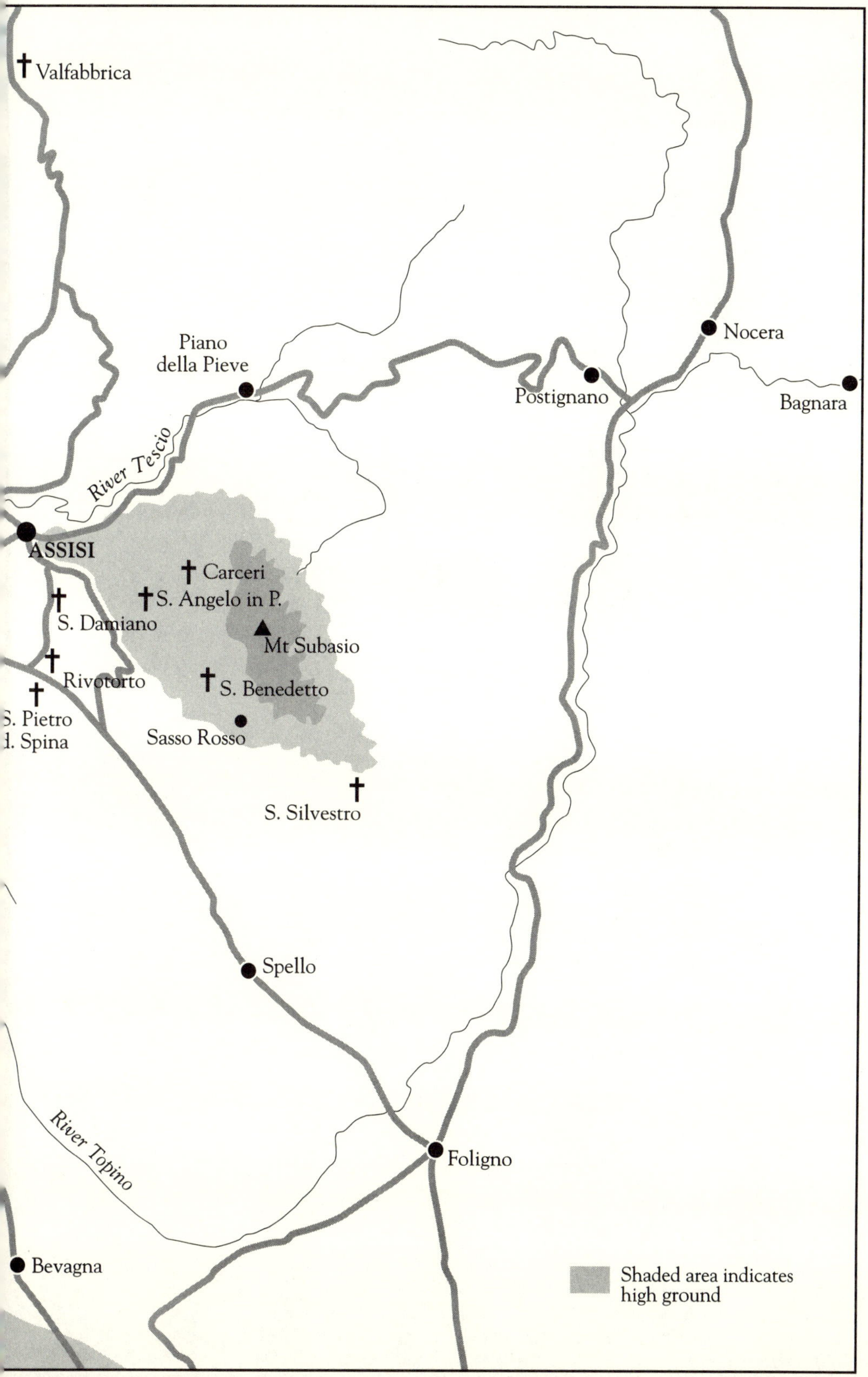

Valfabbrica
Piano della Pieve
Nocera
Postignano
Bagnara
River Tescio
ASSISI
Carceri
S. Angelo in P.
S. Damiano
Mt Subasio
Rivotorto
S. Benedetto
S. Pietro d. Spina
Sasso Rosso
S. Silvestro
Spello
River Topino
Foligno
Bevagna
Shaded area indicates high ground

Foreword

For many people in the Western world—Catholic, Protestant and secularist alike—Francis of Assisi remains one of the most exemplary Christians of any age. At a time when the Roman Church was attaining the zenith of its temporal power and wealth, his adherence to the poverty advocated by Jesus Christ was an eloquent and courageous reminder of gospel values. During the Crusades, Francis reached out to the Muslim world with respect, apparently transcending the self-righteous hatred and rivalry that so frequently afflicts institutional religion, even though he remained a loyal son of the Catholic Church. Francis's experience of joyful harmony with the whole of the natural world has led in the twentieth century to his being declared the patron saint of ecologists. In our skeptical age, three million people each year make the pilgrimage to his tomb in Assisi.

Yet the magnificent basilica which houses Francis's remains, built shortly after his death in 1226, is a violation of everything Francis stood for. Throughout his short life, he insisted that his friars should not live in grand, permanent buildings; his view would have been that the money spent on this church should have been given to the poor and the sick.

In this fresh new introduction to Francis's life, Adrian House writes sympathetically, but does not lard his narrative with a piety that might alienate a secular reader. He weaves the historical background into his story in such a way that it does not impede the flow of events and is thus able to convey the drama of Francis's life: his debauched youth; his conversion; his founding of the new Orders of Friars Minor and of the Third Order of Penitents for the laity; the pathos of his relationship with St. Clare, foundress of the Second Franciscan Order for women; and his visit to Egypt during the Fifth Crusade, when he crossed the enemy lines and preached to the Sultan. The author discusses Franciscan spirituality and gives an intelligent account of Francis's vision at La Verna when, it was believed, his body was imprinted with the five wounds of the crucified Christ, making him the first person in Europe to bear the stigmata.

Later, the scholastic theologian St. Bonaventure (1221–74), one of the most distinguished Franciscans of the period, saw Francis's life as an epiphany, a revelation of the divine in human form. Francis's life was dedicated to the exact imitation of Christ. He took literally Jesus's demand that the Christian give up all earthly possessions and adopt the lifestyle of a homeless mendicant. Like Jesus, Francis sought out people who were marginalized and despised by the Establishment. The appearance of the stigmata on Francis's body, however it is explained, was seen as his final identification with the incarnate Word of God. By contemplating the events of the lives of both Jesus and Francis, Bonaventure believed, we could glimpse the reality of the ineffable and indescribable God in terms that we could understand.

But, as T. S. Eliot reminded us, humankind cannot bear very much reality. Francis's stark message was neutralized even in his own lifetime. The pope and the religious establishment compelled the Friars Minor to modify the extremity of their evangelical poverty: they must no longer rely on alms, must own property, must live in regular houses, and be encouraged to engage in the scholarly pursuits of other monks. Francis resigned as acting head of the Order, retaining only the vague title of spiritual father. The incarceration of his simple tomb in the splendors of the Assisi basilica was the final betrayal of this inspired man.

Adrian House explains this tragedy by pointing out that the popes and bishops, despite their veneration and appreciation of Francis, were ruled more by ecclesiological than by christological principles. They were committed to the survival of the institutional Church and could not countenance a charismatic movement which made the piety of its rulers appear mundane and worldly by comparison. This is undoubtedly true, but the irony of Francis's life also reminds us of the essential extremity of the religious requirement, which many men and women of faith would prefer to forget.

Like Jesus himself, Francis is often sentimentalized. We like the image of the poetical saint, preaching to the birds and exulting in the beauties of the natural landscape. We look back with nostalgia to Francis's time, when the natural world and the Bible seemed not to contradict but to complement one another. But we have no intention of imitating his total self-abandonment which, the masters of the spiritual life in all traditions insist, is essential if we wish to experience the Sacred. A great deal of religion is actually devoted to the propping up of the ego and the establishment of a secure identity. We do not wish to emulate Francis's material poverty, a symbol of his transcendence of the self, and we prefer to keep clear of beggars and the like. Francis's spiritual journey began when he laid aside his visceral disgust for the lepers of Assisi and kissed their hands. This act of compassionate love gave him an immediate intimation of the divine presence.

Religion cannot always be tasteful or confined within the polite restraints of institutional practice, because it aims at the infinite. Like Jesus, Francis showed the difficulty of incarnating a divine imperative in the flawed conditions of human existence. His stringent bodily and spiritual mortifications never degenerated into masochism or narcissism because they were always tempered by a kindness, compassion and gentleness to all creatures which, again, is often sadly missing from the churches that proclaim his sanctity.

Adrian House's goal was to show that "it is unnecessary to share Francis's faith in order to appreciate his soaring achievements." His biography reveals a Francis who is both medieval and modern, and who speaks to readers of any faith or none.

—*Karen Armstrong*

Preface

Books about Francis of Assisi are legion and research on him is continuous. A new biography therefore requires explanation.

The seed of this one was sown while I was at Oxford. Curious to know more about this eccentric young Italian who seemed the most attractive of all the medieval saints, I paid several visits to an Anglican friary in the Dorset hills. It was a converted farm and the surrounding woods were roamed by foxes, badgers and deer. Fellow guests might include a few dusty wayfarers, a bishop, one or two ex-prisoners, a retired general, an alcoholic stockbroker and a couple of potential novices. Because the friars treated all of us identically, it was impossible to know for certain who was who. Intrigued though I was, when the lure and necessity of earning a living took hold, my interest in Francis slowly lapsed.

Thirty years later I used to stay with an old man, George Adamson, in the heart of the African wilderness. We slept in open, thatched shelters; snakes hunted mice in the rafters; hyenas howled at dawn; hornbills and vervet monkeys shared our meals. After supper, in the dark and unarmed, George left the wire enclosure to feed his pride of fifteen wild lions. Inevitably, he attracted visitors – one of his old rangers, the Prince of the Netherlands, Chief Shaba, two girls from England on bicycles, a young man just off cocaine, the Russian ambassador, a human cannonball or Father Nicky, an Irish missionary. Whomever we were, we were all made equally welcome. Reflecting on these evenings under the shooting stars of Africa, I was reminded of starry nights in Dorset and my curiosity about Francis revived. This book is the result.

It differs from others about Francis in several respects. First, I have tried to make the most of the almost continuous drama of his life without sacrificing accuracy. Second, I believe his purpose and impact were directly related to his experience of the social, economic, political, military and religious forces then swirling through Italy; I have therefore threaded these through the story. I have also felt it essential to illustrate how the lives of Francis and St. Clare were interwoven—like the fortunes of their orders—from the day they first met until his death fifteen years later. Most books on Francis concentrate his relationship with her into a single chapter.

Unlike the majority of his biographers I have attempted to write without bias for readers of any faith or none. Although the whole of Francis's life was based on his belief in God and – living where he did when he did – in Jesus as God's Son, few saints if any had less interest in the details of dogma. It is unnecessary to share his faith in order to appreciate his soaring achievements.

It follows from this, as explained in the text, that I have omitted the miracles contained in the two official lives of him by Thomas of Celano and St. Bonaventure. On the other hand, I have repeated without comment a number of stories which require a degree of credulity – Francis's visions, his success in helping others to combat leprosy or the devil, and his legendary encounters with birds and animals. This is because I believe, but am not sure, that many more of them may be literally true than seems probable at first sight; I feel readers should decide for themselves. The most famous and colorful of these episodes come from *The Little Flowers of St. Francis*, which only appeared about a century after the earliest accounts of his life and having grown more fanciful are less reliable.

Throughout his life Francis was almost as responsive to places and landscapes as he was to people and animals. I have therefore followed his footsteps through Italy to France, Spain and briefly to Egypt. The sights, sounds and smells of these places sometimes add an extra, more immediate, dimension to his companions' accounts of his travels and adventures.

I am no scholar and inevitably the foundations of this book rest on the achievements of those who are. My thanks to individuals are expressed at the end, but I would like to acknowledge here my great indebtedness to those whose editorial work, translations, research and publications have contributed to the remarkable range of reliable information about Francis which is now available.

I should make one apology, especially to scholars. To avoid blunting the point of a quotation from an early source I have sometimes rephrased it, or omitted repetitions without always inserting the customary ellipses . . . However, in doing so I have never altered the meaning.

At the age of twenty-four Francis renounced both money and possessions. This, combined with his honesty, humility and courage, released him from the burdens and restraints of worldly conventions and left him free to play God's troubadour and juggler. His song was love and he tossed up society's most cherished possessions – rank, wealth, fame, reputation and power – exposing their flaws, so that their opposites seemed more precious than they. In the line of holy fools and great court jesters he constantly entertained, surprised or stimulated his audiences.

Today Francis may be most widely known for his sermon to the birds; but, however original and characteristic, it conveys as little of his genius as a weathercock does of a great cathedral below it.

Part I

Son

1182–1206

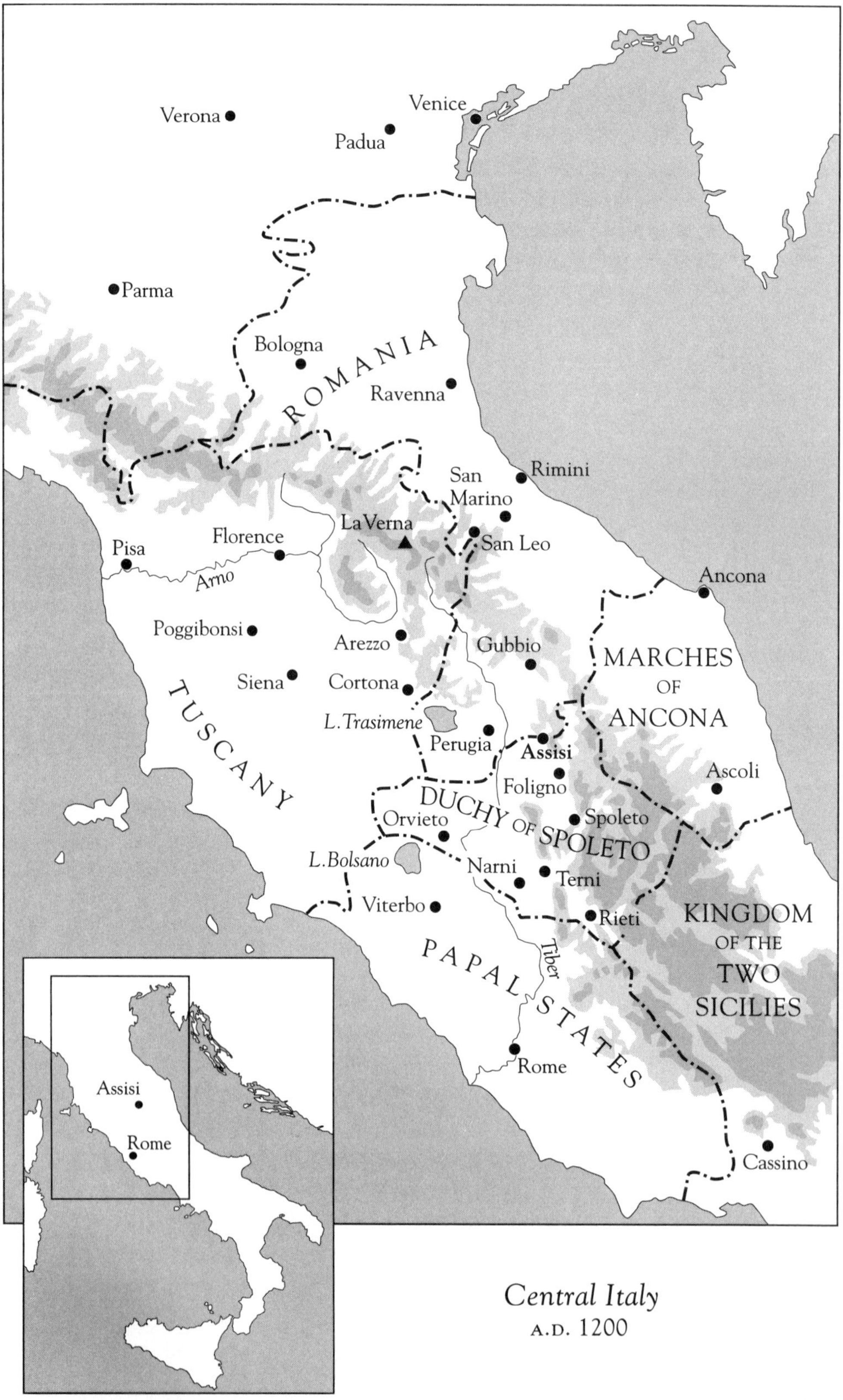

Central Italy
A.D. 1200

1

Morning Star

He shone in his days as a morning star
in the midst of the clouds.
Pope Gregory IX

During his forty-four years Francesco di Pietro traveled all over Italy and to Spain, France, Switzerland, Dalmatia, Syria and Egypt. He died three miles from Assisi, the Umbrian hill town in which he was born.

For some months he had known he did not have long to live but, although he was now blind, ill and suffering acutely, he had been kept away from Santa Maria degli Angeli, the chapel in the woods which had been the one still point in his nomadic life for nearly twenty years. So great was his fame and so high the economic value of a holy man's body that the authorities in Assisi had been determined he should not fall into the hands of their archenemy, Perugia, fifteen miles away. At last, convinced that his time was running out, Francis insisted on being carried down to his little friary of thatched huts around the chapel. The remarkable events of the days that followed were recorded by several men who were there.

Francis died at sunset on Saturday, October 3, 1226, but since the date was then reckoned to change every day at six in the evening, not midnight, his Feast has always been celebrated on October 4. A number of his closest companions, all friars in the order of Brothers Minor he had founded, were with him. They included Elias, his deputy; Bernard, the first brother to join him; Giles, who had followed soon after; and Angelo, a friend since boyhood.

Most unusually, for none was normally admitted to Santa Maria, a woman knelt by the bed. Giacoma de Settesoli, a rich Roman widow, had been the friars' patron for more than a dozen years and was so trusted that Francis liked to call her Brother Giacoma. A few days before he died he had dictated a note asking her to come to him quickly with a length of the ash-gray cloth imported by the Cistercians and some of his favorite cakes; but before there was time for the friars to dispatch the letter they heard the sound of her horses approaching.

The other brothers then at the friary clustered outside the doorway of the hut. Some had crossed the Alps and the Pyrenees, barefoot, with Francis; one had been shipwrecked with him; others had sailed with him to join the Fifth Crusade at Damietta on the mouth of the Nile. It is possible that Thomas of Celano, recently in Germany and soon to be appointed his official biographer, was there, too. Out on the road and among the trees in the wood stood the watchmen and guards posted by the *podestà*, or mayor, of Assisi. Both they and the friars were astonished when, in the last minutes of light, an exaltation of larks – quite uncharacteristically – circled above the roof of Francis's hut, singing.

Still profoundly distressed but consoled by the tranquillity of Francis's dying hours, Elias and Bernard obeyed one of his final wishes. Taking off his shift they laid his naked and emaciated body, as the last expression of his vows of poverty and humility, on the bare ground for "as long as it would take a man to walk a mile." They then washed him, anointed him with spice, and dressed him in a habit quickly cut from Giacoma's cloth, pinning over it some of the coarse burlap he usually wore. Candles and incense, also brought by her, were lit around his bed.

These rites exposed Giacoma and most of the brothers in the cell to a phenomenon of which only a handful of people, among them Elias, were aware. He described it in an encyclical letter he wrote the following night, sending news of Francis's death to friars all over the world; by then friars had already reached Portugal, England, Scandinavia, Poland, the Balkans, the Middle East and possibly India. Elias said that before he died Francis's face – both temples had recently been cauterized by a doctor with a red-hot iron – was wasted and racked with pain while his limbs were contracted and stiff as in rigor mortis. But after his death his face had become radiant and his limbs soft and supple as a boy's.

At the heart of his letter came this revelation:

> I announce to you a new miracle. . . . Not long before his death our Brother and Father appeared crucified, bearing in his body five wounds, the stigmata of Christ. His hands and feet had been punctured right through as if by nails and still bore scars which had the blackness of nails. His side looked as if it had been pierced by a lance and often shed blood.[1]

Francis had taken the greatest care to ensure that these marks, which had never fully healed since their appearance two years before, should be kept secret except to the very few who looked after him.

Giacoma, who was seeing them for the first time, urged Elias to make them known to everyone. When he did so the brothers' grief immediately turned to spontaneous joy. It was the first recorded instance of such stigmata; in subsequent centuries three hundred cases have been reported.

By now messengers had left for Assisi, the first stopping at the convent of San Damiano, two miles away, to break the news to the woman who had been closer to Francis's heart than any other – Clare di Favarone, the abbess. Fourteen years before, at the age of eighteen, she had run away from her family to join him and his friars, at large in the world but committed to a life of apostolic poverty devoted to others. When the church forbade this she had accepted the cloister and founded his Second Order, for women, at San Damiano. Clare knew of the stigmata and had sewn slippers to hide Francis's wounds and protect them. Very ill herself, she had sent a message in the hope of their meeting before it was too late, but in reply he had promised only that she would see him before she died.

Throughout the night the people of Assisi, and large parties from neighboring towns and villages, made their way to Santa Maria by the light of torches and flares. The mood of the friars was so infectious that the whole crowd took up their chants of praise and thanksgiving. Thomas of Celano, much affected by the combination of lights, jubilation and singing, saw it as "a wake of angels."

During the night Elias allowed Francis's most intimate companions to kiss his stigmata, and others to see the marks, but dawn brought the great and the good to verify them and to pay their respects. Among them were a knight who had fought beside Francis, then a young man, at the Battle of Collestrada; Giovanni di Velita, Lord of Greccio, who had given him a sanctuary in the Rieti Valley and was an early member of his Third Order for lay men and women, single or married; and Girolamo di Giovanni, a highly respected magistrate and soldier depicted by Giotto gazing at the wound in Francis's side (Plate 7). Some years later more than a dozen men attested on oath to what they had seen.

When Francis had been placed in his coffin the crowd moved off toward the parish church of San Giorgio where Francis had been to school. They were led by the local clergy; the friars carried the coffin above which a crow was seen flying; great landowners, whole families and the poorest beggars and cripples then followed. Roused by the trumpets and drums, brandishing flags and olive branches, the whole procession joined in the singing.

Faithful to Francis's promise, the friars stopped a mile below Assisi at San Damiano, and bore the coffin into its chapel – once restored by Francis himself. The grille behind the altar through which Clare and her sisters received communion was removed and Francis's body carried over to the window. For "a good hour" the friars held him up and for a time the praying sisters gave way to their grief but then,

> their modesty restrained their great weeping; it wasn't fitting to mourn too much. And so, divided between sorrow and joy, they kissed his most radiant hands; and when he had been taken away the door of the grille was closed to them.[2]

There was no room for all the crowd in San Giorgio during the Requiem Mass and the crow perched on the roof. Most had to remain outside in the piazza, where a few could remember seeing Francis shortly after his conversion, twenty years before, calling them to God for the first time. Now they tried to watch through the doors and listened as the service reached its climax. At last his coffin was taken down into the crypt – its resting place for the next four years.

*

Very soon after the funeral a run of unexpected events profoundly influenced the way in which Francis made his future impact on the world.

First, the friars decided not to elect his able, energetic and ambitious lieutenant, Elias, as their new Minister General, but a far more spiritual man. Second, reports of numerous miracles in response to prayers at

Francis's tomb for the handicapped, crippled and sick reinforced a spontaneous call, from all over Italy, further afield and every level of society, for his canonization. Third, the old pope, Honorius, who had been a great supporter of Francis, died in 1227 – and was replaced by a younger and immensely forceful figure, Ugolino dei Conti di Segni; he was even friendlier to Francis and at his request had become Cardinal Protector of the order. He took the name Gregory IX.

In 1228 riots in Rome caused Gregory to spend time in Perugia where he arranged with his cardinals and Elias to assemble the evidence they needed for Francis's canonization. Normally the process required them to investigate the candidate's life and then to enumerate his or her miracles. Gregory dispensed with the scrutiny on the grounds that Francis was so well known to him; the list of miracles grew longer every week.

The new pope had been frequently in touch with Elias in his role of Francis's Vicar, or deputy, during the previous five years, and had developed a great respect for his gifts, imagination, and devotion to Francis. Now that he had been freed from his time-consuming travels to oversee the order, Gregory set him to work on creating a memorial to Francis of quite extraordinary grandeur. Plans for it were ready by the time the cardinals unanimously confirmed their approval of sanctification.

On July 16, 1228 Pope Gregory rode across to Assisi with a cavalcade of clergy, abbots and bishops, cardinals, princes and Francis's friend and admirer King John of Jerusalem. In the Piazza del Comune Francis was proclaimed a saint. Gregory preached a rousing sermon, taking for his text, "He shone in his days as a morning star in the midst of the clouds," Cardinal Raynerius of Capocci spoke of the miracles, and finally the crowd broke into the *Te Deum*.

The next day Pope Gregory unveiled the plans he had been making with Elias.

Assisi lies along a low spur of Subasio, an imposing mountain with rolling grassland on its summit, below which a dark forest of ilex and pines descends to the city walls (Plate 1). A great fortress, the Rocca Maggiore, stands at the apex of the town; on the terrace beneath churches, convents and tall houses jostle around the cathedral; on the next level stand the civic buildings, the piazza, and other churches. Small houses and shops line the longest streets at the bottom.

Halfway down the hill, outside the wall to the west, there was a rocky knoll on which the town gallows stood. This was where, with typical self-deprecation, Francis had once said he would like to be buried, overlooking the vast expanse of the Umbrian plain and the little fortified towns secure in the folds of the opposite hills. Taking him at his word Elias, with Gregory's blessing, had acquired the deeds of the knoll.

On the day after the canonization Gregory climbed up to it and laid the foundation stone of a basilica to house Francis's remains, honor his memory and astonish future generations for centuries to come. It was to consist of two churches, the lower primarily for the worship of the friars, the upper a tall and vast auditorium in which to preach to the people. In accord with the original design the interior walls of the churches were soon to be entirely covered with frescoes by the finest Italian artists – Cimabue, Giotto, Simone Martini, and Pietro Lorenzetti. The most famous, by Giotto, Cavallini, and others, depict twenty-eight scenes from Francis's life. A small well was cut down into the rock underlying the lower church and made ready to receive the sarcophagus holding Francis's body.

On the northern side, a friary was built adjoining the lower church. To the west, the aspect facing Perugia, a steep retaining wall rose from a riverbank below, like the bluff of a fortress. Later, a set of papal apartments facing south over the valley assumed the style of a palace. This facade of the whole elaborate complex, built entirely of pink and white stone from Subasio, was upheld on the hillside by a superbly engineered tier of arcades.

It is one of the great buildings of Europe through which the Franciscans, with their French connections, introduced the Gothic style on a grand scale into Italy for the first time. It was, however, at total variance with everything Francis stood for. He was explicit that he did not want his friars to live in large, permanent buildings and he would have utterly condemned spending such a fortune, which should have gone to the poorest and sick, on stones, paintings and glass. When Giles – by then famous throughout Italy as a man of exceptional devotion – was shown around the completed buildings by the resident friars toward the end of his life, he is reputed to have remarked sadly, "Now all you need is women!"

The basilica has been shaken by earthquakes many times in its history, but such was the skill of its architects and builders that no irreparable damage occurred. But on September 26, 1997, at 11:42 in the morning, the second of two serious tremors shattered the vaulting over the eastern doorway, bringing masonry down on a team inspecting the effects of the first shock. Four people were killed – including two friars, one a novice and the other his novice master.

The cathedral, and the basilica and convent founded to honor Clare di Favarone – who was canonized two years after her death in 1253 – were even more severely ravaged.

*

However great the reverence with which the Basilica di San Francesco was built and has been lovingly and scrupulously maintained over the centuries, it is not Francis's finest and most appropriate monument. His supreme memorial lives in the three religious orders he founded and which number at least a million members today – mostly Catholics, but also Lutherans and Anglicans.

It is often said of him that he possessed genius, and he certainly exercised an exceptional ability to engage people's spirits with God and each other, so that their capacity for love and their will to help others was constantly strengthened. Of course their hearts and minds were involved in this but his inspiration appealed to the deeper dimension of their souls, though he and his friars exerted their moral influence through an unassuming metaphysical light rather than the ostentatious fire of the zealous.

At the age of twenty-four Francis abandoned his entire inheritance to devote himself as a pauper to relieving the misery all around him. He did this so successfully that the French scholar and agnostic, Ernest Renan, who wrote a best-selling life of Christ, said, "After Jesus Francis of Assisi has been the only perfect Christian."

Evidence that Francis fits into no conventional religious pigeonhole lies in the remarkable extent to which his influence permeates so many aspects of Western culture, even the scientific. For instance Marina Warner, in her study of the Virgin Mary through history, writes, "The Franciscan spirit continues to be considered by agnostics and atheists, as well as believers, as the most genuine expression of Christ's teaching ever approved by the Vatican."

Francis has also been seen by some cultural historians as the morning star of the Italian Renaissance. Johan Huizinga, the Dutch scholar who made a special study of the transition between the Middle Ages and the Renaissance, said this of the first great modern biography of Francis, published by Paul Sabatier in 1893, "Perhaps Sabatier has contributed more than anyone to the shift in the nature and the dating of the concept of the Renaissance. It was no longer a growth of the mind . . . but a growth of the heart: the opening of the eyes and the soul to all the excellence of the world and the individual personality."

Beauty, in all forms, was extremely important to Francis. Henry Thode, a nineteenth-century German art historian, considered he expressed "a new passion for the beauty of the world"; while Professor Ernst Gombrich attached to the wandering friars, "notably St. Francis himself," the shift from the static, two-dimensional, images of medieval painting to the realism, the truth to nature, introduced by the great artists of the Italian Renaissance.

In 1967, Lynn White, professor of history at the University of California, examined the roots of the world's ecological crisis for *Science* magazine. He traced the origins of our suicidal lack of respect for our environment to the dogma of man's dominion over nature. In conclusion he wrote, "The greatest spiritual revolutionary in Western history, Saint Francis, proposed an alternative Christian view of nature and man's relation to it: he tried to substitute the idea of the equality of all creatures, including man, for the idea of man's limitless rule of creation. . . . I propose Francis as a patron saint for ecologists." In a sense the then World Wildlife Fund did just that in 1986. Aware that economic arguments were not sufficiently powerful to mobilize man's defense of the planet, they looked to the spiritual and jointly with the Vatican convened a conference of the world's religious leaders in Assisi.

Francis's sense of beauty – in the human heart, mind, soul, and in every element of the natural world – made an indelible impression on the French philosopher Simone Weil. A Jew, she was never baptized a Christian but underwent a mystical experience in a Benedictine abbey in 1938. She worked in schools, vineyards and a car factory, visited the Republican front during the Spanish Civil War, and joined the Free French government in London shortly before her death in 1943, at the age of thirty-seven. She wrote this:

> The example of Saint Francis shows how great a place the beauty of the world can have in Christian thought. . . . His very choice of places for solitary retreats or for the foundation of his convents was the most

beautiful poetry in action. He stripped himself naked in order to have immediate contact with the beauty of the world.[3]

Spending most of his life out of doors, in all seasons, his vision of man's place in nature and the universe was as intense and apocalyptic as William Blake's or Walt Whitman's. His anthem of praise to God on this theme, *The Canticle of Brother Sun*, composed during his final illness, was one of his last and most memorable achievements. It is also the first poem in Italian to survive, and is said to have inclined Dante to write *The Divine Comedy* in Italian rather than Latin.

*

Dante devotes eighty lines of *The Divine Comedy* to Francis, which begin with an evocation of the Umbrian landscape. It is a good starting point for an exploration of his birthright.

Many see Umbria as the quintessence of Italy. The Tiber flows through it to the west of Assisi and the chain of the Apennine Mountains runs down to the east. Medieval towers in Assisi and its other fortified hill towns – Spoleto, Orvieto, Gubbio, Perugia – rise from Etruscan or Roman foundations. The vineyards and olive groves merge with woodland on its hills and mountains – part of nature and less manicured than the cultivation of Tuscany. But as in so many places nature here has two seasons, faces and hearts.

September brings short, sharp storms of forbidding fury. Black clouds build; winds race in from both ends of the valley, carrying smoke from the bonfires in opposite directions; in their wake sheets of driving rain are pierced by shafts of lightning which strike vertically down on the orchards and fields. Glass rattles in the windows when the thunder explodes, rumbling back and forth between invisible hills. Winter arrives silently with snow from the Apennines; the mountain streams freeze in their beds; the peaks grow white and chilling.

During spring and summer Assisi and the Spoleto Valley are another country. The great Roman poet Propertius, a friend of Vergil and Ovid, lived here in what was in Francis's day, and still is, the bishop's palace. He looked across to the seductive hills opposite – where men hunted "the gentle hare" – and down onto ambling white oxen yoked to the plow, and peasants trimming the vines with their sickles. On fine days the skies are a bright, clear blue, the heat intense. Shutting your eyes you feel the sun on your lids; the air is scented with pine, rosemary and orange blossom; the loudest noise is the soft bellow of pigeons or the ceaseless rasp of cicadas.

In a sense these two aspects of Umbria aptly convey essential features in the two sides of Francis's family. There was something wintry about the character of his father, Pietro di Bernardone; his mother, Pica, radiated the warmth and serenity of summer.

Pietro di Bernardone's direct antecedents in Assisi have been traced back four generations. The Umbrians were a tribe of rough, tough shepherds who migrated down the east bank of the Tiber. They settled on the site of Assisi because it was surrounded by grazing, its elevation offered safety from flooding and disease from the lake and marshes below, and the Tiber was a barrier against a worse menace – the Etruscans, who settled on the far bank where they established Perugia. The two cities had remained enemies ever since.

Although religious, the Umbrians left no signs of artistic achievement or culture. The Romans, when they arrived, drained the lake and the marshes, began farming and started to build their forum, temples and fortifications. Traces of all their work survive, although after four hundred years they were displaced by a series of destructive invasions from the east followed by waves of Lombards, Franks, and finally Germans. Each in turn occupied Assisi, transformed its appearance, and left its stamp on the features of its inhabitants.

Pietro put the talents inherited from these ruthless and acquisitive forbears to such good use that as a successful cloth merchant he amassed one of the largest fortunes in Umbria.

The inference that his wife, Pica, was French rests partly on the absence of any record that she came from a family in Assisi and partly on more positive, if circumstantial, evidence. First, Pietro had ample opportunity of finding a wife on his yearly visits to France to buy cloth. Second, Francis was taught at an early age to sing in French, or rather Provençal – the language increasingly used in fashionable society from the Pyrenees to northern Italy. Third, he also acquired Languedoc's notions of romantic love and chivalry, the culture of its soldier poets.

During the Middle Ages, in the courts and castles of Aquitaine and southern France, romantic or courtly love – a sentiment previously unknown even among the lyric poets of Greece and Rome – suddenly made itself felt. C. S. Lewis, an authority on medieval literature, wrote this perhaps oversimplified account of it:

> The sentiment is love of a highly specialised sort, whose characteristics may be enumerated as Humility, Courtesy, Adultery and the Religion of Love . . .
>
> Many of the features of this sentiment, as it was known to the Troubadours, have disappeared but this must not blind us to the fact that the most momentous and revolutionary elements in it have made the background of European literature for eight hundred years. French poets, in the eleventh century, invented, discovered, or were the first to express, that romantic species of passion which English poets were still writing about in the nineteenth. . .
>
> Real changes in human sentiment are very rare – there are perhaps three or four on record – but I believe that they occur, and that this is one of them.[4]

This romantic love, combined with a commitment to abject service, was usually professed in verse or song by a young man to a married woman whose husband was away on crusade. Its spell was so potent and fashionable that it made troubadours not only of poets and musicians, but of kitchen boys, scholars and princes. As Francis exchanged one mask for another in his early life, the married woman was supplanted in his dreams, as she was among many of the later troubadours who adopted the Virgin Mary instead, while Dante replaced her with Beatrice. Nevertheless whatever role he was playing – dandy, merchant, lover or soldier – and whatever he was doing – preaching, nursing lepers or dying – Francis remained a troubadour. It was his inheritance from his mother.

Romantic and musical, Pica was also a devout Christian; Angelo di Tancredi, who knew Francis as a boy, describes her as an excellent woman. On the other hand, Thomas of Celano, in his first life of Francis, says that she and Pietro, like most of their contemporaries, were flawed and brought up their son shamefully, to be debauched. However, Thomas was shaky on these early years and in his second life he describes Pica as "a friend of all goodness"; he does not say the same of Pietro.

Whatever the differences between them, Pietro and Pica – perhaps united by the attraction of opposites – lived together for thirty years in the merchants' quarter of Assisi, near the main square. At the end of September 1182 (or possibly a year earlier) Francis was born here.

Thanks to his own writings, those of his companions and the research of modern historians, more is known about him than about the personal lives of his most distinguished contemporaries. According to the evidence the likeliest site of his parents' home is now occupied by a little oratory called San Francesco Piccolino. The chapel is said to replace the stable or shop attached to Pietro di Bernardone's house which, like most, was built of stone. The ground floor was vaulted and could be used as a storeroom or stable – the horse, donkey and cows providing the upper floors with heating at night. Next to the stable door was a smaller one, higher from the ground. It gave access to the living quarters above when wooden steps were let down from inside; Assisi was dangerous at night.

Pietro could afford to give Pica the best of everything – attractive clothes, good food, servants, and a warm house with a four-poster bed, soft linen, fur covers, oil lamps, and glass in the windows. It is therefore difficult to believe a tradition that, at the last moment, she insisted on going downstairs to have her baby in the stable, although a fourteenth century inscription in Latin over the doorway reads:

> THIS ORATORY WAS THE STABLE OF OX AND ASS IN WHICH FRANCIS THE MIRROR OF THE WORLD WAS BORN.

Biographers have noted that with each retelling the lives of saints grow increasingly miraculous or embellished with biblical parallels; it is known as the marvel factor. One of the true marvels of Francis's life is that eight centuries after his death four million people every year come to visit his tomb.

2

A Liberal Education

1182–1196

Pietro missed both the birth and the christening of his son. Every autumn he was away for two or three months buying a year's supply of new stock at one of the great European fairs in Champagne – returning through Provence where he had probably met Pica.

The fact that they hadn't chosen a name for their first child before Pietro left suggests that he may have been premature; he was never large and often unwell. When Pica handed him to the bishop for baptism in the font of San Rufino cathedral she asked for him to be christened Giovanni. However, the name didn't stick, for on Pietro's return he wanted to call his son Francesco – reflecting his affection for Pica and his fondness of France, from which he derived so much of his wealth.

On the evening of the christening a pilgrim knocked at the door, begging food. After he had eaten he asked if he might hold the boy in his arms and, to the nurse's amazement, Pica agreed. Looking at the baby he said, "Today two children have been baptized in this city; this one will be among the best of men, the other among the worst."[1] His prediction for Francis came true.

A reviewer once described a biographer as "an artist who is on oath, and anyone who knows artistry knows too that this is almost a contradiction in terms." This doesn't mean that any account of Francis's childhood is an entire fabrication. The brief story of his early life as told by his friend Angelo di Tancredi in the early source known as *The Legend of the Three*

Companions may only be a sequence of anecdotes, but they are carefully selected to lead up to the dramatic moment when his order was founded; and other reliable medieval sources help to fill the gaps – archaeological finds, illustrated manuscripts, frescoes, church records, legal documents, chronicles, epics, poems and local traditions.

Assisi in those days sounded and smelled like a farmyard. Pietro's household, like every other, woke at dawn to a chorus of cocks, donkeys and barking dogs; not long after, the daily procession of goats, cattle and creaking carts left for the fields. Only the pigs stayed behind to clear up the public garbage – until their throats were cut and they were fed to an infirmary, lazar house or one of the convents. Each of the main streets had its chapel or church, and at seven o'clock a clamor of bells rang out for the Mass, their calls to devotion repeated through the day, interspersed with the deep, secular voice of the great town bell.

Pica and a nurse looked after Francis until he was seven or eight. At first the nurse had time to play with him in the mornings but before long Pica had other children. At least two survived; one, Angelo, was a boy. The children of successful parents had plenty of toys – puppets, balls, skittles and hoops, dice games, checkers and chess when they were older.

Until he went to school in the parish church, Pica gave Francis lessons at home. She told him Greek and Roman legends, the lives of the saints, the stories of Alexander the Great and Julius Caesar. On other days she would recite from the *Chansons de Geste* – immortalizing the exploits of Roland and Oliver against the Saracens in the Pyrenees – and the adventures of King Arthur's knights. Like other well brought up children he learned to play a musical instrument – a viol or a harp – but unlike many he was naturally musical. Pica taught him to sing in Latin, Umbrian and French.

When left on his own he would wander through the stockrooms and shop, or play in the courtyard outside. It gave him plenty of time to study his father's customers, neighbors and employees; they came and went like a series of vaudeville acts, mingled with cats and dogs, beggars and drunks, touts and musicians. On a lucky day there could be a juggler, a brawl or a military parade.

In hot weather landowners liked to get away from Assisi. Pietro and Pica rode out to their farms on Subasio or down in the valley. As they left the town swallows and swifts soared between the towers, nightingales sang in the gardens, and nesting hoopoes flitted through the orchards. Further on, when they paused to watch their sheep, peacefully grazing under the silver olives, or the teams of oxen carting sheaves of barley and rye on the hazy slope of the mountain, Pica saw beauty – and Pietro the assets and income of his yearly accounts.

Although these days in the country were the happiest of his childhood, one dark cloud always hung over them. Below Assisi there were half a dozen lazar houses, to which lepers in the town were condemned the moment they were diagnosed as carrying the disease. Throughout his early life Francis was incapable of mastering his horror of these crippled and stinking figures who haunted the roads until nightfall, begging for food or alms. Whenever he encountered them he was relieved to get back to the safety of home with the steps drawn up.

At dusk the town bell tolled the curfew; during darkness no one was allowed to go farther than three houses from their own, except during the corn and grape harvests. The town gates were shut, or like the piazza, closed to traffic with chains. Night watchmen, armed with crossbows, stood guard at key points in the city.

Before he went to bed he said prayers with Pica and perhaps sang a hymn. It was his mother who taught him manners – cheerfulness, generosity, courtesy and deference to his elders. Above all she had to instill respect for his father and a desire to emulate him. Eager and affectionate Francis longed to please, but Pietro was not easily impressed, especially by a son who was small for his age and quite often ill. Francis therefore learned to entertain with his songs and amuse with his antics.

*

When he was eight he went to school in his parish church, San Giorgio, a few hundred yards from home, just outside the southeastern gates of the town. It was his only formal education.

The church and infirmary next to it belonged to the bishop and the canons of San Rufino cathedral. One of the canons was rector of the church, school and also the hospital. This took in not only the sick, but vagrants, pilgrims and families who had lost their homes.

The extent of Francis's learning has always stimulated controversy. Several contemporaries describe him as unlettered or having little education, among them two of his great admirers, Cardinal Jacques de Vitry and the Bishop of Terni. This may have been because he did not go to a university, was never ordained priest, insisted that members of his order should not own books, and said of himself "*ignorans sum et idiota*." Mistakes are pointed out in the Latin of the two surviving texts in his own hand; and his script is unfavorably compared with Leo's, his amanuensis.

On the other hand, Angelo di Tancredi says he grew up "quick and clever"; and a recent analysis of his writing – especially his verse – has led to a much more respectful view of his learning, while his preaching became legendary, even among the most sophisticated.

The rector's first priority was to teach the boys the essentials of their religion – the catechism, the creed, how to make their confession and behave at the Mass. He introduced them to the Bible, explaining the Latin. The story of creation, the Garden of Eden, and the adventures of Noah, Jonah and Daniel – teeming with fish, snakes, birds and lions – had a natural appeal for young boys. Belief in God was universal among the educated. The life of Christ – his birth in a manger, the massacre of the innocents, the miracles, and the mounting drama of his death and resurrection – were as real as any other events in Roman times.

Medieval education otherwise consisted of seven "liberal arts." The three fundamentals that Francis was taught at San Giorgio were grammar, dialectic and rhetoric; he had to pick up the others – arithmetic, music, geometry and astronomy – as best he could. Pica had already given him music and in any case you can't stop an Italian from singing; Pietro would soon expound the mystery of figures; and one day he would learn the rudiments of geometry in a short spell as a builder. His familiarity with the sky would come later still, when he began to travel and sleep under the firmament night after night; the great poem he wrote at the end of his life opens with his praise for the sun, the moon and the stars.

Grammar consisted of learning how to read and write correctly on waxed tablets or boards. Apart from the proper use of Italian, and their own Umbrian dialect, the boys had to write, translate and speak Latin, which was still the universal language of the educated in Europe. Dialectic was intended to train the young in how to think and argue logically. Proof of any proposition was expected to be adduced from one of three sources: reason, authority or experience. In the Middle Ages great store was set by a man's ability to reason. The third art, rhetoric, must have been the one at which Francis excelled and which he most enjoyed. There was a great premium, two hundred and fifty years before the invention of printing, on being able to speak effectively in public – to entertain, announce news, plead a case, lay down laws, rouse an army or win the hearts of a crowd.

About thirty years after Francis died, the church in which he received his basic education was pulled down to make way for a basilica in honor of St. Clare. One of its side chapels is decorated with a lovely fresco – replacing a mural destroyed with the original church – of St. George on his charger, his lance poised at the dragon's throat; the scene is watched by a ravishing princess. It would be difficult to improve on the image of the princess, the knight and the dragon as the epitome of Francis's daydreams.

*

Nowadays children learn much about the shape of the society in which they live from television and the newspapers. At the age of ten or twelve Francis could have picked up the equivalent on a short walk from the Rocca Maggiore at the top of the town to the gate at the bottom; the pyramid of feudal society had adapted itself conveniently to the contours of the hill.

The Rocca or fortress at the top had been built and owned ever since by the most powerful emperors in Europe, first French and then German. In fact most of Italy was now more or less under German control – much to the fury of its principal cities and the pope. The emperor stayed in the Rocca with his family whenever he came to Assisi but throughout the year it was lived in by his permanent envoy, Conrad of Urslingen, Duke of Spoleto, with a powerful garrison.

Just below lived the feudal lords and the knights – a military rank – all of whom had castles and estates in the country. Although they were arrogant and often callous toward their dependants – many no better than slaves – they were the first to answer the call to arms on the rare occasions when pope and emperor made common cause to proclaim a crusade. Their houses in Assisi were large and fortified – many with pretentious towers, like those still surviving in the Tuscan hill town of San Gimignano. These grand families bought their cloth from Pietro, but Francis didn't meet their children. Traditionally, aristocrats' daughters were taught by their mothers at home in the towns, seldom going out and sometimes even kept from the windows. Their brothers, on the other hand, were brought up in the country.

The cathedral was on the same level as the aristocratic strongholds. The bishop was not only a muscular Christian and formidably litigious, but owned or controlled half the property in and around Assisi on behalf of the church.

On the next broad terrace lay the piazza – in several senses a middle ground: it was halfway down the hill; above it lived the privileged pieces on the social chessboard, below it milled the pawns; and the rising middle class of merchants, anxious to make money and wrest power from the nobles, did business all around it.

The streets below the piazza were a jumble of stalls, workshops, ovens, kilns, forges, stores, barns, slaughterhouses, stables and poultry runs, of dilapidated houses, tenements, hovels and lean-tos against the city walls; the whole quarter was alive, crowded, noisy and noisome. Thanks to Roman engineers Assisi was well supplied with water and drains; hygiene is easy to organize on a hill – except for the so-called *minores* who lived at the bottom. In wet weather the lower streets became open sewers, flooding into pools around the doorways.

In summer these slums were sweltering and buzzing with flies; during the freezing winter few could afford fires or warm clothes; whatever the season there were infestations of rats, fleas and lice. Year after year overcrowding, malnutrition and stagnant or polluted water provided perfect conditions for epidemics of leprosy, tuberculosis, smallpox, measles and flu – and for endemic malaria, typhoid and dysentery.

Once a year a mock battle took place between the *minores* and the *majores* who lived at the top of the town. Though weapons were blunted, bones were broken, blood was shed and men died on the streets.

*

Given a current affairs test in his last year at school, and asked to name Assisi's principal enemies or the forces most likely to threaten its peace, Francis could easily have picked four – the Saracens, the Germans, the more obnoxious landowners, and the town's ancient rival across the plain, Perugia.

However far away the actual fighting, the crusades were avidly followed in Assisi. "Saracens" was the name given to the Arabs who, in the eighth century, had occupied the shores of the Mediterranean from the Levant in the east and all along Africa to Spain in the west; numbers were now engaged as mercenaries by the Germans in southern Italy. The resulting confrontation between Christians and Muslims had smoldered for four hundred years; if the Saracens were forced to withdraw in Spain at one end of Europe, they never ceased to keep up pressure on Christian Byzantium at the other.

In 1096–1099 the First Crusade had taken Jerusalem from the Saracens, but a century later, when Francis was five, the city had fallen to them again. Posters of violent scenes in the Holy Sepulchre, and Mohammed humiliating Christ, had appeared in Assisi. Since then a third crusade, under the allied sovereigns of France, England and Germany, had failed to dislodge the Muslims, who still controlled the Mediterranean littoral from Spain to Syria.

While the church, and the rulers of every country in Europe, felt threatened by the Saracens, the cities and states of Italy were also in constant dread of the Germans, who were entrenched in many and menaced the rest, claiming – in defiance of the pope – that they were the legitimate successors of the Holy Roman Empire.

When Francis was thirteen the German emperor, Henry VI, entrusted his wife and newborn son Frederick to Conrad, the Duke of Spoleto, up in the Rocca. Amid scenes of unforgettable splendor, with troops, banners, trumpets and drums, the baby was escorted down to his christening in the cathedral. Because the elderly pope, Celestine III, was then attempting to end the perennial animosity between the church and the empire, the ceremony was performed by a gleaming phalanx of prelates and clergy. The future emperor Frederick II was dipped in the font already used for the baptism of Francis.

> *Baptism by water, the first armour we put on against the assaults of hate, greed and fear on our journey back to eternity . . .*[2]

The armor so defined by the English poet laureate John Betjeman only proved effective for one of these two babies.

In addition to festering with resentment against the Germans, the people of Assisi were increasingly outraged by the offensive behavior of some of the feudal aristocracy who derived their rights from the emperor. Each year the battle between the *minores* and *majores* was becoming less of a ritual and more a trial of strength. It was only a matter of time before the burgesses – the new bourgeoisie – joined the fracas and brought down the scales on the side of political change. When they did, it was certain that the old guard, stubborn soldiers to a man, would not go quietly.

For a thousand years Assisi and Perugia had glared at each other across the Tiber. Assisi had accepted the Romans; the Perugians – originally Etruscans – had defied them. Assisi was dominated by the Germans; Perugia took the part of the pope. In times of famine, Perugia raided Assisi's farms in the valley. Now that Assisi was turning against some of its nobles, Perugia gave them covert support. A conflict was inevitable.

3

The Pleasures of Youth

1196–1197

Life began in earnest for most boys when they left school at the age of fourteen, but Francis was never earnest for long. Although his father worked him extremely hard he still managed to enjoy every moment of his spare time.

If his first three biographers – Thomas, Henri and Angelo – give him little credit for his learning, they allow him virtually none for his early behavior. Angelo's account is the kindest:

> He was a spendthrift, and everything he earned went on eating and carousing with his friends. His parents often remonstrated with him because he squandered a fortune, more like a prince's son than theirs; but they were rich and being very fond of him didn't object for fear of antagonizing him.[1]

Both Angelo and Thomas of Celano agree that Francis was admired for his style, especially his clothes, which outdid those of all his friends; but though his father was unwisely generous, Francis wasn't popular just for his money. He had a magnetic gaiety, loved gossip and was fond of jokes, occasionally wearing eccentric patchworks of the most expensive cloth and the cheapest; he was always considerate and never used foul language.

A much more critical account of his misspent youth is given in a verse life by Canon Henri d'Avranches, written within several years of his death.

Working in the papal secretariat d'Avranches had access to any documents prepared in the process of canonization. His biographical extravaganza dwells, with poetic relish, on the dangers of addictions such as alcohol and sex to which the young sometimes fall prey in their search for new sensations.

Thomas of Celano is even more censorious, but since he too was writing within three years of Francis's death, at the express wish of the pope, and was able to quiz witnesses in Assisi, his version of events – where it does not actually contradict Angelo's – must be accurate:

> Parents everywhere have developed an evil tendency to bring up their children very dissolutely. Even while they are learning to speak, they are taught to say and do detestable things, both lustful and wanton. . . . As soon as they reach adolescence they are therefore embroiled in every kind of debauchery . . . and lend all the members of their body to iniquity.
>
> Francis wasted his time miserably, encouraging wickedness until he was nearly twenty-four years old.[2]

The most plausible explanation of this indictment is that it was designed to deflect responsibility for the saint's youthful debauchery onto Pietro and Pica, although it is far more likely that the real culprit was the louche atmosphere of Assisi itself. In many ways it still retained traces of its pagan foundations, with the Temple of Minerva standing at its heart (albeit by then a Benedictine monastery), its original cathedral, Santa Maria Maggiore, built over the Temple of Jove, and its new cathedral, San Rufino, rising from the foundations of a temple to the Roman earth goddess.

Such traditions die hard. Every December ranks and offices in the town were stood on their heads; a boy bishop was elected and robed in the church of St. Nicholas on the Saint's feast day. It was the prelude to a three-week Saturnalia over the winter solstice, known as the December Liberties. The churches were open to feasting and drinking, erotic singing, dancing and plays.

In May the return of Donna Primavera was welcomed then, as still today, with contests of dancing, drumming, sword play, archery and horsemanship. At night, in the streets lit with fires and blazing brands, the tang of crushed straw and dung mingled with mouthwatering smells from bread ovens and spits. The flickering alleys echoed with hoofbeats and bells; soft, throaty laughter and singing conveyed an erotic impression that the everyday rules of conduct were suspended. Greenmen, sun gods, and giants with flaming scythes strode into the piazza on stilts; at midnight a towering maypole was slowly erected in front of the Temple of Minerva.

It is said that moonlight and love songs are seldom out of date. A few of the songs heard in the streets today were sung by Francis and the troubadours then. Their themes were a girl's beauty, infatuation with her, the long siege of her heart and alarm that her defenses might never fall. In their blithest moments they evoked spring, the soaring flight of a lark, the drawn out throb of the nightingale's song and the richness of summer. Many of them distilled a sense of vitality, wonder, longing and gratitude which was instinct in Francis and remained undimmed throughout his life and his last excruciating illness.

Most of the songs, emanating from the courts of chivalry in southern France, were composed in Provençal, the *langue d'Oc* (*oc* being the equivalent of *oui* in the north of France). Thanks to his mother Francis could pick them up easily; with his strong, sweet, clear voice, he sang them enchantingly.

Although most were addressed to an unattainable beauty whose husband was away on crusade, desires were often frankly expressed. Andreas Capellanus, a chaplain at the Court of Champagne, wrote a handbook on the art of love which, though intended as satire, was imitated by the poets of chivalry. In his view a lover might be progressively rewarded with a token, a kiss, a promise, and perhaps at last with a nude, but unconsummated, embrace.

A married woman only yielded to her lover on the rarest occasions, but when she did the poet didn't gloss over it. This is Chrétien de Troyes's account of how Sir Lancelot and Queen Guinevere gave way to their passion:

> He comes to the bed of the Queen to whom he bows in adoration, for no holy relic inspires him with such devotion. She holds out her arms, hugging him to her breast, and draws him into her bed. Out of the love in her heart she lavishes on him all the endearments of which she is capable. His love for her is a hundred thousand times as great, and he enjoys all he desires as she welcomes his intimacy. He finds her

> lovemaking so sweet and splendid, as they kiss and fondle, that they truly experience such joy and wonder as was never before known.[3]

Songs and verses like these, combined with laughter and wine, were heady stuff toward the end of an evening. Girls were not supposed to go out after dark but the daughters of the burgesses living around the piazza were less restricted than those of the nobles. By the time Francis and his school friends were fifteen they were considered old enough to fight with the army and to marry; their sexual drive was reaching its peak.

Francis, like a number of saints who later achieve strict celibacy, spent his early years loitering at the fabled Ivory Gate of delusion. Siddhartha Gautama, the Buddha, was married, had a son and enjoyed the life of a prince in Nepal until, at the age of twenty-nine, he began his search for Nirvana. St. Augustine of Hippo, before his conversion, took two mistresses and fathered a son; in his *Confessions* he recorded his famous prayer, "Give me chastity but not yet." And in the century before Francis, St. Bernard, the Cistercian Abbot of Clairvaux, had passed through a dissolute phase in his early life.

Both Thomas of Celano and Henri d'Avranches give clear indication that Francis lost his virginity. When money came into general circulation as coinage, it introduced prostitution into Assisi as everywhere else. St. Augustine had taken the pragmatic view that "if you eliminate prostitutes from society you will disrupt everything through lust." St. Thomas Aquinas, born in the year Francis died, believed that prostitution was like a drain in a palace, which allowed sewage to escape and if blocked would give rise to sodomy,* in his view far worse.

Who Francis's early girlfriends were is never mentioned in the sources.

*

By the time Francis left school Pietro had moved his premises closer to the piazza, across from the Temple of Minerva. The square was the center of most of Assisi's official business. It was an arena for the town crier, the city heralds and the magistrates delivering judgment; processions passed

*Jacques de Vitry, the hawk-eyed Bishop of Liège, noticed French prostitutes shouting "*sodomites*" at priests who had declined their offer of services.

through it on election days and festivals; markets were held here. But Francis and his friends were more interested in its other attractions when they escaped from work. A students' drinking song, *Gaudeamus Igitur*, caught their spirit.

Therefore let us rejoice
And give rein to our mirth,
For the pleasures of youth,
Lead to old age uncouth,
And thereafter the earth.

In the evenings neighbors and strangers met in the piazza to drink, gossip and exchange news with pilgrims, travelers, and mercenaries home after fighting the Germans. Sundays apart there were a hundred holidays a year on which young and old could spend hours in the square listening to the troubadours and storytellers. Above all there was wine, which Francis lavished on his friends at every opportunity.

Happily for him, he also began to discover an entirely different set of pleasures out in the country, where Pietro owned a number of farms. Today Francis is best remembered for his love of animals which, as in so many naturalists, probably first stirred when he was out hunting; this was true of his contemporary Frederick II, later the German emperor, a brilliant naturalist, who combined falconry with a scientific study of birds. On the marshes below Assisi a falconer could kill pheasant, quail, waterfowl and, in a hard winter, geese. On Subasio there were partridge, plover and hares.

The mountain is a revelation for anyone, like Francis, with a sense of beauty and exhilarated by altitude. On the climb up through the woods crocus, heartsease and cyclamen flower in profusion on the banks, while in the spring the grassland on the summit is covered, for miles, with orchids and pheasant's eye narcissus. The views up there are breathtaking – fifteen miles to Perugia, farther to the steely glint of Lake Trasimene, and farther still to the Apennines, once described under snow as like the immaculate wings of archangels, fallen in the battle with Lucifer.

Francis could go out with a huntsman and his dogs after the bigger game on Subasio – wolves, wild boar, deer, and even a bear. It was said that hunting was like war, only much more beautiful, even if at the end of the chase the quarry turned, killing one or two of the hounds and maiming their master. Some men acquire an early taste for danger, which grows into habit with age; Francis was one. Hunting was an excellent qualification for a boy who wanted to become a soldier – another passion he acquired in the country.

While he had been at school and learning his father's trade, the sons of the local nobility had grown up on their family estates where, from the age of seven, they absorbed the elements of hunting and knighthood as part of their everyday life. They rode from the day they could sit in a saddle, learned to fence with wooden swords, moved on to staves, and practiced their skill with small bows and arrows on rabbits and birds.

Until now there had been few chances for Francis to meet his more aristocratic contemporaries and these early exercises in the military arts had passed him by. But Tancredi di Ugone, Angelo's father, owned a farm which marched with one of Pietro's; it gave Francis the chance to make friends with the sons of the local nobility. Always competitive, he threw himself into their games – wrestling, fencing, jousting, and improving his archery and horsemanship.

Although his father was only a merchant it didn't disbar Francis from one day becoming a bachelor, a squire and finally a knight. Pietro may have been quietly pleased that his son was acquiring new graces, skills and social connections but had only one life in mind for him – a career in the business.

4

Making Money

1196–1197

When Francis first crossed the threshold of his father's premises as an apprentice he was stepping into a new world – the world of money. Pietro was a pioneer and expert in it. Angelo says he was "absorbed in accumulating wealth"; unlike Francis he had little time for anything else.

Between the collapse of the Roman Empire and the establishment of feudalism little cash circulated in northern Italy. There was no surplus of manpower to produce goods for sale, no surplus wealth to encourage their supply and therefore no real call for coinage; but first the church and then men like Pietro – *nouveaux riches* merchants and their fellow burgesses – found ways of joining or displacing feudal landowners in the exploitation of labor. Until recently the opposite of *pauper* (poor) was *potens* (powerful), now it was becoming *dives* (rich).

The feudal ranks of dukes, counts and lords who derived their rights from the German emperor, each extracted from the level beneath them whatever dues they could in the form of work, produce, military service and other dues. It therefore fell on the lowest class – tenants, villeins and serfs – to support the whole hierarchy with their labor. There had been little incentive to produce more than their quota, but this was now changing as the feudal system began to break down.

It was the clergy, men like the Bishop of Assisi and the Abbot of San Benedetto, the Benedictine abbey halfway up Mt. Subasio, who helped generate the first flow of minted money which cracked open the feudal pyramid, rather as lava bursts through a volcano. The vast monastic estates attracted imaginative monks who applied advances in simple science and technology to create, from their natural and human resources, produce for sale. The church, subject only to its own code of laws, was a more relaxed employer than the aristocracy.

The Benedictines drained and then irrigated some of the marshes below Assisi to cultivate them as vineyards and cornfields. Iron plows proved better than wooden ones; horses worked faster than oxen; scrub was cleared for grazing; pigs, orchards and forests responded to care; a man working a new, broad, horizontal loom could produce more than a woman with an old, narrow, upright one. Wine, wheat, wool, hams, fruit, timber and cloth came on the market, where coinage was more convenient than barter.

However brutal many magnates had been, many others had demonstrated a sense of *noblesse oblige* in a benevolent, if limited, paternalism; others, with uneasy consciences, endowed convents and infirmaries in return for posthumous Masses to be said for their souls; slavery and the strictest serfdom had died out or was waning. The church, too, had frequently exercised charity and regularly helped to negotiate the emancipation of families from the more pernicious conditions of servitude. All this came too late and was too little.

The slow dawn of this enlightenment and the chaos of civil war were enabling a new class of freemen to earn their release or run away from their overlords. These were the men Pietro, with none of the rights of a hereditary landowner, could now employ to develop his business. Other enterprising freemen grabbed the chance to set up on their own – or to work for wages – as millers, bakers and butchers, woodworkers, blacksmiths and masons, tradesmen, taverners and lawyers.

Pietro had inherited a small cloth business begun by his father or grandfather. To achieve the level of his present success he needed not only his single-minded ambition, but luck, courage and the ruthlessness which went with his violent temper. Nevertheless, for a long time he was extraordinarily indulgent toward his new apprentice, although he worked Francis hard during business hours – shifting and checking stock; mastering details of twine, wools, weaves and dyes; memorizing their sources, quality and value. The worst part of the day was going down into the slums, where Francis had to cajole his father's employees into producing even more for the pittance they were paid.

The women, working until long after dark in their dim and smoky hovels, had to spin his wool, weave it into cloth, and then treat it before it was dyed; others cut and stitched it. The dyers' work was literally sweated labor, and sometimes lethal. All day long they stirred their huge bubbling vats, destroying their lungs as they inhaled steam from the solution of dye and the sulfurous salts that fixed it in the cloth. Pietro knew the prices he paid for this work. Francis knew the costs of supplying it; ultimately one of the world's most persuasive exponents of poverty, he first played a part in the birth of capitalism.

It is reckoned that only about five thousand people then lived within the walls of Assisi and about another ten thousand in the countryside around it. In addition to serving customers in the shop Francis therefore had to sell to neighboring towns – Gubbio, Spello, Nocera, Foligno, Spoleto. Even so, cloth alone could not have accounted for Pietro's great wealth; he needed to diversify and invest his profits astutely. The first of these investments was land. The fact that Pietro could actually buy property was a symptom of feudal dissolution – previously land had changed hands only by conquest, grant or inheritance.

The nobility hated the power of money; it was making the new class of entrepreneurs too powerful, and allowing villeins and serfs to escape from the clutches of feudalism. Nevertheless they were desperate to enjoy the luxuries coming onto the market – wines, glass, metal ware, fine weapons and Pietro's best cloth. Having no cash they sold the only asset they had, land, and so accelerated their own decline.

Pietro was able to buy up a dozen farms, down in the valley and all around Mt. Subasio, where Francis spent some of the happiest times of his life. Well managed, the estates yielded produce which fetched good prices in the current famine and integrated rewardingly with Pietro's cloth business. Needing horses and mules for both his farms and his merchandise, he went in for breeding and selling them. His skilled craftsmen made saddlery, bridles and carts for sale. He had to arm, train and maintain a team of men to protect his caravans on their long journeys to France; for a price he could offer protection to others or even hire out his guards.

Pietro was increasingly respected in Assisi; a man so obviously successful was approached with offers to invest or requests for loans on which he could set high rates of interest. It was a short step from this into banking which became an important part of his business.

Angelo mentions Francis's ability as a businessman only briefly. He simply says he was very different from his father, "more high spirited and openhanded." He illustrates this with an example. One day a beggar came into the shop and asked for alms for the love of God, but Francis was "so intent on the business of making money" that he ignored the man. On reflection he realized that if the beggar had asked for money in the name of some prince he would have given it. After that he decided he would never refuse anything asked in God's name, though it has to be said that it took him some time to live up to his good resolution.

*

By 1197 Francis was old enough to join his father's annual expedition to the cloth fair in Champagne for the first time. They were probably away for up to three months and from now on this event became the one activity capable of bringing them close to each other.

To help defray the costs and pay for the year's new stock, they loaded the mules with merchandise for sale at the fair – herbs, dyes, leather, metal work and alum, a ground rock whose salts were essential to fixing dye in a cloth. On the way north Pietro also picked up some of the silk fabrics from the east which came into the great ports of Genoa and Venice.

Before crossing the Alps the Italian merchants buried for the time being their personal rivalries and those between their cities. It was a tough journey, often in very bad weather and the roads were haunted by gangs of discharged mercenaries, known as *routiers*. The merchants banded together in armed convoys and slept under canvas until caravanserais were put up along their routes. At all times in Europe the convention known as the Peace of God was meant to protect priests, monks and hermits, farmers, cowherds and laborers, the old, women, children and merchants. Increasingly the *routiers*, like the castellans, ignored it.

The excitement of these journeys stimulated a passion for travel and adventure that never left Francis. They whetted his insatiable curiosity about places and people, enabled him to show off his skill in handling horses and mules, and gave him a chance to develop the arts of persuasion and to joke with the French in their language.

The mood of even the most hardened merchants would have quickened as their mule trains converged from every direction on Troyes. The Counts of Champagne had created one of the most stimulating courts and successful commercial centers in Europe, organizing fairs in four different towns through the year. Those at Troyes were held in July and September.

The larger houses in the town were half-timbered, many of them so lopsided that they almost met over the alleys; but the foreign merchants congregated with their own compatriots on the outskirts, sleeping in tents or wooden huts. By the time the fair opened, tens of thousands of visitors had streamed into the small town, and Francis found himself at the heart of the most lively, colorful and cosmopolitan gathering in medieval Europe, rivaled only by a coronation or the muster of a crusade.

Spaniards and French brought steel, wine, leather and wool; metals and salted fish came down from Lubeck and the Baltic; bearded Russians arrived from Novgorod with bales of glossy furs – bear, wolf, beaver, fox and marten. Other caravans, from the Middle East, made their way through southern Europe laden with jewelry, silver, gold, pearls and – despite the church's disapproval – slaves, some of them picked up in the Balkans (hence their name). Most arresting of all were the Arabs who crossed over from Africa with spices, ivory and magnificent horses. However, these exotic traders provided only a sideshow at Troyes.

The main business was the commerce in cloth and other materials. The most ravishing and expensive silks were imported from the Middle East – gold and silver brocades, embossed silk, samite or satin, and shot silks, fabulously light, from Mosul; the softest linens and cottons were shipped from Egypt. But Pietro was principally concerned with buying the best woollen cloth from Flanders – heavy for winter use, and light for the summer. The very finest, like the most resplendent silks, were dyed scarlet or crimson, from the kermes insects bred and collected in the Mediterranean oak forests.*

The cloth trade was the dynamic force introducing a new economic age to the whole of Europe, generating not only its infrastructure – new roads, bridges and facilities for river traffic – but a system of credit, in effect international banking, to supersede clumsy and vulnerable dealings in silver and gold. Acting in rare accord, the pope, the Emperor of Germany, the King of France and the Duke of Burgundy joined the Counts of Champagne in promulgating measures to protect these new revenues from

*They gave their name to "crimson."

a variety of threats – credit frauds, plunder by the *routiers*, and demands for excessive taxes and tolls by landowners straddling the principal roads.

Francis already knew how privileged he was in the provincial context of Umbria. Troyes offered him wider horizons. All the resources of Europe and the Mediterranean were on view, and with them the prospect of a lifetime's luxury, travel, patronage and political influence – a way of life soon to become a fine art in Siena and Florence.

At the end of each day's hectic dealing, he could devote himself to pleasure after dark. Troubadours, jugglers and pilgrims, knights and visitors to the court all crowded into the town for the feasts, the drinking, the dancing and the whoring, and to listen to minstrels and dramatic recitals of the epics of chivalry.

About twenty years before, Marie, Countess of Champagne, had commissioned a poet of genius, Chrétien de Troyes, to versify the adventures of half a dozen Arthurian knights. He was so successful that they were soon familiar all over Europe, even in Scotland. Master of the troubadour idiom, steeped in the legends of chivalry, a brilliant storyteller, he was just the man to cast a spell over Francis. The final epic, the adventures of Sir Perceval – who has set eyes on the holy grail and the lance that pierced Christ's side – is not only rich in poetry, psychology, and its observations of nature but, unlike the others, carries the concept of knighthood into the realms of the spirit. The world conjured up by Chrétien de Troyes was far closer to Francis's heart than that of big business.

Closer still were the exploits of two brothers who belonged to one of the great fighting dynasties of France and lived in the Chateau de Brienne, twenty-five miles from Troyes. When their father had been killed on the Third Crusade, attacking the fortified port of Acre in Syria, Walter de Brienne had taken his place, and through sheer courage and skill captured the city from the Saracens; his younger brother John was a soldier of equal brilliance. Such was the influence of these two Frenchmen on Francis that some years later he dropped everything to join Walter on a quixotic campaign in Apulia. Later still he watched John raise his great sword, at the age of seventy, to stem a Saracen charge on the banks of the Nile.

The end of the cloth fair might have been an anticlimax if Pietro and Francis had simply retraced their route over the Alps – about seven hundred miles as the crow flies and taking six weeks or more with the pack animals.

More probably they took an alternative and longer route home, traveling through Burgundy and then floating down the Rhône on barges from Lyons to Beaucaire. After buying more woolen cloth in Languedoc, they set out on the old Roman road, the Via Aurelia, across Provence toward Italy. This was Pica's country and they had relations to visit.

When it came into sight the mule train took the Strada Francesca past two of the family farms and climbed to the welcome gates of Assisi. By the time they reached home they found the town rife with rumor, like every other in Italy, at news of the sudden and unexpected death of the German emperor in Sicily.

5

Civil War

1197–1202

Henry VI's death from fever at the age of thirty-two, without an obvious successor, for his son was only three, raised the town's hopes of breaking his dynasty's stranglehold on Assisi.

Venice and Milan – the two biggest cities in Europe – had long been republics. Smaller towns, such as Pisa and Parma, had recently declared themselves communes or small city-states. The energetic and ambitious new middle class in Assisi were determined to follow suit. All the time they were strengthening their hand by the formation of guilds and fomenting discontent among the ranks of the new freemen; they had also won the backing of some of the more farsighted nobility.

Henry had been loathed in Umbria, partly because he personified a detested occupation, partly for his own sadistic cruelty. He had seated one defeated enemy on an iron throne, heated it until it glowed, and then crowned him with red hot metal. He had blinded and castrated the eight-year-old son of another, imprisoning the boy's mother, Queen Sibila of Sicily, in Alsace.

The Germans had, in fact, achieved the near impossible, uniting against themselves virtually all the factions in Italy normally at continuous loggerheads with each other – the papacy; Rome; many city-states like Assisi; the rising ranks of Pietro's new middle class; and the poorest villeins and serfs, on whom the main brunt of feudalism fell. Even some of the landed aristocracy, whose feudal rights derived from imperial authority, and on whom the emperor relied for support against the pope, had been alienated.

The whole of Italy vibrated as these forces ground against each other like millstones, pulverizing many places and people in the process. Francis, on the other hand, seized the opportunities the disorders offered. Had he been a true soldier he might well have emerged like his heroes, the de Brienne brothers. As it was, the violent fluctuations of his fortunes turned him into a very different kind of soldier.

In Assisi Henry's death rekindled the people's smouldering hatred of Conrad, the Duke of Spoleto, and his garrison up in the Rocca; it also intensified the rancor against the local landowners. For a few months nothing changed, because Pope Celestine III, now well over ninety, was incapable of mobilizing both the will and an army to throw out the Germans. However in January 1198 the reaper removed him. He had wanted to abdicate in favor of an elderly cardinal of great wisdom, Giovanni di San Paolo, but the college elected instead a young cardinal deacon of only thirty-seven; he took the name of Innocent III. Both these men exercised a decisive influence on Francis; Innocent also exercised a decisive influence on the church and Europe.

He had been born Lotario dei Conti di Segni, in about 1160, with impeccable connections. His father's family was German; his mother was a Roman aristocrat; Pope Clement III had been his uncle. He himself was a very clever man, mastering theology and biblical studies at the university of Paris, and perhaps law at Bologna; he had also written a number of books. Deploying his intelligence, energy and courage, his sense of justice, his powers of diplomacy and his willingness to make decisions, he immediately began tackling the mountain range of problems that faced him – fortified by the pronouncements of his predecessor Gregory VII which included:

- The Roman Church was founded by Christ alone.
- The pope can be judged by no one.
- All princes should kiss his feet.
- He can depose emperors.[1]

Having a sense of humor – and of humility – he may have taken another of Gregory's assertions with a pinch of salt: "A duly ordained pope is undoubtedly made holy by the merits of St. Peter."

Within a few months of his election, aware that the Germans now lacked a leader, Innocent began bargaining with Conrad of Urslingen for control of the Dukedom of Spoleto and summoned him to a meeting at Narni, halfway between them. As soon as Conrad left Assisi the communal faction mustered its forces and laid siege to the Rocca. By the time that Innocent heard the news, Conrad had agreed to cede him the fortress, so that the two men were equally affronted and sent envoys ordering the rebels to call off the attack. They refused.

Francis, with so many friends among the young burgesses and so keen to prove himself a soldier, would have been eager to join the final assault which stormed up the escarpment to the Rocca; the walls were scaled or breached, and the fortress was triumphantly sacked. The victors declared Assisi a commune and lost no time in taking over the powers of the *ancien régime* by placing authority in the hands of four consuls, who were supported by priors – city elders – and magistrates.

Pietro is described in a document as "a benefactor and financier of the city-state." The old Roman forum, the Piazza di Minerva, near which he lived and worked, was renamed the Piazza del Comune: it is still called that today. It was the first time for centuries that Assisi was governed by any kind of consensus.

*

For the next four years life in Assisi was fraught. Famine was prevalent in Umbria; civil violence erupted; war lay ahead; and in the background there was a battle for the German throne between Otto of Saxony and Philip of Swabia. For Francis they were years of mounting excitement.

Armed conflicts were then common all over Europe, and whenever possible merchants kept out of them. They were considered more valuable to a community supplying it with goods, lending it money and paying its taxes. Pietro could therefore go on pursuing the relentless growth of his business and wealth. Francis was often free to help him – for instance making the annual journey to Troyes – but, as a younger man, could be called on by the commune to fight in its militia against the city's enemies, including the landowning nobility who began to make trouble.

Although a few of them, including Tancredi di Ugone, had supported the establishment of a commune, the majority resented the fact that without imperial support their prestige and power were draining away. In an attempt to set back the clock and avenge themselves, they turned greedy eyes on the roads, increasingly used by smallholders, traders and the abbeys for the transportation of merchandise. Many of them were dominated by castles, ideally placed for exacting exorbitant tolls, or more simply for ambush, murder and theft.

One of the ringleaders, Leonardo di Gislerio, lived with his family at Sasso Rosso, the castle menacing the road along which Pietro took his cloth for sale in Spello. Monaldo di Offreduccio, another, was head of an even more aggressive clan; he and his brothers owned farmland and castles all the way from Assisi to Cannara on the other side of the valley and beyond. None the less, such was the strength of Francis's magnetism that fifteen years later he drew some of his most devout companions from these two families.

In the meantime, there was only one way for the young commune to protect its food supplies, maintain its revenues and stamp out the malicious opposition of these embittered aristocrats. They launched their militia against each rebellious castle in turn. The owners, remembering how often the emperor had relied on their military support in the past, now looked for reciprocal favors. In vain. Neither of the German pretenders responded.

Sieges great and small dominated medieval fighting. One by one the militia brought down the castles of the dissidents. Sasso Rosso was left in ruins, as it remains today, although its vineyards sell very drinkable red wine. Monaldo di Offreduccio and his brothers were driven from their castles at Cannara and Correggiano. Assisi itself was also rank with smoke, and rubble piled up in the streets, for whenever a castellan fell foul of the commune his fortified house at the top of the town was ransacked and burned.

Perugia took advantage of its rival's preoccupation to launch a series of raids across the Tiber and harass the farms in the valley. At first this was simply an irritation, but the evicted landowners precipitated a full-scale crisis. Those who had escaped with their lives rode across the plain to Perugia with their families. Leonardo di Gislerio led the exodus, followed by the Count of Assisi, most of the other nobles, and a number of knights. The redoubtable Monaldo di Offreduccio took with him two of his brothers and their children, including Clare di Favarone, then aged six.

The émigrés, the cream of Assisi's aristocracy, now pledged themselves and their lands to Perugia, and asked in return that the city should require its ancient rival to restore their properties, compensate them for their losses, and pay them heavy damages.

Assisi braced itself to fight, making diplomatic approaches to its neighbors, organizing its army and reconstructing the walls of its defenses so recently destroyed in getting rid of the Germans. Francis, with every other able-bodied man, threw himself into the building work. Under a master mason the carpenters erected the scaffolding and set up the ramps and pulleys for raising the stones; builders cut, chiseled and laid them, while others mixed the sand, lime and cement into mortar; blacksmiths stood by to provide or sharpen iron saws, hammers, crowbars and shovels. Paradoxically Francis's brief spell now as a mundane builder paved the way for his later initiation and life as a mystic.

In the autumn of 1202 Perugia turned up the pressure by signing a friendly treaty with Foligno, only a dozen miles behind Assisi's back. Next the Perugian consuls announced they would extract their demands by force. The commune in Assisi lost no time in responding. The consuls secured alliances with all the nearby towns – Gubbio, Fabriano, Nocera, Spello and Narni – which had scores to settle with Perugia. They were ready to launch a pre-emptive attack.

6

Into Battle

1202–1203

During the Middle Ages everyone lived close to the cutting edge. You knew how to fell a tree, how to plow a field and reap it, how to butcher a pig and how to trim leather for jerkins and boots.

You watched your children, brothers and sisters being born in a bed or in front of the fire. You nursed the dying and buried your dead. In battle, unless you were an archer or his target, you looked into the eyes of the man you killed or who was about to kill you. The more intensely you were aware of sickness and death, the more you relished your health and your life. Joie de vivre lay at the very heart of Francis's nature but he seemed increasingly convinced that to get the most out of life he should put it at risk.

And he is dead, who will not fight;
And who dies fighting has increase.
The fighting man shall from the sun
Take warmth, and life from the glowing earth.
Speed with the light-foot winds to run,
And with the trees to newer birth.[1]

Every generation has produced its soldier poets but Julian Grenfell, in 1915, came as close as any to expressing feelings about battle which were entirely characteristic of Francis.

The habits of war were a man's second nature. Commanders – kings, counts and consuls – knew exactly what techniques to apply, from the first summons to battle until the final charge or retreat; their dependants were accustomed to follow them. The build-up before the battle against Perugia started slowly, as bands of knights and armed men trickled into Assisi from the nearby towns and the few outlying castles loyal to the commune. Then, on the morning chosen for the attack on Perugia, the town crier went his round, the bells tolled, the gonfaloniers for each district and guild unfurled their banners as their men rallied around them.

Though still not a knight, Francis was well trained for the cavalry. His hauberk and leggings of chain mail, like a close-fitting habit and cowl, protected him from head to ankle; over them went a surcoat painted with his colors or arms; a nosepiece jutted down from his simple steel helmet. Approaching the battlefield he would put on his gauntlets and carry a lance and shield, while his sword, dagger and mace hung at his side.

His parents, his brother Angelo, his father's household, and no doubt several girls, watched him mount and joined the hubbub pressing around the columns. When the first contingents were ready, the heralds raised their long, slim trumpets. The fanfares gave way to the beat of the drums. Echoing off the stone walls, they drowned every other noise and released the adrenalin. As it left the gates, the long procession passed the great wooden carriage of Assisi. Brought out only on special occasions, drawn by a team of white oxen and draped with the red and blue colors of the city, it carried an altar and crucifix. Beside the carriage stood the bishop, notorious for the ferocity of his lawsuits but staunchly loyal to Assisi, although the pope favored Perugia.

So many of Assisi's knights had gone over to the enemy that for the first time untried young men like Francis were riding beside veterans of the Third Crusade or hard-fought battles on Italian soil. Always an exhibitionist, Francis in his showy equipment might have raised a smile among the hard-bitten sergeants and mounted crossbowmen who brought up the rear. Their view of the coming battle was altogether less sanguine than his. The defeated might be shod like mules, have their mouths stuffed with toads, be wrapped in straw and set on fire, or tortured at a banquet as post-prandial entertainment. The Perugians had a particularly gruesome reputation; their emblem was, appropriately, a clawed and snarling griffin.

Starting along the Strada Francesca – now the via Francigena – familiar to Francis from his farm visits and annual journeys to Champagne, the little army left the main road to Perugia a mile or two from the Tiber, and branched up a hill to the hamlet of Collestrada. Today it is possible to see exactly where its line ran along the crest between a church and small castle on the left, to a building, then a leper house, on the right, giving a front about a kilometer wide.

Looking back, Assisi would have been visible on the flank of Subasio, ghostly gray in a late autumn haze. Looking forward, damp fields – a patchwork of bright greens against sodden chocolate plow – sloped down toward poplars lining the banks of the Tiber and the bridge of San Giovanni.

The only reliable account of the battle is part of a long poem by Bonifazio, a Franciscan friar; it was commissioned by Perugia about a hundred years later but is based on the city's records. The Perugians, incensed by the impudence of Assisi's advance, launched an assault. Their decision was more impulsive than wise, for it was against all tactical sense to storm up the hill into a hail of arrows. Both crossbows and longbows were capable of devastating fire – on two occasions popes tried to ban them from military use – and Assisi repulsed the first assaults, prolonging the battle until the late afternoon.

As a cavalryman Francis rode shoulder to shoulder with his echelon; the textbook prescribed that their line should form so tightly that when lowered their lances would prevent a glove from falling to the ground between them. On the order to charge they had to spur their horses into a volley of arrows and then a wall of thrusting pikes, until they were surrounded by a frenzy of axes and swords. The first rule of defense was to unseat the enemy cavalry by killing or maiming their mounts.

In the melee which followed, Assisi lost command of the high ground. The hiss of arrows was replaced by the metallic clash of hand-to-hand fighting, shouted commands by yells of panic and pain, the thud of pounding hooves by the whinny of wounded horses. Both Bonifazio and Thomas of Celano describe the outcome as a massacre; the dead and dismembered bodies of both sides lay strewn across the trampled fields. If Assisi sent only a hundred horsemen onto the field, Francis saw at least twenty or thirty of his companions die that afternoon.

The Perugians pursued the routed army in the chill evening mist – among the reeds by the river, into the buildings on the ridge, up the streams and through the woods toward Assisi. The only lives they spared were those they reckoned would fetch a good ransom. The sergeants may have laughed at Francis's elaborate equipment but it now repaid every penny he had spent, for it so impressed his enemies that instead of cutting his throat they made him a prisoner.

*

Francis was deprived of his horse, stripped of his arms and marched by the light of torches up through the gates of Perugia. Herded through the streets between jeering crowds, the prisoners had no idea if they were heading for execution or torture. The dungeons into which they were finally thrown were part of the city's Etruscan foundations – cold, dark, damp, and soon stinking. For the first time Francis, the spoiled young man, with his troubadour dreams of love and knighthood, had collided with the uglier realities of medieval life.

He himself never wrote anything about the Battle of Collestrada, his time as a prisoner, or the events that immediately followed it. The single reliable witness is Angelo di Tancredi, who says that: "because of his distinguished bearing, Francis was put among the nobles." Angelo knew this because as a genuine noble he found Francis in the same cell as himself.

Unlike the others, Francis never lost his habitual cheerfulness or concern for those less fortunate – a trait already noticed in Assisi. When one prisoner, who was particularly morose and objectionable, lost his temper and injured another, his companions all retaliated and made life wretched for him – except for Francis.

Time hangs heavy in prison. With nothing to read there was little to do other than grumble, argue and listen to the taller stories of old soldiers, but talk and proximity broke down barriers. As the days and weeks ran on into months Francis made allies among his companions. Angelo became his close friend for life. Federico Spadalunga, a cloth dealer from Gubbio, demonstrated the true meaning of friendship a few years later. Giovanni di Simone, a young landowner loyal to the commune like Angelo, kept in touch for the next twenty-five years; on the night Francis died he came down from Mt. Subasio and later attested that he had seen the stigmata on his old friend's body.

A fourth prisoner, a professional soldier, told engrossing stories of his battles in the service of Francis's hero, the great warrior from Champagne, Walter de Brienne. A year or two before, Walter had rescued Queen Sibila of Sicily from her imprisonment by the Germans in Alsace. With the King of France's blessing he had then sworn to recover her kingdom, which included Apulia on the mainland, and married her daughter. In approval of the enterprise Innocent III had created Walter Count of Lecce and Prince of Taranto. It was precisely the kind of career that Francis dreamed of for himself.

There was no privacy in the dungeon except at night, when a prisoner was in the dark with his fears and hopes. Francis longed to be home and out in the countryside, or traveling again, but he knew in his heart that, if he escaped from Perugia, his true ambitions now lay not in business but the field of chivalry.

In Assisi the prisoners were not forgotten. Some were desperately needed back to manage their farmland or continue their trading – but all were hostages for whom Perugia was demanding reparations and ransom. Francis and Angelo were lucky in having proud and affectionate fathers with very deep pockets, while Tancredi di Ugone was one of the three "arbiters" appointed by Assisi to negotiate a settlement.

After nearly a year the Perugians recognized they had won a battle not a war. The reason lay in their association with the pope, who was backing Philip of Swabia – as contender for the German imperial crown. This immediately provoked his rival Otto of Saxony to take Assisi's part, despite the fact that it had thrown Duke Conrad out of the Rocca and declared itself a commune. In return for a few concessions, Otto agreed to recognize the commune – so balancing the scales with Perugia. At the end of 1203, almost a year after Collestrada, Tancredi di Ugone and his colleagues were able to arrange the release of at least some of the prisoners, including Francis, possibly ransomed early on account of his health.

Before the news reached their dungeon, a curious exchange took place between Francis and some of his fellows on a day when most of the prisoners were especially depressed. Francis, on the other hand, seemed more cheerful than ever. Suddenly one of his companions could stand this no longer and acidly sneered at him for looking so happy. According to Angelo, Francis answered, "You may think me foolish, but one day the whole world will come to respect me."[2]

He had never, so far, had a low opinion of himself, had always decked himself out like a peacock, and had naturally taken the lead in any gathering of his friends. It is therefore difficult to tell if this was merely the old Francis speaking, or an intimation that his experience in prison had lit a fuse which would one day project him to fame.

7

Dreams

1203–1205

The prisoners reached home pale and emaciated after their year in a dungeon. It is possible Francis had contracted tuberculosis for he suffered from it later and wrote that he was dogged by sickness when he was young. On the other hand, a bout of illness and "mental distress" commonly attributed to this period did not hit him for another two years.

The Battle of Collestrada had solved no problems for either side. Perugia had not felt strong enough to occupy Assisi and merely continued the border fighting; the *majores* who survived in Assisi went on defying the commune, provoking the destruction of their castles and town houses as before; the famine persisted and violence increased. To strengthen their hand the consuls decided – as other communes had – to elect a *podestà* each year, from outside the city. As chief magistrate, ultimate authority lay in his hands.

If Assisi had not changed for the better, neither, in the eyes of his parents, had Francis. He still lived at home but, if he heard during a meal that a party was going on in the town, he would leave his food on the table and rush off to it. He still worked for his father and traveled with him to France, yet he also began replacing his weapons and armor – and discreetly followed the news of Walter de Brienne's campaign against the Germans in Apulia.

He remained far keener on spending money than making it and was often asked by his group to arrange lavish parties for them, ordering whatever food and drink he liked and inviting any attractive girl willing to risk her reputation in their company. At the age of twenty-one he might well have been married, but perhaps in the interests of the business Pietro preferred him to wait. In any case, as the son of such a rich merchant the search for a bride whose class and wealth were up to expectation, and the negotiation of a contract, might drag on for years.

The prospect of marriage possibly faced Francis with another quandary. The sophistry of courtly love made it a dubious attraction for anyone as romantic as he. Although most of the Arthurian knights were triumphantly married at the conclusion of their adventures, convention held that romantic love could not survive the act of marriage nor be generated between the married, although reality often belied this. Marriage was therefore not entirely enticing to the extreme troubadour temperament.

Nor was adultery an easy alternative even though a troubadour's ideal love was a married woman, lonely in the tower of her palazzo or castle. The act of adultery, if discovered, placed both lovers beyond the pale. One troubadour, caught *in flagrante* by a husband unexpectedly home from the wars, was secretly killed; his liver was then served as a succulent stew to his mistress. Her husband only divulged the ingredients after she had enjoyed it. When King Mark discovered his wife, Isolde, in adultery with Tristan he handed her over, for their pleasure, to a community of lepers. Lancelot's and Guinevere's liaison eventually brought King Arthur's court to its doom, while Dante alludes to it in his canto on the second circle of Hell reserved for carnal sinners.

*

Just as Francis had lost none of his taste for high living, he made no secret of his continued ambition to win his spurs. About two years after his return from Perugia his chance came. One of the nobles in Assisi decided to raise a force to fight in Apulia under Walter de Brienne.

In keeping with his new rank and titles, Walter had filled his court at Lecce with princesses and beauties from all over Europe, and achieved several impressive victories over the German commander, Diopoldo di Vohburg, who still clung on to much of the kingdom. Francis quickly attached himself to a Count Gentile in the hope that he would award him a knighthood, believing like one of King Arthur's young knights that,

"Many high-born men lose through laziness the high reputation they might have if they travelled about the world. It seems to me that repose and reputation don't go well together; for a man of substance who remains idle gains no renown at all."[1]

Francis equipped himself with his usual flamboyance, but almost immediately came across a knight who had fallen on hard times and had to sell his accoutrements. Francis impulsively gave him all his own new weapons and armor (Plate 3).

That night, according to Thomas, he had a very vivid dream – Angelo believes it was stimulated by his generosity to the knight – in which he was shown a large palace, its walls hung with gleaming weapons, shields, chain mail and helmets. When Francis asked whose they were, he was told they were destined for him and his knights. Wishful thinking led Francis to interpret this literally, and he replaced his equipment with such evident pleasure that people questioned him about it. His reply, an echo of his remark in prison, was that he knew he was destined to become a great prince.

When he rode out of Assisi as Count Gentile's squire, their retinue of pages, grooms, chargers and pack animals made a fine sight, but his parents must have watched him go with ambivalent feelings. It would have been only natural for Pietro to have felt both pride and despair that Francis was turning his back on the business yet again. Pica's more sensitive perception was probably disturbed by the contradiction between his generosity and compulsive vainglory.

By the end of the first day Gentile and Francis reached Spoleto, about thirty miles south of Assisi. That night Francis felt unwell and when he was half asleep heard a voice asking him where he was going. He explained his mission and also mentioned his recent dream. According to Angelo the voice spoke again.

"Who do you think will reward you better for this – the master or his servant?"

Francis answered, "The master."

"Then why are you leaving the master for the servant?"

"Lord, what do you wish me to do instead?" Francis replied.

"Return home, and you will be told. The palace and the arms you were shown in your dream were not for your knights but for others, and your principality will be different, too."[2]

Francis was so disturbed that he couldn't go back to sleep and as soon as it was light, rode home to Assisi.

In fact during June 1205, shortly before Francis reached Spoleto, Walter de Brienne had died of wounds in Apulia and some suggest that this is what made Francis decide to turn back. Others feel that the news prompted the dream, which in turn crystallized the decision to return home.

Great respect was paid to dreams in the Middle Ages, and from now on they become a significant feature of Francis's life. Dreaming is a capacity which has evolved in mammals over millions of years; it has also been established that our dream time represents twenty-five percent of our sleeping hours, that is at least five years by the end of an average life. These discoveries argue that dreams make a positive contribution to our essential activities and survival.

More than two thousand years ago Plato pointed out that some dreams express powerful wishes hitherto submerged; for just as long, it has been noticed that they are often triggered by episodes during the preceding day. Occasionally dreams prefigure actual events in the future, as experienced by Joseph in the Old Testament, and by Mohammed, Einstein and Freud.

Today psychologists suggest that dreams enable our unconscious brain to perform two other functions. First, they help it sort our daily experiences, filing what is needed and discarding what would otherwise overcrowd our heads. Second, they provide the brain with the occasion to relate the new material to three components of our psyche: the collective unconscious, a reservoir of universal experience inherited subliminally by everyone; archetypes, the prime concepts dominating our unconscious; and the anima or animus, that is the feminine element in a man's unconscious, and the male equivalent in a woman's.

Dreams offer us surreal glimpses of these processes going on in our unconscious brain where our memory, intellect and imagination interact – so helping us to anticipate or respond to danger, to resolve a dilemma or to plan some new enterprise. It is from this dimension of the mind that painters, poets and storytellers, scientists, philosophers and politicians, prophets and mystics, often draw their inspiration or insight.

If these concepts are considered simply as metaphors – for they are not yet accepted as orthodox scientific facts despite their adoption by many respected psychiatrists – they help throw valuable light, now and later, on the dreams, visions, voices and trances that influenced Francis's behavior during his transition from playboy to saint.

The fact that Francis reported his dreams and that his friends wrote them down implies they thought them significant. The second of the two just related was seen as an early intimation that beneath his sudden whims, sociability, extravagance and ambitions as a knight, a new sense of purpose, humanity, unselfishness and an alternative approach to chivalry were beginning to stir. His simultaneous and contradictory attraction, deep inside, to both war and peace would soon have to be reconciled.

*

After his theatrical departure for Apulia, Francis played down his sudden return and implied he would be going back. His change of mind didn't worry his friends, for almost immediately they formally elected him Lord of the Revels.

Wild evenings of drinking, music and dancing, given by organized circles of the young, were then common in Tuscany and Umbria. In summer the curfew was relaxed, so they could leave the courtyards and gardens where they began and continue in the town. At his first banquet as president Francis sat at the head of the table with his staff of office and when the meal was over watched the others surge into the street. Following them, he soon lagged behind and when they turned to look for him they were surprised to see him standing stock still, lost in a reverie.

"Why aren't you joining us? Are you in love, or thinking about getting married?" they asked.

"You're right," Francis answered. "I was imagining I was courting the noblest, richest, and most beautiful bride ever seen."[3]

Francis told Angelo that a sense of overwhelming sweetness had entirely detached him from the physical world, and even if he were being cut to pieces he could not have moved. His words echo Chrétien de Troyes's description of a knight's infatuation. "New found Love, with its sugar and honeycomb, has brought him fresh sweetness. . . . Never before has Nature succeeded in achieving such an extreme of beauty."

Angelo identifies the bride of Francis's daydreams as dawning faith and, for the first time, some of his actions are most convincingly explained by a growing deference to God, which required him to discard old habits and values. He began to spend time secretly in prayer, sometimes drifting into a trance when he did so.

Since leaving school he had only once given any sign of religious enthusiasm, but when he was a child Pica had lit a spark of belief. He was her favorite child and however badly he behaved she never lost faith in him; when friends asked what she felt about his extravagance, she firmly replied: "Through grace he will become the son of God." The rector of San Giorgio had tried to keep this ember alive.

After leaving school, Francis's churchgoing had been little more than a social formality. Yet he was constantly aware of the ubiquitous clergy, especially the Benedictines, whose abbey was near one of his father's farms, and who owned monasteries, convents and churches in and around the town; as one modern Franciscan authority remarks, in medieval Italy "even the mosquitoes were Catholic." Nevertheless there was little popular admiration of the clergy in Assisi. The pope backed Perugia; the old bishop was aggressive and rapacious; a new cathedral was being built behind the present one, but had not been touched for sixty years; and most of the parish priests were thought to be venal.

Arnaldo Fortini, in his four-volume work on Francis and his times, quotes one of Innocent III's pronouncements on the clergy:

> Many priests have lived luxuriously. They have passed the time in drunken revels, neglecting religious rites. When they have been at Mass, they have chatted about commercial affairs. They have left churches and tabernacles in an improper state, sold posts and sacraments, promoted ignorant and unworthy people to the clerical state, though they had others better suited for it. Many bishops have appropriated the income of a parish for themselves, leaving the parish indigent. They have gone to the enormous abuse of forcing parishioners to make special payments so as to have still more income. They have made a scandalous commerce of relics. They have allowed the illegitimate children of a canon to succeed the father in the benefice.[4]

However, in 1204 there arrived in Assisi a figure who played the role of guardian angel to Francis for the rest of his life – although "angel" is hardly the *mot juste* for the new bishop. He seems to have descended on his throne with a writ in one hand and a bludgeon in the other. Like his predecessor he was a muscular Christian and, to confuse matters, was also called Guido. Since this has only been understood quite recently, the second and more famous Guido has always borne the opprobrium for the litigious excesses of both of them – which has unjustly eclipsed his early recognition and unflinching support of Francis.

Like Innocent III, he was energetic and fearless in deploying his secular authority but also a man of spiritual perception. Some believe he was a personal friend of the pope's, and he certainly maintained close connections with his headquarters at the Lateran Palace – in particular with the wise old cardinal who had been proposed for the throne of St. Peter, Giovanni di San Paolo. At the same time, he kept a sharp eye on the church's front line in his diocese.

It cannot have taken him long, in a small town like Assisi, to get to know his rich and influential neighbors. It must therefore have puzzled him that a merchant like Pietro, respected for his financial support of the commune, with a wife so devout and widely liked as Pica, should have a popular son who spent all his spare time leading the youth of the city astray.

However, after about a year the bishop began to pick up rumors that, although Francis was extremely discreet about it, he was giving away large sums of money, sometimes even his clothes, to beggars he met in the streets or out in the country. If Pietro was not at home Francis would pile loaves on the table and, with Pica's tacit approval, take them down to the poor in the slums. He also made a point of discovering the needs of the meanest churches and supplying them to the priests in charge.

At this moment an unknown hand – perhaps Pica's – brought this straying young sheep and his formidable shepherd together.

8

Nightmares

1205–1206

Late in 1205 Francis suspected that his real vocation was going to be more demanding than his summons to chivalry because the voice now calling him was God's.

From earliest times a classic response to a divine call has been to go on a pilgrimage; the Indians and Egyptians, the Jews and Greeks, all made journeys of prayer, penance or discovery to the places where their deities were thought to reside. In this tradition early Christians made their way to Bethlehem and Jerusalem; and in the fourth century Constantine, the first Roman emperor to adopt Christianity, ordered a church to be built on the reputed site of Christ's sepulchre.

Later, concern for safety and convenience led Christians in the west to extend this observance to the tombs of the apostles, especially those who had been martyred. Rome, outside whose walls St. Peter, by tradition its first bishop, had been buried after his execution, became second to Jerusalem as a center of pilgrimage. His physical relics endowed the place, in the medieval mind, with as much authority as his living presence would have done – an authority invested in every Bishop of Rome, that is to say in each pope. The city was therefore a logical starting point for a Christian's quest for God.

Rome is only a hundred miles south from Assisi, and at the end of 1205 or the beginning of 1206 Francis set off as a pilgrim, in a spirit of inquiry rather than penance or prayer. He headed down the Flaminian Way, which ran beside the Tiber before reaching the city. The view from the northern gates was utterly changed from the great days of imperial splendor. In the time of Constantine the population was over half a million; now it was barely thirty thousand. Once the hub of the greatest commercial and military empire on earth, it now survived on an income from farming, pilgrims and tourists.

Within the twenty-mile circuit of the walls the most striking feature of the view was the skyline. The city had suffered from so many invasions, raids, risings and robbers that its inhabitants had fortified all the principal landmarks, buildings and arches. According to *Mirabilia Urbis Romae*, a twelfth-century visitors' guide, Rome boasted forty-nine bastions and three hundred and sixty towers. A fifteenth-century drawing of central Rome suggests an antique Manhattan.

The city had also been the victim of earthquake. The hills to the west had reverted to fields and vineyards, scattered with ruins and rubble. Ahead, and in a loop of the Tiber to Francis's right, the present population clustered around the tremendous remains of the ancient capital – the Colosseum and the Pantheon, the Forum, castles and palaces, aqueducts, baths and theaters, soaring columns, triumphal arches, and equestrian statues. Beyond them, and close to the far walls, Pope Innocent III occupied the Lateran Palace, beside the basilica of St. John Lateran.

At first the Romans had given the new pope a rough time. The senate was always ambivalent about the pontiff's presence in their capital, feeling it a privilege but also a threat to their autonomy. In 1203 they had forcibly ejected Innocent from Rome, inducing in him depression and an illness from which he almost died – only to find themselves outmaneuvered by his determination and guile into total submission. However, Francis was now intent on visiting St. Peter's, not the pope.

He therefore crossed the Tiber just below the great circular fortress of Castel Sant' Angelo, originally the mausoleum of the Emperor Hadrian, and headed for St. Peter's. About half a mile beyond the river, it stood on the edge of the country at the foot of Vatican Hill.* The approach to the basilica, a large area of rough ground, was crowded and noisy. Currents of pilgrims, sightseers, guides, peddlers and priests eddied backward and

*Two hundred years later a British monk, Adam of Usk, saw wolves fighting in its precincts at night.

forward, pausing at stalls to buy mementos or refreshment. Francis pushed through them all and climbed the steps to the basilica, which Constantine had erected in A.D. 330, over the saint's grave in the hillside cemetery. More pilgrims and beggars jostled in the forecourt as Francis pressed on into the great, aisled, space which could hold a congregation of two or three thousand.

The painted interior stretched away to the sanctuary which was, since this was a sepulchre church, at the western end; brilliant mosaics gleamed from the vault of the apse; the saint's shrine stood at the crossing of the nave and the transepts. Behind a screen, incorporating spiral columns that had originally supported an altar canopy in Constantine's day, stood the marble and porphyry altar containing the confessio, a grating through which pilgrims could look down and throw coins onto St. Peter's tomb. Francis was so shocked by the meanness of these offerings that he pulled a handful of money from his purse and flung it through the grating, startling bystanders with his lavishness and the noise it made.

It cannot conceivably have occurred to him that, within thirty years, a basilica in his honor, with a similar confessio, would be built in Assisi: nor that, on his account, Assisi would become the fourth center of Christian pilgrimage, after Jerusalem, Rome and Santiago de Compostela in north-western Spain, where the remains of the apostle and martyr St. James were said to lie.

For some time, Francis had wanted to experience what it was like to beg. When he left the basilica he therefore persuaded one of the beggars to exchange clothes with him for the rest of the day; standing in the atrium he asked for alms in French, a language he loved but didn't speak well. In medieval stories, as in Shakespeare's plays, an outward change of clothes often indicates an inward change of heart. In Francis's case the frivolous young butterfly was about to shed his colors and return to his chrysalis.

*

Francis's experience in Rome – perhaps the enigma of the contrast between the majestic symbolism of St. Peter's and the abject poverty of the beggars at its doors – confused him. Surreptitiously he went for advice to the one man he now trusted, Bishop Guido, who encouraged him to continue both working and praying for guidance. Enlightenment was granted all too soon, for he quickly sensed he would have to give up all his previous indulgences – nevertheless it was also intimated that if he did so, whatever he had most dreaded in the past would in the future seem pleasurable. It gave him the courage to confront his worst fear, which had haunted him since childhood.

Many lepers on the roads around Assisi were frighteningly and pathetically hideous, their skin discolored and their limbs crippled – they had often lost their hair, fingers, and noses; their bleeding or suppurating sores gave off the stench of putrefying flesh. To protect its inhabitants Assisi, like all other towns, had ejected them, regardless of their background or wealth and however many their dependants. They were forced to lodge outside in a lazar house – named after the biblical beggar, Lazarus, who lay covered in sores at the gate of Dives, the rich man who ignored him and was consigned to the flames. Francis had not merely ignored beggars. Angelo says that, "Besides being incapable of looking at them, he would not even approach the places where they lived . . . and if he gave them alms he would do it through someone else, turning his face away and holding his nose . . ."[1]

Below Assisi there were at least half a dozen lazar houses, chief among them San Lazzaro d'Arce, of which only the chapel known as Santa Maria Maddalena survives today. It was here that lepers were formally admitted by the priest. Standing in the cemetery they were pronounced dead to the world; they were told that this life's worst torments led to the kingdom of heaven and that their present separation was only of the body, not of the spirit, which was more important. Soil from the graveyard was sprinkled on their heads.

Then came their sentence, and the presentation of the ominous insignia of their disease. For the rest of their lives they might not leave the house unless they wore their distinctive gray cloak and sounded their wooden clapper to warn other travelers to keep their distance; they must not enter Assisi or visit fairs, markets and mills; they must not beg for food except wearing their gloves and by proffering their bowl; they must not drink from springs, rivers or wells but only from their flasks; they might only talk with the healthy if they stood downwind of them.

It took Francis a huge effort to stifle his revulsion. One day he met a leper when he was riding near Assisi. Despite his overpowering horror he dismounted, gave the man a coin and kissed his hand. The leper gave him the kiss of peace in return. Francis then knew that to win a complete victory he must follow this first attack on his phobia with a second.

Angelo writes, "Some days later he took a large sum of money to the leper hospital and gathering all the inmates together, he distributed it, kissing each of their hands."[2]

On his deathbed, Francis referred to this episode in the opening words of his Testament: "This is how God inspired me, Brother Francis, to embark upon a life of penance." It was a watershed, and in the next few months he seemed to be racing impulsively down a slope, regardless of the hazards, toward derangement or his destiny.

*

Early in 1206 he began to make secret expeditions to Mt. Subasio. Only one person was aware of them, his best friend who went with him. Their pretext was to look for treasure, but while the friend hunted around for anything worth having, Francis withdrew to pray in a cave – there were several in the gully where the hermitage of the Carceri now stands.

If he expected that in the seclusion of retreat God would quietly provide him with a new sense of direction he was soon disappointed for, like so many spiritual explorers, he found himself enveloped in an emotional maelstrom. In his head the archetypes of chivalry first fought with, and were then replaced by, those of the Christian religion, headed by God and the devil. For instance in the Arthurian Romances a humpbacked hag had turned up to harass Sir Perceval at a crucial point on one of his ventures; now the devil conjured up a similar harridan who lived in Assisi, and warned Francis he would soon look like her if he continued to listen to God.

During these sessions of acute internal strife, he was successively tortured with shame at his previous behavior, exalted by his vision of God's glory and love, and desperate lest his courage fail him in such battles ahead. This was much like the turmoil of one of Chrétien de Troyes's heroes about whom the French scholar Jean Frappier wrote, "His deep reveries and trances, depicted graphically like cataleptic phenomena, had their counterparts as subconscious or pathological states in the actual experiences of religious mystics. Chrétien has modeled the lover's ecstasies on those of the contemplative engulfed in meditation."[3]

Such phenomena were not peculiar to the Middle Ages but have been experienced by visionaries, artists, and thinkers throughout history. Often they have been associated with caves. For instance in *The Republic* Plato examines the concept of a man who starts life in a cave and mistakes the shadows of moving puppets, cast on the walls by a fire, for the activities of actual human beings. To discover the truth he will have to venture outside and face seeing real people in the fierce and painful light of the sun.

Toward the end of the fifteenth century Leonardo da Vinci – said to have been a member of Francis's Third Order – records a confrontation with his own powerful and conflicting sensations when he knelt in the mouth of a cave, at much the same age.

> I shaded my eyes to peer in. . . . After I had remained thus for a moment, two emotions suddenly awoke in me: fear and desire – fear of the dark, threatening cave, and desire to see if it contained some miraculous thing.[4]

This passage occurs between precise observations of nature and imaginative evocations of metaphysical forces at work on man and the earth.

Three hundred years later in *The Marriage of Heaven and Hell* William Blake, who gave expression to his visions with both his brush and his pen, described men and women as shut in the caves of their own bodies, their five senses the only openings. He believed that, "If the doors of perception were cleansed everything would appear to man as it is, infinite. For man has closed himself up, till he sees all things through narrow chambers of his cavern."[5]

On Mt. Subasio Francis struggled to wipe clean and push open the doors of perception.

A young Spanish soldier and rake in the sixteenth century, later known as Ignatius of Loyola, fought much the same battle for purgation (for a time in a cave) after a cannonball hit him between the legs during a siege at Pamplona. Throughout his nine-month convalescence he fought despair at the loss of his prowess as a soldier and lover. He steeled the surgeons to go on operating until he could walk, dreamed obsessively of winning a bride as lovely as any in the epics of chivalry, and read with growing devotion the lives of Christ and the saints; at one stage Francis epitomized everything he wished to become. The two men's characters were quite unalike but after their traumas both embraced poverty, chastity and obedience; they also founded religious orders. The followers of Ignatius, known as the Society of Jesus or the Jesuits, number twenty-five thousand today.

An eminent psychiatrist, Dr. Anthony Storr, has made a special study of the illnesses and psychological disturbances which sometimes presage, even generate, a fundamental change of direction in the lives and thinking of visionaries. To illuminate such episodes he quotes a passage from *The Discovery of the Unconscious* by Henri Ellenberger:

> A creative illness succeeds a period of intense preoccupation with an idea and search for a certain truth. It is a polymorphous condition that can take the shape of depression, neurosis, psychosomatic ailments or even psychosis. Whatever the symptoms they are felt as painful, if not agonizing by the subject. . . . He suffers from feelings of utter isolation, even when he has a mentor who guides him through the ordeal. The subject emerges from this ordeal with a permanent transformation in his personality and the conviction that he has discovered a great truth or a new spiritual world.[6]

It is impossible to define "spiritual" precisely, for a human being's spirit or soul has no exact physical location. During life it is linked to the body and intellect, and is traditionally taken to mean the essential "I," which can control, modify or surrender to the inclinations of these faculties. It can therefore direct them to what is morally good, rather than expedient, alluring, or bad; it can engender the highest form of love; and its conduct is often believed to determine its destination after the death of the body. Paradoxically it is this I, the very nucleus of the spirit, which the most respected mystics of many religions believe must be abandoned at the end before the ultimate purpose of their existence – reunion with God – can be achieved.

According to Angelo, Francis was so drained by the anguish of his inner struggles that, when he rejoined his companion outside the cave on the mountain, his whole appearance seemed radically altered. A close comparison of this passage with Thomas of Celano's account of the severe illness in which Francis underwent "mental distress and bodily suffering," leaves little doubt that the two episodes are one and the same. It was now, and not on his return from Perugia, that Francis collapsed. Thomas adds two graphic touches – that for a time he was so weak he had to walk with a stick, and he was so depressed he entirely lost his perennial delight in the beauty of the countryside.

The psychological pain that Francis endured in these months, and the extreme mortifications he imposed on his body for the rest of his life, bring vividly to mind a modern parallel, prompting the thought that a similar sense of guilt may have contributed to both men's conditions.

As a young man at Cambridge University in England Thomas Merton – later to become a Trappist monk and one of the most widely read Christian writers in the world – was middle class, rich, vain (he flaunted a velvet cloak) and attractive; he used these assets to give good parties and seduce girls of a lower class for whom he had feelings no deeper than sexual pleasure. However in 1933 one of them bore him a son, and he was relieved when his guardian paid off the mother and obliged him to return home to America. There, six years later, at the end of a wild night with his friends he suddenly thought, "I am going to be a priest."

Nevertheless he was excruciated by guilt at his treatment of the girl and their child – both of whom were killed in an air raid on London – and confessed to a correspondent that there was "an impediment to my being a priest. . . . It is something that definitely demands a whole life of penance and absolute self-sacrifice; so that if the Trappists would take me I think I would want to go to them."[7]

If Francis slept with girls, as the first lives suggest, he was in risk of fathering a child – contraception was forbidden by the church and in any case quite unreliable. If a baby was born to him, and harm came to the child or its mother, given his compassionate nature and in the light of his dawning conversion, his remorse would have been no less powerful than Merton's.

Thomas Merton had a wise correspondent to help him through this painful ordeal; Francis had Bishop Guido and Angelo's friendship. Angelo never reveals the identity of the friend who accompanied Francis to the caves on Subasio and it has always been thought strange that anyone so close to him at this critical time should vanish without trace from his life. There is, however, the possibility that Angelo himself was the friend. It would have been entirely in keeping with his character not to say so. In a passage describing the virtues of Francis's close companions Thomas of Celano withholds all their names "to spare their modesty," but the brother he praises as being "known for his outstanding discretion" is generally thought to be Angelo.

From now on Francis continued with his prayers, convinced that details of his true calling would soon be disclosed. He still said nothing of all this to his other friends, except that he would not be setting out for Apulia again; and when he recovered his strength he resumed his riotous parties, although everyone noticed a change in him, and asked him again if he were about to get married.

As before, he answered in a figure of speech. "I shall bring home a bride more beautiful, richer and nobler than any of you have ever seen."[8]

This metaphor for the faith he was about to espouse had the ring of a troubadour's declaration of love, about which it has been said: "it demanded complete obedience and submission to the lady, who in her lover's eyes was the image of beauty, the ideal of all courtly virtues, the source of true joy. . . . Love might derange the lover, but reason and moderation in his role must overcome this folly, and bring sensual desire into harmony with mental and spiritual aspiration."[9]

Francis's moment of submission was rapidly approaching.

9

Trial

1206

Belfries pushed up through the woods and olive groves all around Assisi. The shrines of the original Umbrian settlers were no more than sacred trees hung with incense vases and votive offerings; some were replaced by Roman temples; and about two hundred years after these, the first small Christian stone crosses and tombs appeared. They commemorated among others St. Felicianus, martyred at the age of ninety-three, and the city's first three bishops, St. Rufinus, St. Victorinus and St. Savinus, all killed for their faith in the third century. By Francis's time saints had inspired the building of chapels, churches and abbeys – also cathedrals in Assisi and Foligno containing the remains of St. Rufinus and St. Felicianus.

Many of the abbeys were Benedictine; St. Benedict had been born in Umbria, during the sixth century, only fifty miles away. Since then his order had spread out from his retreat at Monte Cassino, south of Rome, right across Europe. By the twelfth century there may have been as many as ten thousand houses founded in his name. There were at least half a dozen in or near Assisi, some for men and some for women – chief among them the abbey of San Benedetto on Subasio.

Francis had passed most of these churches and chapels, including the lazar houses, on his visits to the family farms with his father. Some were deserted, while the priests in charge of others had no funds to keep them up; these were the men whom he had been privately helping.

One day, in the spring of 1206, he stopped at San Damiano, a simple and decaying little church less than a mile below Assisi, close to where St. Felicianus had once planted a cross. Inside he kneeled down, and looked up at the figure of Christ painted on the crucifix hanging over the altar.* (Plate 4.)

Christ's face expresses resigned serenity; his body has the stillness of an icon; there is no crown of thorns but he bleeds from his hands, feet and side. Angelo says that when Francis began to pray he heard a voice speaking tenderly to him.

"' Francis, don't you see that my house has collapsed? Go and repair it for me.'

"' Yes Lord, I will, most willingly,' Francis replied, thinking that Christ was referring to San Damiano which had fallen into ruin on account of its age.

"It filled him with intense joy to know that Jesus had spoken to him."[1]

There is no suggestion that Francis saw the lips of the crucifix move, or that if anyone else was present he would have heard the voice. The chroniclers simply report what Francis said he had heard. Such phenomena, frequently experienced by mystics, have something in common with dreams, and also with the voices which accompany different forms of mental illness. But whereas the latter tend to coincide with a deterioration of the patient's faculties and behavior, mystics often become charged with a new and urgent purpose, while their conduct, though sometimes eccentric, becomes neither violent nor malicious.

Francis found the priest in charge sitting outside the church. He had been so moved by his experience that he gave the old man some money, asking him to see that the lamp in front of the crucifix never went out. He promised to pay for more oil whenever it was needed.

From this moment the image of Christ and his suffering began to preoccupy his thoughts; sometimes it reduced him to tears of compassion, and he felt a growing need to deny himself all his previous luxuries. Yet he also became extremely practical. His first thought was to raise money for restoring and reroofing the church. In his father's absence he collected bolts of the most valuable cloth from the warehouse, took them to Foligno and sold everything, including his horse. He then trudged back to San Damiano with the proceeds.

*Today it is in the Basilica di Santa Chiara (St. Clare).

The priest was astonished when Francis pressed the money into his hands for the restoration. At first he didn't think Francis was serious – he had seen him only recently at a rowdy party with some of his family and friends. Even when Francis convinced him of his sincerity he still wouldn't accept the coins, probably anticipating that Pietro would be outraged when he discovered what had happened. Disappointed, and having no use for the money himself, Francis tossed the bag through a window where it landed inside on a ledge. Nevertheless, it didn't stop him from repairing the church with his own hands, and while he worked the priest allowed him to stay in his hut.

Francis still kept in touch with his mother but realizing that Pietro would be furious when he came back, he fixed up a cellar or cave – possibly the crypt of the church – in which he could hide if worst came to worst, arranging for a family servant to bring him food there. Pietro was, indeed, so angry that he collected a group of friends and stormed down to San Damiano, loudly calling out for the return of the money and threatening Francis if he didn't repay it; but there was no reply.

Francis was already in hiding and remained so – profoundly shaken but praying continuously. Then, gradually, he experienced a glow of reassurance and a month later mustered the courage to walk into Assisi to face the music. His weeks in hiding had left him haggard, dirty and unshaven; he looked like a madman. He was greeted with jeers and abuse, and when his family and friends came out on the streets they pelted him with insults, filth and even stones.

Perhaps the most telling and original scene in Chrétien de Troyes's romances is one that follows Lancelot's decision to ride in "the cart of shame," driven by a dwarf, because he believes it offers his only chance of finding Queen Guinevere whom he has sworn to rescue. Such carts were the equivalent of a pillory, used to humiliate anyone found guilty of robbery, treason or murder; in it they were led through the streets before their sentences were executed. His lift in the cart was the acid test of Lancelot's dedication to his love and his word. When he reached the town:

> The people were amazed at a knight being carried by the dwarf in his cart; but rather than discuss it quietly among themselves, all of them, great and small, old men and children, shouted abuse at him, filling the streets with their clamour.

> They asked: 'What punishment is this knight going to suffer? Will he be flayed or hanged, drowned or burnt in a fire of thorns? Say, dwarf – is he convicted of theft, is he a murderer?'[2]

Francis, like Lancelot, kept his composure in the face of humiliation, but the commotion grew so noisy that Pietro soon heard it and went out to investigate. When he saw the cause, he fetched some of his men and rushed back – not to rescue Francis but, "like a wolf on a lamb," to knock him about and then drag him back to the house. There, he locked him in a cellar.

Thrifty at heart, Pietro was still smarting at the sale of his best stock for the sake of a crumbling church in the fields. Proud to the core, he was ashamed that his son should provoke his neighbors' ridicule. For so long indulgent, he was bitterly hurt by Francis's ingratitude.

Pietro must have realized by now that his son was no longer committed to the business but felt that his social success was an important asset to it. However neither threats nor blows would change Francis's mind, and at the end of the summer Pietro had to leave on his annual journey to France. After he went, Pica, who had thoroughly disapproved of her husband's behavior, forlornly reasoned with her favorite son, hoping to persuade him to reconsider his future. When she recognized that this was beyond her, she unlocked the cellar and let him go.

*

Francis now had a few weeks' respite in which to make up his mind what to do next, but not wanting to divide his mother's loyalties any longer he went back to San Damiano.

It meant that he was finally shutting the door on his father's world, deliberately and without regret; on the other hand he was still drawn to romance and knighthood. But since marriage seemed out of the question and after his dream at Spoleto campaigning also, it looked as though these gates were closing too. But were they?

There were many rooms in the palace of courtly love – friendship for one; and beyond it a convention adopted by some troubadours that, however passionate, they kept their distance from their beloved; further on still lay *caritas*, a perfectly unselfish love. There were also several dimensions of knighthood – toward the end of his romance Perceval,

Chrétien's ultimate knight, undergoes an experience very similar to Francis's at San Damiano. After fighting in a wasteland, he is guided to a hermitage on Good Friday, sets aside his arms, falls to his knees, and makes his confession to the hermit:

> 'For fully five years I've not known where I was or loved God, or believed in Him, and have done nothing but wrong.'
>
> The hermit hears Perceval out and then gives him a chance to commit himself.
>
> 'Love God, believe in God, worship God. Honour worthy men and women; and stand in the presence of priests – that's a service that costs little and which God truly loves, since it stems from humility. Should a maiden or widow or orphan seek your aid, then provide it. . . . Now tell me if you're prepared to do this?'
>
> 'Yes, sir, very willingly,' Perceval answered.
>
> 'Now I ask you to stay here with me for two whole days and, in penance, take the same food as I have.' Perceval agrees.
>
> That is how Perceval recognised that on Good Friday God was crucified and put to death – and how at Easter he received communion.[3]

Parallels like this and others, between episodes in the literature of chivalry and actual events in Francis's life, not usually traced in any detail, are quoted here for two reasons.

First, it is often thought that Francis must have felt profoundly lost when his dawning vocation obliged him to reject first his father and then the traditional knight as his role model; but this was not entirely so. The daunting ordeals of the heroes in his favorite epics offered inspiring examples as he was steadily drawn into the eternal war between good and evil.

Second, the quotations help explain why, in days to come, Francis often referred to himself and his brotherhood as troubadours or knights of the Round Table. He was not alluding to fashionable young minstrels, despairingly in love with other men's wives, or philistine cavalry officers flocking around Camelot. He had in mind the poets of true love and the warriors whose ultimate allegiance was not to a woman, a code or a king, but to God.

Already he seems to have picked up the fundamentals of Christian doctrine from the priest at San Damiano. With no academic grounding in theology, Francis never looked for anything more, for they were all that was needed to establish his faith and release the full generosity of his love. God the creator of the universe and source of eternal love had given men free will. Through their misuse of this gift they had obscured and obstructed his love, thereby introducing misery and fear of death into the world. God had therefore sent his Son, Jesus Christ, to demonstrate through his incarnation, crucifixion and resurrection that he was prepared to share men's misery and that, if they confessed the misuse of their free will, and were willing to do penance for it, they would find joy amid their present sufferings and could look forward to eternal life reunited with God.

The last supper Christ shared with his apostles, re-enacted in the service of communion, had instituted a perpetual demonstration of this love; and a little later God had released his spirit into the world. The Father, the Son and the Holy Spirit were accessible at all times to all men through the sacrament of communion and prayer.

Francis now committed himself, by way of service, to the bishop who had jurisdiction by a papal decree over everyone living on church property in his diocese. Fortified by this, and no longer alarmed by his father's violence, Francis calmly went back to his building work.

On his return to Assisi, Pietro lost his temper yet again and ranted at Pica for letting Francis go. Rushing down to San Damiano, in the futile hope of bullying him into submission, he turned to his last resort when this failed; he went to the consuls. It was his right, as head of the family, not only to imprison members of his household who disobeyed him, but also to have them banished from Assisi if they persisted. Seeing that Pietro would never relent, the consuls sent a messenger to Francis ordering him to their palazzo near the cathedral.

Francis refused on the grounds that he was now God's servant and therefore subject only to canon law. Unwilling to force the issue the consuls told Pietro he would have to look to the bishop for a judgment.

Wise in the ways of the world, Bishop Guido had a healthy respect for a rich and influential merchant, but he was also alive to the workings of the spirit, and it now looked to him as if Francis was more than a hot-headed rebel. After going into the case with great care, he summoned Pietro and Francis to appear before his court.

His large fortified palace – still standing today – was built on the foundations of a villa once lived in by the Roman poet Propertius. It rose from the walls of Assisi, close to Francis's school church San Giorgio, and just above San Damiano. The bishop often presided in the courtyard, but on this occasion – it was early in 1206 – there was snow on the ground and the trial was held in the hall.

Pietro and his witnesses assembled on one side of the seated bishop. Francis stood alone on the other, dressed in his best clothes and clutching the offending bag of coins, which had lain on the window sill since the day he had brought it back from Foligno. As always there was a crowd of spectators – priests, lawyers, beggars, and petitioners waiting their turn.

Francis was perfectly happy to appear before the bishop and, in Angelo's account, listened attentively when Guido gently but firmly explained that the cloth and horse had been Pietro's, and that if he really wished to serve God Francis must return the money to his father. He ended, "Trust in the Lord, my son . . . for he will provide you with all that is needed for repairing the church."[4]

As soon as Bishop Guido had pronounced his verdict Francis stepped forward with the purse and said, "I will gladly give back this money which belongs to my father."

He had picked up many of the skills of the jongleurs and troubadours – who were often actors as well as musicians – and put them to effective use now. Without warning, he disappeared into the next room. When he returned he was naked.

Walking across to his father, he bent down and placed his bundled clothes at his feet. With his colored cloak, blouse and breeches was a coarse hair shirt. On top lay the money bag.

Straightening up Francis began to speak.

"Please listen, everyone. Because I want to serve God from now on, I am giving back to my father the money about which he is so distressed and also my clothes . . .

"Up till now I have always called Pietro di Bernardone my father. In future I will only acknowledge our Father who is in heaven."

Angelo describes the shocked response to these words, which are accepted as the moment of Francis's final conversion:

> His father, burning with both grief and anger gathered up the clothes and money, and carried them home.
>
> The others present took Francis's part, moved with pity to tears that Pietro had left him there naked.
>
> The bishop, seeing Francis's courage and admiring his resolution, threw his arms open and covered him with his cloak. He realized that a great mystery lay behind the scene he had just witnessed and from now on helped and watched over Francis with loving concern.[5]

Franciscan records side with the spectators in court that morning and spare no sympathy for Pietro. But he had been extraordinarily long-suffering until Francis had sold his finest cloth and one of his horses. It is sad, therefore, that he and especially Pica were allowed to disappear from the story without another word. The old cloth merchant left the palace one of the richest men in Umbria but within a century the only trace of his existence were a few sheets of vellum scratched with his name – and the fame of his son, who had just discovered his destiny.

Part II

Brother

1206–1219

10

Builder

1206–1208

Francis had set out to win his spurs but had relinquished his buckler and sword, had come of age but abandoned his birthright, and his "richest and most beautiful bride" had turned out to be Lady Poverty. In the middle of a bitterly cold winter he had no clothes, food or friends.

The bishop gave him a shift, a rough peasant's tunic which someone had marked on the back with a chalk cross, and a pair of old boots, advising him to keep away from Assisi until the scandal and his father's fury had died down. Francis then headed for Gubbio, about twenty miles away. It was the home of Federico Spadalunga, fellow prisoner in Perugia, whose father, too, was in the cloth trade; and since the bishop's name was Spadalunga he may have proposed the family as a temporary refuge.

The path Francis chose led through mountain forests to the valley of the Chiascio, before climbing to Gubbio on a lower slope of the Apennines. In winter a piercing north wind sweeps down off the range and swirls through the streets of the hill towns, while on the mountains themselves conditions are savage; snow drifts on the moorlands and, after an hour or two's thaw, torrents rampage down the gullies.

About six miles from Assisi, where his track left the woods, Francis was singing to himself in French when he was set on by one of the gangs who took to the forests in winter. They asked him who he was and where he was going: "I am the herald of the Great King. What's that to you?"[1]

Their answer was to search him for money and papers, and when they found nothing, to beat him, strip him, and throw him in a ditch full of snow. As soon as they had gone Francis hauled himself out, bruised, bleeding and wet, but strangely exhilarated.

Before long he saw the Benedictine monastery of Santa Maria di Valfabbrica in the valley below. The monks had a reputation for charity but Francis's appearance went against him. He was made to work in the kitchen, fed on weak broth with no bread and, although he now wore only a shift, wasn't given any clothes. It was several days before the snow melted, the river went down and he could get on to Gubbio. Some years later, when his fame had begun to spread, he met Ugo, the prior, who remembered the incident with great shame and apologized.

Gubbio was a forbidding place under Mt. Ingino. A dark forest, hunted by wolves, came down to its ring of walls, built from the same gray stone as the cathedral, churches and tall, fortified houses. One of these, near the southern gates, belonged to the Spadalungas. Their warehouse was next to it, not far from the river running through the town, beside which the dyers hung out their cloths to dry on tall wooden racks. Pietro and Francis had often done business here.

Federico gave Francis a generous welcome and set him up with clothes suitable for a hermit – a tunic, breeches, sandals, a leather belt and a staff. Nothing else is known about this visit. Anxious to get on with his work at San Damiano, Francis did not stay long.

Federico now disappears from the story, but in the following decades his warehouse became a monastery. A tall church, with plain Gothic arches, also rose beside his house whose front door opened, as it does now, into the sacristy. The church was dedicated to Francis.

*

When Francis reappeared at San Damiano, his hard work and irrepressible optimism quickly overcame the old priest's qualms at seeing him back. Every day he went up to the town in search of materials, cheerfully singing the praises of God before begging for stones. Some people jeered but others were so impressed by the change in him that they gave him whatever they could spare.

It is impossible to know precisely what work Francis did at San Damiano. However, the German art historian Henry Thode pointed out a long time ago that whereas the ceiling of the eleventh-century sanctuary has rounded Romanesque arching, the nave – of much the same date – is roofed with slightly pointed arches, in the early Gothic style, which only reached Italy from France at the beginning of the thirteenth century. Thode argued that Francis, with his quick eye, would have noticed an innovation like this in the new churches and cathedrals then going up in France and copied it. The three other chapels he restored in Umbria and Tuscany all share this feature.

The building work was tough but the lessons Francis had learned on the walls of Assisi now came in useful. Although he wasn't strong, possibly suffered from consumption, and frequently fasted, he humped load after load of heavy timber, stones, sand and cement, to the church. The priest grew seriously worried that he was overtaxing himself and, aware of how well he had fed in the old days, prepared special meals for him; but Francis had vowed to live as the poor did and took to begging for scraps like a leper. At first he retched when he tried to force them down; in the end he professed to find them delicious.

He made such a sorry sight begging through Assisi in his torn and dusty tunic, that his embarrassed father would stop and curse him in the street. In self-defense Francis devised one of his pantomimes. He persuaded a notorious old derelict to come on his rounds, and when Pietro cursed him, Francis would turn to the tramp and say, "Bless me, father." "Bless you, my son," the old man would answer, making the sign of the cross, as Francis had coached him.[2]

Francis also had to endure the sarcasm of his brother, Angelo. He was praying quietly in the country one day, when he was seen by his brother and a friend. "Look at my brother," Angelo said to his companion. "Why don't you ask him to sell you a few pence worth of his sweat?" Francis replied cheerfully, in French: "God gives me far more for my sweat than either of you can afford."[3]

Always the troubadour he often dropped into the idiom when he put on an act, to attract attention or hide his embarrassment. When he was begging for oil to burn in the lamp at San Damiano, he once found his friends gambling and was reluctant to disturb them. Then he plucked up his courage, confessed his embarrassment and asked in French for the oil.

Angelo di Tancredi, who was probably there at the time, describes an occasion when Francis wanted volunteers at San Damiano: "Come and help us finish our work," he called out in French to passersby.

"One day this church is going to be a convent for women, whose life and fame will cause God to be glorified everywhere."[4]

*

When the restoration was complete he must have felt he had fulfilled his obligation and wondered what to do next but, as happened at a number of critical points in his life, he received shrewd advice from the bishop. Guido knew that Francis must occupy both the spiritual and practical sides of his nature. After they had talked, Francis went off to meditate very seriously on Christ's words in the gospels and to restore another building.

An inscription on a stone in the church of Santa Maria Maggiore, beside the bishop's palace, records that Francis did some work there, though it is not dated until eight years later – 1216 – by which time he had become well known in Umbria; however, his next main task was the restoration of San Pietro della Spina, a tumbledown chapel near one of his father's farms.

While he worked he continued to pray, make his confession, do penance and go regularly to Mass at Santa Maria degli Angeli. There, on February 24, 1208 – it was St. Matthias's Day, commemorating the apostle elected to replace Judas Iscariot – he heard the words of the tenth chapter of St. Matthew's Gospel, which Christ spoke to his apostles before he sent them into the world. This is the kernel of what he told them, as they set off two by two:

> Preach as you go, saying "The Kingdom of heaven is at hand." Heal the sick . . . cleanse lepers, cast out demons. . . give without pay. Take no gold, nor silver, nor copper in your belts, no bag for your journey, nor two tunics, nor sandals, nor a staff. . . . As you enter a house, salute it. And if the house is worthy, let your peace come upon it.[5]

Angelo says that Francis listened to the priest's commentary on this passage with "unspeakable joy." It suddenly struck him that the voice he had heard in San Damiano hadn't always belonged to a serene martyr, nailed to a crucifix. It was also the voice of a twelve-year-old boy who had intrigued the elders in the temple with his shrewdness and wisdom, and of a young man perpetually and intensely alive to the miraculous beauty of the world and also to its ubiquitous suffering, which he had set himself to assuage whatever the cost. As the significance of the words sank in, Francis exclaimed, "That is what my whole heart longs to accomplish!"[6]

His certainty had something heady and lyrical about it, like the exaltation of one of Shakespeare's shepherds speaking of love.

It is to be made of all sighs and tears. . .
It is to be made of all faith and service. . .
It is to be all made of fantasy,
All made of passion, and all made of wishes;
All adoration, duty and observance;
All humbleness, all patience, and impatience,
All purity, all trial, all obeisance.[7]

It would be several years before he discovered the burdens which accompany such pellucid faith, demanding the energy of a coalminer, the stamina of a politician engaged in a never-ending election campaign, the compassion of a doctor during a lethal plague, and a devotion to prayer which seldom allowed him more than four hours of sleep.

He immediately gave away his second cloak, his hat, his staff, his sandals, and exchanged his leather belt for a length of rope. In time he adopted a habit – its straight arms and body cut like a capital T – made from the cheapest cloth, ash-gray or earth brown, with a detachable hood. The butterfly had re-emerged from his chrysalis, this time in the colors of a moth.

11

Twelve Beggars

1208–1209

"Preach as you go." Francis was quick to do so, standing outside his old school church, San Giorgio, begging people to thank God for their blessings and follow Christ's example in their everyday lives.

He spoke with such a peculiar mixture of excitement and anguish, solemnity and humor, that people stopped to listen. Many were intrigued and some half-convinced by what he said, including a rich and highly respected notary called Bernard di Quintavalle who owned property all around Assisi.

Bernard sometimes took Francis home to discuss his ideas, and eventually asked him to eat and spend the night. They talked long, deeply and late but when they went up to bed Francis didn't want to make a show of his prayers, and so feigned sleep until he thought Bernard had dropped off; then he got up and spent several hours on his knees. However, Bernard was also dissembling and what he saw convinced him that Francis was entirely genuine. In the morning he asked what a man should do with his wealth if he felt he didn't need it any longer.

Francis was in no doubt, and said so.

"In that case," Bernard replied, "I will give all my worldly goods to the poor, for the love of God and distribution as you think best."

"Tomorrow then," Francis said, "we will go to church and discover exactly what Christ would have told his disciples."[1]

A lawyer whom they both knew, Peter of Catanio, had recently also told

Francis that he would like to adopt his way of life. Francis therefore led both men to St. Nicholas's church, just across the Piazza del Comune, responding to an impulse he describes like this in his *Testament*:

> After the Lord had given me brothers, no one showed me what I was to do, but the Most High himself revealed that I should live according to the pattern of the holy gospel.[2]

Since none of the three men was confident of turning quickly to the appropriate pages of the bound gospel readings on the altar, they first knelt in prayer, and Francis then opened the book in three places. The first time he read out:

> "If you wish to be perfect, go, sell what you have and give it to the poor, and you shall have treasure in heaven" [Matthew 19:21].
>
> At the second opening he read: "Take nothing for your journey" [Luke 9:3], and at the third: "If any man will come after me, let him deny himself" [Matthew 16:24].[3]

Convinced by these texts of their vocation, Bernard and Peter immediately kicked off their shoes and exchanged their clothes for a habit tied at the waist with a rope. The missal, which had thus played its part in the creation of the Franciscan order, later came into the possession of Bishop Guido; today it can be seen at the Walters Art Gallery in Baltimore, Maryland.

While Bernard was distributing the proceeds from the sale of his property with Francis outside San Giorgio they were approached by Silvester, an elderly priest, possibly a canon of the cathedral, who was well known for his avarice. He now came up and unjustly reproached Francis.

"You didn't pay me a proper price for the stones you bought from me."[4]

Francis contemptuously plunged his hand into Bernard's pocket, pulled out a fistful of coins, and thrust them at Silvester, asking if that was enough. His reaction surprised the old priest and set him thinking.

With Bernard and Peter to help him, Francis soon finished restoring San Pietro. He then moved on to the church that became the cradle of his order and his home for the rest of his life.

Santa Maria degli Angeli was a dilapidated little chapel in a forest clearing two miles below Assisi, close to the road between Perugia and Foligno. With the surrounding land it was also known as the Porziuncula or Little Portion; it belonged to the Abbey of San Benedetto. Low-lying, enclosed by oaks and ilexes, near to a stream and the marshes, it could be damp and foggy in winter, airless and humid in summer. The monks had abandoned the church some time ago, but were grateful to have it restored and occasionally came down to say Mass.

Francis and his new friends put up a hut in the clearing, a simple structure of branches to which they attached wattle mats, frameworks of sticks woven with reeds and covered with clay daub. Then they threw themselves into their new existence – helping in the fields, building, preaching and nursing.

Caring for lepers must have been the severest test of "taking up the cross." Leprosy in the Middle Ages, as in the Bible, covered a wide variety of diseases because its early symptoms resembled those of many other complaints – syphilis, gonorrhea, yaws and ergotism or St. Anthony's fire. True leprosy thrives in humid conditions and since it is passed on by prolonged physical contact Francis, who nursed lepers throughout his life, may well have caught it. However, the disease is related to and competes with tuberculosis, whose bacteria are stronger and generate an immunity to the rival disease. Francis was therefore possibly protected by consumption.

The extent to which Francis exposed himself to infection is vividly illustrated by an episode which occurred some years later when a companion named James, who devoted himself to lepers, invited one to eat with his colleagues. Although Francis admired this compassion he also disapproved of it, because it was against every regulation and caused those nearby to shrink away from them. He therefore rebuked James in front of all those present.

Immediately he regretted this, especially for hurting the feelings of the leper, and confessed his lapse of charity to Peter of Catanio. By way of penance he went straight to the leper, sat beside him and placed between them a bowl from which they could both eat together.

> The leper had sores and ulcers all over him, and the fingers with which he fed were eaten away and bleeding, so that whenever he dipped them in the dish his blood ran into it.[5]

By now Francis's reputation was well known throughout Assisi. His work for lepers, like his manual labor, renunciation of self-indulgence and sex, and dedication to every kind of underdog, were an uncomfortable challenge to the people of Assisi, where they fought continually for position, money and power; where the records are littered with public accusations of sodomy, incest, adultery, prostitution, and rape; and where brutal punishments failed to reduce theft, fighting, arson, murder and treason. But his challenge soon struck a chord among some remarkable men, who became as keen to share his crusts and water as others had his banquets and debaucheries.

Bernard and Peter both had reputations as hard-headed businessmen, so that when an enterprising youth, Giles, saw them giving away their money outside San Giorgio he decided to join them at the Porziuncula. Francis found him standing at the crossroads near the lazar house, unsure of the way. When Giles explained why he was there Francis gave him a quick test by asking him to give his cloak to a beggar who had just arrived in search of alms. By handing it over without hesitation Giles won Francis's lasting affection.

During the next few months Francis accepted seven other men into the little community, including Sabbatino, who accompanied him to Egypt eleven years later; Morico, a Cruciger knight working in one of the leper houses whom Francis had nursed through a long illness; and John of Capella whose misguided zeal later led him astray.

Of the remaining four, nothing at all is recorded about Bernard of Viridente; Barbaro is best remembered for his exemplary humility; and Philip, a very tall man nicknamed The Long, played a critical role in the future of San Damiano. The last was, in fact, the earliest of Francis's great friends and the first of many young nobles to join him, Angelo di Tancredi.* As the son of a distinguished consul and important landowner it had been even more difficult for him than for Francis to make an irrevocable break with his family; but once more they became inseparable and remained so until Francis's death.

Throughout his life from now on Francis emanated an almost radioactive energy which seemed to derive from his sense of continuous proximity to God. It was said he didn't love God but was in love with him. To live in his

*Some sources mention that a Giovanni di San Costanzo also joined Francis now.

company was therefore formidable yet also exhilarating, for his conviction was infectious and communicated to many of his companions a faith as luminescent as his. United in everything they did, they quickly discovered a degree of trust, purpose and collective happiness they had never remotely experienced before. It helped to sustain them when they began to encounter a growing hostility in Assisi.

Women, particularly, were often frightened by their uncouth appearance when they begged for alms – food or clothing, for Francis forbade them ever to touch money. Increasingly, rich and poor laughed at them for first giving up all they had owned and then scrounging like dogs. In the aftermath of the famine there was still a shortage of food and sometimes even their families thought them parasites.

Bishop Guido kept in close touch and was well aware of their difficulties although he already had plenty of his own. Only recently, when trying to bring a rebellious abbot to heel, he had been set on, beaten and had his horse killed under him.

Now he sent for Francis and asked him to reconsider his decision not to accept money or to own land on which he and his companions might grow their food; they couldn't expect others to feed them indefinitely without provoking resentment. Francis answered, "My lord, possessions are often the cause of disputes and sometimes violence. If we owned them we would be obliged to carry arms to defend them – and to do that would hinder us in loving God and our neighbor."[6]

The argument rang a bell with Guido, who received a number of reprimands from Rome for protecting his episcopal property too energetically; he accepted the argument with good grace.

With so many hands to help, Santa Maria was soon rebuilt. It then began to dawn on Francis that he had been called to restore something far more fundamental than the church's fabric – the entire institution was in need of repair. To tackle such a task with any chance of success would require an infinitely larger team than his small group of provincials, and since he couldn't rely on any new volunteers from Assisi he and his companions would have to go out and search for them.

*

Before they left the Porziuncula in pairs Francis gave them some advice:

> Dear Brothers, God in his great mercy called us not only for our salvation but for that of many; and so we are to go through the world encouraging all men and women by our example and words to do penance for their sins and keep his commandments.
>
> Don't be afraid to preach penance, even if we appear ignorant and not worth listening to. Put your trust in God who, by the Holy Spirit, will speak through you. . . . You will find some men are devout and kind, others – proud, faithless and blasphemous – will insult and injure you.
>
> But don't be frightened; many noble and wise men will join us; kings, princes and many others will be converted . . . and increase our family all over the world.[7]

He added that, if asked who they were, they should call themselves "penitents from Assisi."

They set out like recruits on an initiative course, without money or food. Francis took Giles up into the Marches around Ancona, a lyrically beautiful landscape of mountains, rich farmland and ancient stone buildings. They stopped to preach in towns, villages and the fields, but were often met with incomprehension, mockery, suspicion or violence. Reckoning the devil had done too good a job in the region they moved on, planning to come back later.

Giles then left with Bernard for Florence, where they were given a similar reception. They could find no lodgings and when a woman reluctantly allowed them to sleep on her porch her husband was furious and wouldn't lend them a blanket. Next morning in church, although they were offered money as alms, Bernard felt obliged to decline it.

Although the principal aim of these journeys was to preach the gospel and enlist colleagues for his ambitious new enterprise, Francis also kept a lookout for retreats to which he and his brothers could return in the future. He found one on his way south, near the top of Monteluco, just beyond Spoleto. Originally the Umbrians had hung their pottery offerings here in the dark ilex forest, so different from the endless expanse of soft browns and greens in the valley below. In the sixteenth century the hermitage was visited by Michelangelo – sometimes claimed as a member of Francis's Third Order – at the age of eighty-one.

Further south Francis explored the Rieti Valley, which became almost as

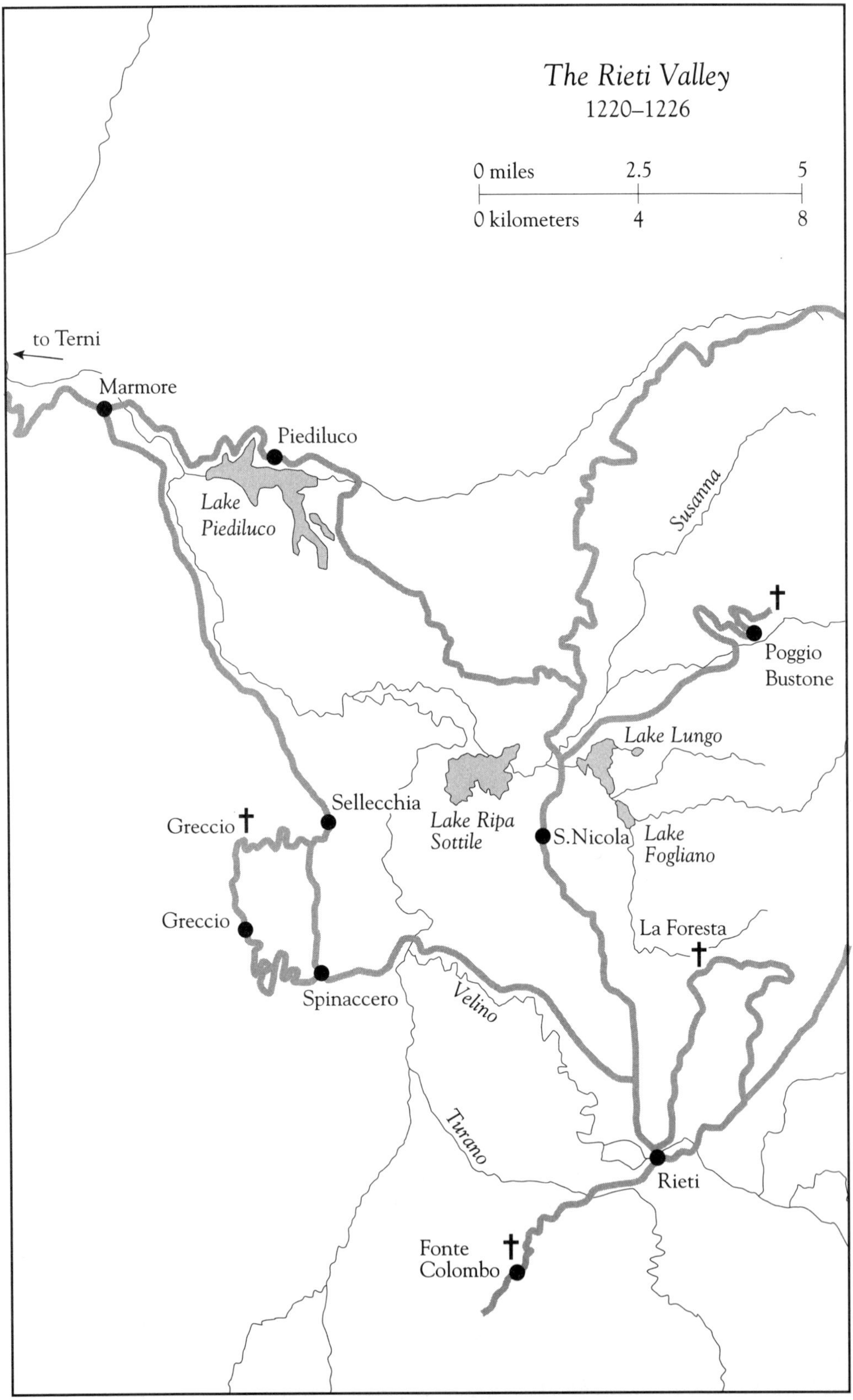

The Rieti Valley
1220–1226
0 miles
2.5
5
0 kilometers
4
8
to Terni
Marmore
Piediluco
Lake Piediluco
Susanna
Poggio Bustone
Lake Lungo
Lake Ripa Sottile
Sellecchia
Greccio
S.Nicola
Lake Fogliano
Greccio
La Foresta
Spinaccero
Velino
Turano
Rieti
Fonte Colombo

important to him as the country around Assisi. It is a spectacular amphitheater, about twelve miles long and nine across, formed by the Sabine Hills and dominated by Mt. Terminillo. From the surrounding peaks, often gleaming with snow, streams race through woods – dotted with anemones, oxlips and cyclamen – to Lake Piediluco in the valley. The more open slopes are either terraced with corn, vines and olives, or bright green meadows grazed by goats, cattle and sheep. Francis eventually left four hermitages around the rim of the valley – they witnessed some of the most poignant scenes toward the end of his life – but in 1208 he stopped at only one of them.

In a shallow cave, just above the village of Poggio Bustone, with a glorious view to the opposite hills, he received two intimations of divine encouragement. The first was a sense of unprecedented certainty that all his previous sins had been forgiven. The second occurred during moments of extra-corporeal awareness, elegantly described by Thomas of Celano:

> He was caught up above himself, and absorbed into a kind of light; the capacity of his mind was enlarged, and he could see clearly into the future. He said to his brothers . . . "I saw a great many men who wanted to share our way of life – the roads, as it were, filled with Frenchmen, Spaniards, Germans, Englishmen and many others, speaking various languages and hurrying toward us."[8]

Just about now Bernard and Giles were crossing France and Spain toward Santiago de Compostela, braving the extremes of the weather. True to their vows they wore no shoes and after Bernard gave his hood to a beggar in shriveling cold he was without one for three weeks; a vivid account of the early Franciscans describes blood in the footprints they left on the snow. Sometimes the road ran through wild, mountainous country, its forests roamed by wolves and bears, its moorlands hunted by foxes and eagles. If Bernard and Giles averaged twenty miles a day, they had neither the time nor the language to preach and must have traveled as pilgrims, for the journey to Santiago and back took them five months.

Waiting anxiously at the Porziuncula for his brothers' return, Francis realized that he hadn't given them a date by which he expected them back; but while he prayed for them they began to turn up. Comparing notes they discovered they had all received much the same treatment. "Wild men of the woods" was the least abusive name they had been called; men, women and children had pelted them with stones and dung; they had been dragged through the streets by their cowls; and occasionally their threadbare clothes had been stolen, leaving them naked.

As a recruiting drive these missions were a failure. As a reconnaissance for remote retreats and training for the future they were an unqualified success. All the sanctuaries still serve Franciscans eight centuries later, while the brothers learned to keep their nerve, their tempers and their sense of humor, so that very soon their strengthened resolve and unfailing goodwill recovered the ground they had lost in Assisi. Some of their previous tormentors even came to ask their forgiveness.

*

Francis's vision at Poggio Bustone and the changing attitude in Assisi gave him fresh confidence, yet the larger his brotherhood grew the more urgent it became to ensure its unity and spiritual stability. The simplest way of establishing these was to give his companions a formal code of life but the suggestion worried Bishop Guido. Similar evangelical movements, with many of the same aims as Francis, had been tarred with accusations of heresy.

The most controversial of these splinter groups, provoked into protest and action by the delinquency of so many clergy, were the Cathars. Their extreme asceticism amounted to dualism – a belief that only the spiritual aspects of man and creation were good, anything earthly or to do with the flesh was evil. Their leaders, known as Perfects, defied the church by administering the sacraments and preaching abstinence from sex and virtually all nourishment. They had spread through Italy, and were found in the Duchy of Spoleto, but one of their most intransigent strongholds was in southern France, around Albi.

Innocent had tried to coax these Albigensians out of their error by dispatching a company of Cistercians to preach to them. Despite the original austerity of their order this particular delegation arrived, plump and complacent, with caravans of luxuries and predictably made no impression. Surprisingly the church's next champion, an austere, saintly and highly intelligent Augustinian from Spain, Dominic de Guzman, made no impact either. Finally the pope sent his personal envoy or legate, Peter of Castelnau, to negotiate the submission of the heretics but in 1208 he was assassinated by a Cathar on the banks of the Rhône. In exasperation Innocent was now mounting a crusade of ferocious retribution against them.

Further north near Lyons, a rich merchant named Waldo had paid for the translation of the gospels into French and given away his wealth to the poor. Members of his movement, known as Waldenses or Poor Men of Lyons, preached along the trade routes – for laymen to do this was regarded as heresy.

Many of the cardinals in the Curia – the papal court – also wanted to brand the Humiliati, a large and thriving evangelical movement of men, women and priests in northern Italy, as heretics. Far wiser, Innocent preferred them as allies not enemies, and had given them an informal license to live in communities and even to preach, provided they didn't dabble in doctrine.

Against this background, if Francis wrote a set of guidelines on the one hand, or failed to do so on the other, he was equally vulnerable to charges of heresy; both the religious and the secular clergy were likely to claim he was picking their fruit. The only safe solution was to adopt one of the rules already approved for the two great orders, the Augustinians and Benedictines.

The Augustinian rule was designed to bring order into the lives of the canons and secular clergy living around cathedrals, churches, castles and courts; they weren't cloistered but were rooted. The Benedictine rule prescribed a life of balanced prayer, work, study, food and sleep; the monks in the order may have been the greatest civilizing influence in medieval Europe but were enclosed and owned vast estates bringing in princely incomes.

Francis regarded neither rule as acceptable for his brothers weren't sedentary, cloistered or owners of property. Nevertheless he was convinced he needed one; and since he always went to the heart of an issue and was happy to take risks, after talking to the bishop, the Benedictines and his companions, he wrote one down. It contained a set of basic principles drawn from the gospels, supported by quotations. Although the text of this first, primitive, Rule has never been found, there is a general consensus that in essence it required: Poverty, Chastity, Humility, Obedience to God, Prayer, Work, Harmony, and Preaching.

The simplicity of these precepts was deceptive. For one thing Francis expected them to be complied with absolutely, to the very limit of human capability. For another he found that this pure distillation of Christ's own teaching sent a shiver down the spines of some of his most eminent prelates. However one senior churchman now performed a *volte face* and asked if he might come and live in obedience to it.

After provoking the scene about the price of his stones, Silvester had reflected on the contrast between his own behavior and the generosity of a young man like Francis. Several nights later he had a dream. He saw an immense cross reaching to the sky; its foot was planted in Francis's mouth, while the arms stretched from one end of the world to the other. On waking he was convinced that Francis's form of religion would spread over the entire earth.[9]

After taking some time to reconsider his whole way of life, Silvester went down to the Porziuncula, apologized to Francis and Bernard, asked to join them and was "kindly received." He was much the oldest brother and the only priest. With Bernard and Giles he is mentioned by Dante in *The Divine Comedy*.

Two years before, abandoning everything including his family, Francis had stood naked and friendless in front of the bishop. Now, in the spring of 1209, he was the moving spirit in a group of twelve devoted companions, some humble, some recently among the richest and cleverest men in Assisi. The thought gave him courage, and he announced one morning that they were leaving for Rome. They would knock on the doors of the Lateran Palace and ask to see the pope with an outrageous request – that he should give them his blessing on their self-appointed mission to restore the church of which he was the God-given head.

12

To the Pope

1209

Before they left, Francis insisted they should choose a leader for the journey; from now on he never traveled alone and always asked someone else to take charge, even if he only had a single companion. On this occasion Bernard was picked.

It was spring and in the defile south of Spoleto the dark forests were brightened by the fresh green of the beeches and chestnuts, and the pink flowers of the Judas trees. The brothers frequently paused to pray, and in the evenings were offered food and shelter wherever they stopped. When they reached Rome they made for the Lateran Palace on the far side of the city.

This expedition was the greatest risk Francis ever took. His presumption in approaching the pope was extraordinary, for over the last ten years he had squandered every worldly advantage he possessed and was now literally a beggar, while Innocent had made himself master of Europe. In the first few years of his pontificate he had been drawn into desperate battles, first to survive and then to stamp his authority progressively on Rome, Italy, Europe and the eastern Mediterranean.

In Italy the Germans had tried to break his hold on the papal lands around Rome by crushing them between their dukedoms in the north and their kingdom of Sicily in the south; but Innocent had turned the tables on them. In the north he had widened the split between the two contenders for the imperial crown, Otto and Philip. In the south he had preempted their threat by crowning his ward, Henry VI's young son Frederick, King of

Sicily, and placing him under the tuition of one of his cardinals.

In the rest of Europe Innocent had asserted his moral and secular authority over the kings of Portugal, Aragon, Leon, Norway, Bohemia, Hungary and Bulgaria. He had placed England under an interdict – denying the country any of the church's services or sacraments – and was about to excommunicate its king, John, obliging him to cede his sovereignty to the throne of St. Peter.

The most extraordinary aggrandizement of his power had resulted from the unexpected outcome of the Fourth Crusade, which he had initiated and promoted with characteristic vigor to recover Jerusalem. Instead the Crusaders, who were dependent on the Venetian fleet, had found themselves drawn into an attack on Constantinople, the capital of Venice's great trading rival, Byzantium. Doge Enrico Dandolo, over ninety and blind, was the first ashore and by April 1204 Constantinople, a Christian city, had been sacked, its women raped, vast numbers of its inhabitants massacred and its treasure looted. Nine hundred thousand silver marks vanished, its four magnificent bronze horses ended up on the facade of St. Mark's basilica in Venice, and it is said a Cistercian abbot made off with St. Cosmas's foot, St. James's arm, and a drop of Christ's blood. The neighboring Saracens were left astonished and unscathed.

Innocent was progressively embarrassed, ashamed and furious at this perversion of his aims, which further widened the schism between the churches in the east and west, that had developed since a breach in formal relations in 1054 arising out of issues such as authority and Rome's incorporation of Christ in the Godhead. But gradually he realized he had been handed temporarily both the eastern half of the old Roman empire and the reins of the Orthodox church. What is more, the Saracens were prepared to sign a six-year truce, leaving Byzantium as an excellent springboard for the next crusade.

The exercise of temporal power was no longer of any consequence to Francis. Rome was its monument: originally built of wood, which had been replaced by brick, and finally marble, it now lay in dust all around him. Goats were grazing in the wasteland of the forum, and on the majestic desolation of the Palatine Hill, once the home of the Emperor Augustus, and commemorated in the name of every palace since. A mile beyond it the road opened out into a piazza in front of the Lateran, the seat of Europe's spiritual power.

The equestrian statue in its center was of Marcus Aurelius, though then thought to be of Constantine, who had established the Bishop of Rome in a series of magnificent buildings here. To the left was his palace; next to it the city's first basilica – its cathedral – known as San Giovanni in Laterano; and on the right an octagonal baptistery, previously a marble bath house. Although detached from the mainstream of city life the papal headquarters, and a cluster of monasteries around it, attracted a constant stream of visitors.

As soon as they arrived the brothers went to pray in the basilica. Dedicated to St. John the Baptist, and named after the Lateran family, its ninth-century facade and interior were highly decorated with mosaics and paintings. The mosaic of Christ the Redeemer still presides from the apse, at the end of an avenue of columns dividing the nave from the aisles on either side. The altar was said to contain relics of the table on which St. Peter celebrated Mass.

When Francis and his companions left the church they walked over to the loggia of the palace, displaying some of the finest bronzes from the ancient world, among them the she-wolf suckling the founders of the city, Romulus and Remus. Just as they were about to ask for an audience with the pope they were greeted by a familiar figure from Assisi.

*

There are several versions of Francis's first encounter with Innocent. The least probable emanates from the thirteenth century English Benedictine chronicler Matthew Paris, who took a jaundiced view of Innocent's nephew, Pope Gregory IX, and of some of the later Franciscans. According to his informant Francis and his companions, bedraggled and smelly from their journey, found their way into the palace and surprised the pope in a corridor. Innocent, supposing from their appearance they were farmhands, brushed aside their petition to preach and told them to save their attentions for swine. Francis quickly led his brothers away, addressed a few words to some pigs they found in the street, and returned. The pope relented and gave him an audience.

The most convincing account is given by Angelo di Tancredi who was almost certainly there. The familiar figure in the loggia was Bishop Guido, who smiled in delight but expressed anxiety that they had left Assisi for good, just as they were becoming a valuable asset in his diocese. He was therefore relieved when he heard the reason for their visit and immediately introduced them to his friend Cardinal Giovanni di San Paolo, the Bishop of Santa Sabina in Rome.

No man was better placed to help Francis. A Roman aristocrat like the pope, he had been a Benedictine monk and subsequently promoted bishop and cardinal by Innocent's predecessor. Universally respected for his learning, piety, and wisdom, he was Innocent's confessor. His special expertise lay in identifying the difference between tolerable if idiosyncratic interpretations of Christianity and treasonable heresy.

The church had become a state with the pope at its head – a priest-king presiding over a Curia or cabinet drawn from the cardinals, who might rank from archbishops, bishops and priests down to deacons. The three principal offices were responsible for liturgy, correspondence and finance; other cardinals administered canon law or represented the pope as his legates.

In talking to Cardinal San Paolo – expounding his own ideas and trying to understand the hierarchy's mistrust of absolute poverty – Francis probably also learned something about another side of Innocent. Two of his books had been on the contempt of worldliness and the sacrament of the Mass; he emerged from them as sympathetic both to indigence and the mystical life. As if to balance massive expenditure on his family's stronghold, the Tor de' Conti, he had established the great hospital of Santo Spirito in Sassia near the Vatican. He maintained tight control of public spending but gave lavishly to the poor. He was reforming the clergy and planning the foundation of university schools to counter a new surge of secular learning. Except on state occasions he simplified the food in his palace, replaced gold and silver with wood and glass, and used lambskin rather than furs.

San Paolo questioned Francis and some of his brothers for several days, probing their beliefs, motives and proposed way of life. The concept of owning nothing in common, and of a religious – especially if he were a priest – begging, was new even to him, but he was well aware that both Bishop Guido and his fellow Benedictine, Abbot Maccabeo of San Benedetto, strongly supported Francis. At the end of his gentle yet firm interrogation he promised to plead Francis's case with the Curia and, "as a special favor," asked to be considered one of the brotherhood.

When he spoke to the pope and his colleagues, San Paolo was unequivocal: "I have found a really excellent man who wants to live according to the gospel, preserving precisely its evangelical spirit. I am convinced our Lord wishes to renew the faith of the holy church, all over the world, through him."[1]

Innocent and his cardinals were surprised by such a wholehearted endorsement for anyone advocating absolute poverty. Many of the Curia were reactionaries and resented any implicit reproach to their comfortable, not to say luxurious, way of life. As bishops and priests most of them had also suffered from the prick of heretical thorns, especially those of the Cathars. Even now, at Innocent's instigation, a new and unscrupulous legate with a bloodthirsty army of mercenaries was setting out to avenge the murder of his previous envoy and smother the spread of their heresy.

Nevertheless, Cardinal San Paolo's words had touched a chord in Innocent. He asked to see Francis the next day.

*

Francis and his companions were conducted through the corridors of the Lateran Palace, past the sumptuous dining hall in which the popes entertained the German emperors after their coronations, and through the vast conference chamber boasting thirteen apses.

At last the twelve unassuming men in their worn, brown tunics were ushered into the Hall of Mirrors, and found themselves facing the pope with a group of his judges and cardinals. They were an arresting sight in their caps or miters, and their robes of white, crimson or gold.

Francis concentrated his gaze on Innocent, a man of medium height whose character and intelligence were easily discerned in his handsome face. While he did so the pope was running his eyes over the penitents from Assisi before taking in their leader.

Even in Italy no reliable portraits were then being painted, but we have a precise account of what Francis looked like. He was slim and of short to medium height by the standards of his time. His face was long and striking, with delicate skin and clear, black eyes; his hair and trim beard were also black; his teeth even and white; his expression cheerful and friendly. He had slender hands with long fingers.

Two elements of this description by Thomas of Celano, who first met him six years later, were recently confirmed in an unusual way. When the sarcophagus holding his body was opened in 1978 his skeleton was in almost perfect condition (Plate 8); doctors calculated that he was five feet three inches tall. Dr. John Moorman, the English bishop who made a life's study of Francis, saw these remains and was particularly struck by the whiteness of his teeth.

Innocent opened the interview, and as Francis answered his questions, a rapport quickly developed between these men at opposite ends of the scale of earthly account. Both were musical, had attractive voices and were extremely articulate. Both had a sense of humor. Innocent's was sometimes astringent (he liked sucking lemons). He had observed, for instance, that every child is conceived and enters this world through the conduits of the human drainage system ("*Inter faeces et urinas nascimur*"), and had once regretted that his bishops were not always able to preach, "due to the surplus of their burdens, not to mention the deficit of their learning." When he received a petition in amusing verse, he sat down and answered in kind.

Francis pleaded his case with growing conviction, transparent honesty and self-effacing charm, but a number of cardinals had supported previous popes in outlawing the Humiliati and Poor Men of Lyons and were opposed to encouraging this group of penitents from Assisi or granting them a rule of their own when they could adopt one already approved. Feeling his way carefully, Innocent spoke his mind.

"My sons, your planned way of life seems too hard and rough. We are convinced of your dedication, but are afraid your rule may be too exacting for those who join you later."[2]

As if to cut short this line of argument Cardinal San Paolo, who had already been over this ground with Francis, now stepped forward to explain that he, too, had been afraid Francis was aiming too high and had therefore urged him to adopt the life of a hermit or monk. However, Francis had declined, not out of disrespect but because he believed his calling was different.

One elderly and influential cardinal, Cencio Savelli, was quickly won over. As chamberlain he had transformed the church's finances by listing all its properties and ensuring that the correct revenues were received from them. However, like the great English philosopher and Lord Chancellor, Francis Bacon, he believed that money, like muck, was "not good except it be spread." The owner of vast personal wealth himself, he was systematically giving it away to the poor. Innocent so trusted Savelli that it was he whom he had chosen as tutor of the four-year-old Frederick II, in

Sicily; others also greatly respected his judgment.

It was later said that while the debate continued Innocent remembered that a few nights before a vivid dream had left him puzzled and depressed; in it he had grown aware that the Lateran basilica was trembling all around him and was being saved from collapse only because it was supported on the shoulder of an insignificant little man. It suddenly dawned on him that this was the man now standing in front of him. His thoughts cleared but, not wishing to rush the Curia into a decision which might split them, he said to Francis, "My son, go and pray that what you ask proceeds from God, so that we can be certain that if we grant it we shall be following his wishes."[3]

When the twelve brothers had left the hall San Paolo addressed the pope and his fellow cardinals again, before they too dispersed to seek guidance in prayer.

"We must be careful. If we refuse this beggar's request, on the grounds that it is new, or that we think it too difficult for his followers, we may be committing a sin, because he is only asking us to approve a form of gospel life. Anyone who says this is unreasonable is guilty of blasphemy against Christ, for he is the author of it."[4]

Despite the weight of his words, the Curia's verdict hung in the balance, but Francis was optimistic. He felt that a recent dream, in which a tall and stately tree had bent down to him, was a favorable omen.

*

During the next few days Francis and his companions devoted themselves to praying for the case they had come to plead, and had time to attend Mass each day at one of the four principal basilicas in the city.

They were now familiar with St. John Lateran, the cathedral of Rome, but not all of them had yet been to St. Peter's, the most sacred of the shrines. Francis himself had a chance to visit St. Paul's (outside the walls), which was scarcely less revered, and Santa Maria Maggiore, dedicated to Christ's mother.

Santa Maria Maggiore would have struck a significant chord in him. Pope Sixtus III had founded it on the Esquiline in the fifth century because he was anxious to counteract the appeal of the nearby temple of the mother goddess which was still attracting Roman women. His basilica was decorated with brilliant mosaics depicting every phase of the Madonna's existence – from the angel's annunciation of her pregnancy, through her experiences as the Virgin Bride of the Holy Spirit and the Mother of God's Son, to her apotheosis as Queen of Heaven.

A secondary theme which increasingly influenced Francis was reflected in the basilica's alternative name, *Sancta Maria ad Praesepe*; just beside the basilica stood the Oratory of the Praesepe – the crib. Resembling a stable in a cave, it contained a relic of the original manger and was seen in the eighth century by an English pilgrim, St. Winibald, who left a description of it. Francis's meditations on the crucifix at San Damiano had disclosed the cost which unlimited love can exact. His contemplation of the nativity gradually revealed to him how much joy and hope God's incarnation had brought into the world, and much later this realization inspired one of his most original innovations – a living commemoration of the Christmas crib.

After Sixtus's initiative in founding Santa Maria Maggiore, Mary's status, and that of women too, made slow progress, probably from a combination of causes: an atavistic feeling that men were superior to women; a superstition that women – especially during menstruation – were unclean; and man's evasion of responsibility for his own lust, by branding woman, Eve, and all her descendants as the tempters. From the beginning God had been a father, Christ a son, priests male, and – in principle – from the fifth century celibate males.

At last, in the twelfth century, the archetypal feminine force in creation began to assert itself and an intriguing reversal occurred throughout Europe. Perhaps it was a reaction against the barbaric male values of the crusades, possibly it was an echo from the culture of chivalry, and no doubt it was because neither women nor men could tolerate any longer some of the church's assumptions about half the human race. The Virgin Mary became known as Our Lady, Notre Dame; between 1150 and 1250 eighty cathedrals were dedicated or rededicated to her in France alone, including those in Paris, Chartres and Rheims; she was celebrated in statues, painted glass and hymns. The use of rosary beads to help count a cycle of prayers, including *Ave Maria*, began to spread.

Hail Mary, full of grace,
the Lord is with thee.
Blessed art thou among women,
and blessed is the fruit of thy womb, Jesus.

These words had to be repeated 150 times, over the course of a week, with each telling of the rosary. While all this was occurring increasing numbers of women joined different branches of the Benedictine and Augustinian orders, formed new, sometimes independent communities, or withdrew from the world altogether as hermits.

Francis had always appreciated women, but during this visit to Rome he began to give expression to the feminine aspect of his own nature, his anima. Its development was one of the secrets that enabled him to understand and influence men and women to a rare degree.

*

While he was saying his personal prayers, either under Cardinal San Paolo's roof or in one of the monasteries close to the Lateran Palace – it is not clear where he was staying – Francis experienced an unusual vision or dream.

> A pure and beautiful girl lived in a desert, and a king who saw her decided to marry her, because he was certain she would bear him some splendid sons. The contract was drawn up, the marriage consummated and a number of sons were born.
>
> When they grew up their mother said, "Your father is a king. Don't be diffident, but go to his court and he will give you all you need."
>
> As soon as he saw the young men, the king admired their looks, and recognized their likeness to himself, and asked them who they were. They replied their mother was a poor woman living in the desert.
>
> At this the king embraced them, saying, "You are my children. You have a greater right here than all these strangers at my table. Go and fetch the rest of the family, and I will look after them."[5]

As soon as Francis had worked out the meaning, he realized that his prayers had been answered and began to feel optimistic about the outcome of his final meeting with the pope.

His first task, back in the Lateran, was to dispel the Curia's fears that he might try to interpret Christian doctrine in his own way, administer sacraments, and preach wherever and whatever he wished. Since these were never his intentions, he succeeded without difficulty.

Questioned further, in case his devotion to poverty and chastity derived from any latent Catharist leanings, Francis convinced his examiners that although he and his brothers were willing to face hunger, however acute, their proposed rule allowed them to eat and drink whatever was offered them as alms. Nor did they have any reservations about marriage and parenthood for those who were drawn to them.

When Innocent asked Francis to state his final position he told the Curia the story of his dream, and ended with these words.

"I am that poor woman, whom God in his mercy has loved and honored, and through whom he has fathered legitimate children.

"The King of Kings has told me that he will provide for all the sons he raises up through me, because if he cares for strangers he will also look after his own children. Since he gives so many of the good things of life to the unworthy and sinners, he will provide even more generously for those who spread his message.

"Please, therefore, confirm our rule taken from the gospels."[6]

At first Innocent was utterly astonished. He must have wondered if he had been listening to a megalomaniac, but as he stared at Francis he saw someone neither boastful nor mad, but humble, sane, alight with his love of God, and passionate to serve him. Then, it was said, he recalled his own recent dream and was convinced that he was speaking with a man who might well save the church from ruin.

It was said of Innocent that in his judgments "he desired only the possible – but all of it." He therefore decided to stretch his pontifical powers to their limit in order to reconcile the aspirations of this disturbing young man with the defensive response of his more conservative cardinals. Stepping down from his dais he took Francis in his arms. "We approve your rule," he said. "Go, Brothers, with the Lord and preach penitence to everyone, in whatever way He inspires you. And when He increases His grace in you and multiplies your numbers, come back and report everything to us. We will then concede more to you, and entrust you with even greater work."[7]

At this Francis knelt on the ground, promising obedience and reverence to the pope. Turning to the twelve brothers Innocent required them – and any who might join them in future – to make the same promise to Francis. He then blessed them all, and they left.

Francis had agreed with Cardinal San Paolo that, if the pope approved his rule, he would be ordained a deacon and be tonsured with his brothers;

it would entitle them to play a part in church services while he might read the gospels, though not administer sacraments. The Roman form of tonsure entailed shaving the whole crown of the head at least once a month.

Innocent's assent to the rule was never confirmed by a bull or even put in writing, and may not then have seemed of very great moment to him, whatever he came to feel later. His stage was, after all, the whole of Christendom, on which he wrestled every day with archbishops, patriarchs, chancellors and emperors.

During his short stay in Rome, with the help of Bishop Guido, Francis had set his new order on the map. He had also made important friends at the pinnacle of the hierarchy including Cardinal San Paolo, who now adopted the brotherhood as its unofficial protector, and the influential Cardinal Savelli.

Some claim he also met the pope's nephew, Cardinal Ugolino dei Conti di Segni, although as Innocent's legate to Otto of Saxony Ugolino spent most of the early months of 1209 shuttling between Rome and Germany to negotiate an accord with Otto. The recent murder of Otto's rival, Philip of Swabia, had persuaded Innocent to crown Otto emperor, provided he swore allegiance in return.

In the meantime Francis said his farewells in Rome, prayed with his companions at St. Peter's and set off for Assisi.

13

Prelude in a Cowshed

1209–1210

From the time they left Rome the memoirs of several brothers and anecdotes collected by Thomas of Celano enable us to watch them moving through the landscape like figures from an early Book of Hours. In the background winding rivers flow through green pastureland and wooded valleys; laborers hoe the root fields, reap the corn, or with baskets strapped to their backs pick grapes off the vines. A bishop with his chaplain, a cavalcade of nobles, a company of soldiers with sloped spears, a beggar on his crutch, make for a castle or fortified hill town.

About forty miles north of Rome the twelve friars stopped below Orte in an attractive meadow by the Tiber. There they stayed for two weeks, discussing how much time they should spend in secluded meditation and how much in helping others and preaching. They took turns to beg for food and stored the leftovers in an empty Etruscan tomb. Prayer convinced Francis that their primary vocation was service and they returned to Assisi.

He felt that as a newly formed order they should not presume to reoccupy the Benedictines' church at the Porziuncula, so he led them to the nearby Rivotorto stream, running through one of his father's farms, where he knew there was an abandoned shed. It may have looked picturesque among the willows and poplars but inside it had nothing in common with the limpid colors and ethereal atmosphere of an illuminated breviary. It was a derelict cowshed, mucky underfoot and extremely drafty until they plastered the cracks in its walls with mud.

Like all country people the friars lived by the sun and kept much the same hours as the animals and birds on the farms in the valley. It is only in the tropics that day and night are conveniently the same length all year, and there are few latitudes which enjoy a constant, comfortable, temperature of 70°F. In Assisi the winter nights were too long and often bitterly cold; there was no room for a fire and seldom enough oil for a lamp. In summer the short, hot and fetid hours of darkness were constantly disturbed by the calls of foxes and owls, and the cries of their prey. The brothers slept on straw, sometimes covered in sacking or rags. Since it was difficult for them all to sit or lie down at the same time, Francis allotted each a space and wrote his name on a beam above it. As summer approached the mosquitoes moved in and one brother said the fleas bit worse in hot weather.

Thomas of Celano, always happy to moralize, writes, "In its shelter those ardent despisers of great and beautiful homes . . . kept themselves from the rains. As a saint once said, you ascend more quickly to heaven from a hovel than a palace."[1]

It was a perfect laboratory in which to test the friars' fitness to live up to their vows. Francis told them that to understand their Rule fully they must frequently discuss it and keep it constantly in their minds, for "the way of the Cross . . . was the hope of salvation, the key to paradise." Properly practiced it could help end decades of bloodshed and lead their generation to heaven when they died. A derelict farm shed may have seemed an incongruous training school for such an operation but centuries before a similar one had been launched in a stable.

Francis's meditations on Christ convinced him there really was only one way of radically reducing the misery in the world and that was by persuading people to love God and their neighbors without reservation. Most great religions agree that unfortunately one massive barrier prevents them from achieving this noble objective – the self. Discussing the purpose of life some years ago, Dame Iris Murdoch, the philosopher and novelist who had made a personal journey through Marxist materialism, logical positivism, and existentialism toward a sympathy with theism, expressed a similar view; she believed our purpose on earth is to conquer the ego.

Francis had no education in comparative religion and never went near a school of philosophy, but he intuitively understood the need to dismantle our selfishness before we can achieve the higher forms of love. The eight most important precepts of his Rule, chosen after his discussions with Bishop Guido, Cardinal San Paolo, and possibly Abbot Maccabeo, were designed for this purpose.

Five of these obligations – obedience, poverty, chastity, humility and harmony – were commitments to self-restraint; the other three – prayer, work and preaching – pledged the brothers to unselfish activity.

*

By his vow of obedience a friar made his submission to God directly, and also indirectly through Francis and the pope. This placed a heavy burden on Francis's shoulders, for it meant he had to see that every friar in his order honored his obligations. Perhaps for this reason he said they must not only obey the text of their Rule, but also carry out at once any instructions they received. They should also try to anticipate his unspoken wishes. When asked to describe the best form of obedience he gave this uncompromising answer:

> Take up a dead body and lay it where you will. It does not resist being moved, complain of its position, or ask to be left alone. If lifted on to a chair it does not look up but down; if clothed in purple it appears paler than before.[2]

Nevertheless he regarded an order given under obedience not as a weapon of the first instance but as a last resort; he said, "The hand should not be laid to the sword too hastily."

Innocent had counted on the friars' behavior and whole way of life to provide an example and corrective to his clergy. For this reason Francis was determined they should never cause a division within the church, and so required them to obey every priest as they would the pope. The friars were to ask a bishop's permission before preaching in his diocese and when staying in a parish should make their confessions to its priest, however notorious. By way of respect for the office of one incumbent Francis went out of his way to receive communion from him although he was well known to be living with his mistress.

Throughout the ages Christians, Hindus and Muslims have found that the practice of poverty has proved invaluable if not essential in releasing the soul from the clamor of self, leaving it free to identify solely with God and his purpose. In his *Varieties of Religious Experience* William James, the philosopher and psychologist, examines Francis's insistence on the total abandonment of money and possessions:

> So long as the surrender is incomplete, the vital crisis is not passed, fear still stands sentinel. . . . A drunkard, or a morphine or cocaine maniac, offers himself to be cured. He appeals to the doctor to wean him from his enemy, but he dares not face blank abstinence. . . . Even so an incompletely regenerate man still trusts in his own expedients. His money is like the sleeping potion which the chronically wakeful patient keeps beside his bed; he throws himself on God, but *if* he should need the other help, there it will be also.
>
> To give it up definitely and forever signifies one of those radical alterations of character which came under our lectures on conversion. In it the inner man lives in a new center of energy. . .
>
> Accordingly, throughout the annals of the saintly life we find this recurring note: Fling yourself upon God's providence without making any reserve whatever – take no thought for the morrow – sell all you have and give it to the poor – only when the sacrifice is ruthless and reckless will the higher safety really arrive.[3]

Just as possessions stand between us and God so they divide us socially and psychologically from each other. Francis maintained that for a brother not to part with whatever he had to someone poorer was tantamount to stealing from him or her – a harsh ruling for the friars had virtually nothing to give except whatever food they had collected and their cloaks.

Cloaks feature in a number of anecdotes – to the despair of the brothers who found it difficult to keep warm clothes on Francis's back during hard weather. For instance he gave his to an old beggar woman who laughed with delight and ran off quickly in case he asked for it back.

"When she cut it up she found there wasn't enough cloth for a dress and went back to Francis to tell him.

"He looked at his companion, who was wearing a similar cloak, and said: 'Do you hear what she says? Let's both put up with the cold for the love of God!'"[4]

A later incident illustrates how far Francis was prepared to go in abandoning any sense of possessiveness. Another destitute old woman came begging for alms at a time when the friars had literally nothing to give but their copy of the New Testament.

"'Give it to her, give it to her,' Francis said. 'I'm sure this will please Our Lord and the Blessed Virgin better than if we kept it to read ourselves.'"[5]

Unless the brothers had been able to earn their food for the day, poverty obliged them to go out and beg before they could eat, which was also an exercise in humility. At first, anticipating their reluctance to do this, Francis went from door to door alone in search of alms but soon realized the friars must learn to get the better of their pride. He "sympathized with their blushes but condemned their confusion," believing that the love of God they offered was a better price than cash, that alms freely given washed stains from the soul, and that there were times when the foot in the door could be holy.

Squatting on the ground, the friars ate whatever came their way – an indigestible diet of occasional crusts, scraps of meat, and raw turnips.

They were startled one night by a voice in the dark.

"' I am dying! I am dying,' one of the brothers cried out.

"' Bring a light,' Francis said. 'What are you dying from?'

"' I am dying from hunger,' came the answer."[6]

Francis then had a meal prepared, and insisted they all eat it together to save their companion embarrassment. Afterward he said he wouldn't make a special dispensation again: "In eating, sleeping and providing for our other physical needs we must look after Brother Body sensibly, so he has no cause to complain: 'I can't go on standing up to pray, putting a brave face on my troubles, or doing all the other things I should, because you don't care for me properly.' "[7]

He added that "the Lord desires mercy, not sacrifice." When Silvester, who was much older than the others, was seriously ill and in need of delicate food Francis took him out into a vineyard before the brothers were awake and gave him the very best grapes.

Nevertheless Francis kept a sharp eye on their eating habits and rebuked a friar who was cooking because he was soaking their beans overnight – they had sworn "to take no thought for the morrow."

In a sense the vow of chastity simply expressed another dimension of poverty. It relinquished a friar's claims to someone else's body and feelings (as well as his own) and in effect deprived him of sexual and emotional satisfaction in rather the same way as poverty robbed him of warmth and repletion. And since we only have one heart with which to love God and our neighbors, it reduced the risk of his dedicating too much of that heart to just one neighbor.

In quarters like the Rivotorto, physical chastity was never really threatened but, mentally, sex remained a frequent and disturbing temptation. Francis warned them with a parable – about two royal messengers, one pure minded, the other less so – against allowing its lures to slip into the mind but few friars were able to keep their sexual fantasies entirely at bay. Their regular antidote, and in moments of failure their penance, was to jump into a ditch of icy water in winter or to scourge themselves with thorns in summer.

The vow of humility took the process of shrinking the self a stage further. It was the true opposite of pride, the ultimate defiance of God's desire for undisturbed harmony in the universe, which had prompted Lucifer – most beautiful of angels – to lead a rebellion in heaven, so incurring his fall and transmutation, some said, into Satan.

Francis had stressed the necessity for humility in naming the friars *Fratres Minores*. He was determined they should identify, like the apostles, with the most despised and worst afflicted men, women or children wherever they found them. Their regular shelter should be the crudest and simplest; when they traveled they should search for lodgings, first in a leper house and then with a priest.

Determined never to let his position of authority undermine his own humility he refused to accept the conventional title of Prior, and finally settled for Minister or servant. He also frequently washed his brothers' feet and expected them to do the same for each other. If a brother were to hurt or provoke another he must kiss his foot in apology.

The attitude toward the clergy which Francis expected in his brothers was an acid test of their humility and dedication to harmony. Whenever they met a priest, however disreputable, they were to bow, kiss his hand, and if he were mounted also to kiss the hooves of his horse.

"We have been sent to help the clergy," he said, "to supply whatever is lacking in them. . . . Winning souls is what pleases God most and we can do this better by working with the clergy than against them. If they obstruct people's salvation retribution belongs to God, and he will punish them in his own time.

"So obey your superiors and let there be no jealousy on your part. If you are sons of peace you will win both clergy and people. . . . Conceal their mistakes and make up for their many defects; and when you have done this be more humble than before."[8]

*

Without Francis's inspiration and the resolution derived from their growing self-discipline, the friars would not have survived their punishing way of life for very long.

Each day began, as it ended, with prolonged and concentrated prayers. At night, rather than risk falling asleep before they were complete, some brothers roped themselves upright. It was difficult to pray in such a confined space and they had no chapel in which to worship together or celebrate Mass. Common services, especially the Office – a sequence known as the Hours said through the day – were the mainspring of monastic communities. Francis therefore put up a reed hut as an oratory in which the friars could all gather. Since Silvester was the only priest, and they owned no books, they couldn't observe the Office; but they listened to recitations from the Bible and joined in saying the Lord's Prayer, the Ave Maria, and a number of Praises composed by Francis from phrases in the psalms. To make good the lack of privacy and peace in the shed, the oratory included a cell for silent contemplation.

Through their prayers the friars discovered new dimensions of life. Its events appeared quite different when viewed in the light of eternity instead of one day. They also found themselves looking at X-ray images, as it were, of their own souls and those of the people they worked with. These new perceptions might lead to unpredictable alternations of guilt and hope, or aridity and exaltation, but often culminated in a catharsis which invigorated their work and preaching.

The rapture of their devotions was sometimes infectious. During a night while Francis was keeping vigil up in the cathedral and his brothers were praying or asleep, one of them saw a chariot of fire sweeping around the rafters inside their cramped shed. When he alerted the others they all professed to see it too, identifying the incandescent charioteer as the soul of Francis at prayer.

The intensity of such prayer could be palpable too. One morning, while

Francis was praying in the cell, Bishop Guido called to see him unexpectedly. He knocked on the door of the oratory, was let in by a friar and, confident in the affection he and Francis felt for each other, pulled back the flap of the cell to look in. As he did so:

> He felt himself being pushed firmly out by divine force. . . . Stepping back, he left immediately, stunned and trembling. He confessed to the brothers he was wrong to have gone in and apologized.[9]

Such an expression of regret didn't come easily to Guido, but it reflected his respect for Francis and his manifest new loyalty to the church.

Confession and regular attendance at Mass were fundamental to his Rule. Frequently the Host – the consecrated bread or wafers offered as the body of Christ to the congregation at Mass – was reserved in churches from one Sunday until the next. Reverence for it became so important to Francis that he constantly stressed it to the friars, spoke of it privately to parish priests, and later wrote a circular letter about it addressed "to all the clergy." Further, he arranged for the friars to forge wafer irons for making the host, and finely made boxes – pyxes – which he distributed for keeping it safe.

By extension any Bible, breviary, psalter or missal – or loose pages from them – found on the floor had to be picked up and put carefully away.

Taking his respect for Christian symbolism almost to its limit he urged brothers on their travels always to stop and pray when they saw a church, a crucifix or even a cross formed by the branches of a tree. Wherever they walked they should be at prayer – "our body is our cell and our soul is the hermit."

To reinforce the importance and habit of prayer, Francis made it part of the Rule that, wherever they were, they should maintain silence from first thing in the morning until noon.

Each day, as soon as they had begged their meal and eaten it Francis set the friars and himself to work. He remembered how easy and pleasant it was, at the end of a meal, to sit and gossip or chew over the news, but considered that "any need revealed by a love of pleasure is the sign of a dead spirit."

Francis was emphatically not a puritan, finding something of delight almost everywhere and constantly stressing the importance of joy, but idleness was anathema to him; brothers were not to "waste God's good time nor become a burden to others." He banished, with a sharp rebuke, one who prayed seldom, did no work, was ashamed to beg and stuffed himself with food.

"Be off with you, Brother Fly. You are like an idle drone, living off the other bees' harvest."[10]

No saint has loved living creatures more than Francis. He lifted a worm off the road in case it was trodden on, and bargained with a shepherd for the life of a lamb he was taking to market. Above all he loved larks, because they reminded him of friars in their habit and hood of brown feathers, humbly gleaning food from the fields and singing God's praises – an affection shared by William Wordsworth, who called them "pilgrims of the skies" and their song more heavenly than the nightingale's. Nonetheless Francis had a dubious opinion of some animals, and "fly" was a favorite term of opprobrium.

He worked every day with his hands, either in a leper house or perhaps using his skills as a builder. A brother who had no trade had to learn one and also take on whatever needed doing – planting, threshing, coping with the aftermath of a fire, nursing families with smallpox or dysentery.

In September 1209, the shadow of the German eagle – symbol of Europe's ultimate pride and power – hovered for a few days over the friars' cowshed, which stood close to the road running south from the Alps toward Rome. Otto of Saxony was making his way down the road with a formidable escort of princes, dukes, archbishops and "a terrible army" of six thousand men. At the end of his journey he was to be crowned King of Rome and Holy Roman Emperor in St. Peter's by Pope Innocent.

Francis didn't want the brothers to waste their time with the crowd waiting along the Strada Francesca to watch the procession. However he let one friar stand on the verge and call out to the columns of swaggering horsemen and barbarous guards that the emperor's glory would be short-lived; the other brothers got on with their jobs.

Apart from the practical dividends of their labor – the help it gave and the food it earned – Francis saw it as a form of prayer, echoed in George Herbert's hymn four centuries later:

Teach me, my God and King,
In all things Thee to see,
And what I do in anything
To do it as for Thee . . .

A servant with this clause
Makes drudgery divine;
Who sweeps a room as for Thy laws
Makes that and the action fine.

This is the famous stone
That turneth all to gold;
For that which God doth touch and own
Cannot for less be told.

Francis often liked to act out with a prop some point he was making and carried a broom whenever he preached in the local churches. If he found one dirty he swept it himself, out of respect for the sacrament reserved in it.

Innocent's parting words to the friars, "go brothers, and preach penitence to everyone," was then a unique injunction to a religious order and they rose to its challenge. Their prayer and work constituted the substance and center of gravity of their lives, yet were never conspicuous: but throughout Umbria their preaching soon rose above the surface of mundane events and shimmered like an iceberg. Wherever they went their work, their prayers and their preaching were inseparable.

In Francis's view:

> The preacher must first draw from his secret prayers what he will later pour out in holy sermons; he must grow hot within before he speaks words that are cold in themselves.[11]

*

During his spell at the Rivotorto Francis sometimes preached in five villages a day. A few of the brothers, traveling in pairs, went farther, into Umbria, Tuscany, the Marches of Ancona and south to Rieti. They frequently spoke out of doors, for in the early days many priests were unwilling to invite them into their pulpits.

In the countryside Francis would preach to laborers, their families and the landowners from a bale of straw in a farmyard, the doorway of a granary or a barrel in a castle wrecked, taken over and restored by the local commune. He once preached so persuasively under a shady tree in a village square that he was given a mountain.

It was much the same in the piazzas of the towns when he climbed on a box, a cart or the pillory in Assisi; into the little open air pulpit at Narni; or onto the steps of the public buildings in Gubbio, Todi and Perugia. Drifters gathered, and as word went around, women hurried from their houses, clerks left their scrolls, priests closed their confessionals and merchants their shutters. Even the signori and magistrates dropped their business to come out and listen. He offered them light at the end of their tunnel of trauma. Marina Warner, in her study of the Virgin Mary, writes:

> The Franciscans spoke for the wretched of the earth, the men and women who during this violent epoch suffered unending injustice, ill-treatment, famine, epidemics, poverty, and the toll of recruitment for the quarrels of noblemen and the crusades of the church.[12]

No one had ever talked to them about God and themselves as Francis did – not even Bernard of Clairvaux who, some sixty years before, had made his way around Europe fulminating against heretics and brilliantly firing kings and their armies with zeal for the Second Crusade. Yet although he recruited for the crusade in French, he normally preached in Latin like the rest of the clergy, and primarily for the educated. Parish priests were largely ignored in the towns, partly because of their lamentable reputations, and partly because their sermons were unintelligible to most of their congregations.

Francis and his friars spoke to them in their own language. They always opened with the words "God give you peace" but the years of demoniac bloodshed had made people so cynical that at first they were angered by the greeting. The friars wanted to drop it, but Francis refused, saying God had put it into his head. He believed this was also true of his sermons; in Thomas of Celano's view he spoke "with the learning and power of the spirit."

If we do not know exactly what Francis said, witnesses graphically describe how he said it. His idiosyncratic delivery made full use of all his skills as a troubadour. His expression was friendly and cheerful; his voice clear and attractive; eloquent and often witty, he became crisp and fiery when he denounced to their faces men commonly known to be guilty of greed, exploitation and cruelty.

He was undismayed by the distractions of wind, rain, cattle, the hubbub of market days, or a flashy young squire racing his horse through the streets. Brother Tebaldo watched a donkey run amok in the square at Trevi while Francis was preaching. No one was able to silence or catch it, until the crowd became seriously frightened. Tebaldo says Francis then spoke to it.

"'Brother ass, please be quiet and let me go on preaching.' To everyone's astonishment the donkey fell silent and stood quite still. Fearing the people might make too much of the miracle Francis began to say funny things to make them laugh."[13]

As a minstrel Francis had memorized scenes from the Arthurian romances and Chansons de Geste, which he quoted to illustrate evil, mercy and courage. As a poet words and images came easily to him. An early list of tips for friars learning to preach recommended the use of similes rather than abstractions. To tell you that if you dip your hand in pitch it will come out dirty, makes more impact than warning you that keeping bad company leads to bad habits.

While mentioning simile the guide added the nice touch that "nothing moves men's hearts more than the behavior of animals." Francis used to tell the story of a family of robins raised by the friars. One of the young, greedier and more aggressive than the rest, grew bigger and finally drove them away. Not long afterward it went to drink from a bowl but was so fat it fell in and drowned. "No cat was found which would touch the bird. Greed in man is surely a horrid evil if it is punished so terribly in birds."

As an actor Francis understood the uses of gesture and mime; he was said "to make a tongue of his body." To express the importance of joy he played an invisible fiddle with a stick; to demonstrate his view of money he told one of his friars, who had just accepted some as alms, to take the coins in his mouth and drop them in a pile of dung.

As a storyteller his imagination was powerful and his language vivid. When he described the nativity the crowd felt that Mary was giving birth to Jesus in one of their stables; the darkening scene of the crucifixion left many of them, and Francis himself, in tears. He was always simple and brief; as a performer he knew when to stop.

Despite the force of his message and his ability to make his words glow, flicker or blaze, Francis might never have been heard of today if he hadn't given proof that the best sermon of all is example.

His intimations of hope held out happier prospects for every level of society. Freedom for those still bound by feudal obligations. Equality for the free who hadn't yet obtained a fair deal from the communes. A new sense of brotherhood for everyone, with the opportunity of help for the poor, of reconciliation between priests and their parishioners, of collaboration between the authorities and dissidents, and even of an amnesty for the more vicious *majores* now threatened with revenge by their victims.

His message was as subversive as the war cry of the French Revolution, but there was an important difference. Although the French agitators disingenuously dropped the end of their slogan "*Liberté, Egalité, Fraternité OU LA MORT*," they didn't discard their use of the guillotine. Francis, on the other hand, set out to undermine the status quo not with violence but with love. Nevertheless he, too, had a black ace up his sleeve – the threat of damnation. Thomas of Celano says he put the fear of God into a number of famous figures. The point he drove home was that a better world now and salvation later were within anybody's grasp but only if they showed genuine contrition for their sins and made ample amends for them. If they didn't the inferno was waiting.

Almost everyone still believed in God; until Francis started to preach many had clearly forgotten him. If some were awestruck by his evocations of hell, others leaped at his offer of salvation. Angelo writes of this time, "A great many people of all classes decided to follow him and copy his way of life. They wanted to give up their worldly affairs to live under his discipline."[14]

*

Three men who appeared in the vanguard of these new followers joined the circle of Francis's most trusted companions.

Masseo di Massignano would have quickly enjoyed a successful career as a burgess had he remained in the world. He was tall, good-looking and a natural public speaker. He also had so much confidence that Francis was not sure what to make of him for the first few months.

Rufino di Scipione's unexpected arrival was the cause of special delight, partly because he was one of Angelo's oldest friends and partly because he belonged to Assisi's most powerful, if most controversial, family. Its head, his uncle Monaldo di Offreduccio, had led most of his relations across to Perugia during the troubles, although Rufino's father had stayed loyal to Assisi. The opposite in most ways to Masseo, Rufino was young and often tongue-tied. He had joined the brothers on impulse, after witnessing the unexpected outcome of a violent quarrel between two of them. Just as they were about to come to blows Barbaro, the more aggressive, suddenly bent down, picked up some dung, shoved it in his mouth and apologized.

The third of these newcomers, Leo, was different again. A priest from Assisi, he soon became Francis's confessor, releasing Silvester to spend more time in prayer, which became his main vocation. Leo also acted as Francis's amanuensis and almost permanent companion. Twenty years after Francis died Leo, Rufino and Angelo pooled their memories of him, which Leo transcribed onto scrolls; sometimes known as *Scripta Leonis* they constitute the most valuable source for the later years of Francis's life. All three men with Masseo are buried a few feet away from Francis, at the four corners of his sarcophagus.

While his brothers, new and old, were asleep Francis often prayed late into the night. Before long their numbers would grow prodigiously but now the addition of even a few newcomers was depriving them of essential peace; conditions in the Rivotorto had become intolerable. Francis desperately needed new quarters, a consecrated chapel in which to celebrate Mass and enough sanctified land around it in which he and his brothers could one day be buried.

Despite his prayers neither Bishop Guido nor the canons of San Rufino cathedral were willing, or perhaps able, to offer such a place, but a day came when he knew that their time at the Rivotorto was up. That morning their silent contemplation was rudely interrupted by a series of thuds and snorts in the doorway of the cowshed.

"In with you, in with you. This is just the place for us," a peasant shouted to his donkey.[15]

For once Francis was ruffled, not because he and his brothers were being ousted from their home, but because they had been disturbed in their prayers.

14

St. Mary of the Angels

1210–1212

Abbot Maccabeo and the Benedictines rescued the brothers by pressing Francis to return to Santa Maria degli Angeli and take over the Porziuncula land around it. They suggested only one condition – that even if the friars acquired others they would always regard this as their principal church. Francis agreed but since they couldn't own property insisted they pay rent in kind, a basket of fish from the river. The monks responded by sending a jar of their oil each year in return.

Leo writes that at first they still had only "a single poor shelter between them, built from wattle and daub, and thatched with straw." Later each brother had the use of a simple hut or cell; another was put up as an infirmary.

The Porziuncula gave Francis a headquarters where he could prepare his brotherhood for their battles ahead. Innocent, in his prolonged war to restore the church's authority, had made impressive progress but most of it political. He hoped that in Francis – as in the Spanish preacher and priest Dominic de Guzman – he had found an inspired irregular leader able to win over people's hearts and minds.

It didn't matter that Francis lacked the repertoire of spiritual experience passed down inside the great religious orders, for he was embarking on something quite new. A Benedictine monastery ran like regulated clockwork inside the casing of its walls; the lives of its monks with their chapel, refectory, library, cloister, garden, workshop and farm, turned precisely with the hours and the seasons.

The friars on the other hand weren't enclosed but nomadic, exposed every day to the vicissitudes of the world. Their devotion to God, the Rule and each other, must therefore ensure their cohesion and take the place of the discipline exerted by an abbot. At the same time their personal faith must be well enough developed to withstand the doubts, confusion and fears they would encounter on a journey or alone on a mountain, in hostile country, a mocking crowd or a storm at sea.

During the next three years Francis made extraordinary progress toward achieving these objectives and in breaking new ground.

*

He and his brothers called Santa Maria degli Angeli the "mother" of their order and it became his home for the rest of his life.

He was fond of it for many reasons, especially as the humblest wayside chapel near Assisi. Today, like an exhibit in a museum, it is enclosed by a vast, domed, Baroque basilica, with a lofty and pretentious porch. The walls of the primitive little oratory, built with stones brought down from Subasio long before Francis repaired them with his own hands, gleam inside and out with gilded frescoes; a terracotta statue and wedding cake tabernacle have been imposed at each end of the roof; sunshine and snow never fall on it; it is insulated from the chirp of crickets and the rustle of mice.

Nevertheless the dignity of this tiny Romanesque shrine, where Francis experienced some of the supreme joys and most poignant sorrows of his life, defies all these distractions. It is one of the most moving places in Assisi.

Francis also loved the chapel for its dedication to the Virgin. He had always associated her with poverty, and was once reduced to tears when a brother reflected there must have been days when Christ as a child went hungry because she couldn't afford to feed him. Emotionally she replaced his mother, never mentioned in the records after his break with his father. Romantically she displaced his ideal inamorata, as she did for so many of the later troubadours; he continually composed and addressed salutations, praises and prayers to her. At least seven times each day the friars chanted her antiphon:

Holy Virgin Mary, you are the daughter of the Father of heaven; you are the Mother of Lord Jesus Christ; you are the spouse of the Holy Spirit. Pray for us with St. Michael the archangel and all the saints . . .[1]

Her constant presence to Francis influenced the way in which his order developed, while her church became the small physical matrix of his great spiritual movement. In it the brothers who had never been formally educated learned about Christ and his church as Francis had in San Giorgio, while all of them explored there the deeper dimensions of their faith. It became their meeting place with God, an encounter experienced by one young man still uncertain of his calling but who hoped for a sign. He was surprised suddenly to find the little church full of people all blind, kneeling with their eyes and hands raised, praying for mercy and sight. Almost at once a shaft of light blazed down and healed them. He joined the order a few days later.

All religions are fundamentally driven by emotion rather than intellect and it is the excitement of the imagination and emotions inherent in divine encounters which often produce the extremes of self-denial and altruism conspicuous in their saints. By now familiar with this stimulation, Francis was anxious his friars should experience it as soon as possible, both through their individual prayers and their worship together.

Prayer takes off from the belief that God is a being with whom we can have a personal relationship. As the creator of the universe he must exist both outside and within time and space, from which it follows that his nature is of an infinite order, beyond the capacity of our mind properly to comprehend or our language to express. Nevertheless, most of the world's familiar religions consider that given practice we can exchange thoughts and feelings with God – especially love – through our actions and the medium of prayer. Prayer is therefore an act of faith and if conversion to this faith coincides with a brainstorm, as happened to Francis, the first steps may be chaotic and frightening. However, as the convert settles into his or her vocation it becomes a regular and controlled activity with the long-term purpose of reunion with God.

A friar's prayer life was nothing like the quiet evening or weekend rambles that we may take as conventional churchgoers. It soon faced him instead with all the challenges and rewards of a long, unpredictable and sometimes hazardous ascent of a mountain – interrupted with pauses to catch his breath, appreciate the widening view, or recover his bearings after getting lost in the dark. There are few safe generalizations to be made about this endeavor; few people talk about it in practical terms to the laity, and the spiritual classics are often above our heads. Nevertheless, priests and close friends sometimes throw out hints which suggest the kind of guidance a new friar may have received.

Two prerequisites were to make enough time and find the right place for prayer. The allocation of time is a good indicator of our motives; we withhold it from those with whom we feel shy, indifferent, suspicious or hostile; we set it aside for those whom we like, wish to work with, or love. Finding somewhere quiet and secluded, especially in the early stages, was also essential; compared with the Rivotorto the Porziuncula was ideal.

The anecdotal evidence suggests that every one of Francis's faculties was engaged during his devotions and that this was also true of his brothers – his body and its senses, his heart and its feelings, his mind and imagination were all placed under the command of his will, itself in the service of his soul. In the everyday postures of our bodies we emphasize our intentions or betray our true feelings; our movements are almost always inherently relevant to what we wish to achieve or hope to receive. Francis would kneel upright or, as often, pray standing with his arms stretched sideways; occasionally he would lie prone, also with his arms widespread.

Since God is imperceptible to the senses, religious communities have always relied on icons as a stimulus or focus of their prayers; the crucifix in San Damiano remained this for Francis. Another aid to the coordination of body and mind during prayer was the rhythmic repetition aloud of phrases, invocations or mantras – "Our Father," in Francis's case, or "My God and my all."

No two devotional lives develop in the same way or at the same pace, but an analogy has been drawn between the metaphysical experience of prayer and an ordinary human friendship. This may progress from initial civility, through engagement in common business, to conversations of mutual interest punctuated with companionable silences; after that meetings may become occasions for sudden outbursts of passionate conviction or declarations of love.

The first stage of this new life was a period of penitence and purgation, clearing the detritus of selfishness which had built up over years and would otherwise obscure the vision of God, distract attention from him, and prove a stumbling block in the service of others. Dante begins his pilgrimage at the opening of *The Divine Comedy* in a dark and daunting forest from which he hopes to escape to a sunlit hill, but his approach is barred by the leopard of sensuality, the lion of pride and a wolf – avarice.

Many guides to prayer suggest dividing it between contrition, petition, thanksgiving, and praise supported by appropriate meditations based on the psalms, gospels or life of a saint. Such devotions were no escapist daydreams but as arduous as the practice of a successful lawyer, engineer or musician; even so, at first, they may have scarcely carried a friar above the spiritual foothills.

A friar's personal devotions were reinforced by services in the little church of Santa Maria. In his early days a new brother might walk into the chapel discrete in his own senses and thoughts – aware of the bell, the heat, a guttering lamp on the altar, his mind playing on some worry or recent delight. He was detached, on his own, as he pressed through the door with the others, identically dressed in their habits. Inside, as he knelt and rose with them to the rhythm of the liturgy, was enveloped in the scented smoke of the incense, joined in the throbbing chant of a psalm and focused on the words of Francis's sermon or the ritual gestures over the bread and wine, his isolation dissolved.

During the silences of the service his soul was released from any physical or mental demand. Like his brothers he was free, in an almost trancelike state, to contemplate his God face to face. On occasions this timeless communion, beyond the power of words to describe, led to a sensation of love in an abundance he had never dreamed of, which afterward drew him closer to Francis and his brothers in whose company, because of whose company, he had experienced transcendence.

The energy of this love, derived from their worship together, a generator more powerful than the sum of their individual prayers, helped give their preaching and work the extraordinary momentum for which they were soon to be famous.

*

Francis learned by trial and error how to choose the right men for his order, make the most of their talents and master the art of their spiritual formation.

Inevitably he made mistakes, sometimes picking a "fly," misreading a brother's behavior, or trying another too harshly, but he quickly became expert at reading their minds and foreseeing their futures. Thomas of Celano regarded this insight as prophecy and gives a dozen examples. For instance several unsuitable men tried to bluff their way into the order. Suspicious of one, Francis discovered he had passed on all his possessions to his family instead of the poor; he was rejected. However, within the next few years he assembled most of his corps d'élite, the cadre around which he would build up the international ranks of friars he had seen in his vision marching the roads of Europe.

He was quick to relax one of his strictest conditions for John, a very simple peasant who struggled to support his family on Subasio. Seeing Francis go into the village church with a broom, John left his plow, took over the sweeping, and said that ever since he had heard of the friars he had wanted to join them. Francis accepted him on the usual condition that he first give away everything he owned to the poor. John promised to do whatever Francis asked and to behave exactly like him. He then went back to his plow, unhitched the pair of oxen and brought back the one which was his for Francis to sell.

The family were distraught for they knew they couldn't survive without John and his ox; his brothers and sisters, all younger, cried pathetically. Over a meal with them Francis therefore made them a solemn promise.

"I mustn't give your son back, but from now on all our brothers will become your sons and brothers. I will also ask John to leave his ox with you, although according to the gospel it should go to others even poorer."[2]

John was true to his word, never failing to imitate Francis, whether he was working, praying, coughing or spitting. Francis was amused at first and then reproached him; but when John reminded him of his promise Francis relented, for he quickly manifested the most exceptional holiness. He didn't live long, but after he died Francis always held him up as a genuine saint.

Masseo and Rufino both came from more sophisticated backgrounds and at first Francis was far less convinced of their virtues than he had been of John's. He therefore tried them out in different ways.

Masseo's family wasn't grand, but from his bearing and youthful assurance Francis felt he was too cocky for a friar, particularly when he put a question to Francis, after one of his more successful sermons.

"Why does everyone want to see you, hear you, follow you, obey you? You're not much to look at, you are not aristocratic and you're not even very well-educated!"

Francis thought carefully before kneeling down to answer.

"I think it must be because God has chosen me, as the most worthless and inadequate sinner on earth, to confound all presumptions of nobility, pride, power, beauty and worldliness!"[3]

Francis applied his first corrective shortly afterward, when they reached a crossroads on the way to Siena and Masseo asked which road they should take. Francis told him to spin around and kept him at it until he dropped from giddiness – he then chose the direction in which Masseo was facing.

Masseo made such a good impression whenever he preached that Francis was anxious it shouldn't go to his head. While the brothers were in retreat one day he therefore told Masseo that since all the others possessed the grace of prayer and contemplation whereas his gift was for preaching, he wanted Masseo to cook for them all, act as gatekeeper and take care of anyone asking for food, clothing or shelter. To protect his brothers from interruptions he should also eat his meals at the gate.

Masseo did exactly as he was told without the slightest hint of reluctance, performing his duties day after day so humbly that his colleagues couldn't bear it for him any longer and pressed Francis to distribute the chores. From then on Francis had total confidence in Masseo, frequently chose him as a traveling companion and used him as a go-between on delicate issues.

Despite his nobility and training as a knight Rufino was the opposite of Masseo. He was shy and frequently lost for words, which caused him to hesitate one day when Francis told him to go up to Assisi and preach in a church. Francis, who mistook this reluctance for arrogance and a breach of obedience, ordered him to strip off his tunic and preach bared to the waist.

The congregation howled with laughter when Rufino arrived and he could barely make himself heard when he struggled to speak. At that moment Francis – now ashamed of humiliating Rufino in the eyes of his friends – appeared in the doorway also dressed only in breeches, which set off further ribaldry while he climbed into the pulpit beside Rufino. Gradually the babble subsided as he opened his sermon with an allusion to Christ's nakedness on the cross. He went on to condemn the crime of nailing him there, pronounced men's need to atone for it, and ended by evoking the raptures of heaven in wait for the penitent.

This remarkable scene so impressed the congregation with the friars' absolute lack of pretension that it removed the last shreds of resentment toward them. It also dispelled Francis's doubts about Rufino and brought home to him that although he himself was capable of unremitting prayer, preaching and work, others might not be able to manage all three.

Rufino wasn't the only brother who needed to balance his work with long periods of undisturbed prayer away from the Porziuncula, which was becoming crowded and increasingly busy – Bernard, Giles, Silvester and Leo were all the same. Once more the Benedictines came to the rescue and offered Francis their hermitage on Subasio – close to the caves of his early conversion – known as I Carceri, The Cells.

From Assisi you can reach it along a path in the woods which eventually joins a road – then a track – winding up through the forest from the abbey of San Benedetto. As the branches close over your head the air grows chilly; in the dim light a blue and white haze of anemones spreads over the forest floor; the silence is broken by cheerful birdsong and a stream which splashes down a gulley.

Round a bend, in a sunlit clearing, the hermitage straddles the dark slash of a ravine. In Francis's day it was little more than a hut made from branches; he slept there curled on a rock; the oratory was a recess in the cliff. Beside the ravine, which was bridged with logs, the brothers found caves in which they could each pray alone.

In remote places like this, especially after a series of long and hungry nights spent wrestling with his worst anxieties, a friar sometimes believed he was, quite literally, being tormented by Lucifer or his attendant demons, whose existence in medieval cosmology was never in question.

Reflecting on a visit to La Grande Trappe, in Normandy, Patrick Leigh Fermor graphically evokes this common experience of monks, hermits and stylites over the ages. At nightfall Satan dispatches his forces against them and they become

> the chief objectives of nocturnal flight; the sky fills with the beat of sable wings as phalanx after phalanx streams to the attack, and the darkness crepitates with the splintering of a myriad lances against the masonry of asceticism.

> Piety has always been singled out for the hardest onslaught of hellish aggression. . . . When the Thebaid* filled up with hermits, their presence at once attracted a detachment of demons and round the pillar of St Symeon the Stylite, the Powers of Darkness assembled and spun like swarming wasps.[4]

These satanic squadrons are unforgettably illustrated in the pictorial life of Francis on the walls of the basilica in Assisi. Francis prays on his knees as Silvester casts out from the towers and chimneys of Arezzo the demons which had taken possession of its inhabitants.

While most people today would regard a friend's assertion he had spoken with the devil as pure delusion, a psychologist on the other hand might consider it a truthful account of what the friend had actually seen and heard. In the imaginative minds of some mystics and artists – not only the sick – their guilt, fears and hatreds, or their loves and ideals, are projected onto an appropriate archetype in their semiconscious or subconscious minds. Satan or an angel is then as real to their senses as the mailman. Equally, anyone who has seen a close friend in such a state will instantly understand how easily his or her radically altered – almost unrecognizable – demeanor can be interpreted as possession by an alien or diabolical force. Before the advent of rationalism and Freud, possession was an intelligent and reasonable, not superstitious, diagnosis.

However traumatic an affray with the devil it could be turned to advantage by a friar and his spiritual director, for no matter how shameful or distressing the issue, it could be confessed and discussed objectively, like a conflict with a notorious adversary rather than one within the friar himself. A means to resolve it was more easily prescribed and accepted.

The most memorable confrontation with Satan, described in *The Little Flowers*, occurred when Rufino was on retreat at the Carceri. The devil's first gambit was to appear to him and predict his damnation; it was not entirely successful but so shook Rufino that he didn't like to mention it to Francis.

For his next assault Satan convincingly adopted the appearance of Christ and regretfully informed Rufino that he, Francis and anyone else

*The desert round Thebes, in Upper Egypt, favored by early hermits as a place of retreat.

who followed him, were indeed destined for hell. Coming from such an authority Rufino accepted the verdict, entirely lost his faith in Francis and decided not to go back to the Porziuncula.

When he stopped turning up there Francis had a shrewd idea of what had happened and sent Masseo to fetch Rufino. Masseo managed to talk him around and together they returned to Santa Maria. When they approached Francis called out, "Rufino you naughty young man, what have you been up to?" He then reconstructed, with great accuracy, the devil's dialectic and concluded:

"Next time he appears and tries it again, say to him quite firmly, 'Open your mouth like that once more and I will excrete in it!'

"You will be able to tell it *is* the devil, because he will rush off immediately."

Rufino went back to the Carceri and followed Francis's instructions precisely. The result was sensational.

> The Devil left so angrily, with a thunder of falling rocks, that for a long time an avalanche hurtled down Subasio, filling the ravine below (as you can still see). The stones gave off sparks as they fell and made such a noise that Francis went out with the others to watch.[5]

After this ordeal Francis repeatedly said of Rufino, who was widely respected for his virtues and almost continuous prayer, that awake or asleep his mind was always on God and that he was one of the holiest men of his times.

Lying on the seismic flaw which runs up central Italy, a century seldom passes in which Umbria escapes an earthquake. If the tremor witnessed by Francis and his brothers that day was spectacular, it was puny compared with some of its sequels, among them the one that brought down most of the basilica at Santa Maria degli Angeli in 1832, and the latest which ravaged so much of Assisi, including the basilica of St. Francis and the cathedral, in 1997.

*

Two other tremors, which shook Assisi in 1210 and the cathedral in 1212, were social and religious, not seismic, and their impact on the city's morale and Francis's order were benign not destructive.

Assisi's long run of disasters was brought to an end by a surprising benefactor, the new emperor Otto. When he and his retinue had reached Rome in the previous year they camped on Monte Mario, not far from Vatican Hill. Two days later Otto processed through crowds waving palms and crosses to St. Peter's. In the basilica, clouded with incense, echoing with anthems and crammed with choirs, acolytes, prelates and the great from all over Europe, Otto made a vow of allegiance to Innocent, who placed the Roman crown on his head, pronouncing him "elect of God and the Pope."

In his own eyes Otto had been elected emperor by the royal houses of Germany but he swallowed his pride and next morning went into Rome to inspect his new kingdom. Unfortunately he had failed to distribute the traditional largesse, so that when he reached the Ponte Sant' Angelo he was greeted by a horde of wolves, eagles and lions, ranged on banners floating above the armed ranks of the citizens; his way was barred.

To avert a battle Innocent rode down from the Lateran and advised him to leave the capital, but Otto unwisely refused and was soon attacked by the Romans who killed or captured a thousand of his horses before driving him north. Renouncing the oath he had so recently made in St. Peter's, Otto set about restoring German authority in Lombardy, Tuscany, the Marches and Umbria, appointing Diopoldo di Vohburg – Walter de Brienne's old adversary – as Duke of Spoleto. A year after he had marched past the Rivotorto in triumph he was excommunicated by Innocent III; his glory hadn't lasted long.

Nevertheless his personal interest in Umbrian affairs radically shifted the balance of power between Assisi and its rival. Otto had a grudge to pay off against Perugia for supporting his opponents, Philip of Swabia and the pope. He therefore sacked the estates of Perugian landowners, ordered the last of Assisi's fugitive nobles to go home, and obliged the two cities to negotiate a peace designed to restore prosperity to the province. In October 1210 he visited Assisi to be sure that the treaty was in place; a few days later it was signed.

Peace changed the mood of the town beyond recognition; everyone started pulling together. A Palazzo Comunale with a tower, the Torre del Popolo, began to go up in the piazza; next to it the Benedictines handed over their monastery in the Temple of Minerva for use as a law court, with a jail in the cellar (Plate 2); the old cathedral was busy with public meetings and transactions to release serfs and convey land; behind it the long delayed work on the new cathedral rushed ahead.

Most of the aristocratic houses around San Rufino had been damaged or destroyed in the troubles. Now the dissident knights returning from Perugia rapidly restored them and contributed to the cost of the new cathedral. Each clan clung together, several families sharing a palazzo, even if they had taken different sides in the civil war. Rufino's father, Scipione di Offreduccio, received back his brothers Monaldo and Favarone (with his wife and daughters) after their years in Perugia. The three men rebuilt their large fortified house next to the new cathedral and, as a concession to public feeling, undertook in writing that their tower would be no higher than its facade.

None of the old families living around the square felt really secure or at ease in this new looking-glass world, where all the old values were being reversed. Nevertheless they still went to Mass and were gripped by Francis's sermons which, like yeast, produced a ferment in the spirits of the younger generation, especially the girls.

In the summer of 1212 this fervor was reinforced by a surprising discovery inside the cathedral. In Roman times St. Rufino had been martyred by drowning in the River Chiascio. Ever since, miracles and legends had been attributed to his relics, whose hiding place was entrusted to a single canon in each generation. However, in July their whereabouts were disclosed in a dream to a second canon, Francis's old teacher at San Giorgio, who reported his revelation to the guardian of the bones.

The two canons consulted Bishop Guido, who felt that this was a sign that the relics should be translated with maximum ceremony to a tomb beneath the altar of the new cathedral. The move precipitated an impressive outbreak of fresh miracles, greatly boosting the prestige of the bishop who meticulously investigated, affirmed and recorded them, a procedure he was to repeat for the miracles attributed to Francis fifteen years later.

Guido's masterly management of St. Rufino's reappearance further fueled the religious revival in Assisi and the countryside around it. The cathedral became a sanctuary to which the privileged took food, money, medicines and offers of practical help, and the desperate came for relief.

*

The wave of goodwill in Assisi, and the concerted efforts to look after the needs of its people, were not being matched elsewhere in Europe that summer. In France, northern Italy and Spain three so-called crusades were being waged or assembled. Their varied consequences, some of them appalling, caught Francis's imagination and concentrated his mind on working out how true Christians should meet the challenge of Islam.

A crusade meant something different to almost everyone – a just war, a war of liberation, a war to save souls, an armed pilgrimage. It was a stratagem by which the pope united the monarchs of Christendom against an empire of infidels, and by which a king distracted his barons from fighting him or each other. It was also the means by which a baron, his knights and their men could win preferment, land, money, possessions, women and the assurance of an afterlife in heaven.

Only one outcome of any crusade was predictable – bloodshed and unspeakable suffering for innumerable so-called infidels, heathens and heretics, just as for the Christians themselves. The crusades therefore became – like the Inquisition – one of the earliest weapons seized on by later generations to kill God, in whose name they were fought.

Innocent III had launched the Albigensian crusade now going on in southern France to punish the murder of his legate, Peter of Castelnau, by a Cathar and to eradicate the heresy. It had quickly grown out of hand to constitute a crime for which he bears heavy responsibility, for he let loose waves of knights from northern France under the leadership of his new legate, Abbot Arnald-Amaury of Cîteaux, who emerged as a homicidal fanatic, and of an able soldier, Simon de Montfort, who turned into a butcher. They destroyed a civilization to which Francis, through his mother, had been an heir. It was more concerned with olives and vines, with the pleasures of poetry, music and love, than with war, and had far more in common with Italy than it had with the French north of Lyons, who spoke a different language.

The crusaders cared very little if those who resisted them were heretics or not; in the church of the Madeleine at Béziers they slaughtered up to a thousand inhabitants indiscriminately. Proven heretics were tossed, sometimes in hundreds, onto mountainous bonfires. Priests were not meant to kill, but some sixty years later St. Thomas Aquinas pronounced that "heresy is a sin which merits not only excommunication but also death." By the end of this campaign the Provençal language and culture were almost mortally damaged.

During the summer of 1212 the tragedy known as the Children's Crusade was unfolding farther east. Thousands of young people, perhaps with children among them, led by a German boy Nicholas, made their way up the Rhine and over the Alps to Genoa, planning to reach Syria and – where soldiers had failed – to occupy Jerusalem. When the sea didn't part for them as they had expected, and ships refused to carry them, many died from illness, exposure or starvation, and numbers of girls were forced into prostitution; the rest returned home.

At much the same time Stephen, a shepherd boy in France, persuaded another army of young to follow him down the Rhône on much the same purpose and with similar results. However two unsavory characters, known as Hugh Iron and William Pig, lured a contingent onto seven ships. Two sank in a storm and the contingent in the others fetched a good price from Barbary slave traders. A handful of these were finally sold on to the Sultan of Egypt, al-Malik al-Kamil, in whose camp near Damietta Francis saw them eight years later.

The third of these crusades was launched by the three kingdoms of northern Spain – Navarre, Castile and Aragon – to drive the occupying Moors from North Africa out of their countries. After a decisive victory in July 1212, at Las Navas de Tolosa about ninety miles north of Granada, they confined the Muslims to Andalusia in the south.

These crusades were, together, responsible for broadening Francis's sense of his vocation. The suffering in Provence – his mother's country whose spirit and language he had adopted – made bloodshed in the name of his religion more repugnant than ever. At the same time it worried him that success in the west, at Las Navas de Tolosa, was distracting attention from failure in the east to recover Jerusalem. He was suddenly impatient to go to the Holy Land in search of a peaceful reconciliation with the Saracens.

Ships normally avoided the passage to Syria during the stormy winter months but in September 1212, at the very end of the season, Francis and one of his friars set out from Ancona. Thomas of Celano maintains that he sailed in search of martyrdom but that is very difficult to square with his commitments to his rapidly growing order; although he was prepared to die there is no reason to suppose he was determined to. Nevertheless he very nearly met his end off the coast of Dalmatia where his ship was wrecked.

He had left the expedition too late, so rather than wait in Slavonia till the spring he decided to return to Ancona whatever the weather. Having no money he and his companion had to stow away, but with an ample supply of food given them by a well-wisher. Again they were blown off course by storms, which delayed them for so long that the crew ran out of stores. Emerging from the hold, Francis offered them his own, so paying his way after all.

It was just as well that he never reached Syria in 1212, for his recent preaching in Italy had sown prolific seed now ready for cropping.

*

The harvest to which he returned included not only young men, eager to take part in the adventure of changing the world but women, too. In Rome, particularly, women had been anxious to help the friars with their work for the derelict. Among them Sister Praxede is a shadowy figure, mentioned only once in the early sources. She is believed to have been a poor penitent – one of tens of thousands of women living in retreat all over Europe, dedicating their lives to prayer and nursing the sick.

Giacoma de Settesoli, on the other hand, always catches the light on the rare occasions she appears in the story. Aristocratic herself, her Roman husband Graziano was a member of the very powerful Frangipani family opposed to the papacy but he had recently died, leaving her with two young sons, a fortune and a long-running lawsuit against Innocent III.

One of the richest women in Italy, Giacoma now adopted Francis and his friars among her other charitable activities. She set up a house for their use in Rome, and later a church, so winning – by her generosity, delightful company and tireless good work – Francis's nickname for her, Brother Giacoma. With him when he died, she afterward settled in Assisi. Her remains now lie in a casket halfway down the steps to his tomb.

Clare di Favarone, the best known of all the women to follow Francis, was both born in Assisi and died there. Today she lies nearby too, but in the basilica raised to her memory as a saint.

15

The Love of Clare

1210–1215

When Clare died in 1253, at the age of sixty, she was so widely admired and respected that Pope Innocent IV, who was staying in Perugia, came over to conduct her funeral at San Giorgio. Carried away by emotion he actually embarked on a form of service which would have committed the church to her sanctification without any form of inquiry whatever. Wisely, to avoid any backlash in the future, the Cardinal Protector of the Franciscans intervened, official proceedings were set in motion and two years later she was proclaimed a saint.

Clare would never have qualified for canonization if she had not, at the age of seventeen, followed Francis and with his help set up a community of women which became his second order. Its foundation in 1212 was one of the great landmarks of his life – yet the early Franciscan sources scarcely mention it.

Fortunately much of its fascinating detail is revealed in two other documents, the Process of Canonization and the official biography of Clare, usually attributed to Thomas of Celano. It is a love story in which Clare's devotion to Francis is strongly reminiscent of the seventeen-year-old Héloïse's to the great theologian and teacher Peter Abelard, a century earlier. Unwilling to contemplate separation the girls were faced with either consummation or uncompromising chastity. Choosing differently they both achieved immortality and both ended their days in a convent, but while one was drawn into tragedy the other emerged as a saint.

The official inquiry was conducted by the Archbishop of Spoleto who went to Assisi with six commissioners – among them Angelo and Leo – and for several days questioned more than twenty witnesses. They included a number of nuns who had been Clare's friends since their childhood, an old retainer and an elderly man who had once proposed marriage to her.

Clare spent her earliest childhood with her parents and sisters in the palazzo they shared with the rest of their family on the Piazza San Rufino. Her father, Favarone di Offreduccio, was a knight and the younger brother of Monaldo; her mother Ortolana was also an aristocrat. Ortolana had stretched to their limits the restraints normally imposed on women by making a series of enterprising pilgrimages to Rome, to Mt. Gargano on the coast of Apulia, where St. Michael the Archangel had once been seen, and far more dangerously, to Jerusalem, sailing either to Acre in Syria or to Damietta on the eastern mouth of the Nile. She always took with her a young cousin, Pacifica di Guelfuccio.

Clare was born in 1193 or 1194 after the last of these expeditions, her sister Catherine in 1197, and Beatrice, the youngest of Ortolana's three children, in about 1205.

In normal times Clare would have had a peaceful and protected childhood confined to the women's quarters of the palazzo. As it was she grew up in an atmosphere of violence and terror. One by one the houses around the square, all belonging to friends or relations, were attacked, ransacked and burned. The first to go up in flames belonged to her friend Philippa, daughter of Leonardo di Gislerio.

When Clare was six several of her relations so antagonized the commune that to protect their lives Monaldo led most of them across to Perugia, where they stayed with a family whose daughter, Benvenuta, became one of her closest friends. While they were in Perugia Ortolana educated Clare in much the same way as the rector taught the boys in San Giorgio. Richer children were expected to learn Latin, history and the poems of chivalry. These included the Arthurian epics; one of Clare's friends – a cousin of Angelo di Tancredi – was christened Ginevra, after Guinevere.

St. Agnes, a Roman, became for Clare what St. George had been for Francis. As a girl, out of devotion to Christ, she had turned down all the pagan suitors her ambitious family urged on her until, in exasperation, they sent her to a brothel. When her hair grew miraculously long, concealing her nakedness, and her body subsequently defied burning, she was beheaded. Later she was canonized as a martyr.

The Offreduccios were able to return to Assisi in about 1207, when a picture of Clare emerges from the evidence given by her friends. She dressed simply, regularly said her prayers, and although attractive, modestly took care not to be seen by men visiting the house. The civil wars in Italy made it impossible to repeat any of her mother's pilgrimages, but she did whatever she could for the poor of Assisi, saving her own food so that her friend Bona, Pacifica's sister, could distribute it to the needy. Sometimes she asked Bona to take money for food down to the Porziuncula where they both knew Angelo and Rufino.

On Sundays Clare and her family went to the cathedral where, like many others, she was swept off her feet by Francis's sermons, but unlike the rest she wanted to discover exactly what inspired him and the other young friars to emulate the early apostles. In about 1211 she became anxious to question him but, as a girl of sixteen and old enough to marry, talking privately with a man of twenty-nine was unthinkable. Her family was determined she should make a match worthy of her beauty, intelligence, wealth and connections; a whisper of impropriety would ruin her chances.

Clare, on the other hand, was convinced there was much more to life than becoming the wife of a provincial knight, and believed that Francis could point her toward it. According to her biographer, her sister Beatrice (who was only about six at the time) and Bona, who accompanied her, she therefore went to a number of secret meetings with him and Philip the Long. They encouraged her to devote her life to Christ so successfully that she was convinced – perhaps intending to enter a convent near Assisi.

While she considered the possibility of joining one of these her dilemma suddenly grew acute; she came into some money, a potential dowry, perhaps because her father had died. The pressure on her to marry, especially from Monaldo as head of the family, intensified. However it looks very much as if Clare had fallen in love with Francis. Despite their difference in class they had much in common. Both had rich fathers; both felt the urge to leave home; Francis had rejected his inheritance and Clare was uncomfortable with hers; they had lived through the same scenes of ferocity and wanted to alleviate the suffering all around them. As their meetings continued Clare became convinced that her vocation lay in leading a life like Francis and as soon as she was eighteen she demonstrated for the first time her independence and will of iron – concealed beneath her gentleness and charm – by making two irrevocable decisions.

First, she gave away to the poor the money intended for her dowry. Her uncle was shocked and did everything he could to dissuade her. Ranieri di Bernardo, a neighbor and friend of her parents, told the inquiry he, too, urged her to change her mind and marry him. Clare refused.

Second, early in 1212 she planned a course so startling that Francis must have pondered it carefully, discussed it with the bishop and on his advice gone to Rome to obtain the sanction of Cardinal San Paolo, if not Innocent, whose parting words had been, "Come back and report everything to us. We will then concede more to you, and entrust you with even greater work."

Not long after Francis returned to Assisi, on Palm Sunday morning, Clare put on her best dress as if for a party or wedding, and went to the cathedral with her family. Everyone in turn walked up to the chancel to collect a traditional sprig of olive leaves, except her. When Bishop Guido noticed this, he stepped down from the altar and brought one to where she was sitting (Plate 4).

That was her last day at home.

*

Clare's flight on Palm Sunday night began like his spirit's tryst with God described by St. John of the Cross three centuries later, in the opening lines of his most famous poem, *The Dark Night of the Soul.*

Upon a gloomy night,
With all my cares to loving ardour flushed,
O venture of delight,
With nobody in sight
I went abroad when all my house was hushed.

In safety, in disguise,
In darkness on the secret stair I crept,
O happy enterprise,
Concealed from other eyes
When all my house at length in silence slept.[1]

Clare crept down the stairs of the tall, echoing palazzo, terrified she might disturb her sleeping uncles and cousins. In order not to alert the man-at-arms keeping watch outside the main door onto the Piazza San Rufino, she struggled single-handed and silently to unblock a smaller door at the back, which finally swung open.

In the lane she found two or three close friends who had promised to accompany her to the Porziuncula. One was probably her mother's cousin and companion Pacifica; Bona had gone to Rome for Easter. Another was a friar – perhaps her cousin Rufino – familiar with the network of lanes threading through the woods. It was possible to avoid any problems at the gates by leaving the town through the grounds of the bishop's palace which was built into the walls, but autonomous.

Francis and his companions were waiting for Clare and came out to welcome her in the glow of their flickering torches. They led her into the church where she made her confession and received absolution from Silvester. Then she exchanged the elegant dress she had worn that morning for a simple habit and made to Francis the vows of penitence and obedience required of anyone joining his order.

As a seal that he had received her Francis cut off her hair in a form of tonsure; some of Clare's curls, the palest gold, almost white, can be seen in her basilica. "I promised him obedience," Clare wrote in her Testament, and this promise to Francis was the inviolable rock on which she founded her order. From it she successfully defied cardinals and popes whenever they tried to deflect her from her vow of poverty during the next forty years.

Clare had not made this drastic break with her old life to become a conventional nun but to work like Francis for anyone in need. Yet she could not remain at Santa Maria degli Angeli for more than a few hours – partly because it would provoke gossip and partly because she knew her family would raise a hue and cry as soon as they discovered where she was.* The friars would be powerless to protect her.

Francis had therefore arranged for her to go to a convent, San Paolo delle Abbadesse at Bastia, a few miles away; it owned vast estates and was surrounded by a large garden in the fork of two rivers. Although

*Her family would have been quite capable of imposing on Francis the same retribution – gelding – as Héloïse's uncle, a canon of Notre Dame, had violently inflicted on Abelard.

Benedictine, the nuns were so rich and well-connected that the pope had taken them under his direct authority; his grant of protection had kept them unscathed during the years of fighting between Assisi and Perugia; it was a safe house.

Its privilege, however, proved no defense against the Offreduccios whose blood was up. Led by Monaldo, seven of them galloped down to San Paolo, demanded to see Clare and forced their way in. When she refused to come home they tried, over several days, to win her back by a series of inducements and threats. At last, breaching her right of sanctuary and San Paolo's immunity, they cornered her in the Romanesque chapel, the only part of the convent still standing. Surrounding her, they attempted to drag her away but she clung to the altar – and it was not until she bared her head that her tonsure convinced them she would never give in.

Unwilling to expose the convent to any further outrage Francis, Bernard di Quintavalle and Philip now escorted her to Sant' Angelo in Panzo, a house and chapel at the foot of Mt. Subasio, on the way to the abbey at San Benedetto. It stood near a stream in the woods and was run as a farm by an informal religious community of women.

The bishop must have believed Monaldo wouldn't dare risk retribution from both church and commune by molesting Clare a second time but, about two weeks after her own flight from home, her sixteen-year-old sister Catherine decided to join her. This time Monaldo led a party of twelve armed men to bring back his nieces. Concentrating on Catherine, they tried to entice her home with ingratiating assurances but nothing would move her. In the end her defiance drove them to frenzy, according to her official biographer: "One of the knights threw himself at Catherine, slapping and kicking her. Then he seized her by the hair and dragged her off, while the others pushed her and then tried to lift her in their arms."[2]

As they slithered down the hill, between bushes and brambles, her clothes were ripped and tufts of her hair left a trail along the muddy path. In desperation Catherine called out to Clare to help her, and her sister dropped to her knees in prayer.

> Catherine's body immediately seemed to become so heavy that they couldn't lift her across the stream, even when they were joined by men who had been working in a nearby vineyard – one of whom remarked that she must have been eating lead all night.

Monaldo, furious, wanted to beat her to death, but when he raised his arm such an excruciating pain shot through it that he couldn't. Clare then walked up to her uncle and cousins, begging them to go and leave her to look after Catherine who, by now, was barely conscious.[3]

When the armed party disappeared toward Assisi Catherine quickly recovered. Nevertheless, yet another home had to be found for the sisters; after a few months the bishop decided to give them San Damiano and the little house next to it. They stood among the olives not far below his palace windows.

According to Clare's Testament she and Catherine did not move in alone. Pacifica, now aged about forty, went with them, her company a great reassurance for the girls (not to mention their mother). Once installed Catherine and Pacifica made their vows to Francis and received the tonsure.

Catherine took the name Agnes, the only saint mentioned by Clare in her writings other than Francis.

*

It is tempting to interpret Clare's vows to Francis, his acceptance of them, the sign of her tonsure and a promise he shortly made always to love and care for her and her sisters, as sealing a union of true hearts, minds, imaginations and spirits – of everything, in fact, except the flesh.

We are often first drawn to each other by the physical and mental attractions of looks, desire, wealth, rank or reputation; when emotion takes over we cross the psychological threshold of falling in love, one of the few transcendent experiences most of us ever enjoy. Yet if the object of our love is not the actual person but a projection of our own dreams and expectations, and if the gap between the two is too wide, love languishes, not because the beloved has changed – as we like to make out – but because we have returned to our senses.

Clare may have fallen in love with Francis at first, as many believe she did. She was young, a virgin and set on sharing his mission through territory far more exciting than the narrow canyons of feudal convention. Neither was an intellectual but they were intelligent, educated and thoughtful, steeped in the culture of chivalry but rebelling against military obsessions while admiring its virtues. As a result Clare was never disillusioned, because the actual Francis and her image of him were almost identical.

Francis's love of Clare was not a precise reflection of hers. He was twelve years older, had experience of women, had struggled and suffered to discover his vocation and was now well established in it. Nevertheless her courage, beauty and devotion to God profoundly moved his troubadour spirit. The Greek poet Nikos Kazantzakis thinks he occasionally had to stifle feelings of desire for her, but his pastoral love was boundless.

At the heart of their enterprise together and the sole source of their inspiration was their faith in God, continuously strengthened by prayer. But most saints find that to maintain their spiritual focus they need the mediation of a divine image, either mental or physical. A couplet under one of the mosaics in St. Mark's, Venice, gives advice on this: "The image represents God, but the image is not God. Reverence it, but in your thoughts worship what it suggests to you."[4]

Francis had been led to his faith by the figure of Christ on the crucifix in San Damiano, an image that helped sustain his prayers for the rest of his life. Clare was led to her faith, and sustained in it, by the person of Francis, yet never mistook the image for God. It was an exceptional tribute to the two of them that the bishop and Cardinal San Paolo allowed them to collaborate in establishing her community at San Damiano. It also shows that, in sharp contrast to the majority of prelates, their attitude to women was admirably level-headed. The church's confusion, first discernible in the utterances of St. Paul and magnified in the fourth century by several deeply respected authorities – St. John Chrysostom considered all women were "weak and frivolous; all feminine nature is fallen into error" – produced outbreaks of paranoia in the Middle Ages. For instance Conrad, Abbot of Marchtal, wrote this at a time when he and his fellow Cistercians decided to disengage from the nuns in their order:

> Our whole community of canons, recognising the wickedness of women is greater than all the other wickedness of the world . . . and that the poison of asps and dragons is more curable and less dangerous to men than the familiarity of women, have unanimously decreed . . . that we will on no account receive any more sisters to the increase of our perdition.[5]

As a professional writer and church propagandist Thomas of Celano swam with this powerful current of bigotry. Not only does his first biography of Francis fail to give any account of his role in establishing Clare and her sisters as his Second Order in San Damiano, but his second volume actually projects uncompromising misogyny onto Francis:

> That honeyed poison, familiarity with women, which leads even holy men astray, should be entirely avoided, for it breaks the weak spirit and weakens the strong. Avoiding such contagion, Francis said, was as easy as walking in a fire without having the soles of one's feet burned. Indeed a woman was so unwelcome to him you would think that his caution was not a warning but a dread or horror. When their importunate loquaciousness caused him difficulty in speaking he would humbly ask for silence . . .
>
> He once said to a companion: "I would not recognise any woman if I looked into her face, except two."[6]

In reality such an attitude was entirely alien to Francis's nature. His whole story makes it clear that women were never "unwelcome" to him, either collectively or individually; they remained – as they had always been – an important element in his life, literally until the moment he died. That is not to say he was not occasionally plagued by longings and sexual temptations which were the opposite of welcome. Leo makes one reference to this. He mentions that sometimes Francis grew upset if people expressed admiration for his strict observance of his vows: he would then murmur, by way of disclaimer, that he still might lapse into fathering children.

Thomas of Celano recounts another, told him by a brother who once saw Francis emerge from his cell on a winter night and make seven figures with the snow; he could tell in the moonlight that Francis was talking to himself. When the brother later asked what he was doing, Francis was appalled he had been watched and swore him to secrecy, but explained.

He had been so tempted by lust while trying to get to sleep that he had finally gone out and made a wife, two sons, two daughters, a servant and a maid. He had then said to his body, "If you really want a family like this, you will have to set off and find them clothes straight away or they will die of cold. If that's too much trouble, go inside and concentrate on God."

As a young man who had, according to two sources, slept with women

Francis could also identify with the group of troubadours who, in the words of a scholar of Provençal literature, "sought refuge from physical desire in the mental joy of distant love or *amor loinh*. Such a controlled love as this, with its attendant courtly virtues of restraint, patience, humility and service, may have provided that love in the sense of *amicitia* . . . recognised as an antidote to the sexual licence of the nobility, a source of serenity in a world of moral confusions."[7]

It is often thought that the church placed too high a value on chastity simply as the avoidance of sensual pleasure. Francis demonstrated that just as poverty and obedience need not represent deprivations but could create opportunity, so chastity could transform sexual drive from a physical force into spiritual energy. The all-embracing relationship between him and Clare was essential to the fullness of their natures as a man and a woman.

*

Monaldo's attempts to snatch Clare and Agnes blew up a family dispute into a cause célèbre; everyone in Assisi soon heard about it. Clare's friends rushed down with food and offers of help; busybodies came to stare and chatter; a few priests, monks and nuns expressed scorn.

Elsewhere in Europe tens of thousands of women had retreated from the dangers and miseries of a turbulent world dominated by men, into religious communities of their own sex, havens for widows, propertied or penniless; orphans, spinsters and unmarried mothers; members of the new artisan and merchant classes, disenchanted by the failure of the new communes to enfranchise them. The convents also became launchpads for a few spirits so dedicated to prayer that they were swept up on thermals of mystical exaltation into the *sanctum sanctorum*.

Assisi was no different; the civil war had shattered the age-old, arrogant assumptions of the privileged but had not broken the spirit of their young. Clare's earliest companions, like Francis's, were drawn from the *majores*. The euphoria induced by the discovery of San Rufino's remains now helped release them in pursuit of the new vision of chivalry preached by Francis – so different from the tarnished original. Once Clare joined him other girls, showing the esprit de corps of their class, started to follow her; they had little idea of what lay ahead, but questing was in their blood.

Nearly a dozen of them survived, forty years later, to answer the commissioners' questions, designed to elicit convincing evidence first of Clare's moral character and virginity, and second, of any miracles attributable to her. A variety of curious and significant anecdotes also emerged in the process.

Agnes was expected to be the principal witness; during Clare's last illness she had been brought from Monticelli, near Florence, where she was abbess, to keep her sister company; but she died too, a week before the inquiry began.

Pacifica, now over eighty, was therefore called first. Like the very old, she remembered the early days better than the later but she was in a unique position to vouch for Clare's virginity and innate goodness, and her assertion that Clare had frequently healed her companions, while saying a prayer and making the sign of the cross, was corroborated by eight other witnesses. Pacifica's sister Bona also testified, though she had not joined the order – she had married Clare's rejected suitor.

Benvenuta, with whose family Clare's had stayed in Perugia, and who took her vows a few months after Pacifica, was the second witness. She was the first to talk about Clare's courage and leadership in confronting a squadron of Arab mercenaries who had once scaled the walls of the convent. Not surprisingly the crisis was etched in the memory of virtually all the nuns giving evidence.

Christina di Bernardo was a latecomer to San Damiano but her family had lived with the Offreduccios and so she had been asleep upstairs on the night Clare left home. She described the general amazement next morning at the superhuman strength Clare had exerted to lift the heavy beams and pile of stones barring the back door.

Agnese di Oportulo – whose father was an important figure in Assisi and became a great admirer of Francis – and Ginevra, Angelo's cousin, also exchanged the *vie de seigneur* for the primitive life at San Damiano. Ginevra took the name Benedetta when she entered the order. She had, like her uncle Tancredi the consul, a gift for authority. After a time Clare sent her as abbess to two daughter houses, in Siena and then Spello. At the time of the inquiry she had recently been elected to succeed Clare at San Damiano but did not testify as she had been away for so long.

On the other hand Clare's youngest sister Beatrice, and her two cousins Balvina and Amata all gave evidence. Like Ortolana, now dead, they had joined the order much later, probably because family opposition held them back.

This is far from a full list of Clare's early companions; many were already dead by 1253. Others were not called because they did not belong to the San Rufino circle and therefore couldn't help the commissioners assess Clare's early life; from the beginning the door of San Damiano was wide open to women from the slums of Assisi, and the farms and hovels in the country around it.

More than six years before Clare moved in, Francis had proclaimed from the top of his ladder that San Damiano was destined to become a convent for holy women. Now that the doves were coming in to roost, the responsibility of looking after them was his.

*

As always when he had some important enterprise in hand, Francis relied on his original companions to help carry it out, sometimes drafting in later ones if they had a special aptitude for the job. He therefore arranged for Angelo, Rufino, Leo and Giles to take care of the sisters, begging food, collecting fuel and providing extra space as their numbers grew.

They were joined by an eccentric newcomer, Brother Juniper. The friars called him this because his good intentions glowed like burning juniper wood; he did nothing by halves. Once, when asked to prepare a simple meal he begged and cooked enough food for a banquet; it would have lasted a week had it not been inedible. Another day he traveled to an important festival stark naked, by way of penance; when rebuked he offered to walk home in the same state to make amends.

All these brothers kept in touch with San Damiano for the next forty years. Angelo, Leo and Juniper sat and prayed with Clare while she lay dying. She was especially fond of Juniper, who invariably raised her spirits.

It has always been assumed that a considerable time elapsed between Francis's original restoration of San Damiano and the construction of the early convent buildings still discernible today. However, Father Marino Bigaroni, an archival and architectural scholar, has recently demonstrated that the expansion must have occurred almost immediately. The crypt of the little church was largely filled in so that the floor of the apse and nave could be lowered and leveled. The roof above them was then leveled and strengthened to provide the floor of an oratory and dormitory over them. A cloister was built on beside the church, giving access to a kitchen and refectory.

Clare quickly accepted it would be unwise for her sisters to go out begging for food, although they sometimes collected it if already offered. Two friars – questors – therefore begged on their behalf and lived in shacks outside the walls, like their colleagues engaged on the building.

The sisters met several times each day to pray in the chapel, where Silvester and Leo also heard confessions and celebrated Mass. Clare spent many additional hours in her oratory above, late into the night or before the others were awake. However tired, she emerged manifestly uplifted unless she had been meditating on Christ's crucifixion, which was apt to reduce her – like Francis – to tears.

For the rest of the day Clare kept her sisters continuously busy – working for their neighbors, weaving, sewing altar cloths, making their own clothes, growing fruit and vegetables. One of the most touching sights in San Damiano is Clare's tiny roof garden, from which she could catch a narrow glimpse of the Umbrian hills.

Francis sometimes referred to her as his "little plant," appropriately, for in the next few years she and her sisters put down vigorous roots; she was joined by fifty companions at San Damiano and invited to take over a second house in Spello. Before long their numbers would run into hundreds, including royalty and half a dozen saints.

16

Innocent's Last Throw

1213–1216

From his palace on the ramparts of Assisi Bishop Guido kept an eye on Clare and watched his neighbors' daughters leave their families for a cheerful if precarious life at San Damiano. He was equally alert to the arrivals at the Porziuncula and was amazed when Leonardo di Gislerio, once the most obnoxious noble in the city, sold his possessions, made his vows to Francis and put on a coarse gray habit. At the same time his daughter Philippa, who had spent several years with Clare in Perugia, entered San Damiano. From his more commanding eminence on the Lateran Hill the pope saw similar communities of poor penitents springing up everywhere, the men preferring a philanthropic to a cutthroat existence and the women to take charge of their own lives.

Among these groups the Humiliati included priests, laymen and women, some enclosed, some itinerant; they now occupied about 150 houses around Milan. The Béguines, consisting only of laywomen, fostered by Jacques de Vitry, the Bishop of Liège, had spread rapidly through the Low Countries. They took no vows but lived in small celibate houses, devoting themselves and their wealth to the poorest and sick. While Innocent and his closest advisers saw the Brothers Minor and Poor Clares, like all these other penitents, as shoots of a spiritual revival, the more reactionary cardinals disliked their competition with the clergy. A confrontation was imminent, but in the spring of 1213 Innocent had reached the climax of his papacy – itself one of the high watermarks of the church in any age – and decided to assert his authority on this and other issues by announcing he would hold a Church Council at the Lateran in November 1215. His agenda included church reform (with a review of its orders), the suppression of heresy, and the summons of a Fifth Crusade to recover Jerusalem.

Reckoning his orders should be safe from interference for another two years, Francis was again tempted by his frustrated urge to preach among the Saracens, convinced that crusades should be fought with words not swords.

He had no qualms about leaving Assisi, confident that Peter of Catanio could supervise the friars in his absence, while Philip and Silvester, with the bishop's help, would see no harm came to Clare and her sisters. Nevertheless he wanted to resolve one old dilemma before he left: should he continue to preach or ought he to devote the rest of his life to prayer? He sent Masseo to ask Clare, and Silvester then at the Carceri, to help him by praying for an answer. Their replies were the same; he should preach.

This time Francis decided to follow up the crusaders' recent victory in southern Spain by trying to convert the Saracens' nazir or provincial governor, known as the Miramolino. But the nazir had retreated to Morocco, and so Francis hurried with Bernard di Quintavalle to Barcelona, where they waited for a ship to North Africa. He was disappointed again; this time he lost his voice and was incapable of preaching.

For weeks, even months, he and Bernard disappeared into Spain, joining – some say – the million pilgrims who traveled across Europe every year to Santiago de Compostela while Jerusalem was in Saracen hands. As always the two companions slept rough, under bushes, against the shelter of a wall, in cowsheds, on the straw of a threshing floor. Spain could be both colder and hotter than Italy; they were woken by chilling downpours and gusts of icy wind, while south of Toledo the blast furnace heat burned their skin, stung their eyes and scorched even their lungs.

At first Bernard, more familiar with the country, had to preach and beg for both of them but Francis could sometimes borrow a fiddle and, as his troubadour spirit revived, set a village singing and dancing. When he stopped he found, like the English poet Laurie Lee seven hundred years later, that a chunk of cheese, a husk of bread or a skin of wine was pressed into his hands. He and Bernard were happiest among the kind of people whose descendants Lee describes living in similar conditions centuries later:

> I seemed to meet no one except the blind and the crippled, the

> diseased, the deaf and the dumb. . . . They told me tittering tales of others even more wretched than themselves – the homeless who lived in Arab drains, who lay down among rats and excrement . . . trapping cats and dogs, and roasting them on fires of driftwood.[1]

Bishop Moorman left his entire Franciscan archive of more than 1500 items to St. Deiniol's College, Cheshire. It includes a handwritten list of a dozen Franciscan houses or hermitages founded all over Spain in 1214. The saint's presence a year or so earlier is a plausible explanation of their sudden, simultaneous, appearance. However by far the most dramatic, if indirect, outcome of Francis's connection with Spain occurred nearly three centuries later, when two senior Franciscans gave Christopher Columbus crucial assistance. One of them, an astronomer, supported his geographical calculations while at the eleventh hour the other – the Queen's confessor – helped him acquire both the finance and the ships he needed for the voyage on which he reached the New World.

Heading homeward, Francis and Bernard crossed the Pyrenees by one of the pilgrim routes, skirted the Albigensian fighting, and made for Arles. There they picked up the road to Italy which Francis had traveled as a merchant with his father who was now on his deathbed. In 1214 Pietro disappears from the records in Assisi and is replaced by his younger son Angelo.

*

On his return Francis quartered central and northern Italy, bringing in new friars like a cheerful retriever – he found thirty priests and laymen in the town of Ascoli alone.

Some were among the most famous to join him. Thomas of Celano, his biographer, was a priest, scholar and professional writer from the Abruzzi; Brother Pacifico, born in Ancona, a composer of erotic songs and the best known troubadour in Italy, had been crowned King of Verses by the Emperor Otto; Brother Elias, an Umbrian school teacher of outstanding energy, imagination and talent, ultimately became head of the order.

Wherever he went Francis lifted people's spirits with practical sympathy and his extraordinary homilies, in which he animated his stories of Christ's life, temptation by the devil, the intervention of angels, and the prospect

1. Assisi today. *Above*, approaching from the west, the Basilica di San Francesco is on the left and Mt. Subasio behind. *Below*, looking down from the east, the Rocca Maggiore is on the crest of the hill to the right.

2. In the Piazza del Comune. The Torre del Popolo, left, was begun in 1212. In Francis's time the Roman Temple of Minerva beside it was first a monastery and then the law court.

3. The young Francis gives his cloak to a poor knight shortly before his final conversion, from the cycle of frescoes designed by Giotto, c.1290, in the Basilica di San Francesco.

4. The 12th c. crucifix from San Damiano. In 1205 Francis heard Christ's voice speak to him from it, telling him to repair his church.

The bishop hands Clare a sprig of olive leaves on Palm Sunday 1212, from a 13th c. wooden panel in the Basilica di Santa Chiara.

5. Francis preaching to the birds by the Maestro di San Francesco, from a 13th c. fresco in the Basilica di San Francesco.

Francis confirms the contract between the savage wolf and the people of Gubbio, from a 15th c. panel by Sassetta in the National Gallery, London.

6. Francis sees the seraph during the night he received the stigmata on Mt. La Verna, from a 13th c. marble relief at the sanctuary.

Opposite, a judge examines Francis's stigmata after his death, from the Giotto cycle of frescoes in the Basilica.

7. *Left,* an early 13th c. likeness of Francis from a wooden panel at Greccio.

Right, Francis, from a 13th c. fresco by Cimabue in the Basilica.

8. *Above*, Francis's blessing for Leo, written in his own hand and signed with the Tau; the red inscription is by Leo. From the parchment in the Basilica.
Below, Francis's bones, briefly exhumed from his tomb in the Basilica during 1978.

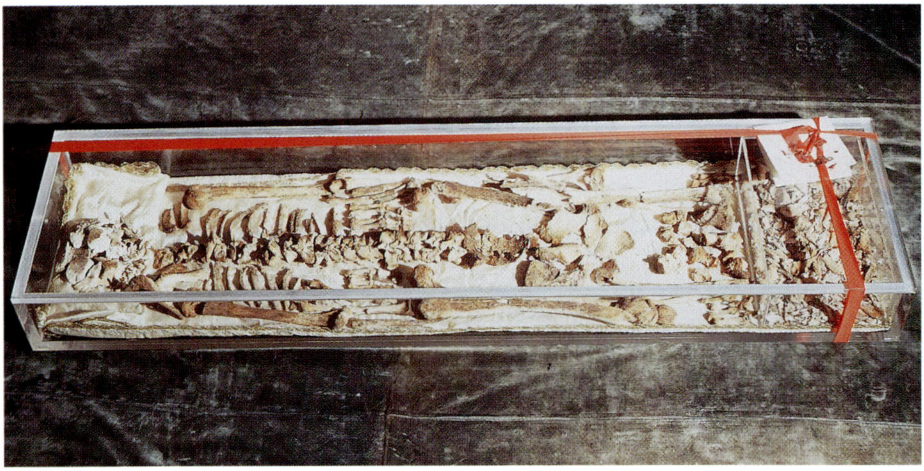

of heaven, with singing and mime. Often, when his tatterdemalion figure appeared, the village bell rang and in a carnival mood men, women and children scrambled to hear him; he seemed able to tug even the richest through the eye of a needle.

One affluent knight in the Abruzzi pressed him to come to a banquet. Francis accepted but, with prescience, suggested he make his confession before they dined. His host did so and dropped dead in the course of the meal.

Leo described how the delicate wife of another rich man, who maliciously undermined all her charitable efforts, raced after them on the road to Cortona. When she reached them, exhausted, she frantically begged Francis to help by giving her his blessing. Touched by her faith Francis obliged her.

"Go back and say to your husband from me that for both your sakes I ask him, for the love of Christ who suffered death on the cross for us, to do whatever he can to save your souls."[2]

Her husband did.

Landowners everywhere offered the brothers properties large and small. Giovanni di Velita, Lord of Greccio, made over a hermitage on his farm above the Rieti Valley, where at the end of his life Francis liked to celebrate Christmas with live animals. Orlando, Count of Chiusi in northern Tuscany, made a more dramatic gesture with a more remarkable result.

He first met Francis on May 8, 1213, when the Lord of Montefeltro invited the local nobility to celebrate the knighting of his son at his castle, set on a stupendous rock in a ring of mountains near San Marino. Francis couldn't resist going to watch the festivities and turned up in the village, now known as San Leo, just below the castle. Its cobbled piazza – little changed over eight centuries – remains the perfect setting for a medieval Mystery or an Italian opera, with a well, the slim tower of its tiny cathedral, a honey colored palazzo, the pink and white stone of the parish church opposite, and soaring above them all the silhouette of the castle.

That day the square was packed with Montefeltro's guests and the excited villagers standing around to stare at them. Seizing his chance Francis jumped on a low wall, under an elm whose successor shades the piazza today, and started to preach on self-sacrifice, taking as his text:

I hope that I so blessed shall be
That every suffering pleaseth me.[3]

The crowd, quickly silent, were soon enthralled. When he finished Orlando immediately asked how he should respond to this appeal. Francis told him to go up and enjoy the party in the castle and afterward meet him in the square. Later, when they were sitting together in the palazzo, Orlando made him an offer.

"In Tuscany I have a remote mountain ideal for anyone wanting to do penance in peace or to spend time alone. It would make me very happy if you and your companions would accept it for the salvation of my soul."[4]

Although he had refused the Porziuncula as an outright gift Francis didn't turn down Mt. La Verna, but accepted it on condition that two of his friars could see it first. The mountain was so wild that Orlando provided an armed escort, who helped them build a shelter near the top, close to where Francis underwent the supreme experience of his mystical life, eleven years later.

However impressive these aristocratic conversions, the essence of Francis's achievement was his devotion to the poorest in society, which was perhaps best rewarded in a village sometimes named as Alviano but now thought to be Cannara, about six miles below Assisi, on the road to Bevagna.

Cannara was a walled village between the swampy banks of the Topino River and the wooded hills on the far side of the valley. Its people were simple but tough, living off the country as fishermen and basket makers, shepherds and cowherds, wheat growers and millers, wolf-hunters, woodcutters and carpenters. Before Francis could start preaching he had to silence a swirl of low flying swallows, chittering after midges; that in itself caught the crowd's imagination. But what he had to say made an even more powerful impact than usual for at the end literally everyone in the village wanted to leave home and follow him with their children.

"Don't be in too much of a hurry," he told them, "and I will let you know, as soon as I can, the best way you can win your salvation." The author of *The Little Flowers* believes that Francis conceived a new, lay order when he made them this promise.

A few miles beyond Cannara he interrupted his journey again, at a hamlet called Pian d'Arce, where his attention was caught by a large gathering of crows, jackdaws and pigeons.* To his surprise they didn't fly off

*An English chronicler, Roger of Wendover, writing about twenty years later, suggests they were attracted by carrion – perhaps discarded by a shambles.

when he went over to look at them, and so he started talking to them quietly, urging them as fellow creatures to praise God. The birds watched him intently, opening their beaks and stretching their wings; when he left they allowed his habit to brush over them (Plate 5). After that he frequently spoke to the animals and birds he encountered on his travels, while his sermon, commemorated now by a wayside shrine in Pian d'Arce, and among the most famous he ever preached, gave expression to his love of creation in much the same way as the poem he addressed to the sun at the end of his life.

The aftermath of the sermon at Cannara exerted an even more potent influence on society, through Francis's Third Order which eventually stemmed from it. Its penitent men and women, married and single, from every level of society, remained in the world but took vows which bound them to the same ends of love, service and peace as his other two. Because it kept no written records we don't know exactly who belonged to it, but serious historians have named King Louis IX of France and Princess Elizabeth of Hungary (both saints), Giotto and Leonardo da Vinci, Dante and Cervantes, Columbus and Galileo. However intriguing the religious and cultural implications if they all did, it emerged later that the political consequences of the order were also profound.

By 1215 the branches of Francis's order embraced large numbers of men and women, whose activities throughout Umbria and beyond had been spotted and admired by one of the church's most critical observers, Bishop de Vitry, now on his way to Rome.

*

The princes of the church reached Rome for the start of the Fourth Lateran Council on November 11, 1215, accompanied by retinues of chaplains, stewards, servants and baggage – like exotic grandees on a spiritual safari. With the cardinals and archbishops came most of the four hundred bishops in the Western church, eight hundred abbots and priors, the affiliated Latin Patriarchs of Jerusalem, Constantinople and Antioch, and the Primate of the Maronite church in Syria, together with a deacon representing the Melchite Archbishop of Alexandria. Cardinal Pelagius of Albano, the pope's arrogant legate in Constantinople, stood out uniquely in this throng, for he had taken to clothing both himself and his horse from head to hoof in scarlet; it made him a laughing stock as well as disliked. Most of the monarchs in Europe – who had by now submitted to Innocent – sent their proctors; these included John of England, Philip Augustus of France, and young Frederick II, recently elected emperor in Germany after the humiliating defeat of his cousin Otto by the French king.

Lodgings were crammed with ambitious priests, monks, deacons and notaries, the streets teemed with sightseers, tourists and touts. The opening Mass had to be limited to cardinals and bishops, while crowds jammed the porticos of the basilica and the papal palace; even so, the Bishop of Amalfi was suffocated in the crush. At night this invasion of visitors and the native Romans were entertained with processions, music, flares, bonfires, acrobats and jugglers. It was the most spectacular Church Council of the Middle Ages.

Francis had refused to adopt the office and title of Prior in his order and therefore had no place at the Council, but his biographers generally agree he was in Rome. Bishop Guido briefed him on the issues which touched him most closely and on the key players he needed to meet. Above all he had to look out for a cardinal willing to fill the place left by San Paolo who had died a year or two before.

Innocent dominated the Council by virtue of his office, his personality and the machinery of government which he had brought to a new peak of efficiency. Through his archbishops, legates and prolific correspondence he handled his relentless problems great and small – from the schism in the church, or the delicate business of undoing the improper marriages of three kings and finding them legitimate wives, to coping with a chapter of grumbling monks in faraway England: "I have had to send you so many mandates and letters concerning the church in Canterbury that I flush to hear about this mouldy business again."[5]

Among the seventy items on the Council's agenda Francis identified with the ends of recovering Jerusalem and eradicating heresy, while utterly deploring the means of military warfare. He remained determined to pioneer a peaceful alternative; and even Innocent now inclined toward leniency in pursuing the Albigensian crusade, which had taken to burning Cathars at the stake.

Nevertheless Francis was wholly at one with Innocent and the Council over their measures for reforming the church, however worried he may have been by an announcement that no new orders (or certainly rules) would receive formal authority, and a declaration that in the future, aspirants could only enter a religious order which was established with a secure and regular income. Neither he nor Clare had a rule authorized in writing and both their orders were penniless.

In this tricky climate Bishop Guido worked hard behind the scenes, and according to Leo the pope declared in Council that Francis's order had been officially authorized – a proposition that has never been seriously challenged, however lively the debates on its rule. The bishop also arranged for Francis to meet the two most important cardinals in the Curia – Cencio Savelli and Ugolino dei Conti di Segni – each in turn to be pope. Cardinal Savelli, who had audited the entire wealth of the church while giving away most of his own, had a natural sympathy with Francis's commitment to apostolic poverty and had supported San Paolo's commendation of his Rule in 1209. He now assured Francis of any help he might need in the future.

Cardinal Ugolino, Innocent's nephew, also offered valuable support. He was very close to Innocent and enjoyed many of his uncle's qualities, but not all. On the one hand he was a clever theologian and expert lawyer; on the other he was an emotional man with a fiery temper yet genuinely moved by Francis's poverty, humility and transparent goodness. Even so the jurist in him was made uncomfortable by Innocent's repeated encouragement of independent-minded evangelists, including Dominic de Guzman fresh from preaching in the Languedoc, who now wanted to start his own order, too.

Although Dominic had failed to win over the Cathars around Albi, he came closest to Ugolino's ideal of a traveling preacher because he and his sixteen followers were intellectuals, believing that theological argument offered a more certain road to salvation than practical example and service. An astute opportunist Ugolino introduced Francis and Dominic, no doubt hoping to regularize Francis's imprecise status and head off Dominic's ambition to found an order of his own, by persuading them to combine under a modification of the Augustinian Rule which Dominic already professed. A Dominican version of the meeting describes de Guzman saying to Francis "Let us be united, for together nothing can prevail against us." Various medieval frescoes show the two friars embracing. Characteristically Dominic is dressed immaculately in his white woollen habit, Francis, the shorter, in a tunic the color of Umbrian earth. Though nothing emerged from their first meeting it paved the way for a new form of ministry which made a radical impact on life throughout Europe.

By the time the Council dispersed at the end of November, its work well done, Innocent had set his seal on the church's affairs.

*

Francis felt so close to Innocent, who chose the Greek letter Tau as the symbol of these reforms, that he adopted it as his personal signature. Like a capital T, it resembled an earlier instrument of crucifixion – the form of the cross which Silvester had seen emerging from Francis's mouth, its arms stretched across the world, in his dream before joining the friars. The only surviving letter in Francis's hand is signed with it, rising from a curious shape he has drawn, like a skull (Plate 8).

A number of the Council's reforms coincided with Francis's aims in his order – the training of more and better preachers, spreading knowledge of the gospels by translating them into the vernacular, regular confession, attendance at Mass, and recital of the Office – which now became possible as more priests joined the order. In addition the Council looked to better control within the orders by requiring them to hold regular chapters. Francis had instinctively adopted this practice from the time he moved into the Porziuncula – assembling his brothers twice a year, at Pentecost in May and the feast of St. Michael in September.

In the early days they were the only form of organization he attempted or needed. Through them he could keep in touch with all his friars (by now there were well over a hundred), receive the vows of each new brother, and make sure that the others were still observing the Rule, which was from time to time modified in chapter if the need arose. These early chapters were intensely happy, remembered by everyone for their unfailing courtesy and the friendships struck up there, which grew steadily deeper through the years. Francis opened them with a glowing welcome, especially for the new brothers.

> The very sight of him, as they listened to his exhortations, banished any worries they had. He spoke to them not as a judge but as a father to his children. Like a doctor among his patients, he suffered with the sick and grieved with the distressed. Nevertheless he knew how to

reprove those who had done wrong and discipline the obstinate or rebellious.[6]

Francis could not escape his duty to exercise authority but was determined it should not displace his humility, so at the start of each chapter he appointed a personal guardian, usually the most junior friar, and meticulously deferred to him.

In his lectures on religious experience William James maintained that the finest fruits of religious endeavor coincide with the highest ideals of civilized morality provided the emotional excitement driving the endeavor is matched with the right inhibitions.

When he spoke to his brothers in chapter Francis balanced like a jongleur at the center of a seesaw, the weight of his concern tilting back and forth between relishing the richness of their blessings but strictly preserving their poverty; between spending hours each night in the realms of the spirit and devoting hours every day to the needs of the world; between the imperatives of squandering their love and restraining their desires.

He never failed to fire a chapter with the passion to love not only God but everyone they encountered, including he said the rich (who were not to be sneered at for living in luxury), their enemies, and the wicked, who might be won over to God in the end.

Nevertheless there were sometimes brothers who lacked the self-control to live up to these counsels of perfection. Then he reluctantly resorted to reproof, penance, an order under obedience or some form of punishment. For gossiping or idleness, "wasting God's good time," the penance was saying a number of Our Fathers or Praises according to the gravity of the lapse. With a brother who suggested a beggar might actually be the most covetous man in the province he was much more severe, although the friar was immediately contrite.

"Take off your tunic," Francis said. "Go naked to that poor man, throw yourself at his feet, tell him how you slandered him, and ask him to pray for God's pardon for you. . . . His poverty and weakness is a kind of mirror in which we can see what our Lord Jesus Christ bore in his body for the salvation of the human race."[7]

The clinching moment of Francis's conversion had occurred in front of the crucifix at San Damiano, and Christ's agony became the pivot around which his prayers and much of his behavior turned for the rest of his life. Leo, who knew his inner feelings better than anyone else, says Christ's anguish was, "a constant source of affliction to him and a cause of interior and exterior mortification; consequently he was utterly unconcerned with his own sufferings."[8]

The friars were quick to recognize this, but many of them did not appreciate that neither abstinence nor mortification were good in themselves but only so far as they helped to suppress appetites and impulses conflicting with their love of God and their neighbors. As a result they took mortification to extreme lengths.

> The first friars and those who came after them used to afflict their bodies excessively by abstinence, vigils, cold, and manual labour. They wore wrist fetters, breastplates and the harshest hair shirts next to their skin.[9]

Although Francis, through his example, was inadvertently responsible for these abuses, he was appalled when he became aware of them. The devices had produced sores, bleeding and septicemia, destroyed the friars' peace of mind and interfered with their prayers. He therefore "bound their wounds with bandages of sensible advice" and ruled in chapter that they should wear nothing of any kind under their habits.

His ultimate punishment, reserved for a flagrant breach of obedience or grave heresy, was expulsion from the order. In the early days it was seldom necessary.

If Francis was imprudent in his manifest mortifications, he was equally inconsistent in his attitude to distress. His own meditations on the crucifixion frequently reduced him to unrestrained tears of compassion for Christ and guilt for his suffering, reported in all the principal sources; yet he told his brothers they must never allow remorse to lead to any open displays of sorrow or depression. This would play straight into the devil's hands, prompting them to find consolation in "vain enjoyments."

"Why are you miserable about your sins?" he asked. "Set them between you and God and pray for your salvation. . . . It is not right for one of his servants to look sad in front of other people."[10]

He thought they should always be cheerful.

"Joy springs from purity of heart and constant prayer; your first concern is to safeguard these. It is the lot of the devil to be sorrowful, ours to be happy."[11]

During every chapter Francis raised the brothers' morale to new heights; his irregulars were turning into the self-disciplined force Innocent needed to stiffen the ranks of the secular clergy.

Angelo, who was probably at most of Francis's chapters, says that when they ended:

> He blessed each of the friars, and gave anyone endowed by God with the necessary eloquence permission to preach, whether a priest or a lay brother. Then, in great joy of spirit they started on their way through the world as pilgrims and strangers.[12]

*

Francis knew that although his brotherhood had escaped the attentions of any post-Lateran inquisitors, Clare and her sisters would come in for close scrutiny.

In recent decades many women had flocked to join authorized offshoots of the two traditional religious orders, the Augustinians and Benedictines. Among the former, ten thousand had taken the vows of a new order originating at Prémonstré under an Augustinian rule, while the most celebrated addition to the Benedictines was the Abbey of Fontevrault, a mixed community on the Loire. Fontevrault consisted of five houses, one each for monks, for the sick, for lepers, for virgins and widows, and for penitent women. Its great patron, Eleanor of Aquitaine – widow of a king of France and a king of England, and mother of the English kings Richard Coeur de Lion and John – chose to live with the penitents who included retired prostitutes. The whole community was ruled by an abbess.

Even orthodox institutions had their critics, among them the great St. Bernard of Clairvaux. In his early years he is said to have been no purer than Francis, in his later ones he was a great deal more outspoken, maintaining, "To be always with a woman and not to have intercourse with her is more difficult than to raise the dead."[13]

The majority of the cardinals were less extreme than St. Bernard, but many shared Ugolino's discomfort at the license given to the Humiliati, who they feared would usurp the authority of their more delinquent clergy.

They were slightly less suspicious of the Béguines, whose reputation had risen rapidly with the fame of their brightest star, the saintly Marie d'Oignies, only recently dead. Even now de Vitry was working on the Curia to give the Béguines official approval.

Francis hoped that despite the hierarchy's ambivalence toward these informal orders there were sufficient precedents for it to endorse the tacit approval he had received from Rome when he had accepted Clare's vows and given her both the tonsure and a primitive rule. This Rule is alluded to by Pope Innocent IV in his Bull dated August 9, 1253, which was shown to her before she died two days later. It contained the words, "We have before Us your humble request that we confirm to you by [our] Apostolic authority the form of life which Blessed Francis gave you and which you have freely accepted." The Bull then sets out the Rule written by Clare herself. The first chapter of it opens:

> The form of life of the Order of the Poor Sisters which the Blessed Francis established is this: to observe the holy Gospel of our Lord Jesus Christ, by living in obedience, without anything of one's own, and in chastity. Clare, the unworthy handmaid of Christ and the little plant of the most blessed Father Francis, promises obedience and reverence to the Lord Pope Innocent and to his canonically elected successors and to the Roman Church. And, just as at the beginning of her conversion, together with her sisters, she promised obedience to the Blessed Francis so now she promises his successors to observe the same inviolably.[14]

Clare recognized that her sisters could not lead lives exactly like the friars. Begging apart, she knew they might not preach because, on the strength of two sentences in a New Testament epistle, an early Church Council and medieval Decretal prohibited women from preaching and teaching.

She was, however, completely taken aback when, following the Council, the authorities proposed to deprive her and her sisters of the fundamental freedom they had been sharing with their brothers – the right to absolute poverty in accord with Christ's words. The hierarchy sought to justify this on the grounds that before Francis every official order had been obliged to accept some kind of endowment in common, and that economic security was essential for any community of women.

Clare saw this not only as an attempt to remove the foundation stone of the apostolic life in which she had joined Francis but also as the thin end of a wedge which might be driven between them. She therefore appealed directly to Innocent to withdraw the proposal. This placed him in an acute dilemma. At any other time his instinct might have prompted him to confirm the rule which Francis had already given her but he could not now fly in the face of a decree issued by his own Council. At the same time he was not prepared to put at risk the loyalty of such a promising and magnetic young religious as Clare.

He therefore sat down and wrote her an unprecedented letter in his own hand, containing these sentences.

> Innocent . . . to the beloved daughters in Christ, Clare and other hand maidens of the Church of San Damiano of Assisi, both present and future, professing in perpetuity life according to a rule . . .
>
> As you have asked we, with apostolic favour, approve your aim of highest poverty, granting with the authority of this writing, that by no one may you be forced to receive possessions.[15]

No contemporary copy of this letter, known as *The Privilege of Poverty* and assumed to have been written between November 1215 and July 1216, has been found but its authenticity has seldom been questioned until recently. A few scholars now condemn it, largely on internal evidence, as a fifteenth century forgery. They claim that a similar letter written to Clare in 1228 by Ugolino, after he was elected pope as Gregory IX, was the first genuine grant of the *Privilege.*

There is one major flaw in this suggestion. However able he was, and however devoted to Francis and Clare, Ugolino always lacked the imagination and flexibility of his uncle; every measure he sought to impose on their orders was vigorously orthodox and as such was either restrictive or undermined their commitment to the apostolic ideal. The spiritual generosity of the *Privilege* was, on the other hand, typical of Innocent's magnanimous vision and allowed Gregory, benevolent but legalistic, to follow his precedent a dozen years later. It is therefore perfectly possible that the original of Innocent's letter – whose existence was known to the author of Clare's official life – was lost, but was needed for some purpose in the fifteenth century, an occasion which gave rise to a reconstruction, now considered questionable, based on Gregory's text.

Clare had won the first of her many engagements with the Lateran on the critical issue of poverty but in doing so she was obliged to concede on a lesser one. Just as Francis had refused the title of Prior, she had declined to become Abbess of San Damiano. Now Francis felt it would be advisable to make a concession to the hierarchy's desire for conformity and urged her to accept the title, at the age of twenty-one. She did. It seemed a reasonable price to pay for her *Privilege*.

*

In July 1216 Innocent made his way north to settle a dispute between Genoa and Pisa over the supply of shipping for his crusade. He and his Curia broke their journey in Perugia.

After eighteen years he was more conscious than ever of the legacy he had inherited – "the Lord left to Peter not only the governance of the church but of the whole world." It is said he saw the church as an ark of salvation in a sea of destruction. Whatever his failings and failures, no pope has ever fought the destructive forces besetting him with a finer array of political, intellectual and moral qualities or with greater success. Although he failed to tame the French king, he thwarted the German emperor's occupation of Italy, outfaced virtually every other monarch in Europe, kept alive the will to recover Jerusalem, did his best to reunite the churches in the east and the west, and clamped down on heresy.

His simultaneous repairs to his ark were equally vital, for without its spiritual credibility his temporal authority would have blown away on the wind, and with it Christendom's hope of salvation in this world and the next. Genuinely devout, his imagination and humanity, combined with a wisdom that saw deeper and further than his prelates – inclining him on the right occasion to relax or temporarily depart from a principle – raised him above his peers and led him to back unorthodox visionaries like Francis and Dominic.

In one of his perceptive letters Bishop de Vitry writes of the pope's high regard for Francis's brothers and sisters, of whom the bishop had observed a great many. He goes on to say that "saintly Brother Nicholas" had left the staff of the Curia to join Francis but, unable to get on without him, the pope had asked for him back. Innocent therefore not only launched Francis on his mission to repair the church but kept closely in touch with it; while, for Francis, Innocent – whatever his faults – was, literally, Christ's representative on earth.

Although still in his fifties, Innocent's concentration on his incessant ceremonies, judicial courts, religious services, sermons, meetings, correspondence, counseling and prayers, inevitably took its toll. "I have no leisure to meditate on supermundane things," he remarked wearily. "So much must I live for others that I am almost a stranger to myself."

During the second week of July, in the middle of business with his court, which was enmeshed in the briefings and arguments that precede all diplomatic summits, he suffered an embolism. Five days later, on July 16th, he died.

Most of the cardinals who mattered, including Cencio Savelli and Ugolino, were in Perugia. By coincidence Jacques de Vitry arrived that day to be consecrated Bishop of Acre in Syria; an inquisitive spectator and prolific correspondent, he has left a vivid firsthand account of what went on in the next few days. A reliable Franciscan chronicler in England, Brother Thomas of Eccleston, writing twenty years later, says that Francis, too, was in Perugia.

In the intensive heat of that long summer day the cardinals and their entourages raced against time to send the news across Europe, to summon and arrange an immediate meeting of cardinals to elect a successor, and to prepare for Innocent's funeral the next day. His body was robed for the last time in his richest and most beautiful vestments, his tiara was placed on his head and his magnificent crozier laid by his side; then, to the chanting of prayers, he was carried into the cavernous cathedral where he lay in state among the treasures of his pontifical office. At last, night fell, the doors were locked and his exhausted guards fell asleep outside.

Early in the morning, when the canons opened the cathedral, they found that thieves had broken in. Everything of value had vanished and Innocent had been stripped of his silk and ermine embroidered with gold thread, pearls and precious stones. "His body was lying in the middle of the church, almost naked, and giving off a nauseating smell," de Vitry wrote. "I went there and saw with my own eyes how brief, vain, and ephemeral is the glory of this world."

Thomas of Eccleston says that Francis was there, too, and immediately took off his habit to cover the corpse of his pope, a man he had loved.

17

A Vision of Creation

Innocent's death, halfway through the breakneck succession of events between Francis's conversion in 1206 and his death in 1226, had a radical impact on his orders. It is therefore a suitable point at which to examine for a moment not what he was doing but how he and his followers did it.

His relationship with his friars, Clare's sisters, and their lay penitents was essentially reciprocal. He was able to lead them to glimpses of heaven, while in return they gave him an ever-widening view of the world – indeed of the universe. Many of his brothers, Bernard and Peter among the earlier ones, Brother Nicholas and Pacifico among the later, were highly educated, and well versed in the seven liberal arts, including astronomy. As a result they could pass on to Francis the medieval image or model of the cosmos which, however grotesque its inaccuracies, was one of the most attractive concepts of it ever devised.

Based on principles proposed by Plato and Aristotle, developed by astronomers in Greece and Arabia, and completed in the fifth century by a Syrian monk – who claimed it owed much to a dialogue between St. Paul and Dionysius the Areopagite – the model answered the questions men and women have asked since the beginning of time. Who are we? How did we, the world, the sun and the stars come into being? What supports us all, what is our purpose and what will become of us when we die?

Because the answers that the model offered were so widely accepted we know what Francis saw when he looked up at the night sky and contemplated the colossal drama of universal existence. True to men's physical perceptions, not to mention their psychological disposition, the stationary Earth was at the center of the cosmos, though smaller than any star. It was a globe, like the sun and the moon, but a barrier of scorching equatorial heat prevented access to the other half of it, on which life existed, moving about like flies on the underside of an apple. Although sophisticated minds did not accept this literally, the fires of Hell, reached by a tunnel, were said to burn at Earth's center; beside the mouth of this tunnel rose the Mount of Purgatory.

The transparent envelope of air enclosing the Earth was the home not only of birds but also of demons, spirits which might be evil (acolytes of the fallen angel Lucifer), neutral or good. Around the orbit of the moon air gave way to ether in which six other planets – Mercury, Venus, the Sun, Mars, Jupiter and Saturn in that order – also circled. Angels, too, moved through the ether. In the region beyond it, also wheeling, lay the *stellatum*, the dimension of the stars and galaxies whose relative stations were constant, unlike the planets. The furthermost element, the *primum mobile*, a total void but rotating like the others, was the last frontier of time and space.

Outside space and time, entirely surrounding the whole system, lay the empyrean, infinite and eternal, the domain of God, the origin of all being. He presided here with Jesus and the Holy Spirit, accompanied by Mary, Queen of Heaven, and a celestial hierarchy of Cherubim, Seraphim and Thrones, Virtues, Dominions and Powers, Principalities, Archangels and Angels. Men could not observe them during the day because their eyes were dazzled by the strength of the sunlight, while at night they were dimmed when the sun passed behind the Earth, whose shadow was cast like a cone of inky darkness up into the firmament. Throughout the upper reaches of the sky the sun's pervading light shone to the continuous and heavenly music of the spheres, expressing their love of their creator, just as their rotation manifested their unceasing effort to approach him more closely.

Looking up at any time of day or night Francis and his brothers could therefore visualize a "revelry of insatiable love" in which they had a vital role to play, for one of the fundamentals of the universe was its unity; every component related to every other in a logical and harmonious pattern. However man's place was pivotal; created when God breathed life into dust, every human soul since had been fetched from heaven at birth and

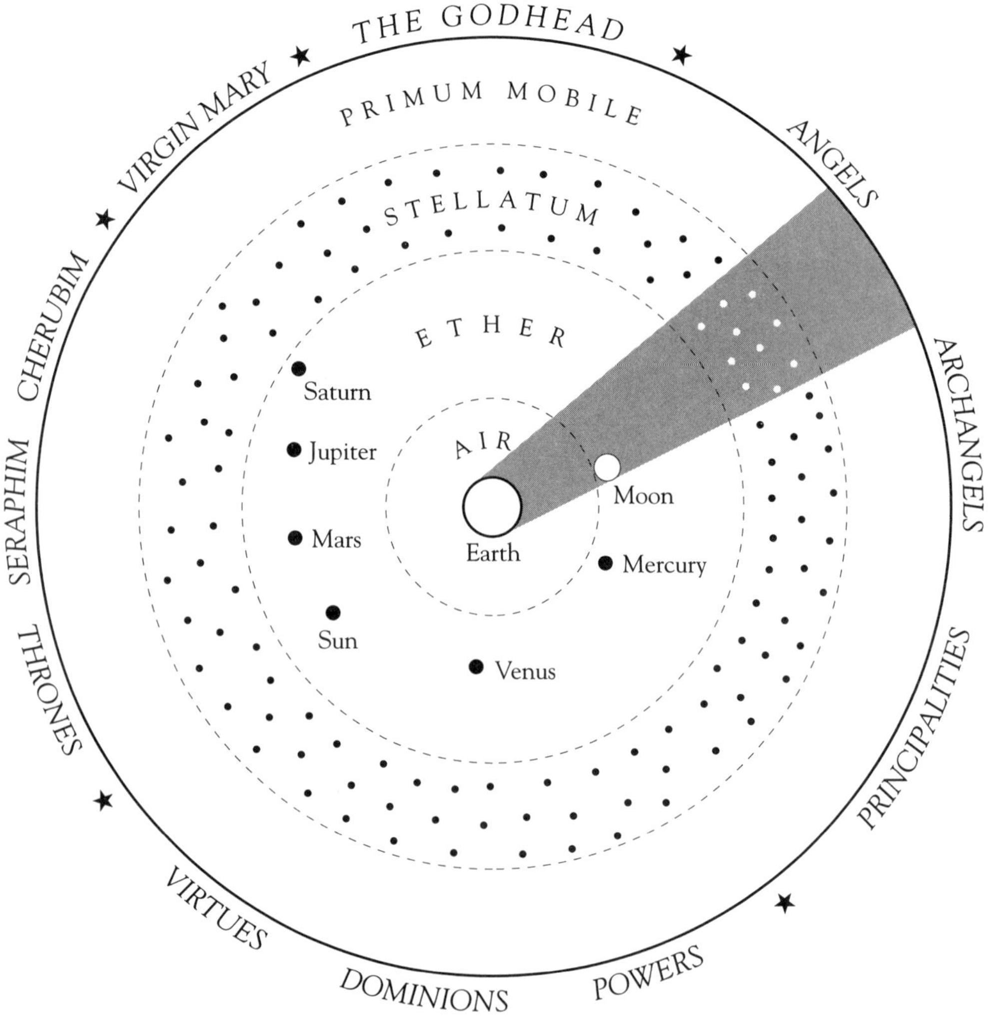

The Medieval Cosmos

The Sun, the Earth and the planets are not to scale

might return there after death. Like stones, plants and animals, men and women were of the Earth, but unlike them though in common with the angels and God, they possessed reason. They therefore had a responsibility for their fellow creatures.

It is possible no one in the west has ever known better than Francis so many of the components of this grand design – the rocks and trees among which he slept, the birds and animals he encountered each day on the road, the men, women and children who flocked to hear him preach and – around or above him – the elements, the sun and the moon, angels and demons, Lucifer and God.

*

The paramount figure in this scheme of creation was of course God. He was not precisely the god of the gospels for the Roman Church had adopted a triune Godhead, defined in "The Apostles' Creed" as a trinity comprising God the Father, his son Jesus Christ, and the Holy Spirit – Jesus being conceived by the Holy Spirit of Mary, a virgin. The apostles might have been puzzled by this definition of God, particularly as Jesus, who may have regarded himself as performing an unprecedented mission on Earth, perhaps referred to himself as "the son of man," never as the son of God.

The complexities of such theology held no problems for Francis. As a deacon he might not expound dogma, and his writings – which comprise less than a hundred printed pages – are confined to his Rules, admonitions, letters, psalms, praises and hymns. Nevertheless he did sometimes find himself pressed so hard to explain a passage from the gospel that he didn't like to refuse. He then relied on his personal experience of God, Christ and the Holy Spirit, and never put a foot wrong.

After hearing him a Dominican scholar in Siena remarked:

> This man's theology, supported by purity and contemplation, flies like an eagle; by contrast our science creeps along the ground.[1]

We can never know exactly how God appeared to Francis in his visions but there is one way in which we can perhaps grasp an inkling of it. The greatest poet of the Middle Ages, Dante Alighieri, was a master of classical literature and medieval theology, a great admirer of Francis, dedicated as he had been to courtly love, and a devout Christian. His trilogy *The Divine Comedy* describes his pilgrimage from the depths of Hell to the Heaven of Heavens, displaying vast knowledge, imagination and command of metaphor. At its culmination Dante attempts to express his spiritual response to the presence of God. It is reasonable to suppose that Francis, with whom he had much in common and who was also a poet, would have understood and shared at least some of his feelings.

Guided by Virgil, the voice of philosophical wisdom, Dante first visits the damned, suffering their agonies in the fires of the *Inferno*. In the second book they climb through the souls struggling to make amends for their sins on the slopes of *Purgatory*. But in the third, when they reach *Paradise*, Beatrice his inamorata and the inspiration of his pilgrimage takes over; she personifies divine illumination. On the way upward she shows Dante the souls gathered on each of the planets. At the Sun a congregation of the church's greatest philosophers and theologians listen to St. Thomas Aquinas, a Dominican, extolling the virtues of St. Francis and telling the story of his love affair with Lady Poverty.

It is a happy interlude; Evelyn Underhill, in her classic study *Mysticism*, writes: "Dante, initiated into Paradise, sees the whole universe laugh with delight as it glorifies God, and the awful countenance of perfect love adorned with smiles. Thus the souls of the great theologians dance to music and laughter in the heaven of the Sun; the loving seraphs, in their ecstatic joy, whirl about the being of God."[2]

Once they have risen above the constellations and the empty *primum mobile* – the first of all the moving elements – Beatrice asks St. Bernard, embodying contemplative vision and the love of Mary, to lead Dante to the climax of his quest. Dante then sees the saints, Francis among them, gathering in the formation of a white rose and presided over by the Virgin, glowing more brightly than the dawn. Bernard advises him to ask her for the grace to gaze directly into the intense, living and eternal light which is emerging from the threefold godhead. In the last lines of his epic Dante seeks words for the ensuing apocalypse.

Like a geometer who sets himself
To square the circle, and is unable to think
Of the formula he needs to solve the problem

So was I, faced with this new vision. . .

But that was not a flight for my wings:
Except that my mind was struck by a flash
In which what it most desired came to it.

At this point high imagination failed;
But already my desire and my will
Were being turned like a wheel, all at one speed,

By the love which moves the sun and the other stars.[3]

The metaphor of light for God, common to so many thinkers, poets and mystics, suggests an analogue between it and the modern concept of energy, fundamental to all existence and activity, terrestrial and astral.

This is a proposition uncannily similar to the view propounded by some of the world's leading physicists in a television series *Universe*, produced in 1999. In it a cosmologist expresses this view: "Studying astronomy provides the basic information each person needs to understand where he or she comes from and where the human race is going. There are universal questions: every religion in the world has a cosmology and they all contain a grain of truth; modern science brings a new and much more complete version of cosmology." The British Astronomer Royal, Sir Martin Rees, then goes on to expound the Big Bang theory of creation. It is reported in a supporting book like this:

> Our universe came into being as a minuscule speck of brilliant light. It was almost infinitely hot, and inside this fireball was contained the whole of space. And with the creation of space came the birth of time.[4]

In fact the theories of modern science are not all so "new." About six years after Francis died, Canon Henri d'Avranches* wrote a versification of

*His brilliance as chaplain to Ugolino (by then Pope Gregory) won him places successively at the courts of three kings, Frederick II, Louis IX and Henry III of England.

Thomas of Celano's life of the saint. In a flight of fancy he evokes the dialogue Francis had with the Sultan of Egypt, which includes this passage.

> *He reasons . . .*
> *How it is that all things come from one source, how a moment*
> *Of that first principle is simple substance, a simple*
> *Moment in the present, a substance simpler than*
> *A mathematical point; how its essence is wondrously present*
> *Wholly, always and everywhere outside of place and time.*[5]

To Francis God was neither as minimalist as d'Avranche's creator nor as ineffable as Dante's. More familiar with Him than the other two he composed a famous Praise for Leo in which he ran through God's attributes in a list whose claims were sweeping yet easy to understand; they included justice, strength, beauty, joy, love, and the highest good, with the power to grant salvation and eternal life. Given the convulsions and cruelty of the age some may have been tempted to question the probability of these assertions. However Francis's continuous effort to emulate Christ, and with such extraordinary effect, offered persuasive evidence that he might know what he was talking about.

The same cannot be said of the church's account of God and the behavior of its clergy. The hierarchy, constantly elaborating its subtle labyrinth of infallible theology, attempted to impose it on the world with ancillary secular obligations. If questioned or defied it set about getting its way by recourse to the crusader's sword and inquisitor's flames. The scandalous aberrations of a great many priests merely confirmed doubters in their doubts.

As time went by the Renaissance, the Reformation and then Rationalism progressively eroded men's faith in religion, the Roman church, and finally God. Nevertheless in the twentieth century an awareness dawned that neither the language of logic nor the measurements of science could either prove or disprove the existence of God, or answer metaphysical questions about our origins, nature and ultimate destiny, although Karl Popper, who had one of the clearest minds of his time, maintained that "only the very greatest thinkers, such as Kant, Schopenhauer, and Einstein, took this on board."[6] Ludwig Wittgenstein, another philosopher also aware of his discipline's limitations, regarded the world's very existence as a "mystical" phenomenon, by its nature beyond normal human comprehension and capability to describe.[7]

From time to time great poets, painters or composers memorably illuminate some aspect of life, love, death or eternity in their work; in a similar way, and also rather rarely, great mystics convey fragments of truth about these mysteries in the way they lead their lives.

*

To the bystander it seems hard on saintly visionaries that they seldom experience God's grace and energy as gentle rain from heaven; more often it descends like lightning – blinding St. Paul, sending some into shock or confusion, and frightening others as it did Francis in his cave on Mt. Subasio.

St. Teresa of Avila, who never minced her words, regretted to her minister provincial that "God treats His friends terribly but does them no wrong for he served His Son in the same way."[8] Equally forthright with God himself, she was overheard telling Him by the river that it was hardly surprising He had few true friends since He dealt with them so badly. Facing Him regularly in prayer therefore required great courage as well as love.

The daily devotions which soon became a friar's second nature at the Porziuncula may have helped purge his worst shortcomings and carried him through the foothills of the spiritual life, but if he aspired to climb higher and find himself in the presence of God, not just within sight of Him, he needed guidance to another level of contemplation. It might not carry him to the summit of the spiritual mountain but was an important part of the journey.

It is impossible to know now exactly what advice he received but since, like Francis, a friar spent up to a third of his waking life in prayer it is worth looking at some of the traditions of devotion which still survive. In contemplation a brother would learn to empty his mind rather than concentrate it, setting aside what William Wordsworth called "the meddling intellect" so that his intuitions and subconscious could lead him closer to God. If he could manage this, sooner or later (according to his temperament) he might acquire not so much "a knowledge" as "an experience" of God – an attainment sometimes known as Illumination to Christians, Hindus and Muslims.

At this point he, and possibly his companions, sensed that he was entering a new dimension of existence, in which he might be overcome by a rapture or trance, and in which the normal limitations of space and time seemed to break down; he might become aware of what was passing through the minds of others, catch glimpses of the future, and understand the forces of nature as never before. In this sphere he was not entirely alone, but probably in the same context of inspiration which later enabled visionaries like El Greco, Blake and Wordsworth to express a sense of immortality, and the early seventeenth-century mystic Jacob Boehme to give his confident answer when asked where the soul goes when the body dies: "There is no need for it to go anywhere." It is simply released from the spatial and temporal constraints of human thinking.

It is only recently that we have begun to explore scientifically connections between our subconscious minds, imaginations and emotions on the one hand and our intellects and mundane senses on the other. The capacity to link them seems to depend on a disciplined relaxation of all the faculties during prayer, so that their inherent organic and electrical rhythms are steadied and in tune with the waves of energy coursing through (in fact constituting) the whole of creation. Traditionally one of the aims of such contemplation is to bring these internal and external pulses into harmony – a process known to the ancient Egyptians, long practiced in the east, adopted by many devout Christians in the west, and now recommended by serious institutions studying our physical and psychological health. It is an activity conducted at the outer edges of our consciousness, on the borders of the physical and the metaphysical.

In Bristol, England, the Cancer Help Centre, originally suspect but now increasingly respected, has pioneered the treatment of cancer and its pain along these lines. Patients are encouraged to generate a benign current by recollecting the feelings, rather than the thoughts, they associate with some episode of exceptional happiness, and then to direct it downward through their bodies, pausing in the region of their tumor. Practiced regularly this form of self-treatment or meditation is frequently shown to alleviate pain, and sometimes to banish it for a time. Occasionally the cancer itself disappears.

At Southampton General Hospital, England, Dr. Alan Watkins has been following up research in the United States on the heart's physical sensitivity to many of our feelings. A generator of electricity more powerful than the brain, it can trigger the release of secretions in our saliva related to these emotions. Anger, misery and guilt tend to raise the content of potentially "destructive hormones such as adrenalin and cortisol," while the level of others known to boost the immune system rise when participants in the study induce in themselves feelings of harmony, compassion and love.

Another study, at Reading University, England, has produced similar findings. While some volunteers inhaled the scent of roses and melting chocolate, others sniffed rotting meat; the pleasant smells led to the release of beneficial immunoglobulin-A into the saliva – a result repeated when the participants were asked to write down some notably pleasant experiences in their lives. The unpleasant smells and recollections produced an opposite effect.

The benign state that these meditations and experiments seek to induce, in order to improve physical or psychological health, has a clear affinity with prayer although it benefits the subject only, lacks the outgoing imperative of Christian love, and takes no account of a being such as God. Nevertheless it has much in common with Francis's insistence that joy, harmony, and gratitude for the ubiquitous beauty of creation, were essential to the proper life of a friar. His own life and work offered a shimmering example.

It is therefore a shock to recognize that the opposite was also true of Francis, though to a lesser extent. His regular contemplation of the anguished and crucified figure of Christ left him haunted by guilt and often in tears – a frame of mind which may have indirectly damaged his immune system and was possibly responsible for what has been called his "dark" side, the mortifications which directly undermined his physical health. Clare followed Francis in both her extreme asceticism and her devotion to the crucified Christ. In the latter she may have gone further, for one religious adviser urged the Poor Clares to place themselves actually within Christ's wounds while meditating on his crucifixion.

During the first millennium the principal images of Christ were as a shepherd and, later, seated in judgment or majesty. The emergence everywhere of his tortured and bleeding figure on the cross, predominant during the second millennium, is an enigma. However admirable the virtue of self-sacrifice, the symbolism of the crucifixion becomes morbid if exaggerated, and the image a deterrent if it eclipses Christ's revelation of love as the essence of God's nature. St. Bernard of Clairvaux was explicit about the unique property of love and Francis would have agreed with him:

> Of all the emotions and affections of the soul, love is the only means of which the creature, though not on equal terms, is able to treat with the creator and give back something resembling what has been given to it.[9]

All of us, searching for light to throw on the mysteries of creation, and a compass to guide us through the mazes of life, instinctively stretch out our hand for help – to philosophy or physics, to biology or psychology, to politics or a metaphysical God.

Karen Armstrong, for seven years a Roman Catholic nun and since then an academic, in her highly acclaimed *A History of God*, maintains that today, for the first time, more than half the world's population does not believe in such a Divinity. This suggests that during the twentieth century, rather than looking to a god for enlightenment about our creation and wisdom in leading our lives, we have turned to prophets such as Marx, Einstein, Darwin, Freud and Gandhi.

In a sense all of them have been on the side of the angels, but it is perhaps too early to tell whether they, in their generation, have been as successful as Francis in disseminating a new sense of purpose, justice, harmony and love. And seven hundred years after their deaths will their followers, like Francis's, still be bringing this spirit to those who most need it – the poor, lonely and old, the sick in body and mind, the distressed and the desperate, and victims of violence as well as those who have fallen foul of the law?

18

The Glinting Diamond

If poets and mystics have so often evoked creation and divinity in terms of light, one of Francis's recent biographers, Raoul Manselli, chose a beautifully apt metaphor to express his capacity to receive and transform the energy of God's love.

> Francis is like sparkling diamonds which, from each of their facets, give off splinters that seem to differ according to the way they are struck by the light.[1]

Like a prism he refracted the full force of the power, dispersing various beams to and through the branches of his order, so that they reached the destinations where they were most needed.

Because the sisters at San Damiano were in Clare's hands, and the lay penitents were living out in the world, the most intense shaft of spiritual light emanating from Francis was directed toward his brothers. It was continuously transmitted through his example and personal relationships with each of them, reinforced twice a year in chapter. Laserlike, it converted a mixture of frequencies – physical, emotional, intellectual and spiritual – into a single beam, burning out the last traces of selfishness.

The fourteenth century Augustinian mystic, Jan van Ruysbroeck, used to tell his students, "you can be as holy as you want to be"; but that is easier said than done. Before it can diffuse unconditional love the will has to mobilize simultaneously the body, heart, mind and soul, each so often in rebellion or at odds with one another, and then surrender them to God's purpose. In his *Salutation to the Virtues*, among them humility, wisdom and love, Francis writes, "There is truly no man in the whole world who can possess one of you unless he first die to self."

Francis followed this precept almost literally, threatening and certainly shortening his life through his severity on his body. Apart from his extreme fasting, in disregard of his Rule – he became increasingly inconsistent as he grew older – he would mix water or ashes with his scraps if he found them too palatable; and when eating at a bishop's table would slip many of the delicacies onto his lap. When he was exhumed in 1978 his skeleton bore the signs of osteoporosis and advanced if not fatal malnutrition.

Leo tells the story of the startling way in which Francis felt he must atone for a lapse in this respect and his dishonesty about it. While he had been laid up with a serious illness he had eaten some chicken; afterward he had thought this self-indulgent and had concealed it from his brothers. Although it was midwinter and he was still suffering from malarial fever, Francis got up, went into Assisi, and preached from the pillory. When he had finished he asked the crowd to wait, went into the cathedral, stripped off his clothes, and told Peter of Catanio to put a rope around his neck and lead him back to the stocks. There he confessed to gluttony and deception.

In a version of his Rule which he later drafted (in 1221) Francis wrote, "From the heart sprout evil thoughts, adulteries, fornications, murders, thefts, avarice . . . false testimonies."[2]

Body, mind and heart had therefore to be kept under the strictest observation but their selfish appetites and ambitions are sometimes easier to spot and control than those attaching to our spirit or superego which must be purged before the purest forms of love can flow freely. As an illustration of the self-effacement he expected, in effect the complete invisibility of the ego, he drew this analogy: "In icons of God and the Virgin Mary they are honored and remembered, yet the paint and the panels ascribe nothing to themselves because they are just pigment and boards."[3]

In attempting to represent Christ and Mary in the world he wanted his brothers and sisters to see themselves as no more than paint and wood.

The presumption of many priests that they belonged to a privileged class was ample warning of the intrinsic snares which lay in wait for the religious. In his *Admonitions*, a document collating some of Francis's *obiter dicta* in chapter, or perhaps offcuts from his drafts for a new rule, he wrote: "Those are all killed who seek to know the words of the scriptures only that they may be regarded as more learned than the others."

An acknowledged master of the spiritual life, the Dominican Johannes Eckhart, is quoted as saying in about 1300 that one of the worst temptations of the professionally religious "was to possess property – not the property shunned by friars but property in prayers, fastings, vigils and mortifications." Francis added to this list "religiosity and holiness which can be seen by many men." He believed prayers should be said discreetly and gave the friars advice about discounting their raptures and concealing any which overtook them publicly or in the street by hiding their faces with their sleeves.

Meister Eckhart, who shared Francis's conviction that such spiritual consolations were of no worth unless they stimulated their work in the world, also warned against these pitfalls:

> If anyone imagines he will get more by inner thoughts and sweet yearnings and a special grace from God, than he could get beside a fire, or with his flocks, or in a stable, he is doing no more than trying to take God and wrap his head in a cloak and shove him under a bench.[4]

Francis's longing for the love of God to flood through him and every member of his order is most perfectly expressed in the prayer which is now said all over the world in his name. Scholars have traced its precise wording no further back than 1912, to somewhere in France, but every phrase bears his hallmark:

> Lord, make me an instrument of your peace; where there is hatred let me sow peace, where there is injury let me sow pardon, where there is doubt let me sow faith, where there is despair let me give hope, where there is darkness let me give light, where there is sadness let me give joy. O Divine Master, grant that I may not try to be comforted but to comfort, not try to be loved but to love. Because it is in giving that we receive, it is in forgiving that we are forgiven, and it is in dying that we are born to eternal life.[5]

The Little Flowers describes an episode which might have been staged to illustrate the application of this prayer and the kind of answer it longed for.

The friars at the Porziuncula were being driven to distraction by an increasingly offensive leper in a nearby lazar house. They managed to put up with his constant but unjustified abuse for failing to look after him with proper compassion and respect, but they couldn't stand his blasphemy when he began to vilify Christ and the Virgin too. They therefore turned to Francis for help, who went to see the leper and gave him his usual greeting, "Peace be with you."

"What peace?" the leper asked. "God hasn't only taken away my peace and everything else worth having, but has also left me rotten and stinking." When Francis urged patience, he began ranting about the indignities inflicted on him by the friars.

After praying for the man, which convinced Francis he was possessed by a demon, he went back to the leper and offered to do whatever he asked.

> "Wash me," he answered, "because I smell so awful and I can't bear myself."
>
> Francis therefore undressed and washed him in warm water scented with herbs, and wherever he swabbed the flesh it started to heal. As the leper's body mended so did his soul, and when he was entirely recovered he apologized and did penance for cursing God and the friars.[6]

Not long afterward he died of some other complaint, shriven and at peace. By then Francis was "very far away because he desired to flee from every glory."

*

The nature of the love Francis directed toward Clare and her sisters was inevitably affected if not conditioned by their gender.

Her simple aim, when she moved into San Damiano, was that she and any sister who joined her should devote their prayers to God and their work to their neighbors in need. Francis's vision of her destiny was broader. He sensed that as her numbers grew, wherever her sisters set up house, working in tandem with his friars, they would make a profound impact on men and women far beyond the precincts of their practical work. There were obvious dangers in men working closely with women, but if the flesh were kept in its place – as he believed it could be – a psychological synergy would be released which would not only motivate every brother, sister and lay penitent in the order, but inspire with their beliefs the mass of ordinary people they had been founded to serve.

Such a partnership between the sexes was not easy for a church so apprehensive of women to conceptualize or put into words, for just as we each only have one heart and soul to love with, we usually have only one vocabulary with which to express our different loves. For instance, the idiom chosen by the sixteenth-century Spanish mystic St. John of the Cross for his devotional poems was erotic.

St. John's relationship with St. Teresa of Avila is the closest historical parallel to the partnership between Francis and Clare. Together they led their Carmelite order back to the barefoot poverty of the gospels; in John his anima, in Teresa her animus, were highly developed; both of them were sustained in the service of others by their remarkable visions which he expressed in verse and she in prose.

Rather as Francis sometimes spoke of himself and his friars as mothers – even as mothers of Christ when they held him in their hearts – St. John frequently describes his soul's encounters with God as a woman's trysts with her lover. It is the theme of the poem already quoted on the night Clare fled from her home, and of another in which his soul searches for her bridegroom. When they meet the groom says:

Beneath the apple-tree,
You came to swear your troth and to be mated,
Gave there your hand to me,
And have new-created
There where your mother first was violated.

You birds with airy wings,
Lions, and stags, and roebucks leaping light,
Hills, valleys, creeks, and springs,
Waves, winds, and ardours bright,
And things that rule the watches of the night:

By the sweet lyre and call
Of sirens, now I conjure you to cease
Your tumults one and all,
Nor echo on the wall
That she may sleep securely and at peace.[7]

In a Hebrew wedding hymn, written two thousand years earlier, there is this exchange between a groom and his bride:

HE
O queenly maiden!
Your rounded thighs are like jewels . . .
Your two breasts are like two fawns,
Twins of a gazelle,
Your neck is like an ivory tower.

SHE
If I met you outside I would kiss you. . .
I would give you spiced wine to drink,
The juice of my pomegranates.
O that his left hand were under my head,
And that his right hand embraced me!

This poem, *The Song of Solomon*, was adopted by Christians as an allegory of the love between God and his church, and later for the betrothal of Christ to each of his nuns. More medieval commentaries were written about *The Song* than any other book in the Old Testament; Clare and her sisters therefore accepted their mystical marriage to Christ as readily as every Poor Clare does today. Erotic idiom is found in the poetry and writings of mystics in every language and century for only allegory of this kind was remotely adequate to express their love of God.

Pledged as they both were to Christ and the Virgin Mary, Francis's bonds with Clare were further strengthened by a shared psychological trait – the possession of characteristics more often apparent in the opposite sex.

When making his final plea to Innocent for the approval of his order Francis had publicly identified himself as a woman in his dream. Later, in a letter to his friars he told them that they should arrange their retreats in hermitages as parties of four, so that two could withdraw in prayer while their companions looked after them "as mothers."

Clare was his complement. She had defied her family at eighteen to join an order of men; she was magisterial in her dealings with Ugolino as cardinal and, later pope; when she was old and crippled she had herself carried into the courtyard of San Damiano to confront a squadron of Arab mercenaries who were scaling the walls and put them to flight. Like Queen Elizabeth of England she had the body of a weak and feeble woman but "the heart and stomach of a king."

The psychiatrist Anthony Stevens warns against the danger of suppressing such cross-gender instincts, which are present to a varying degree in all of us, and says this about the advantage of letting them develop: "As the contra sexual attributes become available to the conscious personality, so a man's *Logos* (reason) is complemented by a refined capacity for intimacy, and a woman's *Eros* (love) is tempered with rational purpose and intellectual understanding."[8]

Clare's subconscious awareness of an exchange of such energy between her and Francis was startlingly revealed by her close friend Philippa to the commissioners during the Process of Canonization.

> The Lady Clare related how once, in a vision, it seemed to her that she brought a bowl of hot water to Francis together with a towel for drying his hands. She was climbing a very high flight of steps, but she did it as easily and lightly as if she had been walking on level ground. When she reached St. Francis he bared one of his breasts and said: "Come, take this and suck." She did so and Francis asked her to suck a second time; what she tasted was sweet and indescribably delicious. After she had finished, the nipple from which the milk had flowed stayed between her lips. When she then took into her hands what thus remained in her mouth it seemed like gold, so bright and shining that everything was visible in it as a mirror.[9]

In her absolute innocence – she was never naive – Clare had felt no embarrassment in confiding her dream to Philippa and two other sisters. Nor did she ever show the slightest reluctance to invite Francis and his brothers to San Damiano. In the early years he felt equally free to come and go.

As founder of his order Francis had adopted the tradition of referring to it as a family; his companions were brothers and he was often their father. In the same way Clare became a mother to her sisters. Giving evidence at the process of canonization her family's old retainer spoke of Clare as "giving birth to a chaste line of sons and daughters." It was an appropriate phrase, for in their unique union Francis drew young women to Clare's order as she did young men to his, while both attracted men and women of every class and calling into their Third Order of Penitents.

For about a thousand million years organisms have been reproducing sexually and as the higher forms of life have evolved their social health and success have depended on maintaining the right sexual balance. In human societies this is as true of their minds and spirits as it is of their physical bodies. The Christian church in the west has tilted too often toward a male orientation, and although the Lord's Prayer opens "Our Father," some scholars hold that the roots of the Aramaic *Abba* or *Abwoon* from which it is translated lead back to a wider expression of parenting. An intuition of this may have led Francis to address an apparently disproportionate number of prayers and praises in his writings to the Virgin Mary.

In 1955 one of the most original and respected priests of his generation, Bede Griffiths, left his Benedictine abbey in England for India, to discover if it might be possible to redress the male bias of Western religion by blending it with the more feminine ethos of Eastern spirituality. Thirty years later, when he was over eighty and living in a Benedictine community run like a Hindu ashram he experienced, simultaneously, a stroke and a vision which nevertheless left his mind intact and finally gave him the solution he had been searching for. A recent biographer writes, "He who had lived so much by his head was now using the language of the centres of power in the body, talking of his energy moving down to the root, the body's connection to sex and the earth. He now saw love as the basic principle of the whole universe."[10]

*

From the day he left Rome with Innocent's blessing Francis was determined that his order would never be confined to a cloister. They were to go out into the world and lead their lives in the full light of day. The canticle he composed not long before he died opens with a salutation to God which continues –

Be praised, my Lord, with all your creatures,
Especially Lord Brother Sun,
To whom we owe both day and light,
For he is beautiful, radiant, and of great splendor;
Of you, most high, he is the emblem.[11]

We are all children of the sun, born on a planet flung from its glowing vapor as a ball of molten gas; children of light too, for the sun's ultraviolet rays then heated up a rich complex of molecules in the sea which one day mutated into the ancestors of all later life on earth, and created the protective layer of ozone that allowed the process of evolution to run its course.

Among the different shafts of light which Francis reflected perhaps the most original lit up the entire natural context of our existence and the creatures we share it with. Before him Christians interpreted *Genesis* as entitling them to treat all other forms of life as their slaves; he, in contrast, believed that as works of God they should be respected and loved no differently from men.

He could not know that all visible life was dependent for its energy on solar power, filtered through the ozone, and trapped by the plants for general circulation through the food chain. Nevertheless observant, responsive to beauty and a visionary, he noticed wherever he went, the miraculous effects of the sun's light, warmth and cycle of seasons.

Many publications and several entire books have scrutinized every aspect of his picturesque encounters with animals and birds. For some they are merely sentimental folktales. The church itself had to step in to refute those who wanted to dismiss them as animist or pantheist heresy. There are scholars who consider the stories merely projected onto Francis a cluster of legends which originated around the lives of early hermits and the Irish saints, who were already well known in Europe as great lovers of the natural world. Others still persist in regarding his sermon to the birds and his negotiations with a wolf as allegorical.

None of these dismissals is necessary for two reasons. The first is that a hypernormal sensitivity to nature, and even authority over it, often seems to accompany the state of spiritual development known as Illumination. Living largely out of doors Francis clearly saw himself as an integral element of God's incarnation in the cosmos. His sympathy with every particle of it, from a gnat to an eagle, a grain of sand to the sun, a dormouse to one of his brothers, was similar to that of many other great mystics. In the ancient Vedic writings of the Hindus:

> All energy in nature . . . is a reflection of the energy which exists eternally in God. All the power of life in nature, of the living organisms, plant and animal, is a reflection of the life which is in God. And so also all the love in human nature.[12]

Francis's contemporary Attar, a Sufi mystic, expresses much the same sentiments in his poem "The Conference of the Birds." In it the lapwing, asked to describe the road which the pilgrim must take to reach the Divine, speaks of Seven Valleys. In the third, Enlightenment: "The mystery of Being is now revealed to the traveller. He sees Nature's secret, and God in all things."[13]

The second reason for accepting many of the stories about Francis and the animal world at face value is that he was not a priest or academic but a countryman. He moved through the lanes, fields and woodlands with the curiosity and sharp eyes of a gardener, shepherd, huntsman, or amateur naturalist. He had grown familiar with the nature and behavior of the creatures he met; they recognized him as a man of peace. Animals often sense our intentions from our movements or postures. Gamekeepers and rangers know that the sight of a gun can frighten off birds or deer; one discovered that unarmed he could approach antelope quite closely and when – as an experiment – he once stood on his head, a herd of wildebeest grazed calmly all around him.

Francis's appreciation of the natural world was universal. When a brother was clearing a plot of ground to grow vegetables, Francis told him to leave a patch for planting flowers; he loved them for their beauty and scent. He asked a brother cutting wood to make sure he left enough of each tree for it to grow again. "He exhorted cornfields and vineyards, stones and forests, all the beauties of the fields and green things of the gardens, to love God and serve him willingly." He would also "see to it that the bees would be provided with honey in the winter, or the best wine, lest they should die during the cold weather."[14]

Leo remembered Francis's delight in a cicada, which sang in a fig tree next to his hut at the bottom of the garden. Each day he lifted it onto his finger where it sang for an hour before he replaced it on a branch. After about a week he felt he should give up these performances in case he drew "vainglory" from them. In Leo's opinion, "God tamed his wild creatures for Francis because he loved them so much."

His care for worms was famous; he quieted noisy frogs (not difficult in Italy where they don't care for human company); and when given a large tench by a fisherman on Lake Piediluco, in the Rieti Valley, he slipped it back into the water where it swam happily beside the boat until he sent it off with a blessing.

A fisherman on the same lake gave him a grebe or moorhen he had netted, which refused to leave his lap until he had finished a long meditation; a wren nestled for a time in his cowl; and he once attempted a duet with a nightingale but was quickly outsung.

There is nothing improbable about the behavior of a pheasant, sent him by a landowner, which he tamed rather than ate. When a doctor in Siena refused to believe that the bird came and went as it pleased, Francis allowed him to take it home to see what happened; very soon the pheasant was back in Francis's cell. Fond of all birds he persuaded a boy to hand over some turtledoves he had trapped. Francis made them nests at the Porziuncula, where they settled and raised their young for many generations. Some lines evoke the Buddha's similar feeling for birds:

Oft times while he mused – as motionless
As the fixed rocks he sat – the squirrels leaped
Upon his knee, and the timid quail led forth
Her brood between his feet, the blue doves pecked
The rice-grains from the bowl beside his hand. [15]

Toward the end of his life Francis made friends with a jackdaw or crow. As adopted crows tend to be, it was fiercely loyal to him. It sat next to him at meals and came on his visits to the sick; when he died it followed his coffin to San Giorgio, refused to leave or eat, and very soon died too.

Some writers believe these stories of Francis's rapport with birds are a form of hagiography, for by medieval convention birds were symbolic of angels; but this may be wide of the mark. There are many practical ways of overcoming a bird's shyness or fear – a quiet approach, familiarization, regular feeding, the provision of a refuge or territory, and above all patience.

During the last world war an Englishwoman, rather like Francis in his huts and caves, kept open house to birds – her doors and windows were never closed. Notices kept even the postman out of her garden and when a patrol of soldiers in training attempted to march through it she barred their way with outstretched arms and had a furious argument with the sergeant in charge. Suddenly the air was filled with fluttering blackbirds, great tits, robins and sparrows, which settled on her head and arms. The nonplussed soldiers retreated.

Wild animals, particularly social species, can often be tamed in the same way as birds, but a few men and women have an exceptional capacity for winning their trust. It usually grows out of love and respect for them, developed through intimations of reassurance, approval or displeasure from both sides. Patiently the animal's suspicions are disarmed with food, a soothing voice or touches of the hand. Finally man and animal arrive at a confident and intuitive sympathy with each other. This understanding enabled Native Americans to handle their horses at speed without bridles or stirrups; good dog trainers and many vets have it; possessing it too, George Adamson could stroll among a pride of wild lions in Kenya unharmed.

Thomas of Celano identified this capacity in Francis: "He was filled with compassion toward dumb animals, reptiles and other creatures. . . . In the most extraordinary manner, never experienced by others, he discerned the hidden things of nature in his sensitive heart."[16]

His delight in animals, "gladly touching and seeing them," enabled him to make friends with mice, rabbits, a hare, a stag, and most memorably a wolf. Wolves were then common in Italy and considered extremely savage, reputed to kill both livestock and people. According to *The Little Flowers*, one of the most notorious was a large male which ranged around Gubbio in a very hard winter, when prey in the forest was scarce, domestic animals weakened or dying, and the townspeople found it difficult to bury their dead. Rumors about the wolf grew so grisly that no one dared leave the city walls.

Wolf packs are formidable hunters and credited with snatching benighted winter travelers from their sleighs, but in fact they seldom if ever attack people. Francis was aware of this and had once disregarded well-intentioned warnings to avoid a stretch of road they were known to haunt. Now, when asked, he agreed to tackle the wolf outside Gubbio, perhaps taking with him a tempting cut of meat.

It turned out to be an elderly animal, perhaps reduced to taking any feeble livestock it found and occasionally scavenging limbs from corpses. The story recounts how Francis, addressing him as Friar Wolf, rebuked him for his reign of terror but acknowledged this was due to hunger. He therefore proposed a pact between the wolf and the people by which they kept him fed, while he promised to stop his attacks on them and their animals.

By now a crowd had gathered, who shouted their agreement; and when Francis held out his hand to the wolf to seal the contract, the narrator endows it with the manner of a dog. He says it stretched out its paw in return, expressing its assent "with movements of its body, tail and eyes" (Plate 5). Two years later it died. In 1872 the skeleton of a wolf was dug up in Gubbio, under the chapel of San Franceso della Pace.

Francis embraced the four elements as warmly as animate creatures. He spoke of Earth as our mother; he praised Brother Wind for bringing us changes of weather; Sister Water was so precious to him that after washing he would not throw it away where it was liable to be trodden on. Nowadays in our age of gas, oil and electrical power his gratitude for Brother Fire seems – perhaps wrongly – excessive to the point of superstition. He loved it for its gaiety, hated putting out candles and lamps or smothering fires, and when the hem of his habit caught light he tried to stop his brothers from quenching the flames.

The Franciscan movement is usually described as urban, but in Francis's lifetime it was rural; he preferred his brothers to live in small houses or hermitages in the country or at the very edge of a town. After he died people were increasingly drawn to the towns for employment and safety, the friars followed, and the light that Francis had shone around the gardens and fields, up at the hills and into the skies, lost its strength, except in the eyes of the great Italian painters inspired by it and among the pockets of friars in the Marches of Ancona, who remained steadfastly faithful to his vision of the world, which they preserved in *The Little Flowers*. However fanciful some of its stories became from decades of retelling, they capture the spirit of Francis so well because they were originally gleaned from some of his most devout and devoted companions – Leo, Masseo, Giles and Clare.

In the following centuries men valued and enjoyed the resources of their gardens, fields, rivers and woods, living off the income from them and with little need to dip into capital. But as the twentieth century progressed it became clear that the world's population was not tapping its natural capital but plundering it irreparably. New watchmen – naturalists, scientists, historians and artists – began to sound the alarm from our farmlands, the rain forests, the African plains and the oceans. We were rapidly destroying our landscapes, whole populations of different species and even the layer of ozone on which our survival depended. It was then that Professor Lynn White of California University proposed that Francis should be elected patron saint of ecologists.

For twenty years the voice of reason failed to halt the tide of commercial and industrial ruination, and its spokesmen recognized that their combined rational, economic, aesthetic and emotional arguments were simply not enough; the professor was right, they needed the additional force of moral and spiritual conviction. In 1986 they therefore convened a conference and retreat for leaders of the Buddhist, Christian, Hindu, Jewish and Muslim faiths from all over the world. It was held at the Basilica of St. Francis in Assisi.

19

New Directions

1216–1219

After Innocent III's death everyone was anxious to fill the power vacuum quickly. There were up to fifty cardinals at any one time, and now twenty hurried to Perugia for a hasty election – just enough to make up the quorum.

The townspeople put pressure on the cardinals by drastically restricting the food and drink delivered to the bishop's palace in the cathedral cloister; and to avoid protracted wrangling the cardinals appointed two of their number – Guido, Bishop of Palestrina and Ugolino, Bishop of Ostia – to recommend a candidate. Well aware that Ugolino was not only strong-minded but irascible, Cardinal Palestrina did not oppose his colleague's proposal – Cardinal Cencio Savelli. It was all over in two days.

The new pope took the name Honorius III. Although now well over seventy he was still clearheaded and highly respected; as one of Innocent's closest confidants his coronation and resumption of business were seamless. He was quick to confirm the summons of the Fifth Crusade and affirm his authority over the sovereigns of Europe. In this he was helped by two strokes of luck, for the most defiant monarch, King John of England, very shortly died, while the most dangerous, young Frederick II of Germany, once his protégé in Sicily, undertook to keep the German and Sicilian thrones separate and promised to make his son, the King of Sicily, the pope's ward.

Honorius had spent much of his career perfecting an inventory of the church's possessions; now he devoted himself to its reforms, including the review of its religious orders. From their first meeting in 1209 Honorius had been extremely benevolent toward Francis and much admired the way in which he both preached and practiced the gospel; although forty years older, he was to outlive Francis.

Honorius's well-known sympathy may account for a Franciscan tradition both mysterious and controversial. Fifty years after Francis died three groups of friars suddenly gave legal testimony to an event which had occurred within a fortnight of Honorius's election. They claimed that a vision had prompted Francis to beg the new pope to grant a full indulgence for their sins to any penitents visiting Santa Maria degli Angeli. Surprised but not entirely dismissive, Honorius asked for how long this dispensation should last . . . one year . . . three years . . . seven . . . ?

When Francis demurred to each of these suggestions the pope finally agreed to an open-ended grant. The cardinals were shocked and antagonized by his decision because it dramatically devalued plenary indulgences, previously reserved exclusively for making a pilgrimage to Jerusalem, Rome or Santiago de Compostela, or as an inducement to join a crusade. Despite their protests Honorius refused to renege on his promise or impose an expiry date on the indulgence but in the end he stipulated that it should only apply for twenty-four hours each year, from vespers on August 2 – the anniversary of Santa Maria's consecration – until the same time next day. When the pope wondered if Francis wished to have this confirmed in writing, his reply was unequivocal.

"Your word is sufficient. This is God's work; let the Virgin Mary be the document, Christ the notary and the angels witnesses."[1]

His request granted, Francis returned to the Porziuncula where he told Masseo, Leo and his other closest companions that they must keep the indulgence a secret until God gave them a sign.

The first problem about this story is that not one of the early biographers refers to it, nor does *The Little Flowers*, nor do any contemporary documents in papal or other archives. Another is that Francis always, and vehemently, opposed privileges for himself, his order or anything to do with them. Third, it was only after the friars notarized their accounts of the episode, in 1277, at the request of the head of their order who later became pope, that pilgrims began to visit Santa Maria in any great numbers, in contrast to the large crowds who had converged every year on Francis's tomb. Since the Basilica was occupied by the faction of friars who took a relaxed view of poverty, the revelation of the indulgence by the faction at the Porziuncula who observed their vows more strictly, drew a mass of new pilgrims to the birthplace of the order, so balancing the books between them.

If Francis did ask for and receive the indulgence, Honorius granted Dominic his wish, too. In December 1216 the pope issued a privilege confirming the approval of de Guzman's order of little more than a dozen men; it was signed by Ugolino and seventeen other cardinals. Dominic had made an attempt to join forces with Francis, even offering to serve under him, but although the Spaniard had given up ownership of all land and property, he had not yet renounced the order's regular income or its observance of an Augustinian rule; Francis therefore felt he must decline the generous suggestion.

A few years later, just before he died, Dominic persuaded his Order of Preachers to abandon their dress as canons and the title of abbey for their houses – both Augustinian – and also to relinquish their revenues. Conversely the Franciscans began to adopt some of the measures devised by the Dominicans to strengthen their administration. Together the two orders – one famous for its service and prayer, the other for its teaching and preaching – became known as the mendicant friars. They were, in their early years, the most distinctive and original force for good in medieval Europe.

Besides Francis and Dominic, a third petitioner also won Honorius's favor. The new pope duly consecrated Jacques de Vitry as Bishop of Acre, and the Curia accepted his request that his protégées, the Béguines, be given recognition. Nevertheless, de Vitry's account of the papal court, in a letter he wrote at the end of the year, was not flattering – unlike his opinion of Francis and his order:

> I saw much that entirely dissatisfied me: all were so taken up with their temporal affairs, political and legal, that it was almost impossible to discuss anything spiritual.
>
> In the midst of this corruption I nonetheless derived immense consolation from discovering a great many men and women who have renounced all their possessions for the love of Christ – Friars Minor and Sisters Minor they are called. . . . I am convinced the Lord has

> decided to use them to save souls and put to shame our prelates who, like dumb dogs, refuse to bark.[2]

The conservative majority of the cardinals were still suspicious of zealous groups among the laity, especially women, seeking formal status from the pope. Honorius therefore had to feel his way carefully in dealing with these cases during the first months of his regime. Nevertheless in early 1217 he felt sufficiently confident to send his most influential colleague, Ugolino, to Florence as his legate.

*

Ugolino's territory comprised the whole of Northern Italy – from the Duchy of Spoleto through Tuscany and the Marches, up to Lombardy and Venice. There he was to preach the coming crusade, keep an eye on the Germans and enforce the decrees of the Lateran Council.

Ugolino was perfectly qualified for the task. Born in about 1170, he had been educated in Paris and Bologna, where he had excelled in Theology and Canon Law. As soon as Innocent was elected pope he had made his nephew a cardinal deacon at the age of twenty-eight, and sent him to southern Italy as his legate, where he evinced qualities of steel in handling the German emperors and their envoys. He was promoted Bishop of Ostia in 1206. A man of stature, both intellectually and physically, he was handsome and robust, energetic and eloquent; yet he was prone to sudden changes of mood and shot through with contradictions. When his anger flared up the dignified prelate would suddenly break into a flow of bad language; he could only cure himself, he said, by wearing a silver locket around his neck, given him by Bishop de Vitry, which contained one of Marie d'Oignies's fingers. A man of formidable presence on state occasions, he was reduced to tears when he saw the friars eating and sleeping on the ground like animals.

One of his main duties was to take over, on behalf of the pope, a number of powers previously exercised by the bishops. These included hearing appeals against rulings given in episcopal courts and the supervision of religious houses in his province.

Ugolino's strength of character served him well in confronting Bishop Guido of Assisi on both these issues. However astutely he had handled his relations with the Lateran in the past, Guido was anything but subtle in dealing with his fellow prelates and the local priesthood, which left him highly exposed to litigation. He was now engaged simultaneously in three lawsuits. One had been brought by the Cruciger knights, in the leper hospital next to the Porziuncula, for seizing their wine; another with the abbot and monks of San Benedetto over the management of their churches and his demands for a share of their funeral fees; and the third by the canons of San Rufino in defense of their right to ordain without his consent and rejecting his assertion that their tithes should be his. Guido had been violently aggressive and in each case Ugolino found against him, obliging him to settle; more than once Honorius himself had intervened.

It was a tragedy that a man so sensitive to the deeper workings of the spirit, and always so robust in his support of Francis and Clare should forfeit the legate's good opinion at this critical moment, for Ugolino's second main objective was to review and where necessary reform all the religious communities for which he was responsible as legate – among them Santa Maria degli Angeli and San Damiano.

The cardinal was still unhappy about the Rule devised by Francis and suspected, quite rightly, that he had a disturbing contempt for all forms of planning, which seemed a perilous attitude when his order was growing so fast. The success of Clare's irregular community worried him even more and he could see no reason to treat it any differently from all the other women's houses in his province. His intentions for them were unequivocal: to ensure their orthodoxy, to find endowment for their living costs, and to protect by enclosure their virginity as future brides of Christ. It looked as though a clash with both Guido's protégés was inevitable.

Ugolino was no stranger to the area round Assisi. As a young man he had been associated with two strict offshoots of the Benedictines – the Cistercians and the more austere Camaldolensians. The latter owned the abbey of San Silvestro on the far slopes of Mt. Subasio. While still a deacon Ugolino had been abbot there; its lovely Romanesque chapel, crumbling but still roofed, survives among the oaks, hornbeams and purple orchids of the steep secluded woodland. He had come to know Abbot Maccabeo at San Benedetto but had left to take up his other appointments long before Francis and Clare had made their names in Umbria. Now, in 1217, his relations with them were to become one of the most fascinating, complex, and formative influences on the evolution of the Franciscan movement.

*

During Ugolino's first two years as legate in Florence Francis did everything he could to honor his vow of obedience by observing the Lateran decrees, however much this meant suppressing his natural inclinations.

He took to heart Bishop Guido's earlier caution that he and his brothers must not become an excessive burden on others, and now that they numbered well over a thousand advised them how to set about making their own shelters and houses instead of always relying on a lazaret, priest or good Samaritan to put them up. When they were offered some land near Siena he wrote and told his brothers that they must ask the bishop's permission before building.

He went on, "Let them dig a ditch around the property and, instead of a wall, plant a hedge along it as a sign of poverty and humility. They should then construct poor houses of wood and plaster, and cells where they can pray.

"Let them also put up chapels, not big churches under the pretext of preaching to the people, because it gives a better example of humility to preach in larger ones elsewhere."[3]

Francis often made use of some natural feature like a cave when he founded a hermitage. Whatever the building it should be small—bricks, stone and tiles were forbidden. He discouraged his brothers from gathering in any number, knowing it would distract them from their prayers and work, and place a burden on the local community.

Francis chose or frequented about twenty-five of these houses, many of them perched high on a mountain or cliff, affording spectacular views, and evoking a sense of silent flight between earth and heaven, lifting the friars from the turmoil and squalor of their days among the wretched and dying to the tranquillity essential for their prayers. Centuries later these first hermitages still induce an almost narcotic sensation of detachment and peace.

Francis's second new measure, made possible by the rising number of priests in his order, was the adoption of the Office, by which the hierarchy set great store. It entailed saying seven Hours or services spread through each day: Matins, Prime, Terce, Sext, None, Vespers and Compline. Brothers were obliged to attend each of them in the chapel or, if traveling, to read them "with moving eyes and lips." The Office ordered the friars' lives like a devotional metronome, providing a rhythm of appropriate prayer. Prime opens with a hymn:

> *Now that the daylight fills the sky,*
> *We lift our hearts to God most high.*

Francis liked Compline, the last, to be said as soon as the light went:

> *The Lord Almighty grant us a quiet night and a perfect end. . . . Brethren, be sober, be vigilant, because your adversary the devil, as a roaring lion, walketh about, seeking whom he may devour; whom resist, steadfast in the faith.*

At the end of the service the brothers drew their hoods over their heads, left the candlelit chapel and made their way in the dark toward their cells.

Like the days, each week had its pattern as the year had its seasons. Wednesday, commemorating the first day of Lent, and Friday, the day of the Crucifixion appointed for confessions, were fast days. Sunday, beginning with the celebration of the Mass, was a feast day. Advent welcomed each new year which, for the Franciscans, was marked by four beacons – Christmas, at the winter solstice; Easter, in the spring; the first chapter at Pentecost which fell, fifty days after Easter, in early summer; and the second chapter on the Feast of St. Michael the Archangel – the leader of the heavenly armies – at the end of September.

As said by the friars, the Hours were not a mere repetitive ritual. For one thing their psalms, readings and prayers rotated from day to day and with the devotional seasons; all the 150 psalms had been said by the end of each week and the entire Bible every twelve months. Francis also composed his own prayers, psalms and antiphons for each of the seven services in a cycle he called *The Office of the Passion*, which he told his brothers to read, learn by heart, say on specified days and pass on to others. It represents about twenty percent of his writings (some of which have been lost). Most were dictated, with extreme care, to Leo. He included 150 quotations from twenty books in the Old Testament, and 280 from over twenty in the New; scholars are amazed not only by the power of his memory but the faultless spiritual and literary judgment with which he wove the phrases into flowing canticles.

He still set his face against possessions but from now on he allowed a few communal books to circulate – Testaments, psalters, missals for the Mass and breviaries containing the Hours. Dominican books of this kind were large and for study, Franciscan versions often tiny, no taller than a finger, for tucking into the sleeve on a journey. One turned up at the Carceri recently, so small that it had slipped through a crack in the boards and lain there for several hundred years.

Shortly before the Pentecost chapter in May 1217 Francis screwed himself up to accept a third innovation. It is often claimed that no leader can maintain personal relations with every member of a group that numbers more than a thousand; should it grow larger his or her control must be replaced by a chain of command if it is to remain effective. In the face of necessity Francis agreed, at what became the friars' first General Chapter, that his brotherhood should be divided into twelve geographical provinces, each under the care of an elected minister. Eight of the provinces were in Italy, the other four beyond the Alps. It meant that he could no longer accept each new brother into the order himself, and that many of the friars would always remain strangers to him and each other; inevitably the majority would no longer experience the charisma of his personal example and so the force of his simple Rule would be weakened; increasingly he found himself addressed as Minister General, and referred to as Father rather than Brother.

The General Chapter also approved another fundamental innovation encouraged by Honorius; the friars would put their growing numbers to good use by establishing missions abroad. One party asked to go to Spain, where a few brothers had already settled, and more adventurous expeditions volunteered for Germany, Hungary and Outremer – the coastal regions of the Levant.

Usually down to earth in dealing with the daily chores of life Francis was otherwise still a Utopian dreamer; to prepare for the morrow was presumptuous. As a result none of the sixty brothers who left for Germany could speak its language. When offered food or a bed they learned to say "*Ja*," but gave the same answer when asked if they were heretics. In Hungary the shepherds set their dogs on these curious ash-gray figures speaking gibberish; the villagers met them with pitchforks and stones until they offered some of their simple clothing in return for food and shelter. To avoid starvation one brother had to remake his breeches fifteen times.

The mission to Outremer – known in the order as Syria – was entrusted to the most dynamic and gifted of the younger lay brothers, Elias. His background is as obscure as his future was dazzling. He had possibly been a schoolmaster, had read law at Bologna, and was versed in both science and the arts. At the end of the chapter he and a few companions took a ship for Acre.

Francis decided that he, too, would lead a mission abroad, choosing France; taking Pacifico, the former King of Verse, and leaving Peter of Catanio at the Porziuncula as his vicar or deputy, he headed north and stopped in Florence to pay his respects to the legate.

Although they did not know each other well, Ugolino was extremely friendly and most interested in the events of the recent chapter; but he expressed serious anxiety about Francis's decision to leave Italy. He urged him to return to Assisi at once, saying that whereas he and the pope supported everything he was doing, many of the Curia were ill-disposed to him. The uncertain status of his order still rankled, quite apart from the fact that Clare possessed no authorized rule, while the phenomenal growth of his lay penitents was resented by many parish priests and communes. If he remained in Italy his supporters in the Curia, like Cardinal Brancaleone, could help him far better.

In any case the friars belonged in Italy. "Why do you want to put their lives at risk by sending them to these outlandish places?" Ugolino asked. Francis was clearly shocked.

"My Lord, do you really think and believe that God chose the friars purely for the benefit of these provinces? I must tell you in truth he sent them for the benefit, and the salvation of souls, of men throughout the world – not only in the lands of the faithful but of the infidel too."[4]

Each took the other's frankness in good part though as yet, according to Thomas of Celano, "they were not joined in that extraordinary familiarity" which later sealed their friendship and affection.

After their meeting Francis returned to Assisi while Pacifico led the mission to France, but very soon he and his companions were mistaken for heretics – Waldensians or Albigensians – and hauled before the bishops and theologians in Paris. The brothers produced a copy of their Rule to demonstrate their orthodoxy but as they lacked a mandate to preach in France the prelates wrote to Honorius for instructions. His answer took some time to arrive.

No two writers agree about the details of the early General Chapters and the missions they sent out, but a Dominican source suggests that in Pentecost 1218 two thousand friars turned up – a dizzying number for Francis to contemplate. It was decided that Benedetto of Arezzo should leave for Greece, and Giles and Eletto sail for Tunis. There Eletto, a delicate but extremely brave young man, was martyred; refusing to let Giles die too, the local Christians sent him home. Meanwhile at the other end of the Mediterranean the Fifth Crusade, initiated by Innocent and adopted enthusiastically by Honorius, was assembling at Acre.

*

As the second order steadily grew during the years 1217 and 1218 Clare valued her close connection with Francis and his brothers more highly than ever.

However uncanonical, the association supplied her and her sisters not only with their worldly needs but also their spiritual lifeblood. A legend was passed down among the friars in the Marches, where Francis and Clare were specially venerated, that he had once invited her and a sister to a memorable meal at Santa Maria; during it the night sky above them flared with heavenly light. Although there is no factual record that Clare ever did visit the Porziuncula, Francis at first went regularly to San Damiano. Clare writes in her *Testament* that he was not content to encourage the sisters with his words and example but also gave them "many writings." On at least five occasions he recommended new sisters to Clare, one of whom she only accepted with great reluctance and the girl soon left. Philip and the other brothers also continued to support her.

She had not plunged into the religious life either as an escape or as a career but as an adventure, which she expected to find among the hovels and hospitals around Assisi. When it began to dawn on her that the authorities might prefer her to remain in San Damiano she discovered her adventure within the walls of its chapel and oratory instead.

The sisters, like the friars, observed the Office, but said rather than sang it; similarly those who could not read said Our Fathers and Praises. The implications of the Crucifixion meant so much to Clare that she paid special attention to Sext at midday – the hour when Christ was placed on the cross; she regularly used Francis's *Office of the Passion*; and, according to her biographer, "frequently prayed the Prayer of the Five Wounds of the Lord." Her focus on the profound grief and the acute pain of Christ's dying hours often left her in tears, but drew her further and further into the dimensions of the spirit. Two of the sisters referred to this in much the same terms. "Sometimes after praying her face appeared more luminous than usual and the words emerging from her mouth were marked by extraordinary sweetness."[5]

Her exaltation and calm were infectious, constantly strengthening the faith of her companions and sometimes physically healing them. One episode graphically illustrates both her remarkable gifts and the close relationship between the friars and their sisters. When Brother Stephen was thought to have gone mad, Francis sent him to Clare in the belief that she could help him.

Her biographer writes, "She made the sign of the cross over Stephen and then she let him sleep for a short time in the oratory where she usually prayed. When he woke up he was healthy, and returned to Francis cured of his insanity."[6]

One of the sisters testifying to this added that, after Stephen came to, Clare gave him something to eat. Thomas of Celano probably condensed the whole process of recovery, for if Stephen was suffering from a nervous or psychological collapse brought on by long vigils and excessive fasting, a woman with Clare's common sense, understanding and touch, given time, would have known very well how to treat him.

Her growing authority and prestige had already traveled well beyond Assisi and Perugia. De Vitry wrote in a letter before he left for Syria that she and her sisters "will accept nothing, and live entirely by manual labor. They are all greatly distressed because they are excessively esteemed by the clergy and laity." According to De Vitry, Pope Honorius and his cardinals shared this admiration. As word of San Damiano spread, Clare was asked to open or take over houses in Spello and Spoleto. Almost simultaneously Cardinal Ugolino wrote to Honorius for instructions because he had been approached with offers for land on which to build houses for holy women in Siena, Lucca and at Monticelli near Florence; the Bishop of Perugia reported a similar offer. Honorius gave his assent for all four projects in consideration of the fact that the women were committing themselves to poverty – and before long the houses became associated with Clare by name. She sent her sister Agnes to be abbess at Monticelli.

The apparently irresistible growth of Clare's and other women's movements decided Ugolino that he could wait no longer to impose his new rule – known as his *Constitutions* – on all their communities in his province, regardless of their origins, lifestyles or virtues. His first move was a sign of things to come. His *Constitutions* required that each convent should have a Visitor or informal inspector attached to it. At the end of 1218 he appointed his chaplain, Ambrose, in this role to San Damiano; he was a Cistercian.

*

The rapid growth of Francis's third order (then still known as Brothers and Sisters of Penance) was peculiarly unpredictable because infectious waves of popular good seldom surge through society with the frequency and speed of unrest and violence.

It is impossible to estimate the numbers of lay penitents who clustered around the houses of the friars and Poor Clares, anxious to devote themselves to prayer and charity but unable to abandon entirely their families and work, for no records were kept. In fact the only documents that survive from the first years of the movement are two versions of *A Letter to the Faithful* dictated by Francis – today "the faithful" are assumed to be his tertiaries. Typically the letters were more concerned with inspiring devotion to God than laying down rigid conditions of membership. Francis's main concerns in them were these: reverence for the church, expressed through confession, attendance at Mass and respect for the clergy; love of God and the penitents' neighbors and enemies; giving alms and making bequests to the poor; restraint in eating and drinking; the avoidance of vice. Finally he urged refusal to obey any order which entailed committing a sin or a crime, offering absolution for such disobedience.

The second letter ends with a gruesome evocation of a defiant figure who has left all his goods to his family and friends but refuses to repent and make amends on his deathbed; as soon as he stops breathing the devil snatches his soul.

There are only a few scattered anecdotes about the lives of the earliest tertiaries who adopted simple gray habits tied by a cord with a single knot. One of them, Lucchesio da Siena, had known Francis when they were both young and had then grown rich by cornering the grain market, from which he made exorbitant profits until civil war drove him and his wife, Buonadonna, to Poggibonsi. There they took pity on the victims of the fighting and distributed everything they owned to the worst hit. After that Lucchesio slaved for the rest of his life to pay for medicines and food which he took around to the sick on his donkey.

Some of the earliest tertiaries, born or married into positions of privilege and wealth, made the most significant contributions to Francis's later life and work. Increasingly he found himself returning to Mt. La Verna in Tuscany, given him by Orlando of Chiusi. Its remoteness, its peace, the beauty of the views from its wooded summit and the company of its birds unfailingly helped recharge his spiritual energy.

He drew similar strength and inspiration from the sanctuary given to the friars by Giovanni di Velita on his farmlands at Greccio. Here many of the country people and inhabitants of the small town – especially the women – took the habit and although they continued to live at home led the lives of penitents. On feasts and holy days they would come and stand outside the friary to sing alternate verses of the psalms and canticles with the brothers. Among the animals on the farms he never shed his distaste for pigs and goats, or lost his soft spot for young sheep – feelings possibly derived from the scriptures. After saving the life of yet another lamb he could think of no better home for it than with Giacoma de Settesoli – Brother Giacoma – now deeply devoted to his Third Order. The lamb took to following her about and nudging her when it was time to go to Mass.

Francis's *Letter to the Faithful* led Giacoma to make an important decision. Ever since the death of her husband she had been fighting a major lawsuit against Innocent III and his successor to protect the interests of her two sons. Now, in May 1217, out of respect for the church, she dropped it. Her gesture was a significant straw in the wind. Ugolino shrewdly spotted that the Franciscans' devotional network could be harnessed to the church's temporal ends. Before long his legal brain was drafting a form of commitment for the tertiaries which, if adopted, would produce historic results. In essence it would give worldly force to the ideals set out in Francis's letters. Many of its provisions echoed Francis's Rule for his friars, but four created a potent political weapon.

The first required every tertiary to make a will within three months of joining the order – with the presumption that the greater part of an estate would be left to the poor or the church but not to the testator's nearest and dearest, while in the absence of a will the church would inherit the lot. The second forbade the taking of all oaths, except to God and the pope. The third was a veto on carrying arms – for their use was bound to lead to the commission of a crime or a sin. Finally, by his or her oath to the pope, a member became subject only to canon law and was immune from a secular action. The genius of this concept was that it could gradually paralyse the sinews running down through the whole feudal system from the emperor to the lowest tenant or serf, for it allowed men, at every level of society, to refuse to fight for a superior and to do so with impunity. It would inhibit, equally, the newly created republican communes from abusing their authority to mobilize a militia and wage war unreasonably.

It naturally took time, while the order of penitents spread from city to city and country to country, for the political nerve gas to make itself felt. Nevertheless within thirty years it helped to put an end to the Hohenstaufen menace.

*

The death of Innocent was a watershed in the lives of Francis and his order although this did not become apparent until 1219 when as many as three thousand friars are said to have made their way to Assisi for the Pentecost chapter. They camped in the woods around the Porziuncula's little chapel and were fed by the generosity of the local population. If there was a superficial resemblance in their appearance – with their tonsures, coarse tunics, knotted ropes and bare feet – they were now utterly disparate at heart. Quite apart from any national characteristics their abilities, education, skills, ambitions and understanding of their vocation were more varied than ever.

Most were attracted by Francis's compassionate ideals, but few had now undergone his stringent scrutiny before taking their vows. As a result some had been able to join the order because they preferred its companionship to struggling through life on their own. Others were eager to bask in the goodwill with which the friars were so often greeted. There were also growing numbers of priests and scholars who had observed the pope's and Ugolino's special regard for the order and joined it as a stepping stone to preferment; they considered their learning an automatic passport to authority or privilege, and already a disproportionate number had been elected provincial ministers.

Peter of Staccia, who held the chair of Jurisprudence at Bologna, the great law school and oldest medieval university in Europe, was now minister for the province. Francis had agreed he might supervise a number of brothers who wanted to study the Bible and liturgy. But Peter had gone further; as if he were still a secular he had accepted a house in which his pupils could live and work. Francis had to rebuke him and tell him to close it. And when one of the novices asked if Francis would sanction his possession of a psalter he refused, saying that a friar's duty was to strive in the world and, if necessary, to die like the Christian paladins, Roland and Oliver; it was not to seek honor by simply knowing and preaching about the courage and virtues of others.

The flood of new colleagues, most of them strangers and many with an agenda quite alien to his own, prompted Francis to confide in Leo an example of the way in which a true friar should welcome shame.

"Imagine the brothers invite me to preach in chapter and I speak as the Holy Spirit teaches me. And suppose that at the end they say to me, 'You aren't eloquent, you are too simple, we are ashamed to have you as our superior' – and they throw me out.

"It seems to me I am not a true Friar Minor if I don't rejoice as much when they disparage and reject me as I do when they honor and respect me."[7]

Although Francis prayed for guidance before any big occasion, at the event itself he always relied on divine inspiration. The pope and his legate, by contrast, had orchestrated meticulous preparations for the General Chapter of 1219, well aware that the friars were planning new missions abroad, despite the setbacks in France, Germany and Hungary. Honorius had already stressed publicly his support for such missions and with typical efficiency Ugolino arranged that the brothers who now pledged to make good the foreign disasters should carry papal credentials.

The chapter also blazed with fresh fervor to preach among the Saracens, for the Fifth Crusade had run up against bitter and bloody resistance. Six brothers were therefore commissioned to go to Morocco in the hope of converting the Miramolino, while Francis announced he would set off to join the crusaders. It was one of the most fateful decisions of his life, the culmination of all his previous, frustrated, efforts to resolve the chronic conflicts with the Muslims and perhaps an attempt to emulate the endeavors of the greatest Christian missionary of all, St. Paul.

On the other hand it was not rational. Many of the considerations discussed with Ugolino in Florence still applied, while his order was being bruised and stressed by many new pressures and strains – its continued expansion, the hierarchy's inexorable enforcement of the Lateran decretals, and the dissent among the ministers. Francis's decision to leave must have therefore been instinctive, an act of impulse or faith, which changed both him and his family, for better or for worse, irreversibly.

This time Ugolino encouraged him not only to go but to take with him his trusted lieutenant, Peter of Catanio, who had always deputized in his absence. The reason for the cardinal's *volte face* was quickly apparent. He persuaded Francis to leave the friars in the hands of two comparative newcomers. Nothing is known about Matthew of Narni, who was to take charge of the Porziuncula and admissions to the order. The same cannot be said of Gregory of Naples who was to keep an eye on the provinces; it is quite clear from his later career that he was clever, worldly, ambitious and sometimes cruel. It has been alleged that he was also Ugolino's nephew.

When the last prayers were said and Francis had given his friars – now more his sons than his brothers – a blessing, he watched them disperse like seeds on the wind, well aware he might never see any of them again. It was the end of a chapter in more senses than one.

Part III

Father

1219–1226

20

The Sultan of Egypt

1219–1220

Francis sailed for Acre in midsummer. Many of the friars wanted to go with him but the captain would accept no more than a dozen; it is said that Francis let a child choose them at random. Apart from Peter of Catanio they included Barbaro and Sabbatino of the original brothers, Leonardo the knight and Illuminato, who was to face almost certain death beside Francis not once but twice.

In Roman times Mediterranean ships had grown so large that the one in which St. Paul was wrecked off Malta carried 273 passengers as well as its cargo of grain. Now they were smaller – either galleys, propelled by banks of oars, or heavier sailing ships, fortified if necessary by wooden castles fore and aft. A brisk summer wind from the south can make a passage to Palestine extremely uncomfortable but the ship was never very far from land. On calm days, between saying the Hours, the friars could enjoy the companionship of cruising seabirds or gaze spellbound over the side to watch

The dancing dolphins with their tails divide
The glittering waves and cut the precious tide

like the Trojans of the *Aeneid.* Among the artists of Francis's day dolphins were the symbols of social love.

Both his official biographers, Thomas and St. Bonaventure, were convinced that Francis was sailing to Outremer in search of martyrdom, the one certain way in which he could share the cost of Christ's passion and make his contribution to human salvation; they present him as the doctrinaire paradigm for the age of crusade. However Francis, although always obedient to the church, was never driven by doctrine; like a good soldier he was prepared to lay down his life at any moment, either for Christ or his neighbor, but there was no point in wasting it unnecessarily. Until it became clear that his time had come he had a great deal to do. Quite apart from encouraging the growth and work of his order, he still hoped to make his pilgrimage to Jerusalem and above all to end the senseless bloodshed between Christians and Muslims.

Almost the whole of the Levantine coast, from Byzantium to Egypt, was now controlled by the Ayyubid dynasty, except for a few isolated states which the Christians had clung onto after the previous sultan, Saladin, had driven them out of Jerusalem. The knights, merchants, farmers and priests, who had settled these little kingdoms, which had included Jerusalem, were known collectively to the Arabs as Franks, after the French who dominated the early campaigns. One of their unique features was the creation of three military orders, the Knights Templar, raised to guard the temple of Solomon, the Knights Hospitallers and the Teutonic Knights – the last two originally formed to care for the wounded as well as fight. Each was a cross between a professional regiment and a religious order. In effect they were an expert standing army, exemplary in their courage, integrity and discipline, one of the few respectable features in the shaming saga of crusade.

Although the present sultan, Saladin's brother al-Adil, was now in his seventies, he had mobilized his empire against this latest crusade with his family's typical vigor and brilliance, denying the invaders any progress in Outremer. The Christians had therefore switched their attack to the Saracens' port and power base at Damietta in Egypt. The setback was a reminder of the Third Crusade, in which Richard Coeur de Lion and his allies had won little more than the right of pilgrims to enter the Holy City.

Richard had, however, captured Acre, which Francis and his friars were now approaching. It was an impressive sight, lying at the northern tip of a long sickle bay, its harbor sheltered by a hook of land and massive groins; above them rose fairytale battlements, castles and churches. The principal fighting powers had been allotted to different quarters of the town, while the Legate, the Patriarch, the Templars and the Hospitallers each had towers of their own on the ramparts. But although the quays were constantly busy with the arrival and departure of troopships and merchantmen, the city was now like a rock pool after the tide has gone out. The captains and kings were two hundred miles away on the Nile with their armies.

Francis soon found Elias with his fellow missionaries and avidly exchanged news with them. Then, anxious to be off to the battlefront, he went back to the port. This time he could only find a captain who would accept him and a single companion. He chose Illuminato and asked the others to follow as soon as they could. He was heading toward the outer edges of geographical certainty, for Europe then shared the northern hemisphere with Asia, China, India and the whole of Africa. The sources of the great river on which he was about to spend six months would remain wrapped in mystery for another six hundred years.

*

Francis's first sight of Africa was sand – the low dunes between which the waters of the Nile ended their three thousand-mile journey to the sea, just below Damietta.

Not far from Cairo the Nile divided, its arteries fanning out to form a triangle on the coast, with Alexandria in the west and Damietta, on one of the two main streams, in the east; each city was about 120 miles from the others. The whole delta was like a vast, flat, fertile oasis, watered by branches of the river and a network of canals. Extensively shaded by thousands of date palms, it was famous for its orange groves, orchards, vineyards and crops of millet and wheat.

Francis was warmly welcomed to the crusaders' headquarters by Bishop de Vitry, whose correspondence and subsequent *Historia Occidentalis* are invaluable records of the Fifth Crusade. Another account, equally precise, was kept by a German schoolmaster in charge of the Rhinelanders, Oliver of Paderborn, who became secretary to one of the two papal legates, Cardinal Pelagius Galvani. A third was compiled by a veteran crusader named Ernoul. Of course Arabs, too, kept their chronicles.

As the respected head of a successful new order, well known to the bishop, Francis moved freely about the allied lines and was privy to the

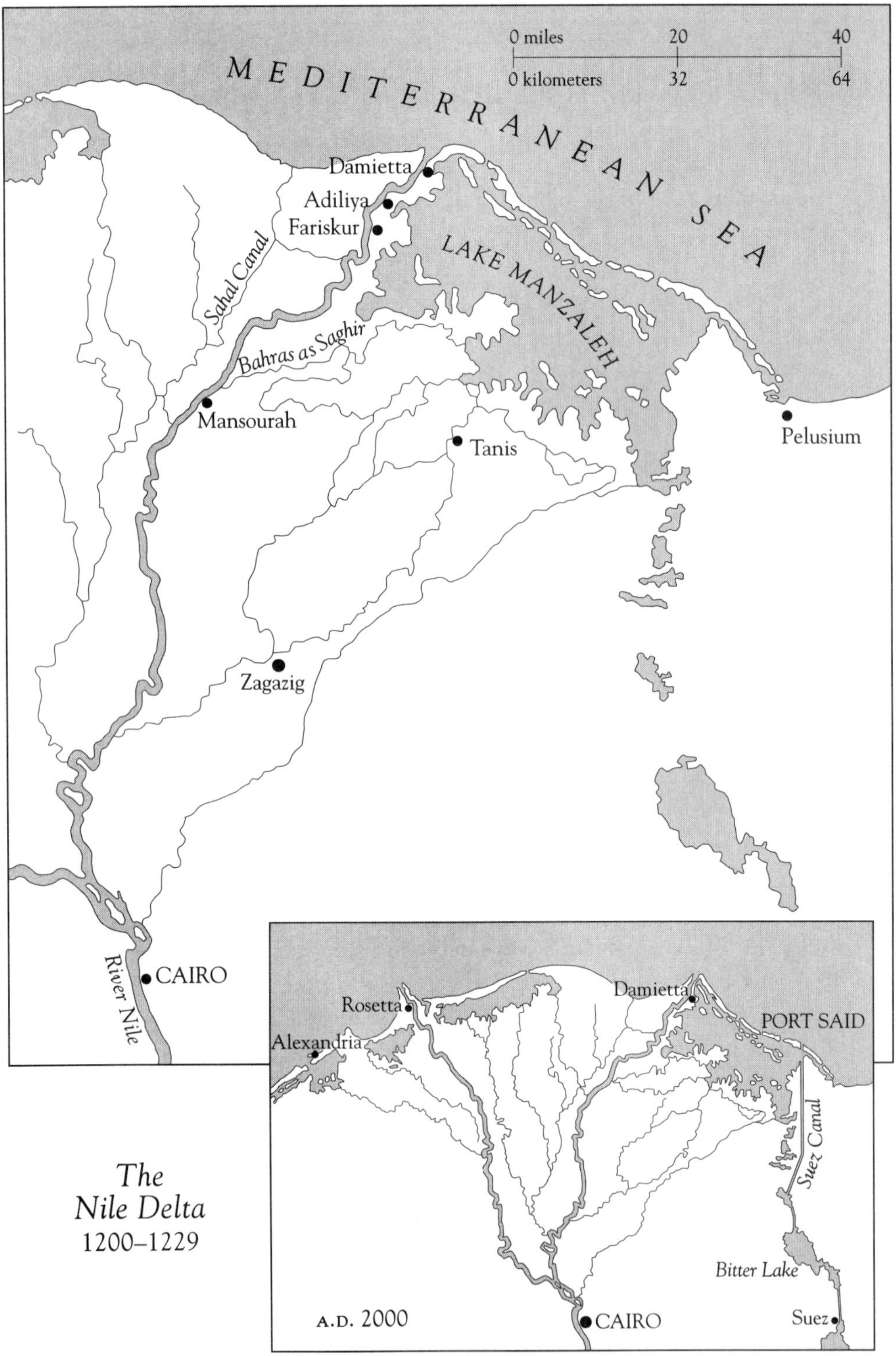

The Nile Delta
1200–1229

counsels of the high command. There he met one of the great heroes of his youth, John of Brienne, whose brother he had set out to serve in Apulia. After fighting in the Third and Fourth Crusades John had become, through his first marriage, King of Jerusalem. A devout man and formidable soldier, tall, tough and courageous, the commanders of the cosmopolitan forces assembled at Acre in the previous year had elected him their leader; they included Duke Leopold of Austria, the Kings of Hungary, Armenia and Cyprus, the Grand Masters of the three military orders of knights, and troops from a dozen other countries. The Earls of Arundel and Chester had reached Egypt but Lord Winchester had died in Acre on the way.

Francis had known nothing like the crusaders' camp which was on the west bank, opposite Damietta, since the great fairs in Champagne. The sights, sounds and smells were much the same – the pavilions and tents, with their pennants and flags, the din of armorers, blacksmiths, bugles and drums, the stink of wood smoke, cooking, horse dung and ordure – though this time the bedlam was set among tamarisks and fig trees, not half-timbered houses, temperatures were up in the nineties, and most of the tracks were no more than packed sand.

The traffic up and down them was almost continuous for the army numbered 40,000 men.* Of these a quarter were knights, squires, pages, mounted bowmen and Levantine mercenaries known as Turcopoles, who needed up to 20,000 horses, mules and donkeys to keep them in the field. In addition there were probably 5,000 well-paid sergeants, archers, engineers and miners. One observer described the 25,000 foot soldiers infesting the delta as "locusts." In all, this was the equivalent of three modern divisions.

But it was not all, for the crusade had gradually attracted another 20,000 sailors and boatmen, priests, doctors and nurses, grooms, husbandmen, merchants and cooks, pilgrims, sightseers and beggars – not to mention some of the knights' families and several shiploads of French and other prostitutes. Once or twice Saracens, stripping the fallen of their armor, uncovered the bodies of women.

When the crusaders had first landed on the delta in May 1218 Sultan

*The figures given in the pages that follow are best estimates only, drawn from the work of military historians. Like all medieval numbers they may well be exaggerated.

al-Adil had been taken by surprise but sent one of his three sons, al-Kamil, to throw the invaders back into the sea. As civilized and intelligent as the rest of his family, al-Kamil was also a resourceful soldier. Confident that Damietta could withstand the first full-scale assault, he set about raising an army in Cairo.

The port of Damietta stood on the east bank of the Nile two miles from the sea. It was suitably imposing for such a valuable center of trade – the maritime gateway of Egypt, once described as the Boulevard of Islam. Its frontage on the river was protected by the double ring of walls which circled the city with forty-two bastions. On the landward side there was a third wall, with twenty-two gates and a moat wide enough for a galley to patrol. Above the busy workshops, brimming warehouses and innumerable houses rose a hundred towers, large and small. Damietta's great mosque was one of the jewels of the Mediterranean.

At the start of the siege there were about 80,000 men, women and children inside the city, half of them its military garrison. Their defensive tactics were well rehearsed and they were amply stocked with supplies. Nevertheless they were thankful when al-Kamil arrived with 7,000 mounted men and 15,000 infantry, established a strongly fortified position on the east bank at Adiliya a few miles upstream, and built a watchtower. From this al-Kamil could exchange signals with Damietta and keep a close eye on the crusaders, who were still confined to the west bank of the river.

Both sides believed that the key to Damietta was a little island in the Nile linked to the town by a bridge of boats and heavy chains to block the passage of enemy ships. A tall fortified tower rose from the island, manned by four hundred soldiers and crossbowmen. The channel on the far side was unnavigable. The crusaders' repeated attempts to destroy the tower, by hurling 100-kilo rocks at it from their trebuchets and mangonels 150 meters away, failed. When King John's boats then approached with ladders and covering archers the scaling parties were driven off by a combination of the crossbowmen's powerful quarrels and Greek fire, a devastating compound of niter, naphtha and sulfur. However in August Oliver of Paderborn lashed together a pair of two-masted cogs, like half walnut shells, and at the top of their masts built a platform with a drawbridge, cladding his ingenious construction with leather to protect it from the Greek fire. A fresh attack was launched and despite its frenzied defense the tower fell.

To everyone's surprise Damietta – by now reinforced and restocked –

held firm, but the loss of the island broke the old sultan's heart and killed him, leaving al-Kamil as the Sultan of Egypt. He immediately unleashed a series of energetic amphibious operations to which King John responded in kind. New bridges were built, only to be captured or wrecked; if the river was blocked, either the barrage was destroyed by fire ships or a canal was dug around it; the fighting flickered and flamed with a vicious intensity.

Meanwhile the forces of nature began to take a hand. The heat of summer and autumn incubated plagues of flies; epidemics of disease and dysentery swept through the crusaders' camp; septicemia and gangrene raged among the wounded. November brought torrential rain and a fierce north wind which built up the sea and drove it inland; the flooded camp was littered with the corpses of fish, donkeys, horses and humans. Although the army had brought provisions for six months it was impossible always to keep the tens of thousands of men, women and horses supplied with adequate fresh water and food, especially through the winter months, and an outbreak of scurvy carried off ten thousand Christians.

When the friars came to recite Psalm 105 during the Office they must have wondered which side God was now on.

He turned their water into blood and he slaughtered their fish
And he increased the frogs in their country,
Even in the rooms of their kings;
He spoke and there were swarms of flies and mosquitoes in all their country.[1]

Perhaps the worst of the crusaders' disasters was that scurvy killed the wiser of the two papal legates but spared the more opinionated – Cardinal Pelagius, the Spaniard, whose arrogance and scarlet buskins had provoked such hostility and ridicule in Constantinople. Overweening and impatient, he began to dispute the military command with King John and, in February, hectored him into advancing his weakened force up the west bank.

This time the cardinal was in luck, because al-Kamil had discovered a conspiracy among his emirs and had quickly retreated about forty miles to Ashmun where he was joined and reinforced by his brother al-Mu'azzam, now Sultan of Syria and Palestine. In less than a month al-Kamil was back in a fortified position at Fariskur, only about six miles from Damietta, but by then King John had his troops across on the east bank. He kept them entrenched around the walls of the city like a steel noose which he never relaxed. In the spring and early summer heat, the fighting rose to a new pitch of ferocity inflicting terrible losses on both armies. Sometimes hundreds or even thousands of men died from wounds, burns or drowning in a single engagement, which might last for a few hours or several days.

By the time Francis arrived there was a lull, but talking to the sick and wounded while he nursed them, and witnessing daily disputes between King John and Pelagius, he quickly sensed a crisis was looming inside the crusaders' camp.

*

It was not long in erupting.

A lifetime of making war had taught King John that blockade, propaganda and patience cost far fewer lives in a siege than a series of reckless assaults. He also knew that cavalry charges, so effective on firm ground in open country, could easily founder in the present conditions. Here the sultan's quicksilver formations of foot soldiers and mounted archers could vanish at will or appear without warning. The king's strategy of persistent attrition was therefore supported by the majority of the military leaders.

On the other hand the rank and file of the army, desperate to get home, were on the brink of mutiny, accusing their superiors of cowardice and sloth. Pelagius, whose lust for action was as pronounced as his ignorance of warfare, took the men's part. Arrogating an authority which Pope Honorius had never intended, he ordered King John to launch an attack on the sultan's position at Fariskur.

Anguished by the prospect of disaster if the crusaders went into action so divided, Francis spent the night in prayer. Next morning he confided to Illuminato:

"The Lord showed me that if the battle takes place it will not go well with the Christians but if I tell them this I will be considered a fool. On the other hand if I remain silent I shan't escape my conscience."[2]

Illuminato's admirable response was that Francis should rate God's opinion more highly than men's, adding that being thought a fool had never worried him in the past. Francis therefore conveyed his misgivings to Pelagius, who dismissed them as he had all the other objections.

On August 29 the crusaders left half their forces investing

Damietta and pushed up the narrow strip of land on the east bank, between the Nile on their right and Lake Manzaleh on their left. As always the advance was led by a detachment of knights from the three military orders. A similar formation brought up the rear with King John; there he could quickly react if the Saracens broke out of Damietta to stab him in the back. Francis and Illuminato watched them leave.

When the vanguard reached the sultan's trenches and palisades outside Fariskur it encountered little opposition; after brief resistance the Saracens fled into the palm groves. Slowly, then faster, the crusaders gave chase through the fields and thickets, constantly confused and delayed by the spider's web of water channels. Suddenly, when they least expected it, al-Kamil sprang his trap; horsemen concealed in the plantations or behind mounds of ancient rubble tore into the Christian flanks. Unnerved, the Cypriot knights faltered, dispersed and turned back; their panic spread. Despite the courage of the Spanish knights, who closed ranks to bear the full brunt of the onslaught, the Christian army broke into chaotic retreat.

Francis, who had spent the time praying, twice sent Illuminato out for news; there was none; but on the third occasion he rushed back to warn Francis that the crusaders, in total disarray, were heading for camp with the Saracens hard on their heels. Nothing could save them from massacre.

Had it not been for the courage and skill of King John, with a cluster of knights from the military orders, Illuminato and Francis would have died in the carnage. As it was the tall figure of the seventy-year-old king, flanked by the Templars, each in his long white surcoat with a red cross on its left shoulder, bellowed his orders to check the stampede. Raising his great two-handed sword, he sliced it down through the head of the first Arab who flew at him. Disaster was averted.

Nobody knows the full number of casualties that day; Francis grieved for them all, but especially for the Spaniards who had fought so bravely, with hardly a survivor among them. Most historians agree that 5,000 crusaders died on the field; at least 1,000 were taken prisoner among whom the Saracens beheaded about 50 knights from each of the military orders. No doubt someone reminded Pelagius that his defeat had occurred on the anniversary of John the Baptist's Decollation.

While the army sought to recover from its worst reverse yet, Francis decided he could no longer delay his own attempt to end the interminable slaughter and misery. He therefore told Pelagius that he wished to go to the

Sultan, in the belief he could persuade him to embrace the Christian religion and abandon his resistance. Inevitably, and with some reason, Pelagius could see no hope of Francis succeeding in this, and refused to consider it. But Francis persisted, doubtless encouraged – in the light of his previous prediction – by King John and Bishop de Vitry. At last, with ill grace, Pelagius gave in.

*

Francis and Illuminato followed much the same route that the army had taken. As the sun rose there was no shade apart from the stands of palm trees and the occasional sycamore. Little moved except for the sheep, grazing on the coarse grass and clover, and parties of restless pelicans and flamingoes, which rose, circled and resettled on the salt lagoons of the lake.

Years afterward Illuminato told St. Bonaventure that as he and Francis had trudged toward the Saracen lines they had chanted "Though I walk through the valley of the shadow of death I will fear no evil, for thou art with me"; and that the sight of two lambs then prompted Francis to quote St. Matthew's Gospel. "I send you out as sheep in the midst of wolves; so be wise as serpents and innocent as doves . . . for men will flog you and drag you before governors and kings for my sake."

Thomas of Celano, Jacques de Vitry, the knight Ernoul and the early Franciscan chronicler, Jordan of Giano all agree that this is exactly what happened. Shortly afterward the two friars were seized by a Saracen patrol; able only to repeat the word "Sultan," when asked who they were and what they were up to, they were roughly beaten, chained and led to the nearest guard post. Briefly their lives hung by a thread for al-Kamil had recently offered the reward of a gold Bezant for every Christian head brought in.

A tone of wry condescension tinges the account of Francis's predicament given by the distinguished scholar Sir Steven Runciman, in his three-volume history of the Crusades.

> He had come to the East believing, as many other good and unwise persons before and after him had believed, that a peace mission can bring about peace. . . . The Muslim guards were suspicious at first but soon decided that anyone so simple, so gentle and so dirty must be mad, and treated him with the respect due to a man who had been

touched by God. He was taken to the sultan who was charmed by him and listened patiently to his appeal.[3]

At Fariskur al-Kamil opened their dialogue by asking Francis if he and his companion were messengers or simply wanted to become Muslims. When Francis replied they were the former, sent by God to save his soul, and that he therefore might like to summon his wise men to witness the event, the sultan showed himself every bit as open-minded as his reputation. He said he would immediately send for the learned doctors without whose presence he could never listen to Christians.

For several days they waited for the theologians in his elegant tented camp, easy to set up and strike but complete with the luxurious diversions in which he delighted. The scent of lilies and jasmine; the gleam of ivory, silver, glass goblets and exotic brass lamps in his personal quarters; the company of his monkeys, parrots and gazelles. Behind the scenes he kept his favorite concubines and, even more fiercely guarded, the coffers of his treasury, stuffed with silver, jewels and coins. Also set apart were his clerks, some Coptic Christians, others survivors of the Children's Crusade seven years before. Farther off, in the shade, stood a line of camels and his pickets of handsome horses.

The sultan held audience in an open space under canopies, with silk cushions strewn around him for the privileged. Here he entertained his emirs and gave them his fighting orders; here he did business with the merchants supplying his armies; and here he now introduced Francis to his holy men.*

They could scarcely believe the Christian's presumption when he repeated his purpose, still less al-Kamil's willingness to listen to him. They therefore arranged a trap. An ornate carpet with crosses woven into its design was laid out in front of the sultan, so that when Francis approached him he must either set foot on the crosses, dishonoring Christ, or would decline to, so insulting al-Kamil. Unsuspecting, Francis walked straight up to the sultan, but when reproached for sacrilege, he immediately replied he was guilty of no such thing. Christians carried Christ's cross in their hearts;

*An Arab source records that at this time Fakhr ad-Din al-Farsi, an Egyptian theologian and jurist who was also spiritual director and a counsellor of al-Kamil, had conversations with a Christian monk.[4]

he had merely trodden on the crosses of the thieves who had died with him – the only ones to which Muslims could lay claim.

After several more days during which Francis continued to plead for the sultan's conversion and an end to the fighting – according to a later source he had to fend off the advances of a beautiful whore sent to ensnare him – the learned doctors reached their unanimous conclusion: al-Kamil must have the friars beheaded immediately. Reflecting on their advice the Sultan recalled that a highly respected Jew, once bidden to pronounce on the relative merits of Judaism, Islam and Christianity, had murmured something about three gold rings which were virtually indistinguishable. He therefore decided that death would be a shabby reward for the friars' good intentions.

Spared execution, Francis made one further effort to win over al-Kamil. He suggested that he and the sultan's advisers should undergo an ordeal by fire to decide conclusively which of their two faiths was authentic. When this proposal was rejected he left his own offer open, on condition that if he emerged from the fire unharmed the sultan would convert to Christianity but, if he perished, his failure should be attributed to his sins and not to any lapse of his God: al-Kamil humanely brushed aside this proposition, too. Some orientalists see these challenges as deliberate echoes of a similar method for resolving an issue put to a group of Christians by Mohammed himself. In that instance it was the Christians who rejected the suggestion in favor of a less hazardous solution.

While al-Kamil had been listening to Francis, enchanted and impressed by his character, arguments and passion to save lives, he had been weighing up the strategic situation. A year before he had proffered the crusaders a tentative truce, and only a few weeks previously he and his brother, Sultan al-Mu'azzam, had agreed that rather than lose Damietta – so politically important and economically valuable – they would allow Christian pilgrims the right to visit Jerusalem and the other places holy to them, provided the Christian armies withdrew from Egypt. Al-Mu'azzam was already dismantling the fortifications of Jerusalem and several Palestinian cities to discourage the Franks from wanting to seize them as strong points.

Skillful questioning of the two friars and some of his prisoners had left al-Kamil in no doubt about the divisions in the crusaders' camp, and after his recent victory he would appear to be negotiating from strength if he were to repeat his offer of peace. Nevertheless he was considering making its terms even more attractive, for in reality he was losing the advantage. Casualties, disease and starvation had almost fatally weakened his garrison in Damietta. He also knew that the Nile, which flooded each year in September as a result of the seasonal rains in the mountains of Ethiopia, would soon begin to fall, exposing the city's defenses.

The sultan had shown himself ruthless in defense of his kingdom and had extended his very sharp claws to rake the crusaders as painfully as possible. Yet fundamentally he was just, civilized and a man of peace. Recognizing these qualities in Francis, and believing there must be others in the Christian camp who shared them, al-Kamil made his strategic decision – but kept it to himself.

He therefore simply told Francis that his conversion was out of the question since it would cost him both his throne and his life. However he would like to present him with what amounted to a prince's ransom of treasure for distribution as alms. When Francis politely declined this al-Kamil gave him instead a laissez-passer to the Holy Land. Then, in the knowledge that they would plead the cause of peace with Pelagius and King John, he sent the two friars back to the crusaders' lines with an escort.

As they took leave the sultan asked them to pray that before he died he would be shown the true faith.

*

Not long after Francis's visit, the sultan sent over a Frankish prisoner proposing a truce during which the sides might explore the possibility of peace. Pelagius agreed to a truce but declined to discuss peace.

Apart from reinforcements, September brought the swallows and swifts back from Europe together with a migration of pilgrims also eager to bask in the sun, and the reflected glory of following the cross. Of considerably more value to the crusade was the arrival of Francis's brothers from Assisi, and Elias with friars from his Syrian province, including Caesar, a new German brother. Bishop de Vitry had once compiled a survey of all the hospitals in France and, with his considerable staff of chaplains and clerks, had kept a close eye on the army's welfare. He particularly appreciated the brothers' expertise in treating the wounded and sick.

By now Francis was extremely unwell himself. He wore himself out with his nursing, preaching and prayer; he slept little; the poor food and water were destroying his physique. He had also contracted trachoma, a viral infection spread by flies, which chronically and painfully inflamed the underside of his eyelids. Nevertheless he never seemed to flag and remained as much a pied piper as he had been in Italy. Jacques de Vitry wrote a few weeks later:

> Sire Rainerio, the Prior of St Michael, has just joined the Friars Minor. . . . The founder of the order is called Francis; he is loved by God and venerated by all men. . . . Colin the Englishman, our clerk, has also entered his order along with two other companions of ours: Master Michael and Dom Matthew to whom I entrusted the parish of the Holy Cross . . . and I am having difficulty holding on to the chanter, Henry and a few others.[5]

In October the sultan decided the time had now come to show the cards he had been holding to his chest. He sent two captured knights with the generous offer he had worked out with his brother: the Ayyubids would cede the whole of Palestine – except for the land beyond Jordan – in return for the invaders' withdrawal from Egypt. King John, the French, the Germans and the English were immediately in favor of acceptance; Pelagius, the military orders and the Italians – each for their own reasons – were opposed to it.

While the so-called allies argued, a few emaciated inhabitants crept out from Damietta after dark and begged the crusaders for mercy. Aware of this the officer in command of the garrison sealed up every one of its gates. On November 2, desperate to bring relief to the city, al-Kamil sent a night raid downriver, but the Templars were quick to detect it. They killed several hundred Saracens and the next morning the heads of six were catapulted into the sultan's camp while their bodies were displayed across the city moat. Pelagius tersely rejected the peace offer.

For forty-eight hours there was little sign of life in Damietta except for the ceaseless circling of vultures and kites above its battlements. Previously the siege tactics – bombardment by trebuchets, assaults from scaling towers and undermining of the ramparts – had been persistently foiled by the defendants' sorties, cascades of Greek fire, and the sultan's diversionary attacks. But on November 4 King John sensed his hour had come. That night a dramatic thunderstorm with driving rain swamped the crusaders' circle of trenches around the city but did not quench the spirit of their assault parties. Scarcely an arrow was fired as they scaled the walls, captured a bastion and smashed or burned their way through the gates.

The scenes which met their eyes in the dawn were more macabre than they had ever expected or seen before – no less disturbing than the first sight of Auschwitz and Belsen to their liberators seven centuries later. Between the two inner rings of walls the earth was ridged with shallow graves which the heavy rains had washed open, exposing a gruesome chaos of disintegrating corpses. Inside the town victims of disease lay unburied and decomposing in the streets, many of them mutilated by rats and birds of prey. De Vitry calculated that of the 80,000 inhabitants and garrison at the start of the siege only 3,000 ghostly men, women and children remained alive; among these no more than 100 were strong enough to put up any kind of resistance.* A French historian says that in the first stunned hour the crusaders wandered through the streets in silence, with tears in their eyes.

Then a kind of hell broke loose, despite the efforts of those in charge. Jacques de Vitry collected all the children to protect them as their elders were beaten or raped before being sold off as slaves. Squadrons of knights attempted to secure in six houses the fabulous treasures discovered in the warehouses and homes of the merchants and emirs. Cardinal Pelagius had an armed cordon thrown around the famous mosque. Nevertheless so catastrophic were the consequences of the slow, strangulating siege, so frightful the atrocities and vandalism of its aftermath, and so protracted the bitter arguments over who should now control Damietta, that it took three months for the authorities to clean up the city and distribute the districts, buildings and booty.

Francis and his friars were given a building for their ministry; their preaching was as badly needed now among the Christians as it would ever be among the Saracens. In language more rhetorical than literal de Vitry wrote of the brothers:

> They are the designated defenders of the ramparts of Jerusalem, for day and night they devote themselves to praising God and preaching . . .

*It is estimated that the atom bomb dropped on the port of Hiroshima, Japan, in August 1945 also killed approximately 75,000 people.

> They know how to bear up under hunger, like wandering dogs. They are, as it were, the salt of the earth which preserves meat and does away with the decay of worms and stench of vices.[6]

The formal occupation of Damietta was celebrated at Candlemas, on February 2, 1220. By then the great mosque, with its lofty dome and handsome carved soffits supported by a forest of marble columns, had been converted into a Catholic cathedral – just as the Orthodox cathedral of Santa Sophia was turned into a mosque when the Turks took Constantinople two hundred years later.

The Papal Legate and the Patriarch of Jerusalem deployed the full repertoire of ecclesiastical and military ceremonial. Candles blazed on all four altars as a seemingly endless procession of prelates, priests, monks and friars, kings and princes, dukes, lords, knights and ladies together with the ranks of the men who had done the killing but survived with their lives, pressed up the aisles for the service of Thanksgiving. Those who were there, with Francis among them, never forgot the music, chanting and prayers of the Solemn Mass, nor the splendor of the robes, cloaks and armor, and the swaying crucifixes, banners and pikes, as the triumphant crusaders finally streamed out through the seven ornate porches into the sunlight.

Within forty years, after the Christians had lost, retaken and surrendered Damietta in yet another crusade, a new Muslim dynasty razed this glittering temptation to the ground.

Nearly eight hundred years later a courteous Franciscan, living in a dusty Cairo slum, doubted if any trace of the old city could still be found; but a Dominican, after a long hunt in his library, unearthed a French archaeological bulletin published in 1902 which contained a description of the great mosque's remains. Despite two world wars and a century of unprecedented urban development, they are still visible in a concrete suburb of modern Damietta, some way from the present course of the Nile.

The red brick ruins, surrounded by derelict tombs, are open to the sky. At their southern end an elaborate porch survives, with a row of small pointed window openings above a fine doorway; a capital carved with lotus leaves crowns a pillar beside the only other entrance. Within the relics of the walls the pavement on which Francis stood with his friends King John, Bishop de Vitry, Illuminato, and so many others, is now eight feet below the level of the cemetery and covered by a stagnant pool of green water.

Warblers sing from the bulrushes growing around its edge and flit up onto the last of the beams rotting on a few lonely columns. *Sic transit gloria . . .*

*

No record exists of where Francis was, or what he did, between the occupation of Damietta and his reappearance at Acre in the summer of 1220; it is the most intriguing gap in our knowledge of his life.

The economic solution of the mystery is that he remained in Egypt, continuing his pastoral work with the army. There was nothing significant to report about these months for the sultan had withdrawn up the Nile to regroup his forces, while most of the crusaders were too busy enjoying, or squabbling over, their spoils to pursue him.

The most tempting solution, adopted by many modern biographers, is that after the occupation of Damietta Francis sailed to Acre with at least one of his brothers and took advantage of al-Kamil's safe pass to the Holy Land, following in Christ's footsteps – from his birth in Bethlehem to his death at Golgotha – and so achieving his pilgrimage to Jerusalem. But had he done this Elias and his other companions in Syria would have known about it, and since the main drive of his life was the imitation of Christ, it would have featured prominently in the works of both Thomas of Celano and St. Bonaventure, yet neither mentions it.

The majority of modern writers do however think that in February Francis sailed back to Acre with King John who was disgusted that Pelagius had denied him sovereignty over Damietta. His respect for Francis, on the other hand, had steadily grown into deep admiration and friendship. He still had two checkered decades to live on in Outremer but eight years later he came to Francis's canonization in Italy, and just before he died he was received into the Third Order. At his own request he was buried in Assisi and his noble effigy, under a handsome marble canopy, reposes just inside the doors of the lower basilica.

Back in Acre Francis may have been too weak to make even the hundred-mile pilgrimage to Jerusalem. His physical health was now chronically damaged, and he could well have collapsed as he had done after his release from prison in Perugia, and later in Spain on his way to Morocco.

He had also undergone a succession of psychological experiences unpleasant enough to crack even a saint. The most obviously distressing were his daily confrontations with the casualties of fighting and disease, compounded by the infernal scenes in Damietta. At a deeper level he had failed to convert the sultan or mediate an end to the fighting. He had also observed in these attempts that the Muslim al-Kamil had demonstrated a greater humanity and desire for peace than his Christian counterpart, Pelagius. Finally, he had to come to terms with shocking news: while he had twice escaped almost certain death he learned that five of the six brothers he had seen off to Morocco had been martyred there in January. At first he and his companions took great pride in their courage, but before long he told his friars that they must not dwell on the virtue of others; they should concentrate on facing their own fears without flinching.

There is no evidence that men and women whose spiritual resources have evolved over years feel the impact of catastrophes less acutely than others – their initial pain and horror are probably just as hideous and costly. On the other hand the confusion, anger and depression which so often accompany trauma seem to dissolve in the context of prayer, which provides whatever is most needed for reparation and healing. As he had helped others in Egypt Francis now had to help himself in Syria.

His meditations during these lost months, combined with his curious gift of foresight, may have convinced him that the sacrifice he had so often anticipated would not be a swift, summary execution like Calvary but would resemble Christ's agony in the Garden of Gethsemene on the night of his arrest, though drawn out over years, not hours.

The herald of this coming ordeal was Stephen, the young friar Clare had helped get over his breakdown. One day in July he appeared at the door of the friary in Acre just as Francis and Peter were preparing to eat. Kneeling down with tears of relief at finding Francis alive, he confessed he had sailed to Syria without permission and blurted out the reason for his journey.

A rumor had reached the Porziuncula that Francis was dead. As a result many of the newer friars, who didn't know him, had urged his vicars, Matthew and Gregory, to bring the brotherhood more into line with the traditional orders. What is more the Cardinal had descended on Assisi at Easter and obliged Clare to accept his *Constitutions*, which required her literally to lock up her sisters in San Damiano for the rest of their lives. The Third Order too had its troubles.

The original friars had been driven to despair at the recent Pentecost chapter when the two vicars passed measures relaxing Francis's strict interpretation of poverty but introducing pietistic regulations on fasting. Stephen produced a copy of them.

Seeing that the meal they were about to eat fell foul of these Francis asked Peter what they should do. He firmly answered that no brother had the authority to override the Rule that he, their father, had given them.

"Let us eat, then," Francis said with a smile.

Talking with his brothers at the end of the meal he realized that if he did not go back to Assisi at once his order might disintegrate. He therefore arranged passages on the first available ship, a Venetian galley, for himself, Peter whom he regarded as his deputy, and Stephen.

Francis also decided to bring two of his brothers from the Syrian province, Elias its Minister, and Caesar, the new brother from Germany. During their months together in Egypt Francis had recognized Elias's exceptional character and talents, including a gift for attracting men to the brotherhood. Caesar was one of them and although originally a preacher he had sailed from the Rhine to Acre as a soldier, where Elias had been delighted to find he was not only a fluent scribe and biblical scholar but a natural friar. Two men of such ability, fresh from the crusade, would be valuable allies in restoring respect for his Rule.

21

The Small Black Hen

1220–1222

However ugly their conduct, the crusades gave back to Europe one symbol of beauty which it had lost since Roman times – the rose. Adopting the varieties they found in the gardens of Persia, the Arabs carried them to the borders of Islam – Kashmir in the east and Spain in the west – while at the end of their campaigns crusaders brought roses home to their castles, delighting poets, artists and the church.

St. Bernard compared the five petals of the single rose to the wounds of Christ's stigmata; because of its purity and loveliness the flower was regularly associated with the Virgin Mary; and at Santa Maria degli Angeli you can see in the Roseto or little rose garden a thornless variety with red leaves. It is said to have sprung from a clump of briars in which Francis rolled after a night of temptation by demons; while the stems promptly lost their thorns the leaves have always kept the color of his blood.

Like any other rose they are most nearly perfect a few hours before they are fully open and become exposed to the hazards of nature or an officious gardener. It might be said that in much the same way Francis's orders were on the brink of bursting into flower at the time of Innocent's death, and that they can be seen or imagined at their best just before Ugolino, as the legate in Tuscany, had taken over their cultivation and Francis had sailed for the east.

The voyage home gave him time to hear more about the blight threatened by the new conditions in Assisi. His vicars, Matthew and

Gregory, had actually removed the gospel injunction, "Take nothing for your journey," from the Rule and had punished some of the original brothers when they had protested. Gregory, able and ambitious but totally at odds with Francis's ideals, had encouraged the friars to set up buildings and libraries to emulate the Benedictines and Cluniacs. Clare's position at San Damiano sounded still more unsettling. Stephen had been taken to see her by Philip, appointed Visitor after Ambrose the Cistercian had died. Nevertheless it looked as if the effect of the Benedictine *Constitutions* imposed by Ugolino would be to sever the connection between the friars and their sisters, for "enclosure" meant that they might neither see nor talk to outsiders except the cardinal, their Visitor and a chaplain, each of whom must be accompanied while inside the convent. The Third Order, too, was being split by John of Capella, who had started a splinter group of men and women with leprosy, keen to found an order exclusively for fellow sufferers.

When the ship reached Venice tradition has it that Francis felt a need to prepare for the confrontations ahead and rowed out to a little island in the lagoon where, under the canopy of sky, he could pray beside the lapping water. The islet, not far from Burano and Torcello, is now known as San Francesco del Deserto. In his *Companion Guide to Venice* Hugh Honour says this about the island:

> Since 1228 it has been owned by Franciscan friars who have made it a haven of peace and otherworldliness for themselves and the numerous birds that nest there unmolested . . . In sight of the distant Dolomites, surrounded by trees and flowers which make the most exquisite works of art look brash and clumsy, you are enfolded in eternity. The island echoes with St. Francis's *Canticle*:
>
> *Thank you, my God, for the moon and the stars;*
> *You have formed them in the sky, clear, precious and beautiful.*
> *Thank you, my Lord, for Brother Wind*
> *And for the air, cloudy and serene, and all weather,*
> *By which you give your children sustenance.*
> *Thank you, my God, for Sister Water,*
> *Who is very useful and soothing and precious and pure . . .*
>
> Here indeed is a place to "worship the Lord in the beauty of holiness."

You don't have to be a saint or a poet to draw inspiration from the elements. A bishop, who had trained as a psychologist, noticed as a chaplain during the Second World War that although he had come across many fine soldiers, few struck him as spiritual men – he had encountered many more in the navy and air force. When he questioned them about this the sailors, and particularly the airmen, said they were conscious that the long spells they spent alone scanning the uncluttered spaces of sea and sky, free from the scramble which crowded their days on the ground, gave them a unique chance to contemplate their lives calmly in a wider perspective.

While many of Francis's retreats seem airborne, others appear to float. He loved Isola Maggiore, a small island on Lake Trasimene, where he survived the forty days of Lent in 1211 on a single loaf. He sheltered at night under the pines in a hollow of brambles overlooking the water – one day bright blue, the next choppy, sullen and gray – which concealed the bones of a Roman army driven there by Hannibal. He was alone with the lizards and salamanders, a few early butterflies, ortolans, finches, and the purple herons which fished the reed beds with great white egrets. The rafts of duck were fewer than the vast numbers flighting into the Venetian lagoon.

There, on his deserted island in 1220 outside the great port, another of Francis's dreams suggested a solution to the problems now racking his order. Angelo writes that in it Francis saw "a small black hen with fluffy legs and feet, like those of a pigeon," who had so many chicks that she was quite unable to shelter or control them. When he woke Francis quickly understood the significance of his vision.

> I am that hen, by nature small and black, whereas I should be simple as a dove, flying up to heaven on wings of love and virtue. The Lord has given me, and will continue to, many children whom I cannot protect by my own strength; I must therefore put them under the control of our holy mother, the church.[1]

As he watched the tides rise and fall over the banks of glistening mud, and the young water birds stretch their wings before flying off to make their way in the world, Francis knew he must let his own children go or they would desert him. His mind made up, he rowed back to Venice.

*

On his way south to Assisi Francis decided to stop at Bologna, but as he approached it he was told that one of his worse fears had been fulfilled; Peter of Staccia was again occupying a comfortable house which he had filled with friars and their books.

It is sometimes said that Francis was entirely opposed to learning; he wasn't, although he was very wary of it. Both Thomas of Celano, who was highly educated, and St. Bonaventure, one of the most distinguished scholars in Europe, emphasize this; four of his closest colleagues – Bernard, Peter of Catanio, Silvester and Elias – had all studied at Bologna; there are also repeated observations in his conversation and writing about the honor and respect due to scholars and theologians.

On the other hand he tended to regard learning like other possessions; it was a potential hazard little different from wealth. For instance the commune in Assisi offered twenty-five gold fiorinis to any citizen returning from Bologna with a doctorate in civil and canon law, and Francis warned his friars against priests who "sell the learning in their sermons for praise." They should value books "not for elegance but edification, not for costliness but their witness to God."

Peter's house in Bologna and its library of books, which he had accepted with the approval of Matthew and Gregory, represented such a flagrant defiance of his explicit wishes and the terms of the Rule that, for the first time on record, Francis lost his temper. He sent a message ordering Peter to empty the house of both the friars and their books and then to dispose of it; even Leo, who was lying there sick, was to leave.

His response to the liberties Peter had taken epitomized the conflict over the meaning of poverty which tortured him and his followers for the rest of his life – and intensified after his death. It angered him that his ministers had enrolled worldly men unable or unwilling to observe faithfully the Rule given him by God. He could not bring himself to modify it but, after his dream, he decided a final decision must rest with God's representative. He therefore avoided Assisi and went straight on to Pope Honorius whose court was then – in early August – at Orvieto.

This spectacular fortified city is set on a massive table of yellow rock which rises six hundred feet sheer from the floor of the Paglia valley. Over the centuries it has been occupied by Etruscans, Romans, Visigoths and briefly by the Byzantine warlord Count Belisarius. Although it then housed only three thousand people the papal court regularly moved out here when the heat or riots in Rome grew too oppressive.

Francis waited patiently at the bishop's palace until Honorius could spare time to see him. The two men had always found each other deeply sympathetic but before they plunged into Francis's business the pope wanted a detailed account of the crusade in Egypt, of which he was the principal architect; then Francis opened his heart. He had to describe the minefield of problems surrounding him with great delicacy because he suspected it had largely been laid, albeit in good faith, by Cardinal Ugolino, the Bishop of Ostia. It was his nephew, Gregory, who had instigated the reforms now dividing the First Order; Ugolino himself who had waited until Francis was safely in Egypt before imposing his Benedictine *Constitutions* on the Second Order; and he again who was encouraging John of Capella to set up a separate order for lepers.

The pope's response was impeccably courteous but unflinchingly firm. He perfectly understood Francis's worries yet made clear that he, Ugolino and the Curia were determined to enforce the decrees of the Lateran Council; with that sole caveat Francis, as Minister General of his Order, could utterly rely on their support. In fact they had already drafted a bull to reduce the number of "flies" creeping into the brotherhood by requiring a year's novitiate before their final acceptance; it meant that for the first time the canonical status of the Order would be acknowledged in a formal papal document.

Grateful as he was for these words Francis knew they failed to address the root of his anxiety, which was the current attempt to dilute his interpretation of gospel poverty and freedom. He also recognized that the old pope was too busy with affairs of church and state to be able to resolve such a fundamental issue. He therefore obtained his broad consent to most of his short-term proposals before kneeling down and addressing the pontiff:

"I am ashamed you should spend so much time on my Friars Minor. . . . For this reason I humbly beseech your Holiness to give us the Lord Bishop of Ostia so that, when necessity arises, the brothers can appeal to him, always saving your pre-eminent dignity."[2]

No doubt greatly relieved by this suggestion Honorius immediately accepted it. Francis possibly based this gamble on two instincts. First, he felt it might be easier to oppose a formidable adversary by getting close to him than by tackling him at arm's length. Second, he had a dawning awareness that Ugolino was fundamentally two men not one – inside the hard line prelate a humble Christian was struggling to get out.

We all plot our courses through life by different means. For Francis Christ was his compass and God his magnetic north; but for rigidly orthodox bishops and cardinals like Ugolino the pope was their compass and church dogma their pole. The two lodestars were miles apart but such was the wisdom and courage of pontiffs like Innocent and Honorius that their compass needles sometimes swung away from canonical north when exposed to an alternative vision of goodness. Would Ugolino's swing too?

The cardinal accepted his appointment as Protector with alacrity. He listened carefully to Francis when he outlined objections to the changes he had sanctioned as legate and immediately demonstrated his respect and goodwill by reversing a number of these decisions. The two Vicars at the Porziuncula would be posted elsewhere; their amendments to the Rule would be quashed; he agreed that Philip's appointment as Visitor to San Damiano should be reviewed; John of Capella would be censured and his lepers disbanded. Finally, with every show of reluctance, Ugolino accepted Francis's decision to stand down as head of his order to make way for Peter of Catanio.

Amicable as they were, these discussions failed to resolve the two most significant issues, the ownership of property and Clare's subjection to a Benedictine rule. Nevertheless an extraordinary rapport immediately developed between the two men. According to Angelo: "When Francis saw the faith and love of the Bishop of Ostia for the friars he was drawn still closer to him in bond of affection. By a divine revelation he knew that the bishop would become pope."[3]

And according to Thomas of Celano: "The bishop testified that he was never so greatly disturbed or upset but that, on seeing Francis or talking to him, every mental cloud would be dispersed and serenity return . . .

"He ministered to Francis as a servant to a master; and as often as he saw him showed reverence to him as an apostle of Christ and, bowing down both the outer and the inner man, would often kiss his hand."[4]

Francis was barely back at the Porziuncula in time for the Michaelmas chapter on September 29. For the older friars it was the most significant and emotional of these reunions; Francis was alive after all. Though obviously unwell he spoke with electrifying effect, talking about the new bull which had been issued ten days before, and asking them to endorse the measures he had agreed on with the pope and their new Cardinal Protector. Leo, Rufino and Angelo recall how, finally, he broke the news of his resignation.

"'From henceforth I am dead to you, but here is Brother Peter Catanio, whom you shall obey.' Then all the friars began to lament noisily and weep bitterly. Francis bowed down before Peter and promised him obedience; after that he remained a subject until his death like any other friar."[5]

For the rest of his life there are ambiguities about who was properly Minister General, but since the pope continued to regard Francis as head of the order, to whom every member ultimately owed obedience, it is easier to reserve the title for Francis, calling Peter and his successor Vicar General.

*

Clare had more reason than anyone else to be happy that Francis was home, even if she was saddened by the signs of his sickness as he was by the burdens imposed by her new way of life.

The issue of Philip also clouded their reunion. Before leaving for Syria Francis had told the friars that to protect the reputation of the order they should spend as little time as possible at San Damiano. He had heard, however, that after becoming Visitor Philip had been there imprudently often; and, again against Francis's wishes, he had obtained privileges from the hierarchy protecting her community in Florence from outside interference. True to her vow of obedience Clare accepted Francis's decision to relieve Philip of his office, but she regretted his loss, for she had always valued his counsel and now delighted in his sermons.

It was clear she had met the imposition of Ugolino's *Constitutions* with a calm, firmness and spiritual maturity unusual in a girl of twenty-five. Matching the cardinal's steel with her own mettle, she had accepted what she must, moderated what she could, and evaded the rest. The fourteen chapters of his regulations bore no resemblance in spirit or style to Francis's simple Rule yet Clare, who had been a natural ascetic since childhood, was content to accept enclosure for many of the sisters, the restriction of visitors, insistence on silence, and also draconian fasting; it is difficult nowadays to imagine the spiritual benefits of the cardinal's new regime which frequently confined women already subsisting on a diet of alms to spells of fruit and raw vegetables or even bread and water. But Clare said men and women could find joy in doing penance and had fasted so rigorously in the past that Francis once asked Bishop Guido to order her to eat more.

Clare was careful to modify some of the cardinal's other provisions. Following Francis she interpreted the role of abbess as that of servant, not superior; she relaxed all the harsher requirements in whatever way she thought necessary for the health of a sister; and she persuaded Ugolino that some of her companions should continue their charitable work in the neighborhood for which there was universal gratitude. Clare also managed to retain the friars' support in providing the sisters with most of their food and any labor they needed.

A great expert on the earliest Franciscan sources, Dr. Rosalind Brooke, and her husband, a professor of Ecclesiastical History, have described Ugolino's transactions with Clare and Francis as "a puzzle and mystery." It is, for instance, tantalizing not to know Clare's response to two glaring omissions from his *Constitutions* – the lack of any reference to poverty and failure to mention Francis. Rather than argue these points, she presumably relied on Innocent's *Privilege of Poverty* and hoped Francis would return before long to speak his mind if necessary.

We do, however, get a vivid impression of Clare's impact on the cardinal's heart from a letter he wrote after his Easter at San Damiano.

> My own dear sister in Christ,
>
> Since that moment when the need to return here separated me from that holy conversation I had with you and tore me away from the joy I had in heavenly treasure – since then I have been overwhelmed with such bitterness of heart, with so many tears and such a weight of sorrow. Unless, at the feet of Jesus, I find consolation in his compassion, I fear I shall always be in such distress that my spirit might even die of it and my soul be quite undone.[6]

Clare's innate goodness could sometimes deflect Ugolino's course from the attraction of ecclesiolatry and bring him into line with the spirit of the gospels. He was well aware of her charisma for in Clare's official biography Thomas of Celano wrote: "It was with good reason that he placed such extraordinary faith in the prayers of this saint because he had experienced their power. In fact when he encountered any new difficulties . . . he often wrote to her asking for her intercession."[7]

The striking warmth and deep respect Ugolino felt for Francis and Clare from now on suggest that he had not previously acted as the order's unofficial protector; this is often assumed but had it been so the cardinal's feelings would not have allowed him to permit the two Vicars to alter the founder's Rule for his first order or have thrust his *Constitutions* so abruptly on the founder of the second.

Between its birth and Clare's death in 1253 the order grew in several ways. Some new houses were inspired by Clare or seeded by the detachment of sisters from San Damiano; some communities, originally founded independently or under other auspices, and observing a traditional rule, opted to join her; and the association of others was promoted by their bishops or Ugolino as legate. The cardinal's role in this process was not one of a founder but of a conscientious legate and protector, whose short-lived *Constitutions* were formally replaced by Innocent IV in 1247 and then, in 1253, by the rule Clare wrote herself. A brief history of the order published by a group of Poor Clares from France, Belgium and Italy, states that: "Even though Clare never claimed any authority over them, in 1253 more than 150 communities referred to themselves as belonging to her form of life."[8]

In about 1263 Pope Urban IV pronounced the movement's official name to be the "Order of St. Clare."

*

Ever since Innocent had first blessed Francis's order the tide of fortune had flowed his way; now it was ebbing. In 1221 Francis was ill; he suffered from his liver – he may have contracted hepatitis or bilharzia in Egypt – and was plagued by spasmodic bouts of malaria. As a result he sometimes gave way to his temper, showed signs of depression and seemed more inconsistent than ever. There were occasions when his confidence waned.

The newcomers' opposition to a literal observance of Francis's Rule drove his oldest companions into temporary retreat. Although Bernard, Giles, Angelo, Rufino, Masseo and Leo emerged for chapters, Francis spent most of his time with the brothers he had brought back from the east. Because of this, and because it seems that Ugolino obliged Thomas of

Celano to skate over these controversies, biographers have to cover the period largely from a chronicle kept by a protégé of Caesar's – Jordan, a young friar from the village of Giano, opposite Assisi.

Francis still traveled with a personal guardian to whom he deferred on all practical matters to leave himself freer for prayer. He frequently chose Stephen, described by the minister in Tuscany as a truthful man. Stephen recounts, without rancor, how Francis once enjoyed a full meal of eggs, gravy and milk, and then complained it was too much. When, the next day, Stephen gave him crusts and water, Francis finished them before asking, "Why so little?"

Stephen's expression was enough to elicit from Francis: "Dear son, discretion is a noble virtue. Remember, you shouldn't always do exactly what your superior tells you, especially when he is troubled by some passion."[9]

The subject of presumption and privilege always roused his passions and Philip's behavior at San Damiano still rankled. When Stephen told him that Philip had asked for the office of Visitor and then personally chosen the friars to look after Clare's convents, Francis burst out, "Until now the ulcer has only been attacking our flesh; there was hope of recovery. Now it is eating into the bone and incurable."[10]

A few days later, walking near Bevagna in the depth of winter, Stephen felt he should ask forgiveness for his visit to San Damiano with Philip. Francis not only reprimanded him but made him plunge, fully clothed, into the icy Topino as a penance.

During that winter Ugolino asked Francis to visit him, ostensibly to discuss the new version of the Rule he was drafting. He therefore took Caesar of Speyer, who was selecting for it suitable quotations from the Bible, and Elias whose natural authority reassured him in this uneasy period of change. They found Dominic de Guzman had also been asked to a meeting – though this may have occurred earlier – for the cardinal was eager to appoint some of the ablest and holiest friars from their two orders as bishops. Both founders were adamant; any form of rank, privilege or dignity would be in absolute contradiction of their calling as *fratres minores*. When they parted for the last time, Dominic – who died that summer – begged Francis for his cord to wear beneath his habit as a token of affection.

Nevertheless once Francis also was dead Ugolino had his way – and Mammon did too. About forty years later Odo Rigaud, a Franciscan but also Archbishop of Rouen and lord of three palaces, with big estates on both sides of the channel, was seen riding to Rome with a retinue of eighty horsemen.

Francis was even less successful in fighting off the clamor for permanent houses and the possession of books. Approaching the Porziuncula after some time away he found a large stone building going up among the trees as a permanent shelter for the ever-growing influx of brothers. Furious, he climbed a ladder with his companion and began tearing down tiles from the roof. Two knights, who were supervising the work, quickly explained that the lodge was being built by the people of Assisi – it was a loan to the friars, not a gift. Francis was mollified, yet it was the thin end of the wedge; before long his Vicar General allowed a small stone shelter and oratory to go up in the woods so that the brothers could pray there in peace.

Meanwhile Ugolino exerted further pressure on Francis to relax his attitudes to property and learning. He had acquired the offending house in Bologna himself to relieve the friars of its ownership and insisted that some of them study there to improve their preaching. Contrary as both moves were to Francis's convictions (when asked he forbade a novice to own a psalter), they were the first steps toward his order providing invaluable pastoral care for young students in the new universities and also producing some of the most celebrated scholars in Europe.

Ugolino perceived that Elias, however loyal to Francis in their frequent debates, privately sympathized with his long-term ambitions as protector. This meant that when Francis suffered another blow in March, the sudden death of Peter of Catanio at the Porziuncula, he and the cardinal were unanimous in wanting Elias as their new Vicar General.

At the Pentecost chapter in May the friars agreed to his appointment and were delighted to hear that Honorius had granted canonical status to what later became known as the Third Order of Penitents. As mentioned previously, it greatly strengthened the political hand of the church, critically tipping the scales against Frederick II and his empire.

One newcomer to the chapter was a young Portuguese of twenty-six, whose fame as St. Anthony of Padua today rivals even Francis's. From the age of fifteen he had studied assiduously as an Augustinian monk at Coimbra. In 1220 when he saw the coffins of the five friars martyred in Morocco, whom he had known personally, brought back to Coimbra for burial, he felt impelled to switch to their order and preach in Morocco himself. But his boat was blown eastward to Sicily, where he was rescued by some Franciscans who had brought him to the Porziuncula. At the end of the chapter the minister for Romagna invited him to join the friars in his province.

During the summer Francis concentrated on drafting his revised Rule with Caesar of Speyer, determined not to dilute his principles, despite the dissent of many new brothers and several of his ministers. He found the work hard, for he had little interest in legal forms and idiom. As a result the document was an ungainly amalgam of his original Rule approved by Innocent, additional provisions since considered necessary, a hundred quotations from scripture, and a flow of exhortations and admonitions which culminated in a lengthy poetic prayer of petition, thanksgiving and praise.

Just before he presented his draft to the Michaelmas chapter news reached Italy from Egypt which saddened Francis but hardly surprised him. Cardinal Pelagius had rejected yet another peace offer from al-Kamil in July, summoned back King John to the Nile and, ignoring his advice, ordered an advance toward Cairo. Biding his time, the sultan waited until he had the crusaders entirely surrounded by his troops and the Nile was in flood – then he blockaded the waterways with his ships and opened the sluice gates. Both cut off and swamped, Pelagius was forced to capitulate.

Al-Kamil's terms were characteristically magnanimous, and after he had given a sumptuous banquet for King John the last of the crusaders sailed away from Damietta on September 8. A Norman troubadour, Guillaume le Clerc, had the last word:

> *We lost this town*
> *Owing to our stupidity and sins,*
> *And on account of the legate . . .*
> *For it is surely against the law*
> *For clerks to command knights;*
> *The churchman should recite his Bible and psalms.*[11]

An inescapable duty, or perhaps a diplomatic illness, prevented the Cardinal Protector from presiding over the September chapter; he sent Cardinal Rainerio Carpocci in his place. Francis read from the Bible, the psalms were chanted by three thousand or so friars, and a bishop sang the

Mass. Francis signaled his refusal to compromise his Rule by prefacing his presentation with the words: "Blessed be the Lord my God who trains my hand for the fight." A long and exhausting battle he had for, content apart, his distended draft ran to about twenty-four modern printed pages – far more than most of the friars could learn by heart. It expressed Francis's full credo better than any other document except his *Testament* and its text was preserved, but even the ingenious Elias failed to extract sufficient concessions from the two sides to achieve a consensus. A decision on the Rule was therefore held over.

Nevertheless peace was preserved and toward the end of the chapter Francis, who was sitting at Elias's feet, twitched his habit and murmured in his ear. Elias looked up.

> 'Our Brother asks me to speak for him as he is tired and cannot talk any more. He says that many good Christians live in Germany and that we often see them walking down the valley with their staves and water bottles, singing and sweating on their way to Rome. But because the first of our brothers in Germany were badly treated no one volunteers to go there any more. Our Brother will therefore grant a special conduct to any of you who now stand up and make the offer.'[12]

Ninety brothers rose to their feet, of whom twenty-five were chosen. Elias and Francis appointed Caesar their leader and minister of the new province. Thomas of Celano was among those included, which meant there was a gap in his personal knowledge of the next few years when he came to write the story of Francis's life. Jordan of Giano admits that at first he was so terrified of the likely danger that he dithered and started quizzing the volunteers to get material for his journal, but was spotted by Elias and felt bound to join the mission. Another eyewitness of the coming events in Assisi was lost.

*

Throughout 1222 and the following year the contradictions in Francis's behavior, and in the characters of the two men now responsible for his order, Ugolino and Elias, threatened disaster.

Francis's energy would slump and then suddenly surge. He would flay a brother for some failing, yet faced by others with faults far more flagrant would say nothing, withdraw to pray and then return, the matter entirely forgotten. His emotional disturbances were often apparent, yet beneath the surface his dedication to Christ and communion with God both steadily deepened. These fluctuations of stamina, passion and mood were not unlike those of the great tubercular composers and poets of the nineteenth century.

His inconsistency must have been even more difficult to live with – his acceptance of money for the sick, but for no one else or any other cause however worthy; his refusal to own either the Porziuncula or the house in Bologna, but his delight in the sanctuaries he had accepted at La Verna and Greccio; his relentless suspicion of books and study, when the former were essential to observing the Office and he was increasingly reliant on men of great learning like Ugolino and Elias. Perhaps it was an unconscious demonstration of the truth that on occasion two diametrically opposite views may both be right. Perhaps it illustrated another – that nothing is absolutely forbidden to man although all things are never permissible to one man or at all times.

Some of the paradoxes in Ugolino's character were much to his credit. He so admired the friars' indifference to all worldly values that now and again he shed his cardinal's paraphernalia and for several days put on a habit, subsisted on slops and slept on bare boards. It was rumored that later, as pope, he housed a leper in the Lateran whom he occasionally nursed himself. The sick man once complained to a visitor that despite being a guest of the pontiff he never saw him, although he was sometimes looked after by an incompetent old friar.

More usually the cardinal conformed to the remorseless dictates of church dogma and protocol. He was, however, far easier to read than Elias, who was imperceptibly sidling toward a similar alignment. Ugolino knew it, many of the ministers and friars observed it, but for some reason Francis's usually infallible flair missed it. Yet for all their brilliance, determination and skill in managing people, Francis still outshone his cardinal protector and Vicar General. His dazzling spirit and love bound them both to him and often took the wind from the sails of the dissident ministers.

All three men were put to the test at Pentecost 1222, the year of an eventful assembly known as The Chapter of Mats, which unfolds like a pageant in the pages of *The Little Flowers;* Leo, and an account of a previous chapter attended by Dominic, confirm the basic authenticity of the story. About five thousand friars from all over Europe converged on the open woodland below Assisi. Clustering around their tiny mother church, they camped in the parties they had traveled with, sixty, a hundred, or several hundred strong, divided by partitions of withies. They sat, as they ate, on the ground, for as long as Francis lived they possessed neither tables nor chairs. Many of them put up shelters of thatching or mats; some slept under the stars.

Every day that week Cardinal Ugolino rode over from Perugia with an imposing escort of churchmen, while counts, lords, knights, gentlemen and hordes of ordinary people arrived from every other direction, chiefly to see "holy Father Francis." When Ugolino approached he dismounted and went humbly on foot to Santa Maria where he preached.

Surveying the vast throng of brothers, praying, chanting the Office, or talking quietly together, Ugolino saw them as "the army of God's knights," fulfilling a vision Innocent had voiced at the Lateran Council. But when he looked closer and saw their beds were no more than hollows scooped in the earth and strewn with handfuls of straw, tears sprang to his eyes; he said they reminded him of the lairs of wild animals and asked, "What will become of the rest of us, miserably addicted to all our excesses?"

Dominic had heard Francis preach to the friars on the lessons to be learned from hunger and thirst, but had thought him improvident in allowing them all to gather without plans to feed them. However he had not reckoned with the feelings the *poverello* now evoked throughout Umbria.

> The inhabitants of Perugia, Spoleto, Foligno, Spello, Assisi and its neighbourhood arrived with pack animals and carts laden with bread and beans, cheese, wine and other good things. They also brought enough table cloths, dishes, bowls, pitchers and glasses for the entire company, vying with each other to serve the friars, until the gentlemen and nobles began to wait on them too.[13]

The climax of the chapter occurred after some of the ministers and more sophisticated priests persuaded the cardinal to ask Francis, yet again, to adopt a conventional pattern of regular life from one of the existing orders. Leo says Francis listened carefully and then led Ugolino by the hand into the great concourse of friars. There he said:

'My brothers, my brothers! God has called me to follow the way of simplicity, and I don't want you to continue pressing some other rule on me – neither St Augustine's, nor St Bernard's, nor St Benedict's.

'The Lord told me he wished me to be a new kind of fool – and doesn't want us to be guided by any higher learning than that. God will confound you for your knowledge and sagacity and I trust that his constables* will punish you for them. Then, to your shame, you will return to your first state.'

The Cardinal was dumbfounded and said nothing. All the friars were afraid.[14]

Perhaps in deference to Ugolino, Thomas of Celano made no reference to this scene in the official biography, yet the cardinal never let it cast a shadow over his relations with Francis. Like the Umbrians he was proud and fond of the saint; like Pope Honorius he saw him leading the church's spearhead of friars in the battle to maintain its moral authority in Europe.

Because, after Francis's death, Elias became such a controversial figure in the order, in the church and even in Europe, his pivotal role in these simmering years is virtually omitted in all the early sources. But despite his surreptitious shift toward the cardinal's camp he remained personally devoted to Francis and took increasing care of his health which grew steadily worse. Always valuable, Francis's life had become doubly precious since Dominic's death in Bologna the previous August.

*

Almost exactly twelve months after Dominic de Guzman's death Francis came to Bologna himself for the Feast of the Assumption on August 15, 1222, and was asked to speak in the piazza. That day his inspiration blazed and his words burned into the memory of the people who listened. Years afterward a priest called Thomas, then Archdeacon of Spalato in Dalmatia, wrote this:

*By "constables" Francis meant demons, who might be good or bad. A whole regiment of devils was said to have swarmed in fury around one of the nearby leper houses during the chapter.

> When I was a student in Bologna I saw St Francis preach in the main square outside the Palazzo Comunale; almost the whole city had gathered to hear him. His theme was 'Angels, Men and Devils'.
>
> Although no scholar, he spoke so well and developed the subject of these three classes of rational and spiritual beings so clearly that he won the unbounded admiration of even the academics in the crowd. Yet it was more of a general address than a sermon.
>
> He wore a tattered habit, his appearance was insignificant, and his face wasn't handsome; but God gave his words such power that they actually restored peace to many of the noble families long torn apart by hatred, cruelty and murder. At the same time ordinary men and women flocked to him out of devotion and respect, afterwards trying to tear a shred from his habit or at least to touch him.[15]

Two of the young nobles, from the Marches, came up to Francis when he left the piazza and asked if they might become brothers. One, Pellegrino, who was extremely clever joined the Third Order and, as a tertiary, became an expert in canon law; Bernard considered him the perfect friar. The other, Riccerio di Muccio, drew very close to Francis toward the end of his life and was finally elected minister of the Marches of Ancona.

The effort of recalling his brothers to their Rule, and of mesmerizing an assembly as large as the crowd in Bologna, was exorbitant for a sick man like Francis. More costly still, if in a different way, was his resolve that having passed the care of his order to others he should now let go of it entirely – a final donation to absolute poverty.

22

Darkness and Light

1222–1223

In the last years of his life Francis fought desperately to convince his brothers that after money and buildings, learning could prove the most dangerous handicap in their pursuit of salvation. He said, "A great cleric must in some way give up his learning when he comes to the order, that he may offer himself naked to the arms of the crucified." Most great religions teach the paradox that to discover who we are and fulfill our unique potentiality we must discard every selfish urge and possession, sometimes even our clothes. In our struggles against the coils of worldliness nudity reduces the enemy's chance of getting a hold.

Bologna was the principal arena in which this and every other kind of moral and philosophical proposition was questioned, defended and fought over, a campus packed with students from Spain, France, Germany, Scandinavia, Poland, Hungary and the Balkans. To combat the surging growth of the university's secular schools teaching Roman Law, Greek philosophy, and science introduced from Arabia, Innocent III had established here the church's own masters to award degrees in canon law and theology and teach disputation. The Dominicans, who quickly excelled in these disciplines and founded houses for their study, represented a challenge which Peter of Staccia had been unable to resist. After his dismissal Francis had labored hard to recover lost ground on this issue of learning.

When the novice who had been so anxious to have his own psalter repeated his request, Francis who was sitting by the fire, demurred.

"When you have a psalter you will hanker for a breviary. After that you will sit in an armchair like a great prelate and say to your brother: 'Bring me my breviary.'"

Then he took some ashes and rubbed them around his head as if he were washing it, saying fervently, "I am a breviary, I am a breviary." [1]

On another occasion he was more explicit.

"My brothers who are being led by their curious passion for learning will find their hand empty on the day of retribution when books, no longer useful, will be thrown out of windows and into cubby holes."

He said this not because he disapproved of scripture study but because he wanted the brothers to be strong in charity rather than superficially learned out of curiosity.[2]

Francis was also worried that some of the brothers merely studied – to the neglect of their prayers, work and service – in order to embellish their sermons.

> "When they have preached and learn that some have been helped and others moved to penitence they will become conceited and congratulate themselves, whereas the penitents will actually have been converted by God through the prayers of humbler brothers secluded in retreats. It is they who are the Knights of my Round Table."[3]

Clear and correct about the dangers of intellectual and spiritual pride, Francis was obscure and possibly misguided in his more general apprehensions about learning which failed to convince his Cardinal Protector – in fact Ugolino soon obliged him to reopen the house in Bologna, though Francis would not do so until the cardinal announced publicly that he, not the friars, was its owner. The cardinal also paid for the friars' books and the materials for their studies which were very expensive. Although this development allowed the persistent novice to have his own psalter at last, he still wanted Francis's personal approval.

This time the *poverello* merely agreed that the brother could do whatever his minister had said; but a few minutes later he ran after the young man:

> "Come back and show me the place where I said that."
>
> When they reached the spot Francis kneeled down and said to the

novice, "I was wrong brother, I was wrong. Whoever wishes to be a Friar Minor should have nothing except a tunic as the Rule allows, with a cord and breeches."

From then on he gave this answer to any friar who came to him for advice about such matters.[4]

In fact Ugolino's encouragement of study was farsighted and quickly successful after Elias, in 1223, appointed the young Portuguese friar later known as Anthony of Padua, to take over the order's teaching and preaching in Bologna. Such was his brilliance that within a few months Francis wrote him a letter of approval, albeit a guarded one.

> It pleases me that you are teaching the brothers sacred theology so long as, in accord with the words of our Rule, you "do not extinguish the spirit of holy prayer and devotion."[5]

Before long the Franciscans so impressed the leading jurists and scholars in the city that three of them – Nicholas of Pepoli, Maestro Bondi the bishop's chaplain, and its most famous professor, Accursius – each endowed the order with a building; while shortly after Elias four other Minister Generals were graduates of Bologna. Very soon every Franciscan province began to take its studies seriously and in 1224 the first friars reached Oxford. By then in Paris, the greatest medieval center of learning in Europe, Brother Pacifico had handed over the province to Gregory of Naples, now rehabilitated after his dismissal as Vicar. Once again authority would go to his head, fulfilling Francis's gloomiest forebodings about the dangers of academia.

On the other hand some years after Francis's death an episode occurred at San Damiano which illustrated the golden mean he strove for. One day a great English scholar, a friar of the order – either Adam of Oxford or Alexander of Hales* – was preaching to Clare and her sisters when Brother Giles was present. Just after the Englishman had started Giles, who was revered as a mystic but famously contemptuous of scholarship and preaching, jumped up and said, "Be quiet, Master, I wish to speak."

*His great work *Summa Theologiae* was said to weigh, in its entirety, more than a horse.

The friar immediately shut up and, with divine fervour, Giles delivered a flow of words, sweet as honey, before ending, "Brother, you can now go on with your sermon."

Clare expressed her delight in what they had just seen: "This fulfils one of Father Francis's great wishes. He once told me he hoped his brothers who were priests would become so humble that a Master of Theology would willingly interrupt his sermon if a lay brother wanted to preach. I assure you I've been more edified by this Master today than I would have been if I'd witnessed the resurrection of the dead!"[6]

*

If Ugolino obliged Francis to withdraw his resistance to change in his first order, his *Constitutions* required the founder's withdrawal from his second order entirely.

Clare had borne most of the regulations imposed on her sisters with great equanimity but when it came to the restrictions on dealings with the friars, Francis showed himself much more amenable than she was. Whereas Elias may have longed for Francis to relinquish entirely his connections with the order's business, Clare constantly sought ways of reviving his association with her sisters, which had lapsed almost completely, especially in the case of the new convents – for which he has sometimes been criticized. In fact a story told by Stephen suggests he may have felt a temporary alienation from these houses, of which Ugolino had declared himself Protector and of which he also claimed to be the founder.

At a time when there was already a move among the Benedictines and Cistercians to shed their women's communities, which had become difficult to support, Francis is reputed to have said, "Sisters. God wished us not to have wives and now the devil has given us Sisters!"

However he seems to have been quickly reconciled to them, for when he was next leaving Ugolino the cardinal remarked, "Brother, I commend these ladies to you." Whereupon Francis's face lit up and he volunteered, "From now on they won't be known as Poor Sisters but as 'Ladies,' since that is the name you have used in commending them."[7]

Although Francis's inclination was to comply with whatever Clare asked, and he communicated with her regularly, there was little he could actually do. Even if he had originally accepted her vows, and had given her and her earliest sisters their first form of life, these had been superseded by their *Constitutions* which made no mention of him. Furthermore the Rule he was now revising for his friars placed stringent limitations on the brothers' relations with women; he also laid down that only the most reluctant brothers should be assigned to the ladies' assistance. For all these reasons and to set his colleagues an example he believed any intervention would be quite inappropriate. For Clare, on the other hand, his involvement with San Damiano was not only appropriate but essential. She made no secret of this, for instance invariably asking to see him whenever he was leaving Assisi. Even so he steadfastly kept his distance and, in the end, without the inspiration of his regular visits the morale in San Damiano sank so low that Elias begged him to go and preach there.

No one forgot the occasion. For a time Francis stood silently among the nuns, his eyes raised to heaven in prayer; then he asked for ashes, which he sprinkled in a circle around him, finally placing some on his head. No sermon followed. After a long time he ended the silence by singing the *Miserere* (Psalm 50), an affirmation that the pleasure of God is not in ceremonies but in the sincerity of obedience, concluding:

> *He who brings thanksgiving as his sacrifice honors me;*
> *To him who orders his way aright*
> *I will show the salvation of God.*

However surprised Clare may have been by this mime, she was not baffled – for practically, mentally and spiritually she and Francis were in perfect harmony. She willingly fasted, sewed her fingers to the bone and washed her sisters' bedpans or toilet stools, yet always remained laughing and cheerful. She mastered the subtleties of the scriptures, the liturgy, and the refinements of her Rule, thus fully comprehending the purpose and rewards of religious practices. And as a mystic she immediately grasped Francis's symbolism; he, she and her sisters were only temporal ashes; their sacrifices now were a preparation for something eternal. Years later she wrote to the abbess of her convent in Prague:

> Since you have cast aside all things which, in this deceitful and turbulent world, ensnare their blind lovers, love God totally, who gave Himself for your love. His beauty the sun and moon admire; of His

gifts there is no limit in abundance, preciousness and magnitude.[8]

Only now, toward the end of his religious life, was Francis making the huge sacrifice of surrendering his order to a superior, his Cardinal Protector. Clare had already made this submission to Ugolino early in hers, yet her humility and obedience had augmented not diminished her stature. This, combined with her intelligence, spirituality and courage gave her a formidable moral authority approaching Francis's own. It is best illustrated by looking ahead to two episodes after Francis's death in which she was forced to cross swords with Ugolino in defense of the integrity of San Damiano. These battles illuminate, too, the reason why the cardinal and Francis never saw eye to eye about the order they both loved so deeply.

The first of Clare's duels with Ugolino occurred after his election as Pope Gregory IX, following Honorius's death in 1227. When he was in Assisi preparing to canonize Francis he so failed to understand her dedication to apostolic poverty that he pressed her to accept both property and endowment for the security of her convents. When she demurred he assumed it was for fear of breaking her Rule and so added, "We will release you from your vow if that is what you are afraid of."

Clare's cool response was simply, "Holy Father, I have no wish whatever to be absolved from following Christ for the rest of my life." Faced with this unblinking affirmation he reiterated in September 1228 her *Privilege of Poverty*, previously granted by Innocent III.

Clare's second obedient protest followed in 1230, when the ministers in General Chapter asked Gregory whether Francis's final Rule or his later, more emphatic, *Testament* should take precedence. In his response he chose to lay down some new guidelines, including a rule that in future no friar might enter a convent without the pope's explicit consent. Hitherto the choice of a convent's chaplains, confessors and preachers had been delegated to its abbess and local minister. According to Clare's official biographer, "She said with a sigh, 'Since those who have nourished our souls are being taken away from us, let's do without the other friars too.'"[9]

If the sisters were to lose the spiritual nourishment they received from the friars, their lifeblood, they might as well lose their daily bread also, and starve. "As soon as Pope Gregory got word of this," Clare's biographer says, "he immediately had the Minister General lift this ban."

Perhaps no other events reveal Ugolino in his true colors as starkly as these do. Despite his genuine devotion to Francis and Clare, and for all his admiring tears of compassion when faced with the penury of the friars at Santa Maria and their equally penniless sisters in their convent at Spoleto, he was marching to a quite different drum. His paramount loyalty was to the Church of Rome established in dogma, theirs to the Kingdom of Christ revealed in the gospels.

*

Francis, normally at ease wherever he was, in a cave, cottage or castle, felt least at home among the lofty towers and gorgeous palaces of Rome. Nevertheless he went there as often as the interests of his order demanded, which they did in the early months of 1223. Sleeping little, he would bridle his senses, shut out distractions, and continue his prayers whether he was sitting, eating or walking through the streets.

Whenever he could he withdrew to the secluded church or his cell in the retreat house which Giacoma de Settesoli had put at the order's disposal. Virtually every friar has some touching weakness for one of the smaller pleasures of life, perhaps chocolate, a hot-water bottle or glass of *vin santo*; Giacoma liked to spoil Francis with his – *mostacciuoli*, the little almond cakes she made. Above all she raised his spirits by the growing generosity of her support for his third order which was expanding with extraordinary rapidity.

As Europe's economy changed, people drifted increasingly into the towns where many found themselves lacking any reliable means of support. Whenever Francis stood up to speak, however ill he felt, he still drew crowds even among the mutinous people of Rome, many of whom were surprised and grateful if someone cared for them enough to preach in their own language. Men and women pressed to join his order of penitents, the least susceptible of the three to clerical interference, the least in need of his protection, and the only one to give him unalloyed pleasure at the end of his life.

When he had to discuss the final text of his Rule with Ugolino in Rome he felt he must accept the cardinal's invitation to stay in his palace. The prospect was not entirely appealing for a few weeks before he had shown his revisions to Elias who is said to have promptly "mislaid" them; it was therefore clear that the ministers, his Vicar and his Cardinal Protector were unanimous in believing the discipline of the gospels was too radical for the thousands of men – especially the priests – now joining the order.

Unwilling to argue with the prelate to whom he owed personal obedience Francis attempted to make his point, as always, by example. Before dinner one day he went out discreetly to beg for some food. When he returned he found that Ugolino and his guests – nobles, knights and chaplains – were already seated. He therefore took his usual place beside the cardinal and after the meal had begun handed out some of his alms to the company around the table, who received them with courtesy. Some ate the crusts while others kept them as mementos of this strange little interlude.

Upset, but too proud to say anything in front of his guests, the cardinal afterward drew Francis into the next room, asking with a smile, "Why, my simple brother, did you shame me by going out begging from my house?"

> "On the contrary, my Lord," Francis replied, "when a servant performs his duty obediently he does great honor to his master. I have to be a model for your poor friars, especially as I know there are some who are too proud to demean themselves by begging or carrying out any other servile tasks.
>
> "I particularly don't want to be ashamed of begging when I am staying with you or other men amply endowed with worldly goods, for I must remember that God came down rich and glorious in his majesty to live with us who are poor and despised in our humanity. I want the friars to know that I find greater consolation in sharing their wretched food than in sitting at your lavish table, for the bread of charity is holy."[10]

This seemed to disarm the sorely tried cardinal who answered, "My son, do whatever seems right to you, for God is with you and you with him." After that they made great progress together on the Rule.

It was only when it came to legislating for the orders that Ugolino argued with their founder, though he never did so openly; he always gave Francis support on public occasions. The most celebrated of these was when he had arranged for Francis to preach before Honorius and his cardinals. Well aware that Francis was no scholar, and that however brilliantly he often spoke he sometimes tailed off in an ecstasy or simply walked away in mid-sentence, Ugolino was on tenterhooks. He begged Francis to prepare his sermon the night before, which he obediently did.

Next day in front of the Curia Francis asked permission to start but, when he tried to, his words flew out of his head. There was a short pause – and then they began to well up from his heart.

> He began fearlessly and spoke with such spiritual fire that he couldn't contain himself for joy. When the words emerged from his mouth his feet moved in time with them as if he were dancing, not frivolously but alight with divine love. This didn't provoke laughter but tears, for those present were deeply touched, astonished by the strength of his devotion and God's grace in him.[11]

This sermon undoubtedly stood Francis in good stead with the Curia when Ugolino later presented his final Rule for their approval. In the meantime one of Francis's greatest admirers, Cardinal Leo Brancaleone, brushed aside his polite refusal to spend a few nights in his palace before going north to Fonte Colombo to finish work on his Rule. Brancaleone argued he should wait for the winter storms to blow over before walking to the hermitage in the Rieti Valley. As added inducements Brancaleone promised Francis that he could eat with the paupers who sheltered in the palace, that he and his guardian could pray and sleep undisturbed in an empty tower which had nine vaulted rooms, and that Angelo di Tancredi, temporarily acting as his chaplain, would look after them.

Unfortunately on the first night Francis felt himself being beaten by demons and called in his guardian, who found him trembling, as if he had a fever. While they sat through the rest of the night talking Francis tried to work out why he had been attacked.

> "Just as a *podestà* sends his constables to punish an offender, God sends his demons. It is feasible to sin in ignorance and, although the cardinal was kind enough to see that I needed a retreat, it is possible that some of our brothers, suffering from hunger and other privations, may hear where I am and criticize the comforts I'm enjoying here."[12]

Feeling that he could no longer remain in Rome after all, Francis explained to his host what had happened and apologized. The cardinal understood, commended his scruples, and blessed him on his way to Fonte Colombo. He also allowed Angelo to go with him.

*

Brancaleone was right about the weather.

> After Francis left Rome it rained throughout the day. As he was very ill he rode a horse but dismounted to say his prayers, during which he got soaked. However he remarked that just as the body, which will soon be consumed by worms, needs time off to eat, so does the soul while receiving its food, which is God himself.[13]

They passed through Terni where Francis preached in the square. At the end the bishop pointed to him and remarked that God had always sent holy men to enrich the church's life but recently he had given it this "lowly and uneducated little man to bring it luster." Francis, sick of so often being called a saint, thanked him for being more honest.

After the politics and intrigue in Rome he was thankful to reach the peace of the Rieti Valley in the company of his most faithful companions, Leo, Angelo and Rufino ("we who were with him" as Leo frequently refers to them in his scrolls). He had also brought a clever canon lawyer to help finish the Rule, usually identified as Brother Bonizzo of Bologna, though some believe this is the name Riccerio took on joining the brotherhood. Others, equally trusted, came and went – Pacifico, Giles, Juniper, Leonardo and Illuminato.

Fonte Colombo, on its wooded heights, is watered by a spring and enjoys a magnificent view across the valley to the snowy summit of Mt. Terminillo. Francis was disturbed here only by pigeons and crows, the bells of browsing goats and woodpeckers drumming in the stands of ilex, beech and sycamore. A simple little chapel dedicated to St. Mary Magdalene already stood there when the friars received the sanctuary but Francis is said to have drawn, with his own hand, the Tau in red ocher by one of its windows. The steps behind the chapel lead down the cliff face – first to Leo's cave and then, below it, to the curving fissure or gallery split open by an earthquake, where Francis lived and worked with Bonizzo for the next six weeks. As each chapter was completed they dictated it to Leo.

Hearing what Francis was up to the ministers were so alarmed he would produce, yet again, a rule too rigorous for their liking, that they persuaded a reluctant Elias to come and remonstrate with him. Francis invited the little delegation into his cave. He had always maintained that God, not he, had laid down the Rule and now, according to Leo, he raised his eyes saying, "Lord, didn't I tell you that they wouldn't believe you?"

> The voice of Christ was heard in the air replying, "Francis there is nothing of yours in the Rule, it is all mine. I want the Rule to be observed to the letter, to the letter, to the letter, and without gloss, without gloss, without gloss."[14]

Francis now looked hard at the ministers and asked if they had heard this; would they like the words repeated? They didn't and very soon left.

Once Francis had led them into his cave it was clear to a pragmatic man like Elias that nothing whatever would change his mind on the true interpretation of gospel poverty, which has exercised the order ever since. The choice was therefore between confrontation or a graceful acceptance that Christ wished the ministers to withdraw their objections. For the time being the second option was preferable; it would also be more readily accepted by the order and the authorities in Rome if the ministers were unanimous that they had actually heard Christ's echoing verdict themselves.

The document that emerged from this long process of attrition skillfully reconciles the opposing forces at work on it. Compared with the version of 1221 it has shrunk from twenty-four chapters to twelve and from about twenty-three pages to eight; over a hundred quotations from the gospels have been cut to eleven. It is clear, practical and can be memorized, but is no longer personal; the passionate exhortations and poetic devotion of Francis's previous version have vanished.

In deference to the Lateran decrees it is harsher – in restricting visits to Poor Clares, prescribing punishment for infringing the Rule, and in depriving brothers who go among the Saracens of the option to observe their faith privately. In deference to the ministers it is more relaxed – in omitting the commands to "carry nothing for your journey" and to offer no resistance to violence; in omitting the brothers' rights against a minister who abuses his office; and in modifying the regulations about working, shoes, the ownership of a breviary and the initial dispossession of goods. On a neutral issue it mentions for the first time the office of *custos*, the friar in charge of a custody or subdivision of a province. Individual houses (and later convents) were in the charge of a guardian.

Angelo, Rufino and Leo who had been close to him longer than anyone else say he was deeply hurt by the opposition of his ministers but that he had made many concessions because he, too, wanted to avoid the scandal of a confrontation. This sacrifice was rewarded when the General Chapter endorsed this new version of the Rule at Pentecost and when Pope Honorius approved it in his Bull *Solet Annuere* in November. It was Francis's last great gift to his order and has defined its way of life, unaltered, for nearly eight hundred years.

*

Although the friars had at last received the papal document which secured the future of their order and laid down the form of life to which they were committed, they were losing something almost more precious – the companionship and guidance of Francis himself.

In one of the early sources, *The Mirror of Perfection*, whose authenticity has been hotly debated, Francis is said to have set out the qualities needed by the Minister General of the order. None of these is surprising for they all reflect the way in which he tried to lead his brothers – with the emphasis on prayer, self-denial, compassion for each one of his friars, and an awareness that his authority must inspire awe as well as love.

There were now plenty of priests in the order to educate new brothers in the practice of confession and communion, and in saying the Office. A number of the friars – Bernard, Giles, Rufino, Silvester, Pacifico and Juniper – were far advanced in mystical devotion. But Francis seems to have had an extraordinary sensitivity to a brother's spiritual difficulties – a wisdom greatly needed if they suddenly found themselves bored by prayer, frightened by the increasing demands it sometimes made, or – worst of all – when they despaired of their failings or the light of their faith seemed suddenly extinguished, and they floundered in a dark night of the soul. In all these situations Francis could advise them from his own spiritual experience, once telling a brother how, in one of his blacker moments, he had been reminded that a mustard seed of faith can shift a mountain of doubt.

There is no more effective advocate of self-denial than seeing it practiced by a man or woman one admires. "Foxes have holes and the birds of the air have nests, but the Son of Man has nowhere to lay his head," he would quote from St. Matthew; and if the friars made a cell specially pleasant for him, or spoke of it as "his" cell, he would move into one smaller. Once when a hermitage caught fire, he let the others quench the flames (he never doused fire himself), while he rescued the fox skin under which he slept out at night. The crisis over, he was bitterly ashamed and vowed never to use the pelt again. His attitude to clothes, food, books and especially money was utterly uncompromising.

Francis's prayers seemed to enrich his understanding as well as his love of his brothers. His companions cite a wide variety of occasions when his pastoral vision and sympathy released a brother from guilt or despair. He *knew* when a senior brother had persecuted his junior, and warned the young man, who was reluctant to divulge this: "Take care that under the pretext of humility you do not lie to me." He told another brother, over-scrupulous on the subject of his temptations, "It is not temptation but giving in to it which requires confession." He reassured a third brother: "The more you are tempted, the more I will love you." However clever, educated, ignorant, simple, well born or humble they were, Francis treated his friars equally. It was the Minister General's obligation to love his brothers and unite them in harmony. And if some deserted the order, they were to be treated with special mercy, for the temptations which led to their betrayal must have been overwhelming.

Above all the Minister General should see his authority as "a burden, not an honor." Could Elias live up to these precepts?

*

Among all the hermitages in the Rieti Valley, Greccio became Francis's favorite, a fondness he passed on to his closest companions who retreated here after his death. Most of the local inhabitants had now joined his order of penitents; in the fields – among their sheep, oxen, horses and mules – he might have been back on his family farmland around Assisi; buzzards and choughs floated on the winds above the woods on the hillside; below them the deer, foxes and occasionally wild boar or wolves crept out from the trees.

Today the hermitage clings to the cliff like a house martin's nest, under the eaves of the trees which lean over the crest. When Giovanni di Velita gave the place to Francis it was no more than a shrine in a cave with a few brushwood huts; but before long these needed protecting from the weather with a facade of stone. Two saints have lived here. Bonaventure, holiest and humblest of great European scholars, occupied a minute wooden cubicle in which he could scarcely lie down or stretch out his arms but which had a tiny window looking over the valley. Francis prayed and slept, sitting up, in a cell which was no more than a recess in the rock.

The brothers lived like a family and like families today enjoyed a party at Christmas. One year they were so carried away that Francis came down from his cell to find a table not only raised off the ground but set with a white cloth and glasses to entertain the minister from Rieti. Creeping out, he borrowed a stick and old hat from a beggar who had just turned up at the door and, when the friars began eating, called out:

> "For the love of God, spare some alms for this poor, sick, pilgrim!"
>
> The brothers immediately recognized him, and the minister gave him bread and the dish from which he was eating.
>
> Accepting them Francis sat on the ground near the fire and said, "When I saw this sumptuous table it didn't look as if it belonged to poor friars who beg from door to door. It's our duty to set a better example of humility and poverty than any other religious, because that is what we have promised before God and man."[15]

Always generous with whatever he had – sometimes only his labor, prayers or encouragement – Francis felt the whole world should be especially open-handed at Christmas. He once said, "If I ever talk to the emperor I will implore him, for the love of God, to decree that no one should trap or in any way harm our sisters the larks. Likewise the lord of every town and village, and every *podestà*, should see that all their people scatter the roads with grain for the birds on Christmas Day."[16]

The connection he makes between the emperor and the birds is fascinating because he and Frederick II cared more about animals than any other two men in Europe. Frederick was then compiling a six-volume study of birds, exploring falconry, the roosting of pheasants, the breeding of cuckoos and barnacle geese, and whether vultures were more dependent on eyesight or smell.*

It was a pity that Francis and Frederick never met, for they had far more in common than birds, a love of music and poetry, and the font in which they were both baptized. In 1225 Frederick was to receive an ambassador from Francis's old friend in Egypt, the Sultan al-Kamil. Their discussions were so fruitful that on hearing about the emperor's exotic menagerie the sultan sent him a shipment of apes, camels, a pair of leopards, a giraffe and an elephant. This gesture opened the way for a political breakthrough four years later. At Jaffa, in 1229, Frederick who was at the head of a small crusade, signed a treaty with al-Kamil which ceded Jerusalem to the Christians; its terms were identical with those that Francis and King John had urged Pelagius to accept ten years before.

Francis's benevolence at Christmas was not confined to birds but was universal.

> Out of reverence for the Son of God . . . all men ought to give a good meal to our brothers the oxen and asses on Christmas Eve. Similarly on Christmas Day the poor ought to be handsomely fed by the rich.[17]

We should all remember with gratitude, Thomas of Celano said, what Francis did at Greccio in 1223. With the pope's permission and Giovanni di Velita's help he arranged an entirely original celebration of Christmas. In preparation Giovanni persuaded his people to build and stock a stable near the hermitage. On Christmas Eve, when darkness fell, the friars around the valley joined the long procession of families climbing up to it.

> Candles and torches light up the night, whose shining star illumines every day and every year. The manger is prepared, the hay is laid out, the ox and the ass are led in. Greccio is made a new Bethlehem.[18]

Shepherds and their flocks gathered at the edge of the crowd gazing into the open stable as Mass was said by the manger. Clothed as a deacon Francis stood beside it, sang the gospel, and preached, suggesting with his

*His investigations and experiments exploded existing theories that these geese emerged from goose barnacles and that vultures pinpointed carrion by smell.

voice each of the animals he mentioned. It was said that one devout man, possibly Giovanni di Velita, saw the sleeping doll open its eyes when Francis bent over the manger to bless it. The night seemed to light up like day and the woods on the hillside rang with the joy of the singing.

That Christmas at Greccio was Francis's last memorable public appearance. Work and preaching were now, with very few exceptions, beyond him. But prayer was not, and as his body – Brother Ass – slowly stumbled to a standstill his soul suddenly soared to the zenith of his spiritual endeavor.

23

Five Wounds

1224

The brothers close to Francis noticed that as his body decayed "the inner man was renewed" and burned even brighter. He withdrew from society, and spent most of his time with a few companions in the mountains. There the daily rhythms of the Office, rotating the focus of their prayers and their meditations on the phases of Christ's life, reinforced their spiritual energy – a power further boosted by the Mass which reassured them, almost daily, of their literal communion with God.

Our reliance on symbols, icons, rituals and sacraments, at the key moments of social, ceremonial and religious occasions, manifests a primal need to express our most potent desires or aspirations through familiar objects and gestures. Vice versa these – a loving cup, raised banners, the lowered sword, a gold ring, the scent of smoke or proffered bread and wine in the Mass – stimulate our senses and through them our minds, imaginations and emotions. These, in turn, activate our wills and stir us to action.

According to the teaching of the Roman Church the bread and wine of the Mass do not represent but actually become, "in substance," Christ's body and blood. This doctrine had taken some time to develop but Francis believed it and Innocent III formally incorporated the term *transubstantiation* in the decrees of his Lateran Council. Since Francis was wholly committed to the imitation of Christ, the symbols associated with his incarnation – the crib, his figure on the crucifix in San Damiano, his blood in the chalice – affected him with extraordinary force.

Although his companions had observed his entranced devotions and occasional raptures during services by the roadside, in a piazza or more formally in a chapel or church, they also knew that his most exalted flights were usually confined to the hours he spent in solitary contemplation. It was then as if he had withdrawn into a darkened room where they must not follow, but while they waited outside they saw a soft glimmer between the door and the frame, which gradually grew until sunlight seemed to stream from the crevices.

By now Francis was close to the summit of his spiritual ascent, reaching a state of self-surrender so complete that it is often known to those who study mysticism as Union with God. He had long been familiar with the subjective experiences of Illumination – visions, voices, music, smells, tastes (as described by Clare) and sensations of subjection to violence or fire. Now he began to experience the kind of objective phenomena reliably witnessed and reported by the companions and observers of exceptional mystics. In *The Varieties of Religious Experience* William James called them automatisms.

These unusual happenings include the effusion of light seen by others, shared visions, speech in a strange tongue, automatic writing, a pervading "odor of sanctity," and the ability to heal. The Bishop of Avila was probably surprised one morning during Mass to see St. Teresa being lifted into the air by some invisible force; Jean Vianney, the Curé d'Ars, was another mystic seen to levitate. Several miracles, including healing, were attributed to Francis toward the end of his life, and many more after his death. They are not included in this book because it is impossible to validate or dismiss now the grounds on which the church accepted them then.

Saints have never accounted any virtue whatever to such episodes, which they see simply as accidents overtaking their spirits. The principal indicator of the distinction between these "accidents" and the delusions of hysteria, dementia or psychosis, has always been whether or not they are accompanied by practical benefits to their fellow human beings. "By their fruits ye shall know them."

Of course these automatisms can be rejected, like many so-called miracles, as fabrications or the unconscious delusions of their reporters. A supernatural explanation – entailing the suspension of, or interference with, natural processes – is no longer acceptable to rational minds. But as historical and scientific research creep forward a sweeping dismissal of such occurrences is as irrational as their wholesale acceptance. Some witnesses turn out not to be frauds or deluded, just as the "laws" of nature turn out to be suppler, more mysterious, or sometimes quite other than previously supposed.

Pacifico described a vision which occurred when he and Francis had gone north toward Ancona and were working in a leper house at Trevi. They spent the night in a nearby church at Bovara, where Pacifico

> . . . was caught up in an ecstasy. He saw a row of thrones in the sky, one higher and more radiant than the others, studded with precious stones. Wondering for whom it was prepared he heard a voice say: "This was Lucifer's throne; Francis will occupy it instead."
>
> It continued: "Just as Lucifer was hurled from it because of his pride, Francis will receive it because of his humility."[1]

Francis had always held St. Michael, who headed the army of angels and archangels against Lucifer, in special veneration and in August 1224 decided to precede his feast with a forty-day fast at La Verna.

*

The Little Flowers tells the full story of the retreat at La Verna. The small party of friars accompanying Francis – Leo, Angelo, Masseo and Leonardo – knew he was too ill to walk there in the heat and persuaded a peasant to lend him an ass. When he handed over the reins he asked, "Are you Francis of Assisi himself?"

Hearing the answer he looked up at the little man in his worn habit: "Well then, try to be as good as you can, because everyone has great faith in you and you mustn't let them down." Francis was so touched that he dismounted and kissed the man's feet.

When the sun rose higher and even the donkey slowed down Francis, reflecting on the peasant's words, turned around to Leonardo who, older than he and once the Lord of Sasso Rosso, was limping behind him.

"Brother, it isn't right that I should be riding while you, who were a noble and so important, have to walk."[2]

Leonardo was both startled and abashed, because exactly these thoughts were grumbling around his head at that moment. They apologized to each other. In fact by the time they were halfway up La Verna even the peasant was exhausted and said he would die without a drink. In one of the so-called Giotto cycle of frescoes he has fallen on his knees to slake his thirst from a spring that Francis miraculously coaxed from the rocks.

Further on, Francis sat for a time under a great oak to see if the birds would welcome his arrival; when each in turn came to sing above his head he was delighted. A hundred and fifty years ago William Wordsworth was also delighted. He had enjoyed the larks, thrushes and nightingales lower down in the olive groves but was so moved by the familiar call of a cuckoo, echoing up here among the beeches, that he wrote an ode in its honor. La Verna still teems with birds, one of the most elegant a kestrel hovering on the wind, or darting to its mate like an arrow.

The friars' huts – Rufino and Silvester were already here – stood on an escarpment toward the top of the mountain. They clustered around the chapel built for them by Orlando which has the same transitional, slightly pointed, arches as San Damiano, suggesting that Francis had a hand in its construction. It is an attractive little church; but three of La Verna's natural features are spectacular – its trees, its views and its rocks. The forest of magnificent beeches and pines, their roots ringed with flowers in the spring, is often quite silent except for the whisper of leaves, the soft, tentative twitter of invisible birds, or the sudden crack of a branch, sharp as a gunshot. Looking down from the summit, La Penna, the eye is led like a swift's over the beautiful Casentino valley and little villages on the slopes of the Valle Santa, to a surrounding circle of mountains, blue ghosts in the distance.

The rocks of La Verna are contorted and haunting. Francis often chose to pray in a forbidding gallery roofed by a ledge, the Sasso Spicco, jutting out from the cliff. A natural cleft at one end slopes down to a deep rock-sided bowl in the mountain. This was the atrium, living branches its ceiling, which led to the cave where he slept on a rock. Some of the scattered boulders have been slashed by a giant's sword, their two halves still only a few inches apart. Elsewhere the blade has sliced a protrusion from the cliff to leave it standing several feet clear, a towering column capped with an island of greenery.

On his first full day at La Verna Francis told the brothers that he wanted to be out of earshot from the friary and needed only Leo to look after him.

The two then searched the woods until they found a spot cut off by a chasm, which they bridged with a log. On the far side they put up a shelter of branches and Leo agreed that for the next forty days he would bring Francis food and water each morning and evening. Francis gave him an instruction.

"Approach silently, and when you reach the log say, 'Lord open thou our lips.' If I answer, 'And our mouths shall show forth thy praise,' come across and we'll say Matins together. If you hear nothing, go away."[3]

During his vigil Francis's sole neighbors were a pair of falcons now raising their young. They called him each morning in time to say Prime, but if he was too weak or tired they let him sleep on; there were lonely hours when their company brought him great consolation.

At first Leo did exactly as he had been told but when he received no answer from Francis one evening – devout, humble and obedient though he was – his curiosity got the better of him and he crept across the log, close enough to see Francis and catch the sound of his voice. He was kneeling in the moonlight, gazing up into the sky with his arms outstretched as if in praise or supplication and murmuring, over and over, "Who art thou, my dearest Lord God and what am I, your vile little worm, your useless servant?" Alone in the beauty and mystery of the night it seemed as if he were attempting to slough off the very last shreds of self-regard which still separated him from his creator.

Among a series of buildings that have risen on the cliff top during the last seven centuries the Chapel of the Stigmata stands precisely where Francis prayed that night. However a narrow little balcony, very close to it, now allows one to stand as Francis did, somewhere between the earth and the sky, simultaneously aware of the sights and sounds of the world and of the prospect of heaven.

It was here, very early one morning in late September 1224, that he experienced a vision of a seraph and an ecstasy uniquely intense even for him – and so startling in its nature that it quickly assumed a historical significance (Plate 6). Several of his companions wrote or handed down their versions of what occurred; historians usually prefer Thomas of Celano's because it was authorized by the pope and the first to be published; yet Thomas was in Germany at the time, he did not hear about the episode for at least another two years, and his account is suspiciously elaborate.

By contrast Leo and Angelo were only a few hundred yards away and later the same morning heard from Francis's own lips what he had seen and felt. Leo never wrote more than a few words about Francis's encounter with the seraph. Much later, long after Francis died, he told the full story of the Michaelmas retreat on La Verna to a spiritual lay brother in the next generation, James of Massa. He in turn passed it on to the friars in the Marches from whom *The Little Flowers* emanated in the fourteenth century.

Leo's own words appear in his neat red script on a parchment already inscribed by Francis with praises and a blessing (Plate 8).

> Two years before his death . . . the hand of the Lord was upon him. After the vision and message of the seraph, and the impression of Christ's stigmata on his body, he composed these praises.[4]

Angelo dictated a slightly fuller account at an unknown date after Francis's death. (Just beneath it a separate section has been interpolated with the complex "official" description of the wounds referred to later.)

> One morning two years before his death, about the feast of the Exaltation of the Cross, while he was praying on the side of a mountain named La Verna, there appeared to him a seraph in the beautiful figure of a crucified man, having his hands and feet extended as though on a cross, and clearly showing the face of Jesus Christ. Two wings met above his head, two covered the rest of his body to the feet, and two were spread as in flight.
>
> When the vision passed, the soul of Francis was afire with love; and on his body there appeared the wonderful impression of the wounds of our Lord Jesus Christ.[5]

For the rest of his life Francis bore these marks on his hands, feet and side, as if he had been crucified and pierced with a lance.

*

Francis immediately decided to conceal his stigmata from the world; at all costs they must not attract attention as a wonder. At the same time it was impossible to keep them secret from his brothers at La Verna; if some knew, all of them should. Apart from that, he had to bandage his hands, wear unaccustomed slippers, and was barely able to walk; more awkwardly still he constantly bled from his side onto his tunic and breeches. They were all sworn to secrecy, but only a few – Leo, Angelo, Rufino, Pacifico and Elias – actually saw the marks, and then by accident.

Claims of a phenomenon like this automatically raise the question, what really happened to Francis that morning? As soon as he died, and the stigmata became common knowledge, men wanted to know more. Some were certain that the wounds were self-inflicted, others that they had been made by the friars postmortem. Even Cardinal Ugolino said he disbelieved their spontaneous origin at first but was convinced by the time he canonized Francis in 1228. Probably the fullest exploration of the question was published by a Franciscan scholar, Octavian Schmucki, in 1991. His 380-page book digests and summarizes his survey of 370 books, journals and articles addressing the subject in ten different languages. He concluded, after considering all the historical and medical evidence, and making full allowance for the adulation Francis inspired at the end of his life, that the only honest verdict is that marks did mysteriously appear on his body two years before he died without any external human agency.

It was the first known case of this kind, but in subsequent centuries another three hundred bona fide instances have been recorded. They include St. Catherine of Siena (1347–80) who, jointly with Francis, is patron saint of Italy; Jean Vianney, the nineteenth-century French priest best known as the Curé d'Ars; and a number of men and women in the twentieth century, among them an English woman, Dorothy Kerin (1889–1963). On May 5, 1999 the pope announced the beatification of the most famous modern stigmatic, the Franciscan friar Padre Pio who died in 1968; the ceremony took place before a crowd of more than 150,000 people in St. Peter's Square; Pio da Pietrelcina was said to have healed a great many people in southern Italy where he lived and frequently to have exuded the scent of violets.

Just as the two men best qualified to describe Francis's condition both chose the simplest terms, so did Elias. He had caught a glimpse of the wounds some time before Francis died, he helped to lay out the body, he had a trained eye and he had been prepared for six months to break the news of their founder's death to the order. He wrote this in his encyclical letter following the funeral.*

*Some scholars are now reviving old doubts about its authenticity but it is too early to evaluate their case.

> His hands and feet had, as it were, the punctures of nails pierced on both sides, retaining scars and showing the black color of nails.[6]

The inference is clear; to the brothers who observed the marks closely it seemed as if Francis had been crucified and taken down from his cross, as in a *pietà*, an image of Christ which had not yet emerged in the work of European artists. For a man who had often prayed to share Christ's suffering it seemed a fitting recognition of his devotion.

In a sense the real problems with the stigmata began when Ugolino and Thomas of Celano put their heads together in 1228 in order to refute the sceptics who suggested the friars had made the nail or stab wounds themselves. For this they needed a description which made it impossible the lesions had been faked. Thomas says this in his first life of Francis.

> His hands and feet seemed to be pierced through the middle by nails, with the heads of the nails appearing on the inside of the hands and on the upper side of the feet, and their pointed ends on the opposite sides. The marks on the palm of the hands were round, those on the outside elongated – pieces of his flesh taking on the appearance of the heads of nails and also their points, bent, beaten back, and rising above the rest of the flesh. In the same way, the marks of the nails were impressed on his feet and elevated above the rest of the flesh.[7]

In a later section of his biography he refers to the stigmata again, rephrasing and modifying the sense of Elias's account.

> It was wonderful to see in the middle of his hands and feet not the punctures of nails but the nails themselves, formed by his flesh.[8]

Thirty or forty years later, in the *Legenda Major*, St. Bonaventure compounded the complications when he not only adopted Thomas's definitions but elaborated on them, writing of the fleshy nails.

> When they were pressed on one side they immediately jutted out farther on the other.[9]

He is more extravagant still in the edition he condensed and revised for use in the Office.

> The curved portion of the nails on the soles of his feet was so big and stood out so far that he could not put his foot firmly on the ground; a man could put his finger through the loop without difficulty.[10]

Although first Thomas, and later Bonaventure, were Francis's official, "canonical," biographers they were propagandists and hagiographers, not historians. Thomas seems not to have consulted the three most obvious and valuable witnesses, Leo, Angelo and Rufino before he wrote his first life of the saint. His imaginative, poetic and often moving account of Francis's activities is light on fact or sometimes wrong. In 1977 Bishop J. R. H. Moorman wrote that it "is in some ways the least satisfying of the early attempts to tell the story of St. Francis." Twenty years later, in 1997, a friar confessed in a Franciscan symposium that Thomas's detailed and didactic account of the seraph's appearance and theological significance convinced him that Thomas not Francis was the original source for its apparition on La Verna that night.[11]

This seems unnecessarily sweeping, just as it would be wrong to dismiss the stigmata altogether. It is possible to accept the wounds were real and spontaneous without being driven to the belief they were "miraculous." Some contemporary stigmatics (recently there were about a dozen cases being investigated in Britain alone) appear to be suffering from either a hysterical or self-hypnotic condition, but experts do not consider that Francis belongs to either group.

Searching for an alternative explanation in 1987 two members of the Franciscan order, Sr. Joanne Schatzlein, a highly qualified nurse, and Dr. Daniel Sulmasy, a physician, were led to the view that a lifetime of nursing lepers had exposed him to the disease and that he had contracted the milder, tubercular, form at about the time he returned from the Middle East with his eye complaint.[12] They make a detailed and plausible case for their conclusion – it would account for the discoloration of his skin, his eye problems, the protuberance of the fleshy "nails" on his hands and feet, the insensitivity of his face to pain when his temples were cauterized, his stomach hemorrhage at Siena, and the fact that some bones at the tips of his fingers were missing when his skeleton was exhumed. However the diagnosis seems to rely too heavily on dubious data from Thomas and Bonaventure and to dismiss too readily the likelihood that Francis may have suffered from a gastric ulcer, been infected with trachoma in Egypt, been subject to bouts of quartan malaria picked up from mosquitoes in the marshes around Assisi or Rome, and had contracted tuberculosis during his year as a prisoner in Perugia (as young Molière later did in a debtors' jail). The doctors also regard finger bones an unlikely choice for the devout seeking a relic from the saint's body. But it was a finger bone that Dr. Moorman chose to hold when he was shown the saint's skeleton in 1978; the privilege so moved him that he did not sleep for the whole of that night. It was a finger bone of St. Marie d'Oignies that Cardinal Ugolino wore around his neck in a locket to tame his swearing. And fifty years ago one of St. Teresa's fingers was on view in a cabinet at Avila.

In a recent history of tuberculosis (*Mycobacterium tuberculosis*) Dr. Thomas Dormandy describes how the human, as opposed to the bovine variety, can attack either the lungs or the lymph nodes. After the French seventeenth-century playwright Molière contracted the disease: "It remained with him for the rest of his life, striking him down from time to time with fever, cough, and extreme weakness for weeks or months. Despite this he kept extraordinarily busy."[13]

He finally died of a lung hemorrhage – a classic symptom – at the age of fifty-one; other regular symptoms are waning appetite, weight loss, poor color, night fevers and sweats, a hoarse voice and sometimes a temporary inability to speak.

Lymph node tuberculosis goes by a number of different names – *Lupus vulgaris*, scrofula or the King's Evil, for a royal hand was thought able to cure it.* Its symptoms include ugly nodules, ulcers and scarring, and resemble *Mycobacterium leproe*, the form of leprosy posited by the doctors in their Franciscan journal. Such nodules may be pink, red or very much darker. However, a characteristic of the disease is that the tissue destruction, the consequent inflammation and the formation of contracting scar tissue may all occur simultaneously with gross and undesirable results. Bonaventure wrote of the wound in Francis's side that it was red, and the flesh was contracted into a sort of circle, so that "it looked like a beautiful rose";

*Francis's contemporary Philip Augustus of France once touched 1500 patients in one session.

perhaps in describing the stigmata he and Thomas were not so inaccurate after all.

There is another dimension of tuberculosis not irrelevant in considering Francis's health. Dr. Dormandy writes that in the middle of the eighteenth century there emerged an "extraordinary procession of artists, poets, writers and thinkers about whom one can reasonably say that they suffered and died from tuberculosis." It was true in the next century, too, of the artists Bonington and Beardsley, the composers Paganini and Chopin, the poets Shelley and Keats, and of the Brontës, Edgar Allan Poe and Robert Louis Stevenson – all of them, like Francis, burning with a hard, gemlike flame, and all extinguished too young.

A final consideration on Francis's apparent immunity to heat – his unconcern when his tunic was burning, his offer to walk through fire in the sultan's camp and his insensitivity to the doctor's irons at Fonte Colombo – is that his transcendental meditations may have taught him how to neutralize the normal effects of burning, in much the same way as achieved by Hindu or Muslim fakirs.

At this distance of time it is impossible either to diagnose reliably the precise cause or causes of Francis's ill-health or to explain what brought about his stigmata. The latter, in particular, defy scientific analysis because the time scale of their appearance is unknown. Thomas of Celano implies they occurred almost immediately after the apparition of the seraph, which would rule out a leprous or tubercular origin; on the other hand if they gradually emerged over the full forty-day retreat, or longer, the conclusion might be different.

Today many doctors find themselves faced with the symptoms of psychosomatic disturbance and the more open-minded accept that some elude precise diagnosis. In Francis's case the possibility that Jesus may have been roped, not nailed, to the cross is irrelevant; the image of the crucifix in San Damiano was the one that inspired and sustained his entire life. Had he lived five hundred or a thousand years earlier or been born into the Eastern not the Western church, his guiding vision might have been of Christ the shepherd or Christ in majesty, transfigured as the light of the world.

As it was, given the intensity of his nature and his rare ability to unify and concentrate his spiritual, mental, emotional and physical faculties, it is perhaps not surprising that his identification with Christ should ultimately manifest itself visibly. Octavian Schmucki quotes a study which ascribes the phenomenon to an ecstatic experience of the crucifixion which enveloped Francis so powerfully that it "focused an overexcited neural activity on the tissues of his hands, feet and side."[14]

*

Although Francis often called Leo his "little lamb," his confessor had the spirit of a lion. Once, when Francis wished to be vilified as a form of penance and had grown persistently more reproachful when Leo refused to cooperate, it was the lamb who won the day; after that they came to know each other inside out. St. Michael's Lent 1224 bound them together more closely still, and Francis suddenly became aware that Leo had an unspoken longing to be given a few uplifting words, written in his hand, to help keep his fears and temptations at bay. After writing out some Praises he told Leo to guard them carefully until his death. This was the parchment on which Leo recorded the stigmata; faded and creased from years of rubbing against his habit, it is now in the basilica at Assisi.

In the seventeenth century a letter by Masseo turned up at La Verna, which described Francis's final farewell to the sanctuary; it is no longer considered authentic, but it preserves an ancient tradition. In it Francis bids goodbye to Masseo, Angelo, Silvester and Illuminato; he thanks the mountain, the Sasso Spicco which protected him during his prayers, and the kestrels for their kindness; and then he sets out for Assisi.

Progress was slow because Francis was extremely unwell. The party stopped first in the hermitage at Borgo San Sepolcro, where several of the friars had an unusual background. A few years before, the brothers living there had been constantly importuned by a band of robbers who treated them as their call of last resort when villainy failed. The friars gave all they had, as they would to any other beggars, but the gang never reformed in return for their charity.

Francis therefore told the brothers to go an extra mile – seek the robbers out in the hills, take them bread and wine, lay out plates and glasses on a cloth in the forest, feed them eggs and cheese, too. After that he suggested asking them why they led such boring, dangerous and unpleasant lives when they could earn a good living on the land. Before long the gang were bringing down firewood to the friary; not long after, three of them joined the order.

Orlando had lent Francis a horse for the journey but Leo still walked as they moved on to the hermitage at Monte Casale. After that they stopped at Citta di Castello where Francis was so ill that they had to stay for a month. Yet such was his resilience when they were back at the Porziuncula that he insisted on riding around Umbria and the Marches to preach. Elias, who was genuinely fond of him and especially concerned to keep an eye on his health, would occasionally join him for a few days on his travels. Several years later he told Thomas of Celano about a night he and Francis had spent in Foligno. After he had gone to sleep he was visited by "a white-garbed priest of very great age and a venerable appearance." The old man looked down at him and spoke to him.

"Arise, brother, and say to Brother Francis that eighteen years have now elapsed since he renounced the world, and that in another two he will go the way of all flesh."[15]

Elias did as bidden, and Francis took the spectral message to heart. From then on he was constantly aware that his days were numbered and when he was too unwell to go out preaching he put the time to good use dictating letters to Leo, for he was now nearly blind and could do little with his own hands; yet he never gave into despair and – like St. John of the Cross – he thought disquietude a useless vanity.

The champagne sparkle of joy, on the other hand, had always been important if not essential to him since his days as a troubadour. The Joy of the Court, extolled in the Arthurian romance of *Erec and Enide*, is a distillation of the harmonies of music and song, the love experienced in courting, marriage and friendship, and the happiness all of us search for and occasionally find. Toward the end of their quest for this courtly joy a few of the later troubadours abandoned it, as Francis had, for the joy of God's love they had discovered instead.

Francis gave a new twist to the courtly concept when he defined joy to Leo like this:

> If I were told that every scholar in Paris, all the bishops and archbishops beyond the Alps, and the kings of France and England had joined the order, that should not bring me joy. Nor should it if I discovered that my brothers had converted every infidel, while I was

able to heal the sick and perform miracles.

But if I walked back from Perugia, through the mud on a dark night in winter, and my legs bled from the icicles on the hem of my tunic; and if I had to knock twice at the door of the Porziuncula when I got back and was twice turned away; and if the third time I knocked I was told to go off and find shelter in the Cruciger's leper house – I tell you that if I could stand all this and not be upset, that would be perfect joy.[16]

Elias grew increasingly alarmed that Francis wouldn't take any of his maladies seriously, declining all medicines and medical advice. He therefore asked Ugolino to intervene from Rieti, where he was staying with Honorius and the Curia, and Francis received this letter in his little rush hut at the Porziuncula.

Brother, It isn't good to refuse to have your eyes treated, for your health and your life are very valuable – to yourself and other people. You, who have always shown such sympathy for your brothers when they were ill shouldn't be so callous toward yourself, for your illness is serious and clearly needs treatment. That is why I command you to submit to it.[17]

Put like that Francis could no longer refuse to talk to a doctor. He would have to go to Rieti, where Ugolino wanted him to see the physicians attending the Papal Court.

24

Sunset

1225–1226

The soul's dark cottage, batter'd and decay'd,
Lets in new light through chinks that time has made.
Stronger by weakness, wiser men become
As they draw near to their eternal home.

Edmund Waller
1606–1687

During his last two years Francis was continuously cared for by his closest and most devoted companions, all experts in nursing the sick, all familiar with the problems of his stigmata and the agony from his lungs, stomach and eyes. Several times he thanked them formally, once apologizing for the trouble his pain and fatigue were causing. He went on to assure them that in the end God would reward them on his behalf and credit them with the good work they would have otherwise done.

Clare as always was anxious to see him before he left Assisi again, never knowing how long he would be gone or if he would ever return. Now, perhaps as much for his own sake as hers, he called at San Damiano to say goodbye and to reassure her of his unwavering care and affection. However she immediately recognized that it was he who needed affectionate care, and provided it with her characteristic confidence. Turning a blind eye to

Ugolino's *Constitutions* and Francis's own injunction against familiarities between the friars and their sisters, she had a lean-to of rushes put up for him in her garden. There, under her watchful eye, his companions could help build his strength for the journey to Rieti.

Instead, as the late spring weather grew hotter, his symptoms – especially the inflammation of his eyes – became increasingly serious. He couldn't stand sunlight and found it impossible to see by the glow of a lamp or candle at night. Imprisoned in darkness, his pain was so intense that he seldom rested or slept, and if he did drop off was soon woken by the field mice that scampered all over him. Shocked to discover he was giving way to self-pity he concentrated harder on his prayers.

They were soon rewarded with an intimation that his illness and suffering were worth far more than the value of the entire earth if it were solid gold and its stones jewels. What is more, he told the friars in the morning, "God deigned to assure me, while I'm still here in the flesh, that there will be a place for me later in heaven. I therefore want to compose a song praising him and thanking him for all his creatures on earth, because we cannot live without them and we daily offend him by our lack of gratitude for them."[1]

This was his song:

Most high, almighty, good Lord,
Yours be the praise, the glory, the honor and every blessing;
To you alone, most high, do they belong
And no man is worthy to utter your name.

Be praised, my Lord, with all your creatures,
Especially Lord Brother Sun,
To whom we owe both day and light,
For he is beautiful, radiant and of great splendor;
Of you, most high, he is the emblem.

Be praised, my Lord, through Sister Moon and the stars,
You have made them in the heavens, bright, precious and beautiful.

Be praised, my Lord, through Brothers Wind and Air,
Through cloud, clear skies and all other weather
By which you give your creatures sustenance.

Be praised, my Lord, through Sister Water,
So very useful, humble, precious and chaste.

Be praised, my Lord, through Brother Fire,
By whom you enlighten the night;
He is beautiful, merry, robust and strong.

Be praised, my Lord, through our sister, Mother Earth,
Who sustains and looks after us,
Producing the different fruits, colored flowers and the grass.[2]

Leo, who recorded the whole period at San Damiano, says that after Francis had completed this great song of praise he arranged with Elias that Pacifico, once the emperor's King of Verse, should take a band of friars around the country and sing it after they had preached, saying to their audiences, "We are the Lord's minstrels and you can repay us for our performance by leading a life of penance."

He gave these praises the title of *The Canticle of Brother Sun*. It was composed in the Umbrian dialect, then emerging with others from Latin into Italian. Some scholars say it is the earliest poem in a modern European language to survive, others that the original reveals great artistry not only in the choice and arrangement of its images but also in the subtlety of its rhythms. Although its refrain of praise echoes the *Benedicite*, sung at Matins – itself drawn from the song of the three young men in Nebuchadnezzar's burning, fiery furnace – its vision of our family relationship with the whole of creation is entirely original. It is one of the shafts of light which opened the eyes of the great Italian artists to nature and expresses a lively concern shared by science and popular feeling today.

The Canticle's immediate success brought Francis such sweet relief that his rising spirits enabled him, in July, to confront a dispute then tormenting Assisi. The nobility and citizens of its old enemy Perugia were at each other's throats, causing so much local unrest, that the *podestà* of Assisi felt obliged to intervene, against the express wishes of the Perugians' historic patron the pope. As a result Honorius had angrily ordered Bishop Guido to excommunicate the *podestà*, Oportulo di Bernardo. Oportulo, a brave and honorable man, was so outraged by this that he declared no one in Assisi was to sell to, buy from, or have any dealings whatsoever with the bishop.

The conflict deeply saddened Francis. Guido, now an old man with only three years to live, had first backed him in Assisi and then launched him in Rome; while he had long admired Oportulo, whose daughter Agnese had joined Clare at San Damiano five years before. He therefore composed another verse to his canticle.

> *Be praised, my Lord, through those who pardon for thy love,*
> *And bear infirmity and tribulation.*
> *Blessed are they who uphold peace;*
> *By you, most high, they will be crowned.*[3]

Francis then sent a friar to the *podestà* with a personal message asking him to go to the small piazza outside the bishop's palace while two other brothers went to Guido and explained that Francis wanted some of them to sing the new canticle to him and Oportulo: "He asks you to listen very devoutly." The protagonists and their supporters assembled in their official uniforms and full regalia, surrounded by an excited crowd who quickly fell silent when the friars began to sing.

> The *podestà* stood up and listened intently as if to the gospel, with his hands joined and tears in his eyes, for he was very fond of Francis. At the end he spoke. "I wouldn't give in to our bishop whom I ought to acknowledge as my lord." Then kneeling at the bishop's feet he went on, "I am ready to make satisfaction to you in whatever way you please, for the love of Jesus Christ and his servant Francis."
>
> The bishop bent down, raised him to his feet and answered, "My office requires me to be humble but I am, by nature, quick-tempered and you must make allowances for me."
>
> At that they embraced and kissed each other with grace and affection, resuming their former warmth after this acrimony.[4]

Immensely heartened by the détente between his two great friends, Francis was ready to leave Clare and make his reluctant way to Rieti. This was his last visit to the grounds of the little church he had first repaired twenty years before, and as a parting gift he composed a fifteen-line *Canticle of Exhortation* for her and her sisters, which he asked his companions to give them as he did not feel he could take it into the convent himself.

Now he braced himself for the hot, dusty journey to Rieti, dreading the inevitable crowds besieging the papal court and the medical treatment he neither wanted nor believed in.

*

Francis had walked the long winding and often steep road to Rieti many times; now he had to ride. To reduce his suffering his companions sewed a strip of linen to his large floppy cowl which protected his face from the glare, dust and flies. Even so his eyes wept continuously as they do in the very early painting of him now at Greccio (Plate 7). Some believe it is a contemporary likeness commissioned by Giacoma de Settesoli.

Although the principal episodes of the next twelve months were recorded by Francis's contemporaries their precise chronology is uncertain, and since they were not written down until after his canonization – by which time a stream of miracles had been attributed to him – suggestions of the supernatural are apt to creep into the narrative.

Francis was so warmly welcomed to Rieti by Honorius and Ugolino, and his prestige within the Curia was so great, that Bishop Rinaldo invited him to lodge under his roof with the pope and his entourage while Elias immediately urged him to take advantage of the skills of the society doctors clustering around the powerful but elderly prelates. During his years as legate in southern Italy, Honorius had discovered how much more the Arabs knew about medicine than their European counterparts. In particular he seems to have patronized a doctor called Tebaldo de Saraceno, whose father was either an Arab or had picked up his knowledge in the Middle East, and with whom Francis immediately struck up a friendship. Tebaldo treated him with bloodletting and eye salves but was reluctant to go further, which suited Francis admirably; he mistrusted the drastic surgery recommended by some of the Italian doctors and favored by Elias. His daily needs were looked after, from now until his death, by Angelo, Rufino, Leo and Masseo, "on whom he rested like a house on four columns."

However modest he was about his achievements, and especially his exploits in Egypt, he was conscious that he excited irresistible curiosity among the grandees and hangers-on in Rieti. Men would break off their business to ask his advice or hear him talk, listening with apparent respect; yet he suspected that when many turned away it was to gossip or laugh about him. Nevertheless he could never refuse a cry for help and when a notoriously dissolute priest, who was dangerously ill, asked for his blessing he gave it, but concluded with a warning, "Beware you don't return to your vomit or you will incur a very harsh judgment." Gideon recovered but failed to mend his ways. He was killed when a roof fell in, leaving everyone with him unharmed.

For a time Francis could escape from these unwelcome crowds to the newly built cathedral next to the bishop's palace. Its simple, beautifully proportioned Romanesque columns and vaults – still intact – were a perfect refuge for contemplation. However the atmosphere in Rieti remained so oppressive that he fled three miles to the little country church of San Fabiano, where the priest's house stood peacefully in his garden and vineyard. Yet even here Francis's personality and reputation attracted a procession of visitors. Parties of cardinals, bishops, their retainers, and other well-meaning clergy turned up every day, all eager to meet him. Pushing into the little vineyard they settled in its shade and quenched their thirst on the grapes – it was now September. Very soon most of the crop had been eaten, trampled or simply taken. Powerless to prevent it the priest, whose wine was his only source of income, was first angry and then distraught.

Francis consoled him, asked what yield he had hoped for, and assured him that God would make it up with half as much again. The priest was not disappointed, and today visitors can see the stone vat in which the remains of the plundered harvest were pressed, to produce the promised twenty barrels of wine. Visitors are also shown, just below the house, a cave in which some, believing that early scribes misread San Fabiano as San Damiano, maintain that Francis wrote *The Canticle of Brother Sun*. Tracks in the dust around the cave confirm it is still occupied by mice but otherwise there is no tangible evidence for their claim.

The daily invasion of San Fabiano (now known as La Foresta) forced Francis to move on to the hermitage up in the woods at Fonte Colombo where he had completed his Rule. Tebaldo frequently came out to see him but being successful and rich declined the friars' invitation to share their hard-won scraps. However, Francis embarrassed his brothers one day by insisting that the doctor should stay and eat. Tebaldo brushed aside their apologies but Francis was seriously nettled by their lack of faith in him, for just as they were putting their crusts of bread and some wine on the table, a peasant appeared at the door with a large basket from the chatelaine of a nearby castle. It was full of "bread, fish, crab pâté, eggs seemingly fresh from the nest, honey and grapes."

Although his eyes failed to improve Francis managed to postpone the operation recommended by one of the specialists in Rieti, Master Nicholas, which entailed cauterizing the veins in his temples to stem the flow of tears and pus, for it was thought inadvisable to undergo this in the cold winter weather. He therefore probably spent some of the time at Greccio, celebrating Christmas once more with a living crib. Otherwise, barely able to see, he devoted himself to prayer, the Office, and dictating to Leo, conscious that he was no longer strong enough to work or go out preaching.

His surviving letters are not dated and many are lost, including a number to Clare. It may have been now that he wrote to "The Rulers of the Peoples," urging them to reflect on the approach of death and to promote the love of God among their subjects; the pope, who had left Rieti in January, and the young emperor Frederick II, who had recently married King John of Jerusalem's daughter, were at loggerheads, threatening the peace of Europe. And it was certainly now that he wrote to "The Entire Order," as "a useless man and unworthy creature," begging them to observe their Rule inviolably.

When the warmer weather came in the spring Elias persuaded Francis to endure the operation for his own good and that of the order, emphasizing he would like to be present for it. But as the weeks went by he was constantly on the move with Ugolino or visiting the provinces and Francis could no longer wait. In a tall bare room upstairs Leo and the others waited with him while the brazier was lit and Master Nicholas plunged his branding irons into its heart until they grew red hot.

> So that he wouldn't be too frightened Francis said to the fire: "My brother, noble and useful among all other creatures as you are, be courteous to me in this hour for I have always loved you and still do. I beg our Creator, who made you, to temper your heat so that I can bear it."
>
> As for us who were with him, we all fled out of love and pity; only the doctor remained.[5]

Carefully but firmly Nicholas pressed his red-hot irons into the skin on Francis's temple, searing a three inch furrow into the smoking flesh between the top of his ear and the corner of his eye – first on one side and then on the other.

Outside the four friars heard nothing until the doctor opened the door. Then Francis turned his head toward them and said, "Why were you such cowards and so lacking in faith as to go out? I felt neither heat nor pain – and if I'm not properly singed I had better be branded again."[6]

The astonished doctor said that he had never come across a man before, however strong and healthy, able to stand the pain of such extensive cauterization without flinching or even a twitch. It is one of the arguments used by the Franciscan doctors who suggest that Francis may have contracted the tubercular form of leprosy, which has been known to numb areas of the head. It is equally possible that during his twenty years of mortification, self-discipline and meditation, Francis had learned aspects of physical and mental control comparable to those acquired by eastern fire-walkers, or masters of yoga, Zen and the martial arts, who seem impervious to certain physical traumas and the normal experience of pain. If so, it would explain, among other things, his insouciance when his habit caught fire.

Tragically, as Tebaldo had predicted, the operation gave Francis no relief whatever and treatment by another doctor, who insisted on piercing his eardrums, proved excruciating and futile; some pain he couldn't outwit. Tebaldo therefore invited him to stay in Rieti where he poulticed and bandaged the burns on his head.

One evening, as a distraction from his pains and discomforts, Francis asked Pacifico to borrow a zither so that together they could compose and sing praises to God. Oddly, Pacifico demurred, explaining he would be suspected of vainglory if he practiced his old skills and Francis felt obliged to bow to his scruples. But the next night, while lying awake, he caught strains of music more beautiful than any he had known in his life; they came and went as if a minstrel were pacing up and down outside the house. In the morning he found no one else had heard the playing or was able to explain it, for after the nine o'clock curfew no one was allowed in the streets.

When Francis heard that Tebaldo was treating a woman's eye trouble without charge because she was utterly destitute, he gave signs that his spirit, if not his health, was recovering. He told his companions to take his cloak, beg some loaves, and – under the pretext that they were repaying a loan she had made to a poor man – hand them over to her. She was naturally bewildered at first and refused them. When they finally prevailed Francis saw to it that she was fed every day when she came to see the doctor.

Then he was off. Always restless and no longer able to stand his confinement at Rieti, Ugolino and Elias agreed his companions should take him to Siena. There he could consult some of the finest doctors in Italy, stay with his brothers in their friary at Alberino just outside the city, and enjoy the long, slow ride in the spring sunshine.

*

The Rule obliged the brothers to travel everywhere on foot unless they were unwell. For choice Francis now rode an ass but for the long journey to Siena he was put on a horse.

Throughout these last six months of his life he was regularly looked after by his four "pillars," though Illuminato and Pacifico frequently appear in the story, and occasionally a John of Lodi. At one point some of the other brothers revealed just how far they were failing the spirit of their vows, by criticizing him for favoritism. Willing to change his ways Francis remarked, "Recently I saw a blind man who only had a little dog to guide him and I don't want to seem more important than he"; but Elias saw that he kept his closest companions. Leo remained his confessor, reader, amanuensis and confidant, while a discreet and devoted companion was needed to wash him and his clothes after his frequent sweats and recurrent bleeding from the wound in his side; Rufino offered to do this. At first he had been puzzled by the patch of blood which always appeared in the same place on the tunics and when he finally asked what it was, Francis pointed to his eye and said, "If you don't recognize this as an eye ask me again what it is." By the time the little party left Rieti they all knew his secret and were expert at keeping it hidden from strangers and other colleagues in the order, including their cardinal protector.

Before leaving the valley they stopped to spend Lent and Easter at Greccio, only a dozen miles off. After dreaming of a new way to celebrate here the first hours of Christ's incarnation there was nowhere better to commemorate his last moments in the flesh. Ever since his call from the cross in San Damiano Francis's desire to emulate Christ was driven by the image of the crucifixion, but as time went on this was balanced by his understanding of the nativity, so that Christmas became for him the supreme day of the year. Easter, too, was a glorious feast on which, he said, even the walls should be fed with fat. The focus of his prayers, behavior and preaching was always concentrated on Christ's example during the span of his life here on earth. This was the ultimate inspiration of his selflessness and love; there are curiously few references in his writings or conversation to the resurrection.

The weather grew steadily warmer as they made their way to the friary just north of Siena, where a large crowd clustered around Francis. Predictably he started giving away to beggars the spare cloaks, habits and breeches his brothers had painstakingly collected to keep him decent. Sadly neither the famous physicians nor the climate of the city made any difference to his health, and throughout the whole of one night he vomited blood from his stomach. Believing that this was the end, his companions sent a message to Elias and begged Francis to leave them all some words by which they could remember him on his deathbed. According to Leo he therefore began dictating to the guardian of the friary, Benedict of Piratro, who had taken to saying Mass at his bedside. In essence Francis expressed three desires.

> Since I cannot speak much because of my weakness and pain I wish briefly to make my purpose clear to all my brothers present and to come. I wish them always to love one another as I have loved them; let them always love and honor our Lady Poverty; and let them remain faithful and obedient to the bishops and clergy of holy mother church.[7]

After a few days Francis began to recover but during the scare two more of the friars contrived to catch a glimpse of his stigmata. Pacifico is alleged to have induced Francis to hold out each hand in turn to be kissed so that a friar from Brescia had time to see them; while Elias, who had rushed to Siena and sensed that something was being kept from him, found a pretext for helping Francis remove his tunic and so saw the wound in his side.

Elias hurried the party toward Assisi but, when Francis suffered a relapse, they had to break the journey at the hermitage of Le Celle in the hills outside Cortona. The symptoms, described by Leo as bleeding from the stomach and an enlarged liver and spleen, suggest that, apart from chronic undernourishment and possible TB, he was suffering from a peptic or stomach ulcer and the side effects of malaria. His abdomen began to swell – his legs and feet too – from dropsy; he could take no solid food.

Nestled beside a stream in a steep gorge Le Celle is the most picturesque of all the early Franciscan retreats. From the top of the short track down to it there is a sweeping view of the plain, and the depth of the ravine is accentuated by tall green poplars and the dark shafts of the cypress trees which flank its sloping path. In the sanctuary at the bottom a blind man must succumb to the spell of honeysuckle and roses, oregano and thyme, and the unearthly silence, broken only by the trickle of water, the song of blackbirds and sometimes the cackle of a laying hen.

Francis was terminally ill, but after some days in the serenity of Le Celle he felt well enough to travel again. Yet, weak as he was, because the body of a saint was so valuable and Perugia regarded as so perfidious, Elias decided to make a long detour through the hills around Gubbio. The humid June heat in Assisi and airless huts of the Porziuncula were totally unsuitable for a man in Francis's condition, so after only a few days there Elias sent him, with his companions, to a new little hermitage in the hills at Bagnara, just outside Nocera, about eighteen miles east of Assisi.

Nothing is recorded about either his brief stop at the Porziuncula or the next few weeks at Bagnara, but Elias used the time to make plans with his colleagues, Ugolino, Bishop Guido, and the new *podestà*, Berlingerio di Jacopo, to ensure the dying saint's safety and organize suitable arrangements to cope with the demonstrations of popular grief which were bound to erupt the moment Francis died. Before this happened Guido decided to make a quick pilgrimage to Mt. Gargano in Apulia.

However Francis, who had arrived in this world a little sooner than expected, was about to leave it earlier too, and in the first week of September the *podestà* received an urgent message that he should be brought home. Berlingerio therefore dispatched an escort of knights and burgesses – some of them Francis's friends from his days as Lord of the Revels – to carry him back to Assisi. Although blind and too feeble to sit on a horse, he was still mentally alert when Angelo and Rufino hoisted his limp little figure up into the arms of the soldiers with whom they, too, had grown up as boys. Soon after dawn the cavalcade, heavily armed against ambush, headed west through the autumn farmland, around the hilltop castle of Postignano on its pinnacle of rock, and then toward Mt. Subasio.

Francis saw nothing; he missed the froth of old man's beard on the bushes, the cheerful pink rock roses and the blues of chicory, scabious and flax. But he caught the sound of men and women working in the fields, the soft chime of cowbells, the bleat of goats and the voice of brother wind gently tossing the invisible branches above him; and he picked up the scent of broom, thyme, and wild mint crushed by the horses' hooves.

Occasionally the riders paused to pass him from one pair of arms to another, and at midday they stopped in the village of Satriano on a spur at the back of Subasio, thirsty, hungry and tired after riding nonstop to Bagnara on the previous evening. A poor man quickly took Francis into his cottage but when the knights went from door to door trying to buy food and drink they returned empty-handed. Laughingly they told Francis they would have to rely on his charity. Suddenly fired up he answered, "If you found nothing it was because you relied on the flies in your purses, not God. Go back to those houses, swallow your pride, and ask for alms in his name. The spirit will move them."[8] It did, and they gave whatever they had, with joy and generosity.

Sadly no vestige of Satriano's castle, church, farmsteads or cottages is left standing today, but every year, on the anniversary of that occasion, a cavalcade mounted on thoroughbreds, hacks, skewbalds, gypsy ponies and sometimes a mule, commemorates Francis's last journey home. The horsemen pause here to say prayers in a chapel resurrected from the hamlet's ancient stones; then they ride on, under holm oak, acacia and holly, in through the gates of Assisi and down to the bishop's palace, which Guido had left at the friars' disposal.

*

A few hundred yards from his parents' house, and close to his school at San Giorgio, Francis had returned to his roots. From the palace windows his companions could look across the valley toward the Porziuncula woods, Clare's convent at San Damiano and the village of Cannara, where the inhabitants' clamor had inspired him to raise his host of lay penitents.

Now Elias, his Vicar, was responsible for looking after this vast and growing family which was about to lose its father. No one could have been better fitted to mastermind a funeral certain to arouse the emotions of the three orders, the religious hierarchy, the civil authorities and the local people of Umbria and the Marches. In the meantime he had to ensure

Francis's safety. Visitors were screened and guards were posted around the palace at night.

One of his oldest friends, Bongiovanni di Marangone, a doctor, was among the first to see him, and Francis asked him straight out if he would recover from his dropsy. Bongiovanni prevaricated but Francis was firm.

"Tell me the truth. Thanks to God's grace I feel so united with him already that I'm as happy to die as to live."[9]

When the doctor gave him until the end of the month or a few days into October Francis simply opened his arms and said with obvious pleasure, "She is welcome, sister death."

However old, ill and apparently feeble, the dying sometimes express with startling precision what is closest to their hearts – so disposing of great wealth or power, revealing deep emotional attachments, or craving something trivial. In his last weeks Francis articulated with crystalline clarity everything he wished to say about death, his order, the service of God, and his closest companions. He even humored – for the first time – the whims of his long suffering body.

First, he addressed death, by adding a final verse to his *Canticle*.

Be praised, my Lord, through our sister, the Death of the Body,
From whom no living man escapes.
Woe to them who die in mortal sin,
But blessed are they who do your holiest will,
For them the second death shall never harm.

Praise and bless our Lord, and give him thanks,
And serve him with great humility.[10]

The completion of his hymn gave him so much pleasure that he repeatedly asked the brothers to sing it with him, both to keep up his spirits and, at night, to boost the morale of the guards outside. Before long this disclosed the spiritual chasm between him and Elias. After hearing the anthem float down from the windows yet again Elias came in to talk to Francis about it.

"Dearest brother, this show of joy in your sickness is very edifying but the people of Assisi, who venerate you as a saint, are convinced you are going to die soon and must wonder if you ought to sound so cheerful when you should be contemplating death."

"For the last two years," Francis answered, "I have thought about my end night and day. . . . So please leave me, brother, to rejoice in the Lord and to praise him for my illnesses."[11]

A little later he gave the first hint that he was having second thoughts about the wisdom of Elias succeeding him. Brother Riccerio and others questioned him about the future, and one friar asked whom he thought should become the next Minister General.

"My son," he is alleged to have replied, "I don't know of any leader suitable for so great and varied an army, or any shepherd for so vast and scattered a flock."[12]

This led one of his companions to blurt out his anxieties for the future: "You know how in the old days the whole order flourished in their perfect observance of holy poverty, whereas nowadays many of our brothers excuse themselves from it on the grounds that it is impossible because we are so many – well, some of us wonder why you put up with it and don't correct them?"

The question seemed to sting Francis, for his answer was quite uncharacteristic in its asperity.

> "God forgive you, for you speak like an enemy who wants to involve me in something which no longer concerns me. . . . When some of our colleagues, whose numbers were growing, began to disregard their duty, and my health prevented me from exercising pastoral care of them, I renounced my office.
>
> "My authority is now purely spiritual and if I cannot influence my brothers by example and preaching, I don't intend to flog them like a worldly executioner. In fact I believe God will send his invisible constables to punish, in this world or the next, those who break his commandments. Nevertheless I will try to set them an example so that I may not be held accountable for them."[13]

Aware that this did nothing whatever to allay their fears he dictated a document known as his *Testament*. Many find its forty simple sentences the purest and most moving distillation of his *modus vivendi* because it emerged straight from his heart without benefit of Ugolino's canonical intervention.

The first half reminded the brothers of how his earliest Rule, given him directly by God, came into being; the second exhorted them passionately to be faithful to those precepts in the final one which were in jeopardy of being diluted or ignored altogether. Obedience – they must honor, absolutely, God, the priesthood and their Minister General, ensuring that any friar in breach of his vows be taken as a prisoner to the Cardinal Protector for correction. Prayer – he commanded observance of the Office and scrupulous respect for the sacraments. Humility – he forbade any suit for privileges from the hierarchy. Poverty – they were to abandon all possessions and accept no permanent houses or churches.

However unequivocal this *Testament*, it bequeathed the friars an acute dilemma, for while Francis enjoined them, in half a dozen instances, to respect his words "under obedience," he also categorically ordered them, "Do not say this is another Rule." Four years later it fell to Ugolino, as Pope Gregory IX, to give a formal judgment on this apparent contradiction.

By now Francis was exhausted and seldom able to eat, but at the end of one long day he felt an inconvenient longing for fish. No sooner had he mentioned this, however, than a brother arrived from the minister in Rieti with an offering of a pike and some crayfish. On another night he asked for some parsley to chew, which upset the brother then cooking who confessed he wouldn't know where to find it by day, still less in the dark. Francis told him gently to go out and pick what first came to hand in the garden; he did and it turned out to be parsley.

Toward the end of September Francis was aware that Bongiovanni's prognosis left him only a few days to live. Determined to die at the Porziuncula he had himself carried down the hill on a litter. When it reached the crossroads by the house now known as Casa Gualdi (then possibly a lazaretto), he asked the brothers to pause and turn him to face Assisi which he could no longer see. There he thanked God for changing the hearts of its people and begged his blessing on the city in the future.

*

He had now endured two years of continuous physical pain and discomfort, combined with prolonged distress at the divisions in his order. Together they had once reduced him to crying in anguish, "Who are they, who have torn my order and my friars from my hands? If I get to the next General Chapter I will make my feelings very clear."[14]

Yet even at this point his prayers restored his equanimity after he heard God's voice asking:

> "Why are you so sad; who planted the order of friars? Surely I? I want you to know I so love it that if any friar dies outside the order I will send another in his place. And suppose in the whole order there remained only three friars I would never abandon it."[15]

For all his disappointments there had also been several oases of light on his journey through this long, dark night of the soul. The final approval of his Rule, the success of his imaginative celebration of Christmas, and his ecstatic experience at La Verna, had sustained and deepened his faith, just as they have inspired generations of Christians ever since.

His brothers listened carefully as he told them they should never abandon the Porziuncula of Santa Maria degli Angeli, their mother and home, and that only members of their order should enter it. Then he eased himself off his bed in the small reed hut where he lay, sat on the bare earth and struggled out of his clothes. For a time he remained there, quite still, holding his left hand over the wound in his right side to hide it. After a time his guardian handed him a tunic and breeches, saying: "Father, I lend you these and it is my will that you have no power to give them away."[16]

Under obedience, Francis accepted them but told his companions that as soon as he was dead they were to place his naked body on the ground once more "for as long as it takes a man to walk a mile."

Now, during his last week, the flow of love he had lavished on the world for twenty years was concentrated on the men and women nearest to his heart who had done so much to establish and extend the three branches of his family. He knew that Giacoma de Settesoli in Rome would be distressed if she had no warning of his death and a few days before the end dictated a letter asking her to bring what would soon be needed, a length of ash-gray cloth worn by the Cistercians and some candles; he added a request for the little almond cakes he loved so much.

Just as a messenger was leaving with it there was a knock at the door of the friary and she arrived with one of her sons, prompted by a premonition while praying. When Francis told the gatekeeper to waive the rule against admitting women Brother Giacoma carried in the gray cloth needed for his shroud, wax for the candles, almonds and honey for the *mostacciuoli*, and also incense, which Francis had forgotten to mention. Immediately the brothers set about making the habit and molding the candles while Giacoma prepared the sweetmeats.

Clare, too, was in Francis's mind. She had been ill ever since he had received the stigmata and, weeping bitterly, she now sent a friar to say she was frightened she might die without seeing him. He therefore sent back a note to San Damiano with his blessing and an absolution for any possible failings, saying to the friar, "Take this letter to Lady Clare and tell her that she is to set aside all sorrow that we cannot meet now; but reassure her that before she dies she and her sisters will have the consolation of seeing me."[17]

The taste of an almond cake reminded Francis of Bernard; he had enjoyed them, too. So he sent for Bernard and some of his other early brothers, including Angelo, Rufino and Leo who left a detailed account of these last days. Francis could hear Bernard's voice among the kneeling friars but couldn't see him and, when he stretched out his hand to give him his blessing, realized it had fallen on the head of Giles, the third of his original brothers.

Bernard moved closer. Francis then placed a hand on his head and said to Leo:

> "Write as I tell you. Brother Bernard was the first friar the Lord gave me and the first to give all his goods to the poor. Because of this and for many other reasons I am bound to love him more dearly than any other. Therefore I wish and command you – as far as I can – that whoever is Minister General love and honor him as he would me, and the friars of the whole order are to regard him as myself."[18]

After a sleepless night, Francis summoned all the brothers at the Porziuncula to his bedside next day.

> When they were seated he considered they represented the entire order. Laying his right hand on each he blessed them, also blessing every brother in the order, including all those who would join it until the end of the world . . .
>
> After that he called for loaves, blessed them and because of his weakness told a friar to break them. Then he gave a piece to each, just

as on Maundy Thursday the Lord wished to eat with his apostles, for Francis thought it was Thursday although it was not.[19]

Elias later told Thomas of Celano that Francis asked him to read St. John's account of the Last Supper in Chapter 13 of his gospel. He also said that, barely whispering, Francis broke into the words of Psalm 142.

. . . Bring me out of prison
That I may give thanks to Thy name;
The righteous will surround me,
For thou wilt deal bountifully with me.

As the afternoon wore on, at his wish, the brothers exchanged his shift for a hair shirt and sprinkled him with ashes. The rest was silence.

Death sometimes approaches like a shadow or cloud, even the onset of night, and it must have seemed so to the brothers who prayed around Francis in the fading light. But he was moving into another world, growing closer to his God whose emblem was the sun. Blind, he was looking up into the cloudless blue sky of a perfect summer morning which suddenly blazed with a dazzling light as he died. For the others it was just after sunset on October 3.

Epilogue

Epilogue

Francis's bequest to future generations is all the more remarkable for surviving the turmoil that followed his death.

Ugolino, elected Pope Gregory IX in March 1227, reaffirmed with his usual incisiveness the church's policies of reform in the west, reunion with the east, the recovery of Jerusalem and the frustration of German imperialism. In response to irresistible popular demands and to encourage others in pursuit of his first objective, Ugolino canonized Francis in 1228,* commissioned his official biography and appointed Elias – passed over by the friars as their new Minister General – to build a handsome basilica in the new saint's honor.

Many friars were surprised by the grandeur of the shrine, shocked when Elias badgered his provincial ministers all over Christendom to collect money for it, and outraged when Gregory announced, in disregard of Francis's explicit wishes for Santa Maria, that the basilica would become *caput et mater* – head and mother – of the order. On the other hand a significant number of their brothers entirely approved of the enterprise.

The politics of the basilica and the emotions they released were symptomatic of widening divisions in the order. To Francis's original companions – later labeled spirituals – the attitudes of Gregory and Elias were abhorrent; distressed that the Rule of 1223 had diluted the crucial requirement of absolute poverty, they had been reassured when Francis restored its original force in his *Testament*. However for many priests,

*Bishop Guido lived just long enough to witness the service of canonization, dying on July 30, 1228.

scholars and ministers, who eventually became known as conventuals, Gregory's liberal interpretation of the Rule was a *sine qua non.*

Hoping to heal these rifts, the new Minister General, John of Parenti, a man of devotion and humility, asked the pope to decide whether *Testament* was as binding as the Rule. Anxious to retain the loyalty of the cleverer and more ambitious young friars, on whom he was relying to help consolidate his reforms, Gregory issued a bull *Quo Elongati* in September 1230. The Rule was to be paramount; he further made it clear that from now on money might be held on behalf of the friars for convenience as well as necessities, that the buildings they occupied might be large and permanent structures, and that they should be allowed books and other personal effects.

Reflecting on Gregory's verdict Bishop Moorman wrote that with it "he quietly destroyed the very foundations upon which Francis had built, and shattered the whole ideal." When told of the bull, John of Parenti stole a page from Francis – he took off all his clothes as if in resignation of his office.

Two years later, after an unseemly demonstration by Elias's supporters in chapter, John did stand down and Elias was elected Minister General in his place.

Opposition among his friars, especially the ministers, may have induced in Francis feelings of betrayal which echoed Christ's anguish on the Mount of Olives before his arrest; yet Francis had told Leo that rejection by his brothers was good cause for perfect joy. The wounds of his stigmata were painful; yet, crowning his efforts to emulate Jesus and share in his suffering, they were a form of apotheosis.

By contrast three exceptional men whose lives were interwoven with his found few or no compensations in their last few years. Gregory's international problems proved more ferocious than any he had previously faced in a lifetime's diplomacy. He made no progress in bridging the chasm between the churches in Rome and Constantinople, while his overtures to Frederick and plans for a crusade were quickly and bitterly disappointed. He therefore felt obliged to excommunicate Frederick, which soon led to war between the Hohenstaufens and the papacy; and, although a fragile peace was restored in the 1230s, hostilities were renewed at the end of the decade and Gregory excommunicated the emperor a second time.

The gloves were now off and, to mobilize every possible moral and military advantage, the pope convoked a general church Council in Rome for 1241. But the so-called Holy Roman Emperor threw a ring of troops around the papal states to prevent its assembly. As they worked their way toward the Lateran Palace, Gregory died.

It was a tragic finale for a man of courage, huge ability and personal goodness, who genuinely loved Francis, Clare and their orders. His decisions to release the friars from their vow of absolute poverty, so as to sustain the momentum of their growth, and to build a monument to Francis which he never would have wanted, may have been wrong. Or, since the order still thrives and millions of people visit Assisi each year, it may have been right. Perhaps, unlike Francis, his love and his faith pulled in different directions – an occupational hazard afflicting many who devote their lives to religious institutions.

For nearly ten years Frederick fought for supremacy in Europe and to establish the succession of his sons in Germany, Italy and Sicily, but ultimately the combined opposition of his enemies led by the new pope, Innocent IV, proved too powerful for him. His spirit broken, he died in 1250.

Brilliant patron of music, poetry, medicine and science, a scholar of philosophy, mathematics and history, master of six languages, sympathetic to Jews, Muslims and Christians, he survived three wives, kept an attractive harem, and was recently found to be sharing his coffin with two women. But however active his mind and his libido, he also had a heart, which he claimed he lost to one of the two princesses whom he courted in vain – Agnes of Bohemia, who founded a house for Poor Clares in Prague, later becoming its abbess, and Elizabeth of Hungary.

Elizabeth's husband (the Margrave of Thuringia) died on crusade, and she subsequently took the vows of a Franciscan tertiary, devoting herself to prayer and nursing the sick in the hospital at Marburg. Four years after she died Gregory canonized her, and when she was translated to the cathedral in 1236 Frederick laid his iron crown on her coffin and walked beside it barefoot to her tomb, saying: "I was never able to crown her on earth but I can, at last, now she is an immortal queen in heaven." In the Basilica di San Francesco a bust allegedly of Frederick gazes down from a capital outside one of the transepts. In the other an altar was dedicated to Elizabeth; she is patron saint of the Third Order.

In the meantime Elias had been playing a dangerous game. Gregory's patronage, the successful completion of the basilica, and his election as Minister General had gone to his head. When not overseeing work on the basilica he spent much of the time after 1232 at Cortona with a cook, a liveried servant and a magnificent horse, visiting the rich but never the poor. Furthermore his behavior toward the friars became so high-handed that in 1239 Gregory had to call a chapter which replaced him. It coincided with Frederick's second excommunication, and when Elias joined his court at Arezzo he received a similar sentence.

After the emperor's death Elias retired in disgrace to Cortona. Three years later his remorse and public penitence won him papal absolution on Easter Sunday, 1253; within twenty-four hours he was dead. He had been trusted in turn by three great men, Francis, Gregory and Frederick. For a time he worked for each of them faithfully and shone in their service but the light he transmitted was really theirs, not his own. Nevertheless the basilica in Assisi was largely his personal creation and for at least ten years after Francis's death he retained the absolute respect of the greatest of all the saint's followers, neither a friar nor a prelate – but Clare.

*

Apart from the dramatic moment in 1240 when Clare repulsed Frederick's Saracen mercenaries, bursting over the walls of San Damiano "like a swarm of bees," the last twenty-five years of her life were outwardly peaceful. But she alone possessed the status, the will and the courage to resist the hierarchy's persistent attempts to thrust financial endowment and the ownership of property on San Damiano and the other houses closely associated with it. In fighting this cause she also rallied the morale of the more spiritual friars and kept alive their hope that one day their order would return to the ideal of poverty established by Francis and approved by Innocent III.

The elevation of Innocent IV as pope in 1243 raised her expectations and although the Germans drove him into exile at Lyon he gave her a new Rule which officially restored her order's Franciscan connections. Nevertheless, on the issue of poverty it was too ambiguous for Clare, and she therefore began drafting a version of her own.

It was lucky for her that when the papal court returned to Italy in November 1251, conditions in Rome were still hazardous and consequently it settled in Perugia. Here Innocent and the Cardinal Protector of the Second Order, Rainaldo dei Segni, could keep a solicitous eye on San Damiano. It was soon obvious that both men were extremely impressed by the proliferation of Clare's followers all over Europe. They were also captivated by the combination of her intelligence, goodness and charm; and although she was now in constant pain and frequently close to death as she worked on her Rule, she always made light of her physical struggle.

By December she had completed her draft – a blend of essentials from Innocent's, Gregory's and Francis's versions, with contributions of her own. When Cardinal Rainaldo rode over from Perugia to discuss it, she begged him with tears to have it approved by Innocent and the Curia. But nearly a year went by before Rainaldo confirmed his own approval in writing and after a further six months, when Clare was actually dying, there was still no news of the pope's decision. She hovered on the edges of consciousness while the nuns, including her sister who had been brought back from Florence, nursed and prayed for her. They were joined in their vigil by Giles, Angelo, Rufino and Leo; and when Juniper came to sit by her she would suddenly perk up and ask him: "What's the news from heaven?" He would then console her with a radiant report from his prayers.

At the end of July or in the first week of August 1253 Innocent visited Assisi. As soon as he heard there was no hope for Clare he hurried to San Damiano, walked straight to her bedside and held out his hand to be kissed. She asked if she might kiss his foot, too, and when he raised it on a stool she pressed her lips to its toe and sole. Finally, Thomas says in his life of her:

> Her face looking angelic, she asked the pontiff for the remission of all her sins. "Would I had as little need of pardon," he exclaimed, and gave her full absolution.[1]

Innocent and Rainaldo hastily drew up a bull formally approving Clare's Rule; it was signed and sealed on August 9, and the following day a friar carried it across to San Damiano. When she heard that her last wish had been granted Clare took the parchment in her withered hands and kissed the seal. She died the next day.

Innocent was then in Assisi and stayed the night in order to conduct her funeral at San Giorgio in the morning. By now his devotion to her was so intense that Cardinal Rainaldo had to restrain him from declaring her a saint there and then. Innocent therefore waited two months before initiating the formal process of canonization, but before the procedure had run its full course he, too, was dead. It was left to Rainaldo, who succeeded him as Pope Alexander IV, to make the official proclamation of her sanctity in August 1255.

*

The evidence of Francis's legacy is immediately and impressively visible wherever you go in Assisi. As a center of Christian pilgrimage, next only to Jerusalem, Rome and Santiago de Compostela, it became frozen in time; inside its walls many of the buildings and streets are still medieval. We cannot share Bishop Moorman's experience "It was about six o'clock on the evening of February 18, 1978 that I saw St. Francis"; but we can see in a single day Francis's birthplace, the battlefield of Collestrada, the caves of his conversion on Mt. Subasio, the Rivotorto, Santa Maria degli Angeli and his tomb. At the basilica we can also look at the parchment on which he wrote his blessing for Leo, one of his habits and the fresco of him by Cimabue (Plate 7). It is the portrayal which perhaps captures best his spirit and likeness, for his nephew, Picardo, was procurator at the time and would have guided the artist.

The Basilica di Santa Chiara, and the convent next to it, were built at the other end of the town on the site of San Giorgio, which was cleared to make way for them; Clare's body was moved there seven years after her death. There it could be seen in the crypt, while displayed in a chapel above were the crucifix from which Francis heard Christ speak to him in San Damiano, and one of the slippers Clare made for him.

Evocative as all these sights are, magnets for millions of visitors every year, the essence of Francis's life lay not in his affection for places and things but in his devotion to God and love of his fellow human beings. His lasting achievement is therefore best gauged through the lives of the friars, Poor Clares and members of the Third Order dedicated to the aims of their founders all over the world. These ideals were so deeply rooted in the souls of their most loyal followers that, however bitter and even violent the disagreements created by Gregory and Elias after Francis's death, the harmony he prescribed in his original Rule has prevailed. Courtesy, charity and a refusal to engage in controversy have become hallmarks of the orders.

The thirty thousand brothers of the First Order now fall into three groups, the Friars Minor Conventual, Friars Minor, and Friars Minor Capuchin, differentiated by their observances and degrees of asceticism; on most fundamentals they are as one. In Assisi the Conventual Friars in the Sacro Convento maintain the basilica while the Friars Minor at Santa Maria degli Angeli look after the Porziuncula.

Of the eighteen thousand Poor Clares in the world only four sisters were able to live in the grounds of their convent in Assisi at the time of writing, so serious were the effects of the earthquake in 1997. Both convent and basilica are now undergoing radical restoration.

The Third Order is now divided into two. One element, the Third Order Regular, numbers over a hundred thousand men and women living under strict vows and some of them cloistered; they therefore effectively more than double the strength of the First and Second Orders. The others, known as the Third Order Secular, live in the world, as their forerunners did in the time of Francis, and number a million worldwide.

In 1922 a Franciscan order – known as the Society of St. Francis – was founded within the Church of England. Its brothers were diffident about going to Assisi but while two of them were visiting the basilica in 1960 they were greeted with characteristic warmth, and some surprise, by a friar attached to the Sacro Convento. Father Maximilian Mizzi, a Maltese, had no idea that the Franciscan family extended beyond the invisible boundaries of the Roman Church. That meeting, and the friendship which grew from it, led Mizzi to pursue the concept of dialogue between faiths initiated by the conversations between Francis and Sultan al-Kamil outside Damietta.

The Franciscans, and the authorities in Rome, supported his attempt to build bridges and in 1972 he opened a Centro Francescano Ecumenico in Assisi.* Then, in October 1986, the pope agreed to preside at the celebration of a World Day of Prayer for Peace outside the basilica. For perhaps the first time in history leading Buddhists, Christians, Hindus, Jews, Muslims, Zoroastrians, and representatives of traditional African religions prayed as one congregation for peace.

*In 1989 this became known as the *Centro Francescano Internazionale per il Dialogo*.

*

With Pope Innocent III and Emperor Frederick II, Francis was one of the three pre-eminent figures in medieval Europe, but his achievement was even more remarkable than theirs, not least because while they were born into their crimson and purple his career began in a shift of dirty, old burlap. Innocent was a great pope, in fact one of the greatest; Frederick's ability and scintillating talents won him the universal sobriquet *stupor mundi*, Wonder of the World; yet a higher claim still can be made for Francis.

For instance the French nineteenth-century critic, historian and philosopher Hippolyte Taine, a determinist, maintained that Francis "marks the summit of civilization in the Middle Ages." In his study *Civilisation* Lord Clark went considerably further, writing, "Everyone recognised that St Francis was a religious genius – the greatest I believe that Europe has ever produced." Historians frequently refer to his genius and there are many definitions of the attribute which *Encyclopaedia Britannica* has called the highest conceivable form of original ability, beyond even supreme educational prowess, different in kind from talent. Since official sanctity is no guarantee of such merit, it is worth considering how Francis's achievements relate to those of men who unquestionably possessed it.

In Marcel Proust's view "all the greatest things we know have come to us from neurotics. It is they and only they who have founded religions and created great works of art."[2] However vivid the message of Francis's public charades, there probably is a degree of neurosis in his compulsive sweeping of churches, his flagrant inconsistencies, and his sudden urge to confess a peccadillo naked, on a pillory, with a rope around his neck. Perhaps it was simply one of the irritants often said to produce pearls in the oyster of genius – adversities such as imprisonment, ill-health and depression. Prison was as unwelcome to Francis as it was to Cervantes and Molière, yet it left in all three a lasting stoicism, wisdom and warmth which underlay creations as unalike as the order of Brothers Minor, *Don Quixote*, and *Le Malade Imaginaire*.

While Francis, who lived so much through his eyes, went slowly blind, Beethoven, in despair, lost his hearing. Both were self-disciplined, original, controversial, even revolutionary in their work, which expressed love and ranged from lyricism to passion; and both were implacably opposed to the imperial ambitions that drove Frederick and much later Napoleon, regardless of human cost, toward the domination of Europe. The notable music critic Desmond Shawe-Taylor once wrote of Beethoven that "he lived in a period of war and revolution; a passionate believer in freedom and the brotherhood of man. . . . He continually created affirmations of divine order out of a world of disorder – hope out of despair."[3] His Oratorio was devoted to Christ's suffering on the Mount of Olives; he chose as the words of his final, choral symphony (composed when he was deaf as Francis composed his *Canticle* in blindness) Schiller's "Ode to Joy."

The qualities that Francis shared with Beethoven, combined with his interest in every man and woman as a unique human being, his driving curiosity about our natural environment, and a mystical sense of creation's holistic unity, link Francis in different ways with Giotto, Leonardo, Dante, Cervantes, and Galileo (whose telescope demonstrated conclusively, to the pope's dismay, that the sun not the Earth is at the center of our little galaxy).* Beethoven apart, all of them are alleged to have joined the third Franciscan order. Fundamentally they and Francis developed their perception of the world's actual or potential rhythms and harmonies – physical, musical, visual, intellectual – to benefit mankind through their creations of beauty, revelations of truth or demonstrations of goodness.

It is harder to assess a saint than an artist for genius, but from the day he first entered the Lateran Palace, Francis showed himself to be a communicator and persuader of prodigious ability, far beyond any skill the schools of Bologna or Paris could teach. His vision and energy galvanized society – vertically from three popes all the way down to the lowest beggars and peasants, horizontally across Italy and the countries of Europe. His motivation, inspiration, of his three orders was no less astonishing.

More impressive still was his distinctive influence on so many dimensions of medieval life. His friars' pastoral work helped to redress permanently many social injustices and radiate enlightenment from the new universities; their fidelity to the gospels contributed crucially to the hierarchy's success in fending off the Reformation for three hundred years; and toward the end of his life Frederick II acknowledged that the lay

*Galileo placed both his young daughters in a house of Poor Clares. The elder, Marie Celeste, helped restore his peace of mind and confidence after an ordeal at the hands of the Inquisition in 1633.

orders' refusal to bear arms had deprived him of vital recruits in his conflict with Gregory IX.

George Holmes edited *The Oxford History of Medieval Europe* and in 1986 wrote a book exploring the origins of the Renaissance in Italy. One of its ten chapters, "The Model of Francis of Assisi," opens like this:

> The most prominent figure in the Italian imagination in the thirteenth century was not a pope or a politician but a saint: Francis of Assisi. There are few cases in European history of individuals whose lives have been so generally accepted as an inspiration by [a] whole country. . .
>
> He was a preacher who embraced complete poverty but expressed a delighted love of the physical world, a man of superhuman power who attracted simple brothers to establish a new way of life which would excite the enthusiasm of ordinary people in a strife torn society.[4]

Extraordinary people, too. Within little more than a hundred years of the deaths of Francis and Clare, the patrons, protectors and members of their orders included four more popes and a variety of monarchs and saints.

Agnes of Prague was the sister of "Good King Wenceslas" and cousin of St. Elizabeth of Hungary. Elizabeth, in turn, was cousin of St. Hedwig, Duchess of Silesia, St. Elizabeth the Queen of Portugal, St. Ferdinand, King of Castile, and St. Louis IX of France, who asked to kiss the pillow on which Francis's head was lying when he died. All of them were tertiaries. Clare also inspired every other level of society. In the next generation or so, St. Rose of Viterbo, St. Margaret of Cortona, Blessed Oringa of Menabuoi and St. Clare of Montefalco, lived within fifty miles of Assisi or belonged to the Third Order – or both. Though several were mystics and their visions ethereal, their work was down to earth.

Francis's influence was no less diverse. The career of his friend John of Piano Carpine was as bizarre as any. He began by opening up houses in Germany with Caesar of Speyer and went on to establish the order in Bohemia, Hungary, Poland and Norway. Next, in 1246 Pope Innocent IV sent him as his emissary to Genghis Khan's grandson at Karakorum, then the capital of the Mongolian empire. Middle-aged and fat, the intrepid friar was obliged to make the three-thousand-mile journey there at breakneck speed by horse, and return (often sleeping out) in the middle of winter. All this twenty-five years before Marco Polo set foot on the silk route.

In 1288 Brother Jerome of Ascoli was elected Pope Nicholas IV and sent a number of fellow Franciscans on a mission to China. Three other friars won international reputations for their pioneering intellects rather than their missionary stamina – Roger Bacon as a scientist, William of Ockham as a philosopher, and Jacopone da Todi as a gifted and original poet whose moving dialogue between Christ on the cross and his mother Mary, *Stabat Mater*, has been set to music as an anthem by great composers ever since. Then there were the brilliant artists of the early Renaissance who reflected his vibrant vision of nature in the new realism of Italian painting.

Like the work of supreme artists, composers, scientists and original thinkers, Francis's legacy transcends distance and time. It survives with theirs to offer us illumination, guidance or instruction, to encourage, console or delight us on our individual journeys through life toward oblivion – or back to eternity.

The Rule of 1223

Honorius, Bishop, Servant of the Servants of God, to His Beloved Sons, Brother Francis and the Other Brothers of the Order of Friars Minor, Health and Apostolic Blessing.

The Apostolic See is accustomed to accede to the pious requests and to be favorably disposed to grant the praiseworthy desires of its petitioners. Wherefore, beloved sons in the Lord, attentive to your pious prayers, We confirm for you with our apostolic authority, and by this document ratify the rule of your Order herein contained and approved by our predecessor, Pope Innocent of happy memory, which is as follows:

1

The Life of the Friars Minor begins

The rule and life of the Friars Minor is this: to observe the holy Gospel of our Lord Jesus Christ by living in obedience, without anything of their own, and in chastity. Brother Francis promises obedience and reverence to the Lord Pope Honorius and his canonically elected successors and to the Roman Church. And let the other brothers be bound to obey Brother Francis and his successors.

2

Those who wish to embrace this life and how they should be received

If there are any who wish to accept this life and come to our brothers, let them send them to the ministers provincial, to whom and to no other is permission granted for receiving brothers. The ministers should diligently examine them concerning the Catholic faith and the sacraments of the Church. And if they believe all these things and are willing to profess them faithfully and observe them steadfastly to the end; and if they have no wives, or if they have wives who have already taken a vow of continence and are of such an age that suspicion cannot be raised about them, and who have already entered a monastery or have given their husbands permission by the authority of the bishop of the diocese, let the ministers speak to them the words of the holy Gospel that they should go and sell all that belongs to them and strive to give it to the poor. If they cannot do this, their goodwill suffices. And let the brothers and their ministers beware not to become solicitous over their temporal affairs, so that they may freely dispose of their goods as the Lord may inspire them. But if they stand in need of counsel, the ministers may have permission to send them to some God-fearing persons who may advise them how they should give what they have to the poor. Then they may be given the clothes of probation, namely, two tunics without a hood, a cord, short trousers, and a little cape reaching to the cord, unless at some time it seems proper to these same ministers before God to make other provisions. When the year of probation is ended, let them be received into obedience, whereby they promise to observe this life and rule always. And in no way shall it be lawful for them to leave this Order, according to the decree of the Lord Pope, since, according to the Gospel: No one having put his hand to the plow and looking back is fit for the kingdom of God. And those who have already promised obedience may have one tunic with a hood, and, if they wish, another without a hood. And those who are forced by necessity may wear shoes. And let all the brothers wear poor clothes, and let them mend them with pieces of sackcloth or other material, with the blessing of God. I admonish and exhort them not to look down or pass judgment on those people whom they see wearing soft and colorful clothing and enjoying the choicest food and drink; instead, each must criticize and despise himself.

3
The Divine Office and Fasting and the way the Brothers should go about the world

The clerical [brothers] shall celebrate the Divine Office according to the rite of the holy Roman Church, except for the Psalter, for which reason they may have breviaries. The lay [brothers], however, shall pray twenty-four Our Fathers for Matins, five for Lauds, seven for each of the hours of Prime, Terce, Sext, and None, twelve for Vespers, and seven for Compline. And they shall pray for the dead. And [all the brothers] shall fast from the feast of All Saints until the Nativity of the Lord. May those who fast voluntarily for that holy Lent which begins at Epiphany and continues for forty days, which the Lord consecrated by His own fast, be blessed by the Lord; and those who do not wish to keep it shall not be obliged. But they shall fast during that other Lent which lasts until the Resurrection. At other times, however, they are not bound to fast except on Fridays. But in times of manifest necessity the brothers are not obliged to corporal fasting.

I counsel, admonish and exhort my brothers in the Lord Jesus Christ, that, when they go about the world, they do not quarrel or fight with words, or judge others, rather, let them be meek, peaceful and unassuming, gentle and humble, speaking courteously to everyone, as is becoming. And they should not ride horseback unless they are forced by manifest necessity or infirmity. In whatever house they enter, let them say: "Peace to this house." And, according to the holy Gospel, they are free to eat of whatever food is set before them.

4
The Brothers are never to receive money

I firmly command all the brothers that they in no way receive coins or money, either personally or through an intermediary. None the less let the ministers and custodians alone take special care to provide for the needs of the sick and the clothing of the other brothers through spiritual friends according to places and seasons and cold climates, as they may judge the demands of necessity; excepting always, as stated above, they do not receive coins or money.

5
The Manner of working

Those brothers to whom the Lord has given the grace of working should do their work faithfully and devotedly so that, avoiding idleness, the enemy of the soul, they do not extinguish the Spirit of holy prayer and devotion to which all other things of our earthly existence must contribute. As payment for their work they may receive whatever is necessary for their own bodily needs and those of their brothers, but not money in any form; and they should do this humbly as is fitting for servants of God and followers of most holy poverty.

6
The Brothers shall not acquire anything as their own; begging alms; the sick brothers

The brothers shall not acquire anything as their own, neither a house nor a place nor anything at all. Instead, as pilgrims and strangers in this world who serve the Lord in poverty and humility, let them go begging for alms with full trust. Nor should they feel ashamed since the Lord made Himself poor for us in this world. This is that summit of highest poverty which has established you, my most beloved brothers, as heirs and kings of the kingdom of heaven; it has made you poor in the things of this world but exalted you in virtue. Let this be your portion, which leads into the land of the living. Dedicating yourselves totally to this, my most beloved brothers, do not wish to have anything else forever under heaven for the sake of our Lord Jesus Christ.

And wherever the brothers may be together or meet other brothers, let them give witness that they are members of one family. And let each one confidently make known his need to the other, for, if a mother has such care and love for her son born according to the flesh, should not someone love and care for his brother according to the Spirit even more diligently? And if any of them becomes sick, the other brothers should serve him as they would wish to be served themselves.

7
The Penance to be imposed on the brothers who sin

If any of the brothers, at the instigation of the enemy, sins mortally in regard to those sins about which it may have been decreed among the brothers to have recourse only to the ministers provincial, such brothers must have recourse to them as soon as possible, without delay. If these ministers are priests, they shall impose a penance upon them with mercy; but if they are not priests, they shall have it imposed by other priests of the Order as it seems best to them according to God. They must take care not to become angry or disturbed because of the sin of another, since anger and disturbance hinder charity in themselves and in others.

8
The Election of the Minister General of this Fraternity and the Chapter of Pentecost

All the brothers are bound always to have one of the brothers of this Order as the minister general and servant of the entire fraternity and they are bound strictly to obey him. Should he die, the election of a successor should be made by the ministers provincial and the custodians at the Chapter of Pentecost, for which the ministers provincial are always bound to convene in whatever place it has been decided by the minister general; and they shall do this once every three years or at a longer or shorter interval as decided by the aforesaid minister. And if at any time it should become evident to the body of the ministers provincial and the custodians that the aforesaid minister is not qualified for the service and general welfare of the brothers, then the same brothers, to whom the election is entrusted, are bound in the name of the Lord to elect another for themselves as custodian. After the Chapter of Pentecost each minister and custodian may call his brothers to a Chapter once in the same year in their territories – if they wish and if it seems expedient to them.

9
Preachers

The brothers shall not preach in the diocese of any bishop when he has opposed their doing so. And none of the brothers shall dare to preach to the people unless he has been examined and approved by the minister general of this fraternity and has received from him the office of preaching. I also admonish and exhort these brothers that, in their preaching, their words be well chosen and chaste, for the instruction and edification of the people, speaking to them of vices and virtues, punishment and glory in a discourse that is brief, because it was in few words that the Lord preached while on earth.

10
The Admonition and Correction of the Brothers

The brothers who are the ministers and servants of the other brothers should visit and admonish their brothers and humbly and charitably correct them, not commanding them anything which might be against their conscience and our Rule. On the other hand, the brothers who are subject to them should remember that they have given up their own wills for God. Therefore I strictly command them to obey their ministers in all those things which they have promised the Lord to observe and which are not against [their] conscience and our Rule. And wherever there are brothers who know and realize that they cannot observe the Rule spiritually, it is their duty and right to go to the minister for help. The ministers on their part should receive them with great kindness and love and should be so approachable that these brothers can speak and deal with [the ministers] as masters with their servants; for this is the way it should be: The ministers shall be the servants of all the brothers. At the same time I admonish and exhort the brothers in the Lord Jesus Christ that they beware of all pride, vainglory, envy, avarice, cares and worries of this world, detraction and complaint. And those who are illiterate should not be eager to learn. Instead let them pursue what they must desire above all things: to have the Spirit of the Lord and His holy manner of working, to pray always to Him with a pure heart and to have humility, patience in persecution and weakness, and to love those who persecute us, find fault with us, or rebuke us, because the Lord says: "Love your enemies, and pray for those who persecute and slander you. Blessed are those who suffer persecution for the sake of justice for theirs is the kingdom of heaven. But whoever perseveres to the end, he will be saved."

11
The Brothers are not to enter the monasteries of nuns

I firmly command all the brothers not to have any associations or meetings with women which could arouse suspicion. Moreover, they should not enter the monasteries of nuns, except those brothers to whom special permission has been granted by the Apostolic See. They should not be godfathers of men or women so that scandal not arise on this account among the brothers or concerning them.

12

Those who go among the Saracens and other nonbelievers

Those brothers who, by divine inspiration, desire to go among the Saracens and other nonbelievers should ask permission from their ministers provincial. But the ministers should not grant permission except to those whom they consider fit to be sent.

In addition, I command the ministers through obedience to petition the Lord Pope for one of the cardinals of the holy Roman Church, who would be the governor, protector, and corrector of this fraternity, so that, always submissive and prostrate at the feet of the same holy Church, and steadfast in the Catholic faith, we may observe the poverty and the humility and the holy Gospel of our Lord Jesus Christ which we have firmly promised.

No one, therefore, is in any way permitted to tamper with this decree of our confirmation or to oppose it rashly. If anyone, however, should presume to attempt this, let it be known that he shall incur the indignation of Almighty God and of His blessed Apostles Peter and Paul.

Given at the Lateran, the twenty-ninth day of November, in the eighth year of our Pontificate.

[This version of the Rule from *Francis and Clare: The Complete Works*, translated by Regis J. Armstrong OFM Cap. and Ignatius Brady OFM, published by Paulist Press, New York, 1983, is printed here with grateful acknowledgment.]

Acknowledgments

I am immensely grateful to the innumerable people who have helped me during the preparation of this book.

At the outset the Rt. Rev. Michael Fisher SSF, Minister General of the Anglican Franciscans 1985–1991, Br. Purfield OFM, at the Franciscan Study Centre, Canterbury, and Dr. Rosalind Brooke, a leading authority on the early Franciscan sources, gave me invaluable advice. My first thanks are therefore to them.

In Assisi I must thank especially Fr. Maximilian Mizzi OFM Conv. and Fr. Pascal Magro OFM Conv., both attached to the Sacro Convento and Basilica di San Francesco, who gave me indispensable guidance and much of their time; while Sr. Chiara Anastasia OSC at the Convento di Santa Chiara talked most helpfully about St. Clare and the nature of her order. I also owe special thanks to Giancarlo Ronci, then in charge of the city's information office, for his warm friendship and practical help in opening so many doors both literally and figuratively. Similarly Dr. Ezio Mancini made my wife and me welcome whenever we came to Assisi; his introductions included one to Maria Marcucci Gubbiotti, whose house we rented on each of our visits. For notes on the flora and fauna we saw together in the mountains of Umbria and Tuscany I am grateful to Stephen and Susan Druce.

I am much indebted to Rebecca Porteous for taking me on a magic carpet to the remains of the great mosque at Damietta in Egypt; to Fr. Anthony Carrozzo OFM, Vice President for Franciscan Mission, University of St. Bonaventure, NY, for his help and hospitality during my visit to the Franciscan Institute there; and to Dr. Peter Meyer of Bern for coming to take photographs in Assisi regardless of the continuous rain and ubiquitous scaffolding. I would also like to thank for their help the Warden and staff of St. Deiniol's Library at Hawarden, home of the Moorman Franciscan collection; Br. Francisco for giving me several hours of his time in Santiago de Compostela; and Br. Samuel SSF, the Guardian, for the hospitality of the friary near Cerne Abbas in Dorset, to which I was first introduced by Br. Denis Marsh long ago in the last millennium. Toward the end of the whole enterprise Julia Chappell, the Rev. Simon House, Bill Swainson, the Rev. David Scott and Dr. Ronald Williams very kindly ran their expert eyes over some or all of the chapters. For permission to quote passages of text and verse acknowledgments are made in the *Source Notes*; photographic acknowledgments are made below the *List of Illustrations*. There are many others whose different forms of assistance I would like to acknowledge and much regret that I cannot name them all here.

As a layman, in every sense, I am deeply grateful for the generosity and patience of three scholars who read the completed script – Sr. Margaret Carney OSF, Dean and Director of the Franciscan Institute, University of St. Bonaventure, NY; Professor Christopher Brooke, Dixie Professor of Ecclesiastical History, Cambridge, 1977–1991; and the Very Rev. David Edwards, Dean of King's College, Cambridge, 1966–1970 and later Dean of Norwich. Their invaluable comments have saved me from many errors; any mistakes and dubious opinions which remain are entirely my own.

I cannot thank Pat West sufficiently for her mystical intuition and technical skill in repeatedly transforming my illegible longhand into impeccable typescript, and am indebted to Myrna Blumberg for her skilled copyediting, to Roger Walker for his maps, and to Douglas Matthews for his index. For the place of peace in which it has been possible to write the book, I am eternally grateful to Lord and Lady Sainsbury of Preston Candover. The enterprise would have foundered halfway through without the unfailing love and encouragement of my wife Perella.

ADRIAN HOUSE

Source Notes

The notes that follow indicate the sources on which this book and its individual chapters are primarily based. They are set out in three parts:

1 **EARLY SOURCES**
2 **GENERAL BIOGRAPHIES CONSULTED**
3 **CHAPTER SOURCES**

The abbreviations used in the notes are given in parentheses.

1 EARLY SOURCES

ST. FRANCIS

(1) *St. Francis of Assisi: English Omnibus of the Sources for the Life of St Francis.* Edited by Marion A. Habig, Franciscan Press, Quincy, Ill., 1991 (*Omnibus*)
The Writings of St Francis
The First Life of St Francis, Thomas of Celano (1 *Cel.)*
The Second Life of St Francis, Thomas of Celano (2 *Cel.*)
The Major Life of St Francis, St Bonaventure *(Major Life)*
The Minor Life of St Francis, St Bonaventure *(Minor Life)*
The Legend of the Three Companions (Leg. 3. Comp.)
The most reliable account of Francis 1182–1209, thought by some experts to be the work of the saint's close companion, Brother Angelo.
The Legend of Perugia (Leg. Per.)
The Mirror of Perfection (Mir. of Perf.)
The Little Flowers of St Francis (The Little Flowers)
Thirteenth Century Testimonies.

(2) *Scripta Leonis*. Edited by Rosalind Brooke, Clarendon Press, Oxford, 1970
The carefully edited recollections of the saint's life thought to have been written down by Leo, Rufino and Angelo. Earlier versions of these were called *The Legend of Perugia* and (in a less authentic form) *The Mirror of Perfection.*

(3) *The Saint. Francis of Assisi: Early Documents. Vol. I.* (*The Saint*). Edited by Regis Armstrong et al., New City Press, New York, 1999. The first volume of a planned trilogy of new translations which will supersede the *Omnibus*.

(4) *The Versified Life of Saint Francis* by Henri d'Avranches, included in *The Saint* (above)

ST. CLARE

(1) *St Clare: Process of Canonisation (Proc. Can. Clare)*
Included in (3) below

(2) *The Life of St Clare* Trs. C. B. Magrini, Editrice Minerva, Assisi *(Life of Clare)*
The author of this is unknown, though many assume it to be Thomas of Celano. Included in (3) below.

(3) *Clare of Assisi: Early Documents*. Edited by Regis Armstrong, Paulist Press, New York, 1988 *(Clare Documents)*

2 GENERAL BIOGRAPHIES CONSULTED

Although these lives inevitably cover much the same ground they are only mentioned among a chapter's sources if they throw special light on its content.

ST. FRANCIS

Luciano Canonici, *Francis of Assisi*, Assisi

G. K. Chesterton, *St Francis of Assisi*, Hodder & Stoughton, London, 1923

Father Cuthbert, *Life of St Francis of Assisi*, London, 1921

Omer Englebert, *Saint Francis of Assisi*, Franciscan Herald Press, Chicago, 1965

Arnaldo Fortini, *Francis of Assisi*, Trs. H. Moak, Crossroad, New York, 1981
This biography, by a lawyer and mayor of Assisi who devoted decades to his research, contains invaluable information about every aspect of life in Assisi during Francis's time.

Chiara Frugoni, *Francis of Assisi*, Trs. J. Bowdon, SCM Press, London, 1998

Julien Green, *God's Fool*, Fount, London, 1993

Johannes Jörgensen, *Saint Francis of Assisi*, Trs. T. O'C. Sloane, Image Books, London

J. R. H. Moorman, *St Francis of Assisi*, SCM Press, London, 1950

Michael Robson, *St Francis of Assisi*, Geoffrey Chapman, London, 1997

Paul Sabatier, *Life of St Francis of Assisi*, Hodder & Stoughton, London, 1904
The first biography of modern times, written by a French Protestant scholar in 1894. Its brilliance has stimulated a century of research into Francis's life.

ST. CLARE

Marco Bartoli, *Clare of Assisi*, Darton, Longman & Todd, London, 1993

Margaret Carney, *The First Franciscan Woman*, Franciscan Press, Quincy, Ill.,

Ingrid Peterson, *Clare of Assisi*, Franciscan Press, Quincy, Ill., 1993
Chiara Lainati, *Saint Clare of Assisi*, Edizioni Porziuncula, Assisi, 1994
Nesta de Robeck, *St Clare of Assisi*

3 CHAPTER SOURCES

Details of the books cited below are given in the Bibliography.

1 Morning Star

5 1 Elias, Encyclical Letter, October 1226, see *Omnibus* p. 1894
6 2 1 *Cel.* 117
11 3 Weil, *Waiting on God*, p. 94
13 4 Lewis, *The Allegory of Love*, pp. 2, 4, 11

Early sources 1 *Cel.* 117; Elias, Encyclical Letter, October 1226.

General sources Adams, *Umbria*; Dante, *Paradiso*, XI; Huizinga, *Men and Ideas*, pp. 263–264; Lewis, *The Allegory of Love*; Moorman, *A History of the Franciscan Order* and *The Sources for a Life of St Francis*; Paciocco, *Sublima Negotia*, preface by André Vauchez; Renan, *Nouvelles Etudes d'Histoire Réligieuse;* Rowdon, *The Companion Guide to Umbria*; Weil, *Waiting on God*.

2 A Liberal Education

15 1 *Leg. 3. Comp.* 1
21 2 Betjeman, *Coming Home*, p. 500

Early sources *Leg. 3. Comp.* 1.

General sources Betjeman, *Coming Home*; Gautier, *Chivalry*; Green, *God's Fool*; Lewis, *The Discarded Image*; McNeill, *Plagues and People*; Paterson, *The World of the Troubadours*.

3 The Pleasures of Youth

23 1 *Leg. 3. Comp.* 2
24 2 1 *Cel.* 1
26 3 Chrétien de Troyes, *Arthurian Romances*, "Lancelot," l. 4651

Early sources d'Avranches, *Versified Life of St Francis* (see *The Saint*); 1. *Cel.* 1, 2; *Leg. 3. Comp.* 2, 3.

General sources Barber, *The Knighthood and Chivalry*; Chrétien de Troyes, *Arthurian Romances*; Fortini, *Francis of Assisi*; Haskins, *Mary Magdalen*; Viscardi, *L'Italia nell' Eta Comunale*.

4 Making Money

Early sources 1 *Cel.* 1, 2; *Leg. 3. Comp.* 2, 3.

General sources Bautier, *The Economic Development of Medieval Europe*; Duby, *The Early Growth of the European Economy*; Frappier, *Chrétien de Troyes*; Gautier; Topsfield, *Chrétien de Troyes*.

5 Civil War

37 1 see Southern, *Society and the Western Church in the Middle Ages*, p. 102

General sources Barber; Bautier; Fortini; Green; Southern, *Society and the Western Church in the Middle Ages*.

6 Into Battle

41 1 Grenfell, *The Times*, 1915, "Into Battle"

45 2 *Leg. 3. Comp.* 4

Early sources *Leg. 3. Comp.* 4.

General sources Brown, *The Roots of St Francis*; Contamine, *War in the Middle Ages*; Englebert, *Saint Francis of Assisi*; Fortini; Gautier; Mundy, *Europe in the High Middle Ages*.

7 Dreams

49 1 Chrétien de Troyes, *Arthurian Romances*, "Cligés," l. 154

49 2 *Leg. 3. Comp.* 6

51 3 *Ibid.* 7

52 4 see Fortini, p. 252

Early sources *Leg. 3. Comp.* 6, 7.

General sources Chrétien de Troyes, *Arthurian Romances*, "Cligés"; Cristofani, *La Storia d'Assisi*; Fortini; Lewis, *The Discarded Image*; O'Donoghue, *The Courtly Love Tradition*; Pazzelli, *San Francesco e il Terz'Ordine*; Ranke-Heinemann, *Eunuchs for Heaven*; Stevens, *Private Myths*; Storr, *Feet of Clay*.

8 Nightmares

57 1 *Leg. 3. Comp.* 11

58 2 *Ibid.*

58 3 Frappier, *Chrétien de Troyes*, p. 104

59 4 see Bramly, *Leonardo*, p. 86

59 5 Blake, *The Marriage of Heaven and Hell*, "A Memorable Fancy"

60 6 see Storr, p. 161

61 7 Furlong, *Merton*, p. 112

62 8 *Leg. 3. Comp.* 13.

62 9 Topsfield, *Chrétien de Troyes*, p. 109

Early sources *Leg. 3. Comp.* 11, 13.

General sources Blake, *Marriage of Heaven and Hell*; Bramly, *Leonardo*; Frappier; Furlong, *Merton*; Hetherington, *Medieval Rome*; Masson, *The Companion Guide to Rome*; Moore, *The Foundation of a Persecuting Society*; Ozanam, *The Franciscan Poets of Italy of the 13th Century*; Plato, *The Republic*; Storr; Topsfield.

9 Trial

64 1 *Leg. 3. Comp.* 13

66 2 Chrétien de Troyes, *Arthurian Romances*, "Lancelot," l. 409

67 3 *Ibid.* "Perceval," l. 6364

69 4 *Leg. 3. Comp.* 19
70 5 *Ibid.* 20
Early sources *Leg. 3. Comp.* 13, 19, 20.
General sources Campbell Ross, *Umbria*; Chrétien de Troyes, *Arthurian Romances*, "Lancelot" and "Perceval"; Robson, *St Francis of Assisi*.

10 Builder
73 1 *Cel.* 16
75 2 *Leg. 3. Comp.* 23
75 3 *Ibid.*
76 4 *Leg. 3. Comp.* 24
76 5 *St Matthew's Gospel*, 10: vv. 7–13;
77 6 *Leg. 3. Comp.* 25
77 7 Shakespeare, *As You Like It*, V, ii, 90
Early sources 1 *Cel.* 16, 17, 18; *Leg. 3. Comp.* 23, 24, 25; *Leg. Per.* 15.
General sources Canonici, *The Land of St Francis*; Jörgensen, *Saint Francis of Assisi*, p. 298, n. 19; Matthew, St, *Gospel*, 10: vv. 7–13; Santini and Valigi, *Perugia*.

11 Twelve Beggars
78 1 *Leg. 3. Comp.* 28
79 2 St Francis, *Testament*, 14, see *Omnibus*, p. 65
79 3 *Leg. 3. Comp.* 29
79 4 *Ibid.* 30
80 5 *Ibid.* 22
82 6 *Ibid.* 35
83 7 *Ibid.* 36
85 8 1 *Cel.* 26
88 9 *Leg. 3. Comp.* 31
Early sources 1 *Cel.* 26–32; Francis, St, *Testament*, 14 (see *Omnibus*); *Leg. 3. Comp.* 22, 25–31, 33–45; *Leg. Per.* 22, 67; *Scripta Leonis*, pp. 309–15, 319–21, 323–25.
General sources Moorman, *Sources*, pp. 39–54; Robson, *Laurentianum*, 1993, pp. 124–28 and *St Francis*.

12 To the Pope
93 1 *Leg. 3. Comp.* 48
94 2 *Ibid.* 49
95 3 *Ibid.* 49
95 4 *Leg. Maj.* III, 9
97 5 *Leg. 3. Comp.* 50
98 6 *Ibid.* 51
98 7 *Ibid.* 49
Early sources 1 *Cel.* 32–34, 83; *Leg. 3. Comp.* 46–53; *Major Life*, III, 9.
General sources Anderson and Zinsser, *A History of Their Own*, I; Gregovorius,

Rome in the Middle Ages, V; Highet, *Poets in a Landscape*; Kelly, *The Oxford Dictionary of Popes*; Krautheimer, *Rome: Profile of a City*; Mann, *The Lives of the Popes in the Middle Ages*; Sayers, *Innocent III*; Warner, *Alone of All Her Sex*.

13 Prelude in a Cowshed

101 1 1 *Cel.* 42
102 2 *Mir. of Perf.* 48
103 3 James, *The Varieties of Religious Experience*, p. 320
103 4 *Mir. of Perf.* 29
104 5 *Leg. Per.* 56
104 6 *Ibid.* 1
104 7 *Ibid.* 96
106 8 *Ibid.* 15
107 9 *Ibid.* 6
108 10 *Ibid.* 62
109 11 2 *Cel.* 163
110 12 Warner, p. 181
111 13 *Archivum Franciscanum Historicum*, see *Omnibus*, p. 1882
112 14 *Leg. 3. Comp.* 54
113 15 *Ibid.* 55

Early sources *Archivum Franciscanum Historicum*, see *Omnibus*, p 1882; 1 *Cel.* 34–36, 40–47, 82–83; 2 *Cel.* 155, 163; *Leg. Per.* 1, 3–6, 15, 18, 41, 56, 60–63, 67, 78, 80, 96, 102, 110; *Leg. 3. Comp.* 54–58; *Mir. of Perf.* 29, 47–49, 51, 86.
General sources d'Avray, *The Preaching of the Friars*, pp. 230–31; James, *The Varieties of Religious Experience*; Warner.

14 St. Mary of the Angels

116 1 St Francis, *The Office of the Passion*, see *Omnibus*, p. 140
119 2 *Leg. Per.* 19
120 3 *The Little Flowers*, 10
122 4 Leigh-Fermor, *A Time to Keep Silence*, p. 70
123 5 *The Little Flowers*, 10, 29

Early sources 1 *Cel.* 55; Francis, St, *The Office of the Passion*; *Leg. 3. Comp.* 55, 56, 60; *Leg. Per.* 8, 19; *The Little Flowers*, 10, 29.
General sources Dalrymple, *Letting Go in Love* and *Simple Prayer*; Gibbon, *The History of the Decline and Fall of the Roman Empire*; Leigh-Fermor, *A Time to Keep Silence*; Ramon, *Franciscan Spirituality*; Robson, *Laurentianum* and *St Francis*; Runciman, *A History of the Crusades*, 3; Sumption, *The Albigensian Crusade*.

15 The Love of Clare

132 1 *Poems of St John of the Cross*, Trs. Roy Campbell, "The Dark Night of the Soul" with acknowledgment to Teresa Campbell
134 2 *Life of Clare*, 25
135 3 *Ibid.* 26

136 4 Ozanam, p. 18
136 5 see Southern, p. 314
137 6 2 *Cel.* 112
138 7 Topsfield, p. 109

Early sources 2 *Cel.* 112; *Life of Clare*, 25, 26; *Proc. Can. St Clare*; *Clare: Documents; Sainte Claire d'Assise: Documents.*

General sources Bartoli, *Clare of Assisi*; Bigaroni, *Franciscan Studies 47*, 1987, "San Damiano"; Carney, *The First Franciscan Woman*; John of the Cross, St, *Poems of St John of the Cross*, Trs. Campbell; Ozanam; Southern; Topsfield.

16 Innocent's Last Throw

144 1 Laurie Lee, *As I Walked Out One Midsummer Morning*, Ch. 8
145 2 *Leg. Per.* 27
145 3 *The Little Flowers*, "Considerations on the Holy Stigmata, I"
146 4 *Ibid.*
148 5 see Southern, p. 118
151 6 *Leg. 3. Comp.* 59
151 7 *Leg. Per.* 89
152 8 *Ibid.* 37
152 9 *Ibid.* 2
152 10 *Ibid.* 97
153 11 *Spec. Perf.* 95
153 12 *Leg. 3. Comp.* 59
153 13 see Southern, p. 314
154 14 *Rule of St Clare*, 1253, I see *Clare Documents*
155 15 Fortini, pp. 360–361

Early sources 1 *Cel.* 58, 59, 62; 2 *Cel.* 125, 128, 160; *Leg. 3. Comp.* 57–59; *Leg. Per.* 2, 27, 37, 89, 96, 97; *The Little Flowers*, 16, "Considerations on Stigmata, I"; *Major Life*, XII, 2; *Mir. of Perf.* 47–49, 95.

General sources Brooke, *Early Franciscan Government*; Lawrence, *The Friars*; Lee, *As I Walked Out One Midsummer Morning*; Moorman, *History* and *Research Notes*, 160 (Public Records Office, Clwyd); Morris, *The Papal Monarchy*; Sayers; see Southern, pp. 118, 314.

Second Order *Leg. 3. Comp.* 60; *Rule of St Clare*, 1253, I, see *Clare: Documents*; *Ste Claire d'Assise: Documents*; Anderson & Zinsser; Bartoli; Carney; Fortini; Maleczek, *Greyfriars Review, 12*, 1998; Robson.

Third Order *Leg. 3. Comp.* 60; *Leg. Per.* 27; *The Little Flowers*, "Considerations on Stigmata, I"; Adams, p. 90; Goodich, *Vita Perfecta*, pp. 165–68; Ramon; *The Saint*, pp. 599–600.

17 A Vision of Creation

161 1 2 *Cel.* 103
162 2 Underhill, *Mysticism*, p. 438
163 3 Dante, *Paradiso XXXIII*, ll. 135–45
163 4 Couper and Henbest, *Universe*, pp. 20, 24

164 5 d'Avranches, *The Versified Life of Saint Francis*, VIII, ll. 151–60, see *The Saint*, p. 487
164 6 Magee, *Confessions of a Philosopher*, p. 116
165 7 *Ibid.* p. 48
165 8 see Sackville-West, *The Eagle and the Dove*, pp. 81, 100
168 9 see Huxley, *The Perennial Philosophy*, p. 98

Early sources *2 Cel.* 103; d'Avranches, *Versified Life*, VIII, see *The Saint*; Francis, *Salutation to the Virtues*, *Omnibus* p. 132.

General sources Couper and Henbest, *Universe*; Dalrymple, *Letting Go in Love* and *Simple Prayer*; Dante, *The Divine Comedy*; Gautier; Huxley; John Paul II, *Faith and Reason*; Lewis, *The Discarded Image*; Sackville-West, *The Eagle and the Dove;* Shanahan, *Franciscan Studies*, 1988, "Henry of Avranches"; Underhill, *Mysticism*.

18 The Glinting Diamond

169 1 Manselli, *Chi era Francesco d'Assisi*, in S. Gieben, *Francesco d'Assisi nella Storia* (see Magro, p. 5)
170 2 *Rule of 1221*, XXII, *Omnibus* p. 47
170 3 *Leg. Per.* 104
171 4 see Southern, p. 301
171 5 *St Benedict's Prayer Book*, p. 117
172 6 *The Little Flowers*, 25
174 7 *Poems of St John of the Cross*, Trs. Campbell, "Songs between the Soul and the Bridegroom." See Ch. 15, note 1
175 8 Stevens, *Private Myths*, pp. 215–216
175 9 *Proc. Can. Clare*, III, 29
176 10 du Boulay, *The Tablet*, 12 Sept. 1998
177 11 St Francis, *The Canticle of Brother Sun*, *Omnibus*, p. 130
178 12 Griffiths, *The Marriage of East and West*, p. 96
178 13 Underhill, *Mysticism*, p. 131
178 14 1 *Cel.* 80
179 15 see de Watteville, *Speak to the Earth*, p. 205
180 16 1 *Cel.* 77, 81

Early sources 1 *Cel.* 51–54; Francis, *Admonitions* 7, *Omnibus* p. 47; *Rule of 1221 XXII*, see *Omnibus* p. 47; *Leg. Per.* 39, 104.

General sources "Francis's Prayer," see *St Benedict's Prayer Book*; Huxley; John of the Cross, St, *Poems*, Trs. Campbell; Manselli, *Chi era Francesco d'Assisi*, see Magro, *Saint Francis Luminous and Illuminating*; Southern, pp. 301–5.

Second Order *Proc. Can. Clare*, III, 29; Bartoli, pp. 125–29; du Boulay, *Tablet*, 12 Sept '98; Carney, pp. 38–61; John of the Cross, *Poems*; *Solomon, The Song of*, IV, 10; Stevens, pp. 215–16.

Nature 1 *Cel.* 58–61, 77–81, 111, 165–71; Francis, *The Canticle of Brother Sun*, *Omnibus* p. 130; *Leg. Per.* 49, 51; *The Little Flowers*, 21; Armstrong, *St Francis Nature Mystic*; Fortini, pp. 541, 664 n. 43; Griffiths; Sorrell, *St Francis of Assisi and Nature*; Underhill; de Watteville, *Speak to the Earth*; White, *Science*, March 1967, "The Historical Roots of our Ecologic Crisis."

19 New Directions

184 1 See Fortini, p. 381

186 2 de Vitry, *Lettres*, see *Omnibus* p. 1609, also Fortini, p. 380, and Jörgensen p. 142

188 3 *Leg. Per.* 16

191 4 *Leg. Per.* and *Scripta Leonis*, 82

193 5 *Life of Clare*, 20

193 6 *Proc. Can. Clare*, III, 15, and *Life of Clare*, 21

197 7 *Scripta Leonis* and *Leg. Per.*, 83

Early sources 1 *Cel.* 74, 75, 94; *Leg. 3. Comp.* 65; *Leg. Per.* 16, 79; *Scripta Leonis* and *Leg. Per.*, 82, 83; de Vitry, *Lettres*, see *Omnibus* p. 1609; *Life of Clare*, 20, 21; *Proc. Can. Clare*, II, 15; *Ste Claire: Documents*.

General sources Bartoli; Brooke, *The Coming of the Friars*; Canonici; Carney; Edwards, *Christian England*; Englebert; Fisher, *A History of Europe*; Fortini, pp. 380, 381; Jörgensen, p. 142; Kelly; Knowles, *The Religious Orders of England*; Matura, *Francis of Assisi: The Message of his Writings*; Moorman, *Sources*; Sayers, Southern.

20 The Sultan of Egypt

207 1 *The Psalms*, Trs. Peter Levi, Penguin, London, 1976

208 2 2 *Cel.* 30

211 3 Runciman, *A History of the Crusades*, 3, pp. 159–60

211 4 Manselli, *St Francis of Assisi*, p. 221

214 5 de Vitry, *Lettres*, see *Omnibus*, p. 1609

216 6 de Vitry, *Historia Occidentalis*, see *Omnibus*, p. 1613, and *The Saint*, p. 585

Early sources 1 *Cel.* 57; 2 *Cel.* 30; *Major Life*, IX, 7; de Vitry, *Lettres*, see *Omnibus*, and *Historia Occidentalis*, see *Omnibus* and *The Saint*.

General sources Basetti-Sani, *Muhammed, St Francis of Assisi and Alvernia*; Contamine; Daniel, *The Franciscan Concept of Mission in the High Middle Ages*; *Encyclopédie de l'Islam*, Picard; Fortini, pp. 395–439; Grousset, *Histoire des Croisades*; Lane-Poole, *A History of Egypt in the Middle Ages*; Manselli, *St Francis of Assisi*; Marshall, *Warfare in the Latin East 1192–1291*; Mayer, *The Crusades*; Mockler, *Francis of Assisi: The Wandering Years*; Runciman; Salmon, *Rapport sur une Mission à Damiette*, Inst. Arch. Orient., Cairo, 1902.

21 The Small Black Hen

222 1 *Leg. 3. Comp.* 63

224 2 *Ibid.* 65

225 3 *Ibid.* 67

225 4 1 *Cel.* 101

226 5 *Leg. Per.* 105

227 6 see Bartoli, p. 83

228 7 *Life of Clare*, 27

228 8 *Clare of Assisi: Light for the Way*, p. 33

229 9 Thomas of Pavia, see *Omnibus*, pp. 1837–38

229 10 From *Archivum Franciscum Historicum*, see *Omnibus*, pp. 1849–1850
231 11 See Mayer, p. 227
232 12 Jordan of Giano, *Chronica* 17, see Fortini, p. 477
234 13 *The Little Flowers*, 18
235 14 *Leg. Per.* 114
236 15 Thomas of Spalato, *Historia Salonitarum*, see *Omnibus*, p. 1601

Early sources 1 *Cel.* 99–101; *Leg. 3. Comp.* 62–67; *Leg. Per.* 11, 12, 105, 106, 114; *The Little Flowers*, 7; *Mir. of Perf.* 43; *Major Life*, VIII, 9; *Arch. Franc. Hist.*, see *Omnibus* p. 1849, Thomas of Pavia, *Omnibus*, pp. 1830, 1837, Thomas of Spalato, *Omnibus*, p. 1601; *Life of Clare*, 27.

General sources Brooke, *Early Franciscan Government*; Desbonnets, *From Intuition to Institution*; Englebert; Fortini; Honour, *The Companion Guide to Venice*; Jordan of Giano, *Chronica* 17, see Fortini; Maalouf, *The Crusades through Arab Eyes*; Mayer; Moorman, *Sources*, pp. 31, 121; Runciman; Southern, pp. 190–91.

Books and Study *Leg. Per.* 38, 69–73; *Mir. of Perf.*, 5, 6, 72.

Clare *Leg. 3. Comp.* 60; *Mir. of Perf.* 84; *Major Life of Francis*, IV, 6; *Proc. Can. Clare*, II, 15 and III, 12; *Bull Can. Clare*, 13, see *Clare: Documents*; *Life of Clare*, 32; *Ste Claire: Documents*, pp. 273, 364; Bartoli; R. and C. Brooke, *Studies in Church History, Subsidia*, I, 1978, "St Clare"; Carney; *Clare of Assisi: Light for the Way*, Editions du Signe; Esser, *Origins of the Franciscan Order*.

Chapter of Mats 2 *Cel.* 63; *Leg. 3. Comp.* 61; *Leg. Per.* 33, 114; *Mir. of Perf.* 68; *The Little Flowers*, 18; Englebert pp. 187–189.

22 Darkness and Light

238 1 *Scripta Leonis* (and *Leg. Per.*), 73
238 2 2 *Cel.* 195
238 3 *Leg. Per.* 71
239 4 *Ibid.* 74
239 5 Francis, Letter to Anthony of Padua, see *Omnibus*, p. 164
240 6 *Ste Claire: Documents*, p. 288
240 7 From *Arch. Franc. Hist.*, see *Omnibus*, p. 1849
242 8 Clare, Third Letter to Agnes of Prague, see *Clare of Assisi: Early Documents*
242 9 *Life of Clare*, 14
244 10 *Scripta Leonis* (and *Leg. Per.*), 71
245 11 1 *Cel.* 73
245 12 *Scripta Leonis* (and *Leg. Per.*), 92
246 13 *Leg. Per.* 95
247 14 *Scripta Leonis* (and *Leg. Per.*), 113
250 15 *Leg. Per.* 32
250 16 *Scripta Leonis* (and *Leg. Per.*), 110
251 17 *Ibid.*
251 18 1 *Cel.* 84

Early sources Francis, Letter to St Anthony, see *Omnibus*, p. 164; 1 *Cel.* 73,

84–87; 2 *Cel.* 195; *Leg. Per.* 32, 71, 74, 95; *Scripta Leonis* (and *Leg. Per.*) 71, 73, 92, 110, 113; *Arch. Franc. Hist.*, *Omnibus*, p. 1849; *Life of Clare*, 14; Clare, Letter to Agnes, *Clare: Documents*; *Ste Claire: Documents*.

General sources Jenkins, *The Naturalists*, pp. 13–17; Lawrence; Maalouf; Moorman, *Sources*; Sabatier.

23 Five Wounds

255 1 *Leg. Per.* 23
255 2 *Ibid.* 30
257 3 *The Little Flowers*, "Second Consideration on the Stigmata," *Omnibus*, p. 1441
258 4 Leo, note on parchment from Francis, *Omnibus*, p. 124
258 5 *Leg. 3. Comp.* 69
260 6 Elias, Encyclical Letter, October 1226, *Omnibus*, p. 1955
260 7 1 *Cel.* 95
260 8 1 *Cel.* 113
260 9 *Major Life*, XV, 2
261 10 *Minor Life*, VI, 3
261 11 Wayne Hellmann, "The Seraph in Thomas of Celano's *Vita Prima*," from *That Others May Love*, Ed. Hayes
261 12 Schatzlein and Sulmasy, *Franciscan Studies* 47, 1987, "The Diagnosis of St Francis"
262 13 Dormandy, *The White Death*, p. 10
264 14 Schmucki, *The Stigmata of St Francis of Assisi*, p. 49
265 15 1 *Cel.* 109
266 16 *The Little Flowers*, 8
266 17 *Leg. Per.* 42

Early sources 1 *Cel.* 94, 95, 98, 103, 113; *Leg. 3. Comp.* 69, 70; *Leg. Per.* 23, 30, 42, 90, 93; *Major Life*, XV, 2; *Minor Life*, VI, 3; *The Little Flowers*, 8, "First Consideration," *Omnibus*, pp. 1432–36, "Second Consideration," *Omnibus*, p. 1441; Leo's note on parchment, *Omnibus*, p. 124; Elias's Encyclical Letter, *Omnibus*, p. 1958.

General sources Dormandy, *The White Death*; Fortini, p. 559; Frappier; Harrison, *Stigmata: a Medieval Mystery in a Modern Age*; Hayes, *That Others May Love*; Sackville-West, p. 57; Schatzlein and Sulmasy, *Franciscan Studies*, 47, 1987, "The Diagnosis of St Francis"; Schmucki, *The Stigmata of St Francis of Assisi*; Topsfield.

24 Sunset

268 1 *Scripta Leonis* (and *Leg. Per.*), 43
269 2 Francis, "The Canticle of Brother Sun." This translation attempts to capture accurately the sense of the original after considering it carefully together with a number of previous English versions. See *Omnibus* p. 130.
270 3 *Scripta Leonis* (and *Leg. Per.*), 44

270 4 *Ibid.* 44
273 5 *Ibid.* 48
274 6 *Leg. Per.* 48
276 7 *Ibid.* 17
278 8 *Ibid.* 59
279 9 *Ibid.* 65
279 10 See *Leg. Per.* 100
280 11 *Leg. Per.* 64
280 12 *Mir. of Perf.* 80
280 13 *Scripta Leonis* (and *Leg. Per.*), 76
281 14 *Mir. of Perf.* 41
282 15 *Scripta Leonis* (and *Leg. Per.*), 86
282 16 *Scripta Leonis*, p 297 and 2 *Cel.* 215
283 17 *Leg. Per.* 109
283 18 *Scripta Leonis* (and *Leg. Per.*), 107. Thomas of Celano (1 *Cel.* 108) describes a similar blessing given to Elias while Francis was still in the bishop's palace. Doubtful that both benedictions occurred; some authorities prefer Thomas's version, others the testimony of Francis's closest companions Leo, Angelo and Rufino.
284 19 *Ibid.* 117

Early sources 1 *Cel.* 88-111; 2 *Cel.* 215; *Leg. Per.* 17, 48, 59, 64, 65, 100, 109; *Scripta Leonis* (and *Leg. Per.*), 44, 48, 76, 86, 107, 117; *Mir. of Perf.* 80.
General sources Fortini, pp. 590–96.

Epilogue
Text References

291 1 *Life of Clare*, 41
294 2 Proust, *Le Côté de Guermantes I*, p. 418
295 3 *The Record Guide*, Collins, London, pp. 77–78
296 4 Holmes, *Florence, Rome and the Origins of the Renaissance*, p. 45

Early sources Life of Clare, 41; *Scripta Leonis*.
General sources Bartoli; Carney; *Catalogo delle cose d'Arte e di Antichità di Assisi*; Clark *Civilisation*; Englebert; Fisher; Holmes, *Florence, Rome and the Origins of the Renaissance*; Moorman, *The Franciscan*, January 1979, *History* and *Sources*; Lunghi, *The Basilica of St Francis*; *La Ricognizione del Corpo di San Francesco*, Casa Editrice Francescana, Assisi; de Robeck, *St Clare of Assisi*, p. 100; Robson; Sobel, *Galileo's Daughter*; Underhill; Vauchez, *Sainthood in the Middle Ages*.

PERMISSIONS

The author expresses his gratitude to all the authors and translators whose works are quoted and referred to above, and to all their publishers, agents, executors or copyright owners who have given their consent to such use.

Bibliography

For lists of the biographies of St. Francis and St. Clare please see *Source Notes*.

Adams, M. *Umbria*, Bellew, London, 1964
Anderson, B. & Zinsser, J. *A History of Their Own, I*, Penguin, London, 1990
Armstrong, E. A. *Saint Francis: Nature Mystic*, Berkeley, 1973
Armstrong, K. *A History of God*, Mandarin, London, 1994
Baccelli, R. *Non ti chimaro piu Padre*,
Barber, R. *The Knighthood and Chivalry*, Boydell Press, Ipswich 1974
Basetti-Sani, G. *Muhammed, St Francis of Assisi, Alvernia*, Fiesole, 1975
Bautier, R-H. *The Economic Development of Medieval Europe*, Thames & Hudson, London, 1971
Betjeman, J. *Coming Home*, Methuen, London, 1997
Bigaroni, Meier & Lunghi. *La Basilica di S. Chiara in Assisi*, Quatroemme, Perugia, 1994
Bramly, S. *Leonardo: The Artist and the Man*, Michael Joseph, London, 1992
Brooke, R. *The Coming of the Friars*, Allen & Unwin, London, 1975
Brooke, R. *Early Franciscan Government*, C.U.P., Cambridge, 1959
Brown, R. *The Roots of St Francis*, Chicago, 1982
Campbell-Ross, I. *Umbria*, Viking, London, 1996
Chrétien de Troyes. *Arthurian Romances*, Trs. Owen, Everyman, London 1991
Clark, K. *Civilisation*, BBC/Murray, London, 1969
Contamine, P. *War in the Middle Ages*, Blackwell, Oxford, 1984
Couper, H. & Henbest N. *Universe*, Channel 4 Books, London, 1999
Cristofani, A. *Delle Storie d'Assisi*, Assisi, 1875
Cusato, M. & Coughlin, E. (Ed.) *That others may Know and Love*, Franciscan Institute, St Bonaventure, NY, 1997
Cuthbert, Father. *The Romanticism of St Francis*, Longmans, London, 1915
d'Avray, D. L. *The Preaching of the Friars*, Oxford, 1985

Dalrymple, J. *Letting Go in Love*, Darton, Longman & Todd, London 1986
Dalrymple, J. *Simple Prayer*, Darton, Longman & Todd, London 1996
Daniel, E. R. *The Franciscan Concept of Mission in the High Middle Ages*, Kentucky, 1975
Dante. *The Divine Comedy*, Trs. Sisson, OUP, Oxford, 1993
Davies, N. *Europe: A History*, Pimlico, London, 1997
Desbonnets, T. *From Intuition to Institution*, Trs. Duggan, Chicago, 1988
Dormandy, T. *The White Death*, Hambledon Press, London, 1999
Douglas-Klotz, N. Trs. *Prayers for the Cosmos*, Harper & Row, S. Francisco, 1990
Duby, G. *The Early Growth of the European Economy*, Weidenfeld, London, 1974
Edwards, D. *Christian England*, Collins, London, 1981
Edwards, D. *Christianity: The First Two Thousand Years*, Cassell, London, 1997
Encyclopédie de L'Islam, Picard & Fils, Paris, 1913
Esser, C. *Origins of the Franciscan Order*, Franciscan Herald Press, Chicago, 1970
Fisher, H. A. L. *A History of Europe*, Eyre & Spottiswoode, London, 1938
Fisher, M. *For the Time Being*, Gracewing, Leominster, 1993
Frappier, J. *Chrétien de Troyes: The Man and his Work*, Trs. Cormier, Ohio U.P., Ohio, 1982
Furlong, M. *Merton: A Biography*, Darton, Longman & Todd, London, 1980
Gautier, L. G. *Chivalry*, Trs. Dunning, Phoenix House, London, 1965
Gibbon, E. *The History of the Decline and Fall of the Roman Empire*
Goad, H. E. *Franciscan Italy*, London, 1926
Goodich, M. *Vita Perfecta, The Ideal of Sainthood in the Thirteenth Century*, Hiersemann, Stuttgart, 1982
Gregorovius, F. *History of the City of Rome in the Middle Ages V*, Bell, London, 1897
Griffiths, B. *The Marriage of East & West*, Fount, London, 1983
Grousset, R. *Histoire des Croisades*
Harrison, T. *Stigmata: A Medieval Mystery in a Modern Age*, Fount, London, 1994
Haskins, S. *Mary Magdalen: Myth & Metaphor*, Harper Collins, London, 1993
Hetherington, P. *Medieval Rome*, Rubicon Press, London, 1994
Highet, G. *Poets in a Landscape*, Hamish Hamilton, London, 1957
Holmes, G. *Florence, Rome and the Origins of the Renaissance*, Clarendon Press, Oxford, 1986
Honour, H. *The Companion Guide to Venice*, HarperCollins, 1965
Huizinga, J. *Men & Ideas*, Eyre & Spottiswoode, London, 1960
Huxley, A. *The Perennial Philosophy*, Chatto & Windus, London, 1946
James, W. *The Varieties of Religious Experience*, Penguin, London, 1985
Jenkins, A. C. *The Naturalists*, Hamish Hamilton, London, 1978
John of the Cross, St. *Poems of St John of the Cross*, Trs. R. Campbell, Harvill, London, 1951
John Paul II, Pope. *Faith and Reason*, Catholic Truth Society, London, 1998
Johnson, R. A. *The Psychology of Romantic Love*, Arkana, London, 1987
Jörgensen, J. *Pilgrim Walks in Franciscan Italy*, Sands, Edinburgh, 1908

Kaftal, G. *St Francis in Italian Painting*, Allen & Unwin, London, 1950
Kazantzakis, N. *God's Pauper: St Francis of Assisi*, Faber & Faber, London, 1975
Kelly, J. R. N. *The Oxford Dictionary of Popes*, O.U.P., Oxford, 1986
Knowles, D. *The Religious Orders of England*, Cambridge, 1959
Krautheimer, *Rome: Profile of a City 312–1308*, Princeton U.P., New Jersey, 1980
Lane-Poole, S. *A History of Egypt in the Middle Ages*, Frank Cass, London, 1968
Lawrence, C. H. *The Friars*, London, 1994
Lee, Laurie. *As I Walked Out One Midsummer Morning*, André Deutsch, London, 1969
Leigh-Fermor, P. *A Time to Keep Silence*, Murray, London, 1982
Lempp, E. *Frère Elie de Cortone*, Librairie Fischbacher, Paris, 1901
Lewis, C. S. *The Allegory of Love*, O.U.P., Oxford, 1958
Lewis, C. S. *The Discarded Image*, C.U.P., Cambridge, 1964
Lunghi, E. *La Basilica di San Francesco di Assisi*, Scala, Firenze, 1996
Maalouf, A. *The Crusades through Arab Eyes*, Trs. Rothschild, Al Saqhi Books, London, 1984
McEvedy, C. *The New Penguin Atlas of Medieval History*, Penguin, London, 1992
McNeill, W. H. *Plagues and Peoples*, Penguin, London, 1979
Magee, B. *Confessions of a Philosopher*, Weidenfeld and Nicolson, London, 1997
Magro, P. *Saint Francis Luminous & Illuminating*, Greyfriars, Kerala, 1995
Mann, H. K. *The Lives of the Popes in the Middle Ages*, Kegan Paul, Trench, Trubner, 1925
Marshall, C. *Warfare in the Latin East 1192–1291*, C.U.P., Cambridge, 1992
Masson, G. *The Companion Guide to Rome*, HarperCollins, London, 1965
Matt, L. von & Hauser W. *St Francis of Assisi: A Pictorial Biography*, Longmans, London, 1956
Matura, T. *Francis of Assisi: The Message of his Writings*, Franciscan Institute, St Bonaventure, NY, 1997
Mayer, H. E. *The Crusades*, Trs. Gillingham, O.U.P., Oxford, 1988
Mockler, A. *Francis of Assisi: The Wandering Years*, O.U.P., Oxford, 1976
Moore, R. I. *The Formation of a Persecuting Society, 950–1250*, Blackwell, Oxford, 1987
Moorman, J. R. H. *A History of the Franciscan Order*, Clarendon Press, Oxford, 1968
Moorman, J. R. H. *The Sources for the Life of St Francis of Assisi*, Manchester University, 1940
Morris, C. *The Papal Monarchy: The Western Church from 1050 to 1250*, O.U.P., Oxford, 1989
Mundy, J. H. *Europe in the High Middle Ages 1150–1309*, Longman, London, 1991
Musker, R. (Trs.) *The Poems of Propertius*, Dent, London, 1972
O'Donoghue, B. *The Courtly Love Tradition*, Manchester University Press, 1982
Ozanam, F. *The Franciscan Poets in Italy of the 13th Century*, London, 1914
Paciocco, R. "*Sublima Negotia,*" Pref. A. Vauchez, Padua, 1996

Paterson, L. M. *The World of the Troubadours, c.1100–c.1300*, C.U.P., Cambridge, 1993
Pazzelli, R. *San Francesco e il Terz'Ordine*, Emp, Padua, 1982
Plato. *The Republic*, Trs. Lee, Penguin, London, 1987
Pounds, N. J. G. *An Economic History of Medieval Europe*, Longmans, London, 1994
Ramon, Brother *Franciscan Spirituality*, SPCK, London, 1994
Ranke-Heinemann, U. *Eunuchs for Heaven*, Trs. Brownjohn, Deutsch, London, 1990
Raymond, E. *In the Steps of St Francis*, Rich & Cowan, London, 1938
Renan, E. *Nouvelles Etudes d'histoire Réligieuse*, Paris, 1884
Rowdon, M. *The Companion Guide to Umbria*, HarperCollins, London, 1969
Runciman, S. *A History of the Crusades 3*, Penguin, London, 1978
Sackville-West, V. *The Eagle and the Dove*, Michael Joseph, London, 1953
Salmon, G. *Rapport sur une Mission à Damiette*, Inst. Franc. Arch. Orient., Cairo, 1902
Santini, L. & Valigi, C. *Perugia*, Plurigraf, Terni, 1992
Sayers, J. *Innocent III*, Longman, London, 1994
Schmucki, O. *The Stigmata of St Francis of Assisi*, Franciscan Institute, St Bonaventure, NY, 1991
Sobel, D. *Galileo's Daughter*, Fourth Estate, London, 1999
Sorrell, D. *St Francis of Assisi and Nature*, O.U.P., Oxford, 1988
Southern, R. W. *The Making of the Middle Ages*, Pimlico, London, 1993
Southern, R. W. *Western Society & the Church in the Middle Ages*, Penguin, 1970
Stevens, A. *Private Myths*, Hamish Hamilton, London, 1995
Storr, A. *Feet of Clay*, Harper Collins, London, 1996
Sumption, J. *The Albigensian Crusade*, Faber & Faber, London, 1999
Topsfield, L. T. *Chrétien de Troyes: A Study of the Arthurian Romances*, C.U.P., Cambridge, 1981
Underhill, E. *Mysticism*, Methuen, London, 1930
Vauchez, A. *Sainthood in the Later Middle Ages*, Trs. Birrell, C.U.P., Cambridge, 1997
Viscardi, A. *L'Italia Nell' Eta Comunale*, Editrice Torinese, Torino, 1966
Waddell, H. *Peter Abelard*, Constable, London, 1987
Warner, M. *Alone of All Her Sex*, Picador, London, 1990
de Watteville, V. *Speak to the Earth*, Methuen, London, 1935
Weil, S. *Waiting on God*, Fount, London, 1977
Zanotti, G. S. *Francesco e i Francescani*, Casa Editrice Francescana, Assisi, 1994

Index

Index

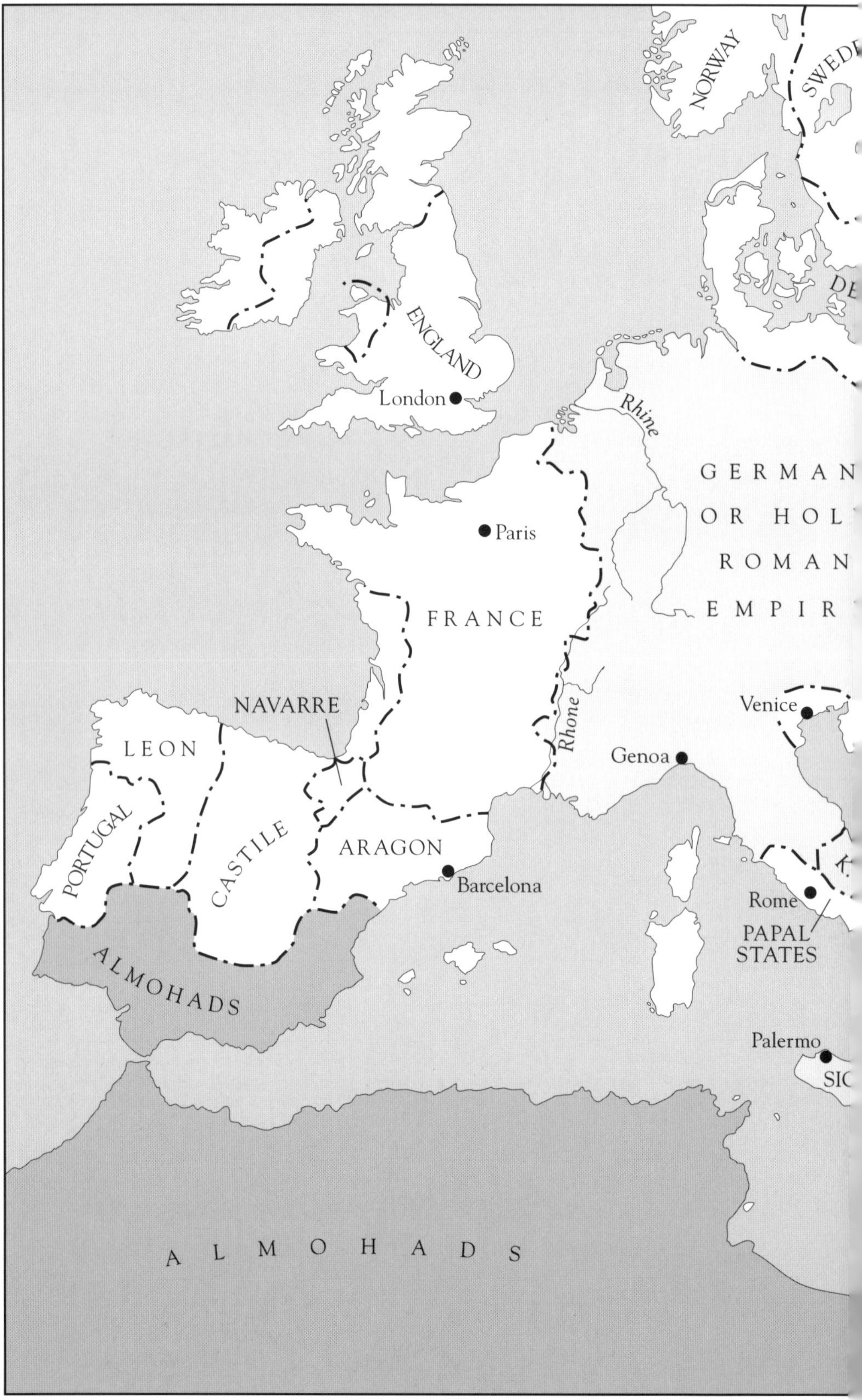
NORWAY
ENGLAND
London
Rhine
GERMAN
OR HOL
ROMAN
EMPIR
Paris
FRANCE
NAVARRE
LEON
PORTUGAL
CASTILE
ARAGON
Barcelona
Rhone
Venice
Genoa
Rome
PAPAL STATES
ALMOHADS
Palermo
ALMOHADS

Europe and the Mediterranean
1200–1220
OLAND
HUNGARY
BULGARIA
LATIN EMPIRE
Constantinople
NICAEA
RUM
Antioch
CYPRUS
CRETE
Acre
Jerusalem
Damietta
Nile
AYYUBIDS